Pearl

The Obsessions and Passions of
JANIS JOPLIN

A Biography by
ELLIS AMBURN

WARNER BOOKS

A *Warner* Book

First published in the USA in 1992
by Warner Books, Inc.
First published in Great Britain in 1993
by Little, Brown and Company
This edition published in 1993 by Warner Books

A CIP catalogue record for this book
is available from the British Library.

ISBN 0 7515 0856 X

Printed in England by Clays Ltd, St Ives plc

Warner Books
A Division of
Little, Brown and Company (UK) Limited
165 Great Dover Street
London SE1 4YA

Ellis Amburn is the bestselling author of *Dark Star: The Roy Orbison Story* and has collaborated with Shelley Winters on her autobiographies, and edited and collaborated on the bestsellers *Priscilla, Elvis and Me* and *Up and Down with the Rolling Stones*.

Also by Ellis Amburn:

DARK STAR
The Roy Orbison Story

To Al Lowman

Best Agent in the World

Contents

Acknowledgments

Most of *Pearl* is based on original interviews with Janis Joplin's friends, lovers, schoolmates, roommates, neighbors, and her professional colleagues: bands, impresarios, costume designers, songwriters, roadies, rock-festival promoters, record-industry executives, and managers of hotels where she stayed on the road. I traveled 33,000 miles to find them—crossing the country several times and living in Port Arthur, Beaumont, Houston, Austin, San Antonio, and El Paso, Texas; New Orleans, Lafayette, Vinton, Starks, and Toomy, Louisiana; Juarez, Mexico; Tucson and Prescott, Arizona; San Francisco, Monterey, Aptos, Larkspur, Sonoma, Occidental, Guerneville, Cazadero, Santa Rosa, Vacaville, Palm Desert, and Los Angeles, California; Seattle; and New York.

This book's true parents are listed below. I am deeply grateful to them all for generously sharing their memories of Janis, often opening their homes and their hearts to me: James Langdon, David Moriaty, Grant Lyons, James Gurley, Chet Helms, Richard Hundgen, Kim Chappell, David Getz, Linda Gravenites, Travis Rivers, Nick Gravenites, Sam Andrew, Clive Davis, Michael Lang, Stanley Bard, Henry Carr, David Columbia, Charles Conrad, Stanley Mouse, Dave Richards, Mark Braunstein, Bob Seidemann, Howard Hesseman, Milan Melvin, Powell St. John, Pat (Sunshine) Nichols, Kenai,

Richard Bell, George Hunter, Carl Gottlieb, Michael Pritchard, and Jack Jackson.

Shelley Winters, Elaine Dundy, Anna Hull, Linda Higginbotham Carroll, Rev. Darrell Evans, V. J. Harper, Charles Williams, William N. McDuffie, Roy Murphy III, Ms. Roy Murphy, Jerdy Fontenot, Sara Maxfield Jordan, Rev. Neil E. Lindley, Mary Lindley, Rev. Bill Hauck, Bill Wilson, James Ray Guidry, Nona Kettrick, Ruth Day, Michelle Sorenson Johnson, Paul Bartlett, Lorraine Gee, Irene Richardson, Lloyd Russell, Homer Pillsbury, James Dattalo, Deborah Taylor, and Mike E. Howard.

Gayle Blakeman, Ronald Colichia, Albert Fink, Jim Tipton, Sr., Lynda L. Mills Youngblood, Carolyn Dodds, James W. Smith, David W. McFadden, Janice Hays-Cavada, Mike Gracey, Danny M. Sessums, Dick Burke, Frank E. Andrews, Annette Irwin Feemster, Glynn Lyons, Dr. Hyler J. Bracey, Sidney Long, Rillie Ann Mahaffey Davis, Carolyn Black Ratliff, Alice White Fletcher, Carol Scalco, and Joseph LeSueur.

Frances Duvall, Amy Boullion, Milton Haney, Jim Salling, Tim Berryman, Jack Pullen, Judy Blanton Hollinger, Erin Linn Scheller, Pat Flowers Newman, Nancy Hebert, Cliff Hodges, Susan Sherwood, Linda R. Pulliam, B. J. Hughes, Louis Andrews, Alice White, Bill McCuistion, Carolyn Black Ratliff, Merilyn Milam, Wanda Dionne, Carol Thomas, Pat Allen, Ginger Brown, Ann Grossfield Page, Gladys Lacy, Lavern McMillan, Jean Lusk Forsythe, Paul Brown, Mark Horne, Mona Liby, A. C. Hebert, Faye Stewart, Jane Hebert, Brenda LeBoeuf, Mary Hantz, Celestine Hebert, Clama Hebert, John Richard, Betty Richard, Bill Hada, and Pat McCarthy.

Allen LaFleur, Bobby Lynch, Jerry LaCroix, Sharon Irby, George Arena, Jr., Sandra Lacey Sierra, Madeline Oliver, Dorothy Bailey Fink, Adrian Haston, Kathy Patrick, Steve Watson, Susan Sherwood Pearson, Herb Greene, Peter

Acknowledgments

DeLucca, Danny Fields, Joe Hawkins, Steve Paul, Michael Klenfner, Helen Richards, Elliot Mazer, George Hampton, Bill Perez, Pat Brown, and Darragh Doiron.

John Palmer, Bill Graham, Zenobia Wilson, Steve Hodges, Bobby Mayhem, Joey Dukes, Cheryl Carroll, Thomas Gladysz, Dave Willis, Judy Davis, Tony Secunda, Don Howell, Seabourne Stokes, Jr., Jessie Seward, Lisa Ghm, Ken Strum, Mary Kay Benson, Harry Koutoukas, and Jim Brennan.

For their constant encouragement and advice, I am also grateful to my agent, Al Lowman; my editor, Maureen Mahon Egen, Publisher, Warner Hardcovers; Nanscy Neiman, Publisher, Warner Books, Inc.; and Laurence J. Kirshbaum, President, Warner Books, Inc. Maureen Egen and her team at Warner are among the most gifted and dedicated people in publishing: her assistants, Anne Milburn and Anne K. Hamilton, kept the manuscript and supporting documents together through many changes; Nancy Trichter guided me through the legal reading of my manuscript with skill and patience; and my former editor, Charlie Conrad, inspired me with his enthusiasm and faith.

Loyal friends have supported me through this book with unflagging understanding and love. They are Cy Egan, Sandford Birdsey, Wendy Tucker, Bill Manville, Polly Siwek, Dick Burke, Michael Browning, Karen Luknis, Jon Phillips, Mary Ann Masterson, Clay Gregor, Fred Aanerud, Chris Stone, Jean O'Neill, Dennis Lannon, and Carol Lannon of Key West, Florida; Mark Stough of Port Arthur, Texas; Jim McCulloch and Ruth Ellen McCulloch of Fort Worth, Texas; Steven Gaines of Wainscot, Long Island; Susan Blond, Judy Feiffer, Betty Prashker, Patricia Soliman, and Michael Pietsch of New York City; Esther Mitgang, Sam Mitnick, Allston James, and Pepper James of San Francisco, California; Nell Crisante of Carmel, California; and Shelley Winters, Jack Larson, Jim Bridges, David Columbia, Pat Loud, and Lance

Loud of Los Angeles, California.

My mother, Belma Amburn, was the messenger who gave me the news that *Pearl* was to be published by Warner Books, and I'm glad that I could share that happy moment with her. She died on August 18, 1991, at the age of ninety-six, and will always be missed. I am blessed with a wonderful brother, Bill E. Amburn of Columbia City, Florida, and sister, Lu Bradbury of Fort Worth, Texas. Their spouses, Joyce Amburn and Bill Bradbury, are as close as blood kin to me, and as dear.

This book is also based on written material. The legwork done by Janis's previous biographers was a help to me, and I wish to acknowledge Peggy Caserta's *Going Down with Janis,* David Dalton's *Janis* (also published as *Piece of My Heart*), Myra Friedman's *Buried Alive,* Gary Carey's *Lenny, Janis and Jimi,* Deborah Landau's *Janis Joplin,* and George Frazier's 'Brief Candle' in Robert Somma's *No One Waved Goodbye.* The work of journalists who cover the rock scene, I found of inestimable historical value, and I am grateful to David Dalton, Chet Flippo, John Bowers, Michael Lydon, Richard Goldstein, Robert Christgau, Tony Glover, Ben Fong-Torres, and Ellen Sander.

Ray Cline helped me at the Port Arthur Public Library; Sam Monroe and his staff were courteous to me at the Janis Joplin exhibit, Gates Memorial Library, Port Arthur; and the Joplin files at the Lincoln Center Library for the Performing Arts, New York, and the Margaret Herrick Library of the Academy of Motion Picture Arts and Sciences, Los Angeles, were also useful. I owe a special debt of gratitude to the enterprising and resourceful staffs at the County Library in Marina del Rey, California, and at Rogues and Records, Key West, Florida.

1

Town Without Pity:
1943–1962

On a sweltering street corner in Port Arthur, Texas, home-town of Janis Joplin, the greatest female singer in the history of rock 'n' roll, I watch a construction crew demolish the twelve-story Goodhue Hotel, scene of Janis's last public appearance twenty years ago. A crane with huge claws jerks at steel rods supporting a roof of elegant Spanish tiles, which suddenly come loose and clatter to the ground. The Goodhue is a handsome 1930s structure, a Latino-styled Art Deco jewel that merits landmark status and preservation, but all of downtown Port Arthur looks like bombed-out Berlin after World War II – abandoned buildings with boarded-up windows, some of them caving in, most of them firetraps.

Only a few places such as Woolworth's, Walgreen's, the Keyhole Klub, and a porn shop remain in business; even the Greyhound bus station is closed. City Hall and a few other municipal agencies are clustered along the Intercoastal Canal, which runs through the heart of the downtown area. It's a far cry from the Port Arthur of Janis's day – a bustling seaport full of bars, whorehouses, and gambling dens. In the 1960s, the middle class fled out toward the highways, Central Mall, and surrounding swamps, leaving the inner city to poor African-Americans. The town's total population is 61,195.

For Janis, in 1970, the Goodhue Hotel had been a scene of

crushing disappointment, the tenth reunion of her high school class of 1960. She'd been so unpopular at Thomas Jefferson High, as a wallflower with acne and the town's first beatnik, that she said, 'They laughed me out of class, out of town, and out of the state.' At the peak of her fame in 1970, she saw the reunion as a chance to flaunt her success and get even with the people who'd ostracized her in high school. 'I'm going to show up with bells and feathers,' she told reporters, 'and I'm gonna say, "Remember me, man? What are you doing? Still pumping gas?" ' At the same time, she was crying out for the love and approval she'd been denied in Port Arthur and had never ceased to crave.

At the reunion, she wanted to bury the old plain-Jane Janis forever and be reborn as Pearl, the lovable, quintessential good-time girl. Ever since she'd first discovered that she couldn't compete with the high school beauty queens, she'd been trying to carve out a new definition for herself. Instinctively, she knew that only by being totally loose could she grab her share of kicks. If she couldn't be pretty, she could at least be outrageous. It was an act that had flopped miserably at Thomas Jefferson High, where they called her a slut and threw pennies at her, but it had worked ever since – as a beatnik runaway, folksinger, hippie queen of Haight-Ashbury, and now as an international rock 'n' roll star pulling down fifty thousand dollars a night.

'She was devastated,' says Robert Rauschenberg, a Port Arthur native who went on to become a world-renowned painter and a winner of the grand prize at the Venice Biennale. 'She needed confirmation from home and that's what got her into trouble. She wanted to rub it in and on the other hand she wanted to be loved. That's an acid combination. One's just going to dissolve the other.'

For Janis, already burned out on drugs, booze, and sex at twenty-seven, it was a blow from which she'd never recover.

Not everyone agrees: Her sister, Laura, who was present, heard a former classmate assure Janis that no one had minded that she'd been 'different, had a weight problem, had skin problems . . . "We liked you." ' Then, says Laura, they sat down and muddled through a rendition of the class song. Sounds jolly, but unfortunately history contradicts such efforts at revisionism. Just seven weeks later, Janis Joplin lay dead in a Hollywood motel room of a drug overdose. She had gone home, a star in quest of the self-esteem denied her in adolescence, but it had proved unrecoverable.

After the reunion that night, she was observed walking alone on the dark streets of Port Arthur, finally going into a bar called the Pompano Club. 'She kept sending back drinks,' says a man who was tending bar that night. Twenty years later, I interview him in the alcohol-recovery club on Lewis Avenue and he tells me that Janis had said, 'These are shit drinks.'

'I guess she wanted them stronger.' He laughs. 'I drank them myself and went home blind-drunk.'

Many of the young people I see in the Lewis Avenue recovery club were just kids when Janis died, but having grown up in Port Arthur, they all have stories to tell. The way to see the ghost of Janis Joplin, schoolchildren are told, is to 'go into a dark room, say "marijuana" three times, and turn around and look.' The derivation of the 'Dialing for Dollars' reference in Janis's song 'Mercedes Benz,' I'm informed, is a 1950s call-in show that gave away color TVs. 'They would call people during the show,' a young man tells me, 'and you had to be at home watching if you wanted to get the call and win a color TV. Everybody in Port Arthur watched it.' Janis wrote the song herself, in collaboration with poet Michael McClure, and she sang it a cappella on *Pearl*, her final album.

I'm reluctant to leave the Lewis Avenue recovery facility.

Though I'm a stranger in town, all the locals here are warm and friendly, treating me like a member of the family. How different they seem from the heartless rednecks Janis hated. But then I remember what it was like for me, growing up in Fort Worth, Texas: bloody hell. I am spending the rest of my life putting together the pieces of a personality that was shattered on the playgrounds of William James Junior High and Polytechnic Senior High. To be different in Texas is to be lower than dirt, a nonperson. Forgiveness has been as hard for me as it was for Janis, and it did not begin until I realized that self-respect comes only from the inside and it never matters what people say about us.

Out on the street, the Texas sun is like a blast furnace and people are darting from air-conditioned cars to air-conditioned houses as if fleeing a hailstorm instead of a bright day. I drive the short distance from Lewis Avenue to Procter Street, looking for the little house where Janis was born. All I find is a vacant lot with nothing to indicate it's Janis's birthplace. Still, there's something nice about it – a quiet, cool, grassy nook with flowering purple bushes and a towering tree in back. A curving sidewalk leads to the empty space where the house once stood, and a lone concrete porch step is all that remains. Later, a local man named John Palmer tells me he tried in vain to persuade the city to save Janis's house. When it was destroyed, he asked them to create a meditation garden here so visiting fans could sit under the tree and quietly pay their respects. Again the city turned a deaf ear.

Returning to the downtown ghetto, which is about a mile down Procter from Janis's birthplace, I duck into the Keyhole Klub to escape the heat. Ordering a Coke, I sit down at the bar and strike up a conversation with the middle-aged man next to me. 'Yeah, I worked with Janis once,' he says. 'I play guitar, and we were shooting a TV commercial, some bank around here; this was the sixties. She was carrying her bottle with her. Fine girl, Janis.'

The following day is Sunday, and after breakfast at Beverly's diner on Twin City Highway, I drop into a Protestant church. Only a dozen people are in the congregation, and after the service I ask the minister whether he can suggest local people for me to interview about Janis. Blinking and taking a step backward, he says, 'No. She got into a lot of trouble here. I'd be careful if I were you. You'll find that people around here don't like her – at all.'

'Not everyone is so judgmental,' I say. 'I met a man in the Keyhole Klub who thought she was a fine lady.'

'Excuse me,' he says, turning away.

In the parking lot, a woman and her daughter tell me that Port Arthur has never forgiven Janis for criticizing the city and the state in public, still disapproves of her lifestyle, dislikes her voice, and hates rock 'n' roll. That's when it hits me: This is the Texas Bible Belt and twenty years haven't made a dent in the town's prejudice against Janis. It's as if the triumphs of the sixties counterculture – the civil rights breakthrough, the downfall of Johnson and Nixon, the end of the Vietnam War, the sex revolution, women's and gay lib – had never happened. A strange feeling comes over me. It's as if the edge of the universe came up as far as the Port Arthur city limits and abruptly stopped.

On Monday, accompanied by a schoolmate of Janis's named Cliff Hodges, I visit the high school Janis attended her sophomore and junior years. It's now a junior high, and some cute girls out front flirt with us and want to know all about my car, a new 5.0 Mustang GT convertible; they hint for a ride. They're a bunch of bold, beautiful little Lolitas, straining at the starting gate of life, just as Janis had been at their age. Inside the graceful redbrick colonial building, I get into a terrible fight with a woman employee who attacks

Janis mercilessly. Suddenly, the place seems ugly and sinister, exactly as it had to Janis, and I beat it out of there. In 1959, the high school moved to a new campus over on Twin City Highway. That is my next stop.

Thomas Jefferson High is a sprawling 1950s structure of glass and steel, typical Eisenhower-era architecture. Beside the main structure stand two huge, round concrete mounds, housing the gym and auditorium, often referred to as 'Twin Titties.' Several personable staffers in the principal's office greet me and bring out copies of the yearbook. All of Janis's pictures have been cut out, but a framed photograph of her is displayed in the hallway, along with other prominent TJ alumni, including Rauschenberg (class of 1944); Jimmy Johnson, coach of the Dallas Cowboys; Allan Shivers, governor of Texas, 1949 to 1957; and the actor G. W. Bailey, who appeared in *Police Academy*.

A young man whose mother went to school with Janis tells me that TJ is as rough today as it was in Janis's time. 'I'm gay,' he says, 'and some guys told me that they'd kill me if I ever walked in front of the school. I'm dropping out and taking an equivalency test for my diploma.'

After lunch, I go into the strip mall record shop to buy all of Janis's tapes. Ted Primeaux, the owner, points to a stark concrete courtyard just outside the store and says, 'She used to hang out there. Kids would come over here during the lunch hour and eat at a little restaurant off the courtyard. Then she'd come in here to look at records.'

Ted tells me about the Janis Joplin exhibit at Gates Memorial Library on the Lamar University–Port Arthur campus, and the next day I call on the president, Sam Monroe. He insists that she'd never been unhappy in Port Arthur and only knocked Texas to enhance her image as a rebel. 'Look at her yearbooks in the exhibit,' he says. 'From her friends' inscriptions, you can see she had her support group.'

The Janis Joplin exhibit is housed in an imposing white stone classical building across the street. Janine, the librarian, takes the yearbook, called the *Yellow Jacket,* out of a glass case, and I begin to read the messages Janis's friends wrote some thirty years ago. Tarry Owens, 'Esq.,' penned a chilling note advising her that she would live longer if she was wicked and reminding her of the fun they'd had in 'Old Witch Dunn's' class. Dee Dee wrote that despite Janis's controversial reputation, she turned out to be okay. Karleen bragged about how terrific two guys named Jim and Kenneth had been and what a pity Janis hadn't been around for the fun. Brent (Buddy) Burney congratulated Janis on having reformed. Someone who signed himself 'Ace' told her she was boy-crazy and ought to cool it.

Janis had her support group, all right, but somehow only one inscription strikes me as having come from a happy person. 'You are the nicest hunk of junk in the school,' wrote blond, crew-cut, burly Billy McDuffie, 'but just the sweetest girl.' He meant it. A few weeks later, I contact him in Greenville, Texas, and he tells me how he used to carry her on his shoulders at the homecoming bonfire. Then they'd drive across the Intercoastal Canal to Pleasure Island, where they'd park and make out.

'Why don't you have a Janis Joplin Street?' I ask the chic woman in the mayor's office. 'You've got a Martin Luther King, Jr., Highway, and he didn't even live here.'

'No one has asked us,' says Yvonne Sutherlin, unflappably polite. The mayor's office has a panoramic view of the Texaco refinery, Gulf Island, Sabine Pass, and the swamps of Louisiana. Mayor Mary Ellen Summertin is not in today and I'm interviewing her assistant, Yvonne, who says, 'As for the Martin Luther King, Jr., Highway, five members of the city council are black. Come, I'll introduce you to the city manager.' She takes me into the office of Cornelius (Curt) Boganey, an African-American, and I put the same question to him, adding, 'Your high school is named after Thomas Jefferson, who was from Virginia. Doesn't anyone realize that Janis is the only major celebrity to come out of Port Arthur?'

'Yes,' he says, 'but with her lifestyle, how could we set her up as someone for young people to emulate?'

I start to tell him he should be focusing on Janis's achievements as a singer, but something in his common-sensical attitude stops me. It would be political suicide for these people in City Hall to promote any kind of memorial to Janis, the most hated person in town. While Memphis rakes in millions from Graceland, home of a bigger junkie than Janis, Port Arthur would rather sit and rot in this swamp than collect one penny from fans wanting to visit the birthplace of Janis Joplin. The city is casting about for other ways to pull itself out of the bog of unemployment and recession. Though the local clergy are against it, there's talk of legalized gambling and making Port Arthur the wide-open town it was in Janis's day, when more than thirty whore-houses were in operation.

Later, when I visit the Uptown Barber Shop on Austin, Jerdy Fontenot says, 'This was a boomtown till '68. Before Saudi Arabia and the Mideast took over oil production, the Gulf and Texaco refineries here produced more petroleum than anyplace in the world. Marcella's was the town social center, if a port town full of crazy sailors could be said to have such a thing.'

'Marcella's?' I ask.

'Yeah,' says a customer in the next chair. 'Port Arthur was known as the cathouse capital of Texas. Marcella Chadwell, she run a great whorehouse over yonder a block or so away.' Another man looks up from his magazine and says, 'Janis and a bunch of girls stole a sign somewhere and put it in front of Grace's Wood Yard [another whorehouse]. It read "Men at Work." '

Children and parents are often perfect strangers, joined only by the accident of birth. So it was with Janis Joplin, a future beatnik born into a Republican family. Dorothy Bonita East Joplin gave birth to Janis Lyn at 9:45 A.M. on January 19, 1943, at St. Mary's Hospital. Dorothy Joplin originally came from Nebraska, and in a photograph of her as a young woman, she appears well groomed, fashionably attired, petite in stature, and with an average-looking face, just a shade too long and on the horsey side to be called pretty. On two separate occasions, I make the trip to her present home in Prescott, Arizona, an old mining town with swinging-door saloons. On the first trip, when I call her from my hotel, she's blunt and businesslike but fairly responsive. 'I cooperated with a writer once,' she says, 'but when I tried to read the book, I quit after forty pages and just sat there laughing. She missed the whole point.'

'What *is* the point?' I ask.

'Well, I knew Janis,' she says, but lets it hang there.

I mention that I've been in Port Arthur, talking with Sam Monroe, who'd told me she'd been registrar of Port Arthur College. 'Registrar?' she says. 'I was vice president.'

She volunteers that she's seeing a doctor the following day for a bladder infection, 'very unfortunate for a woman of my age.' Returning to the subject of my book, she says, 'It's an imposition for me to go over all this again, but since you have come all this way to see me, would you like to come to my house tomorrow? How's that?' We arrange to meet at four in the afternoon and she asks me to bring along samples of my writing. 'Even high school themes will do,' she says. Further, summaries of my interviews to date would be required, together with some biographical material about myself.

The next day, I locate her house on Plaza Drive, which winds through one of Prescott's better residential areas. She'd alerted me on the phone to look for the house with 'a real front yard – it's kind of unusual to have grass growing in Prescott.' The house is a low, rambling ranch-style structure made of stone and several kinds of timber, painted green. A late-model luxury import sits in the open garage.

She greets me cordially in her doorway and apologizes for not asking me in, explaining that she is barely on her feet and should be in bed. We speak of Janis for a minute and I mention that *Pearl* is now recognized as the best album made by a woman. 'I see you like Janis's music,' she says, her blue eyes twinkling. 'I liked one of her songs.'

'Which one?'

'It was on the first album.'

I ask if it was 'Summertime,' but she's not sure. Her eyes tear and she says, 'I guess I'll be grieving till the day I die.'

Trying to be of some comfort, I say, 'Janis may be better off than we are. God may have needed a good strong voice.'

She smiles and says, 'Maybe so. I was always very active in the church.'

When I tell her I've brought along all the material she'd requested, she reaches out for it with an eagerness bordering on avidity. Once she has it firmly in hand, she says something that makes me feel as if I've just been outsmarted. 'My daughter Laura is something of a writer,' she says. 'I won't be able to talk with you anymore until I've checked with my family. And there's a lawyer involved.'

Weeks pass and I hear nothing from her, but the lawyer writes me a stern letter. The family objects to the fact that I'd mentioned I'd visited with Mrs. Joplin in a questionnaire I'd circulated to the TJ class of 1960. A couple of months later, in Port Arthur, Janis's classmate Linda Higginbotham Carroll shows me a letter from Laura Joplin to the TJ class of 1960, in which she seems to have misunderstood the circumstances of my meeting with her mother. Laura claims I arrived without notice, but, in fact, I had called Mrs. Joplin the day before.

Laura's letter concludes by urging everyone to send their memories of Janis to the Joplin family. Laura had decided to write her own book in 1988 and was currently offering it to New York publishing houses.

Subsequently, on another visit to City Hall in Port Arthur, Yvonne Sutherlin tells me that Mrs. Joplin is 'upset' with me. Nevertheless, I drive once again to Prescott and call Mrs. Joplin, but this time she's curt. 'Who are you?' she demands, and when I remind her, she says, 'Oh, that man who stood in my door for four minutes.' She refuses to see me this time, explaining, 'It's not good for my mental health.' She has obviously had difficulty coming to terms with Janis's death, but she coldly informs me, 'I don't need someone like you to talk to.' Less curt at the end of our conversation, she says, 'I wish you well with your book.'

The Joplins had moved to Prescott following Mr. Joplin's retirement in 1976. According to a Port Arthur neighbor named Bodie Pryor, Janis's notoriety had driven them from Port Arthur. 'It got to the point where I couldn't bring up anything about Janis, good or bad,' Pryor said. 'Mr. and Mrs. Joplin got cancer when they were living here. They both recovered from it, but I think that was another reason they wanted to leave.' In Prescott, they 'lived the life of a retired couple,' he added. 'They enjoyed playing bridge. They were bridge instructors out there.' In 1987, Mr. Joplin died at the Yavapai Regional Medical Center in Prescott at the age of seventy-seven.

As a young man, Seth Ward Joplin had received a degree at

Texas A&M University before coming to Port Arthur from Amarillo to work as a mechanical engineer in Texaco's case-and-package division, where he rose to the position of supervisor-foreman. 'One of the nicest gentlemen I ever worked with,' says Gladys Lacy, who sat across from him at Texaco from 1942 to 1944. 'His motto was live and let live and he certainly lived it. I liked him very much: He was Christian in his dealings with others, and he never used suggestive speech.'

Seth had married rather late, hoping to accumulate a nest egg first, and then he and Dorothy delayed having children. In Texas, the Great Depression lingered on well into the 1940s. When Janis was born, Seth was thirty-three, somewhat older, and perhaps less flexible than many new fathers. Another daughter and a son were born within a few years, and the first lesson the children were taught was to renounce, refrain, and abstain. On Janis, who grew into a cotton-headed, gray-blue-eyed little girl, the lesson was wasted.

Janis not only expected to get her own way, but felt everyone should applaud her for bulldozing through any and all obstacles. Her first setback occurred when she was four years old. Bill Wilson, a nursery school playmate, recalls how unhappy she was when the family moved from the little house on Procter. They didn't go far away, just up to 4330 Thirty-second Street to a larger house, but in Port Arthur in the 1940s, that was like moving to the country. 'Janis cried and said they were moving too far away for her to come to church,' Wilson remembers. Then the Wilson family moved, too, and Bill and Janis attended Tyrrell Elementary School together. 'She was shy and sweet,' says Bill.

Janis's mother taught a Sunday school class at the First Christian Church [Disciples of Christ] and one of her little pupils was named Linda Parker. When I meet Linda's mother at the church one day in 1991, she recalls, 'Dorothy was wonderful with the children. I remember Janis wearing a white lacy embroidered dress, and being average-looking as a little girl.' Bill Wilson's mother, Zenobia, was in the Christian Women's Fellowship with Dorothy, and once a month they'd meet at a different member's home. Dorothy 'was very intelligent and could express herself very well,' says Zenobia. 'I enjoyed her. She was very nice.' At Dorothy's house, the women were served sandwiches, ice cream, cake, and Kool-Aid, and Zenobia recalls seeing Janis around. 'She was a shy little girl. So was Bill. He wouldn't talk for hours and then he'd cry when it was time to go home.'

James Dattalo, who was in the same elementary school class with Janis from the second through the sixth grades, calls her 'a typical little freckle-faced girl and extremely smart.' James Ray Guidry remembers her as an excellent grade school student. There were three sections in each of the reading groups, he says, 'the smart, the normal, and the "tardos," and Janis and I were in the highest one. She was someone I'd remember even if she hadn't become famous. She approached me in grade school and said, "I like you." We decided we were going to get married when we were twenty-one and talked about it on the phone. By the third grade, we got engaged. I visited her house a lot of times, and she went around on stilts. I was there one day when they were all getting ready to go on some kind of vacation and Janis was stalking around on wooden stilts and it became very hectic and even frantic. But she was a real sweet little girl from a nice family. She came over to my house and I tried to kiss her, but she put her hand up and said, "No." I said, "That's okay. I don't know how to, anyway." One day, she came up to me and said, "Now I like Bill Bailey," but we remained friends. Bill was chubby, kind of like Sluggo.'

The First Christian Church ran a one-week summer camp

for kids in Woodville, Texas, and Roy Murphy III, who today is a Houston attorney, recalls getting into a 'Coca-Cola pop-spewing contest' with Janis. The girls and boys occupied six cabins and devoted themselves to Bible study, volleyball, and buying candy bars and soft drinks at the camp's canteen. Roy calls Janis 'a normal little girl from a Bible Belt family that went to church every Sunday.' Roy's folks had a spread with cows and horses and he says Janis came to visit and enjoyed the animals.

As a small child, as well as later in adulthood, Janis saw the world as a glittering palace of delights to be consumed in the here and now. In this quest, she was often thwarted by her mother, whose strength and will more than matched her own. The love between mother and daughter was intense and would survive incredible tests in the years ahead, but, almost from the start, they were at war. Janis turned into a rebellious child.

'One time, Janis showed up for Sunday school in jodhpurs,' says Roy Murphy's mother. We are chatting before the morning service at First Christian just before Christmas 1990, on my second trip to the city. 'Jodhpurs?' I say, trying to picture them. 'You mean riding breeches?' She nods affirmatively, and I ask, 'But didn't everyone laugh? Why would Mrs. Joplin let her do that?'

'She thought she should encourage self-expression. She didn't realize the ridicule that would come later on.'

Though Janis was a knockout in the little-girl frocks her mother dressed her in, she persisted in wearing pants, an anomaly in Port Arthur and just about everywhere else in the 1940s and 1950s. Jerdy Fontenot, who cut Seth Joplin's hair regularly, recalls, 'Janis always came along with her dad when he got his hair cut, and I'd trim her bangs for her. Even as a child, she wore pants.'

She was also developing a very foul mouth. 'Janis told dirty jokes in the car,' says Marie Lowther, who ran a car pool to the elementary school. 'The other kids were surprised. Janis had been well behaved, but on some days this cute little girl shocked us.' Marie estimates Janis was in the fifth or sixth grade at the time.

Janis inherited her love of music from both parents, though it filtered through to her in an unfortunate way. Seth would round up his children and make them listen to his recording of Pablo Casals playing 'Kol Nidre,' stressing how sad it was. Her mother sang in the church choir, and she'd once held a music scholarship to Texas Christian University in Fort Worth. When Janis was a young girl, her mother had a thyroid operation, and the surgeon accidentally severed a nerve connected to her vocal cords, ending her singing forever. Seth sold her piano.

Her mother's sad experience with music had a profound impact on Janis, who'd later develop ambivalent feelings about singing. As a child, though, she loved the sound of her own voice, and she'd often sing herself to sleep at night, using the folk songs and African-American spirituals she was taught at Tyrrell Elementary. In time, she joined the First Christian Church choir, and it was here that she got everything in one package – both God and sex. At her class reunion in 1970, Janis would say to Bill McCuistion, a classmate who'd become a minister, 'So you're on the other side. I'm just kidding. You're really on the same side. We're just doing it differently.' To Janis, God and sex – spirituality and freedom and pleasure – were the indivisible essence of life. She was as happy being baptized and singing hymns as she was letting boys play with her breasts after choir practice. She loved life and something told her that if it felt good, do it. Says Rev. Darrell Evans, who today is pastor of the Westbury Christian Church in Houston, 'Janis and I sang in the church choir together. She was very active in church, and word went around among the boys, "If you want to make out, take Janis Joplin home." After choir practice, the boys tossed coins to see who'd get to hit on Janis.

'I knew her well and she was unique – complex and caring, concerned about people. If you were down, she'd always see what she could do to help you. She was shy in a crowd, but she'd try anything. Her parents were good people. Seth occasionally attended church. He was an oddball with a strange, twisted way of looking at things. Dorothy's attitude was "don't rock the boat." Janis did not get along with her mama; it was a love-hate relationship. Janis loved her but embarrassed her, and the more critical people were of Janis, the more rebellious she became. The whole basis of Port Arthur's resentment of Janis can be stated as, "She did things I wanted to do and didn't have the courage to do." '

At Woodrow Wilson Junior High, Janis emerged as a bright student – a clever writer on the school paper, the *Sea Breeze,* and the mimeographed literary magazine, the *Driftwood,* and an outstanding painter. As a volunteer worker at the library, she created a series of posters illustrating *The Wizard of Oz* for the library's summer reading program. After work, according to classmate David W. McFadden, 'She had a reputation for going out behind the public library on school nights to make out with boys.'

At school, when she saw a really cute, nice guy she wanted, like blond Tim Berryman, she tried to charm him with bawdy wit. Tim and Janis had taken a junior lifesaving course together and he'd dragged her across the Woodrow Wilson swimming pool in a cross-chest carry. 'She was a little flat-chested nothing at fourteen, just like all the other girls down here,' says Tim. But Janis was not easily discouraged when she set her sights on a boy. One day, Tim was standing in the hall outside Ms. O. Flummerfelt's home-room class when Janis came up to him and handed him a box. 'Look at this,' she said. It was labeled 'The Family Jewels,' and when Tim opened it, he saw two English walnuts with sequins sprinkled over them and suspended and held together by golden ribbons. Says Tim today, 'A young lady of fourteen in Port Arthur just didn't do that sort of thing.'

Janis's trashy style and coarse features did not go over well in junior high. The boys shunned her, preferring the pretty, demure girls. Years later, in an interview with *Playboy*'s John Bowers, she compressed the tragedy of her adolescence into a single sentence: 'I didn't have any tits at fourteen.' Says her classmate James Ray Guidry, 'I was surprised when she said they threw rocks at her, because beginning in junior high she was more ignored than anything. She had been a sweet and pretty little girl but did not grow up with curves and a tiny waist and a pretty face. Junior high is the most horrible time in life, the time of puberty and sexual identity and self-image formation. Here it is determined who are to be full-fledged persons and who are to be the nerds among the boys and who are to be the princesses and the wallflowers among the girls. Janis Joplin got a category all to herself: slut. She was in disgrace from junior high on.'

The boys' rejection drove her to delinquency. According to Guidry, she started 'running with the rough kids.' Milton Haney saw her at a Procter Street dance during the summer of 1957 and says they decided to steal some booze. 'I got Southern Comfort and Janis got Johnnie Walker Black, and then we ran to the seawall. I took a swig of Southern Comfort and said, "Too sweet." She said, "I'll take it." I took her Johnnie Walker and we stayed at the seawall and partied. I finally went off with another girl and Janis stayed there and drank by herself.'

When Janis later told *Playboy*'s John Bowers that she used coat hangers 'to bust into cars down in Texas,' she did not specify exactly when, but it was probably around this time. In

17

Sidney Long's yearbook, she identified herself as a problem child, adding that it was the roughest of rows to hoe. A doctor she saw warned that she would be jailed or locked in a psycho ward by twenty-one unless she changed.

Rumors inevitably began to spread, partly due to Janis's own indiscretions. Despite her mother's warning to 'think before you speak,' she saw no reason to be less than honest about everything. After all, she felt good about her developing body and its new and pleasurable sensations. As she'd later say in her recording of 'Tell Mama,' she knew from the time she was fourteen years old that life was about love and sex.

In 1957, the summer between junior and senior high, James Langdon met her when he and Janis appeared together in *Soldier Woman*, a little theater production. 'Her mother struck me as very straitlaced, critical, rigid, and cool – not a warm person,' says Langdon. 'Janis revered her father, loved him very much, thought he was a cultured man musically. He once sat down and played Casals for me, a seventy-eight record of the Bach cello suites, and cried.'

Her parents, Janis once complained to a reporter, had written her off as a 'goner' when she was young and did not revise their opinion of her until she became a star. Glad to have her mother's respect at last, she said they'd been at loggerheads since she was fourteen. Evidently, that was the age at which some very tough love was tried on Janis, because she later stated unequivocally to journalist David Dalton, 'My mother threw me out of the house when I was fourteen.' To jazz critic Nat Hentoff, she protested, 'My mother would try to get me to be like everybody else . . . and I never would.'

Says Roy Murphy III, the Houston attorney, 'Janis went a separate path when she was fourteen. Most people after that thought of Janis as a bad girl. The rumor was that she went to an old abandoned drive-in near the high school – the Surf Drive-in Theater – became an artist and set up her easel and did artwork there. She was wild and strange and unusual.'

In the fall of 1957, she entered Thomas Jefferson High. 'It was obvious something had really gone wrong with her,' says her old friend Charlie Williams. 'Talk around the halls was that she'd gotten drunk and gotten laid – and there went her reputation. Her personal hygiene had gone to shit. She'd been cute and all of a sudden she was ugly. It was like her total self-respect had taken a broadside.'

Desperate for attention, Janis had to face the fact that she didn't have a chance of winning any of the popular elections in high school, such as cheerleader, Posture Queen, Miss Ideal Secretary, Football Sweetheart, Most Typical, or CavOilCade Queen. What she coveted most was membership in the elite drum and bugle marching corps, the Red Hussars, who performed at the Cotton Bowl and inaugural parades in the nation's capital. Fortunately for Janis, Red Hussars were selected on the basis of talent rather than in an election. Since she had energy to burn and loved to sing and prance, she felt she'd be chosen.

Annette Irwin, who sat directly in front of Janis in sophomore English, also tried out for the Hussars. It was a grueling five- or six-step process that lasted over a period of two months in the fall, and candidates were tested on posture, memory, marching, dancing, singing, and instruments, and they could be eliminated at any stage. Out of 150 candidates, only 24 made it. Even Janis's friend Carol Scalco, a cheerleader, Most Popular Girl, and Pilot Sweetheart, was rejected for the Hussars because she didn't meet the height requirement. In fact, there was a saying around TJ that went, 'Every cheerleader is a disappointed Hussar.'

Annette recalls, 'Janis and I were called at the same point – around step five. I remember her checking the list in the gym and crying when her name wasn't there. I hugged her and told her it was okay. I've often wondered if she had been accepted into the Hussars if her life would've been different. Maybe that was a rejection that was very important to her.'

Indeed it was. Says her friend Grant Lyons, who was on the football team, 'She's supposed to have taken off her blouse at a pep rally. Certainly she wanted to give the impression that she was a wild, wild girl, a slut.' She was not without friends and admirers. Says David McFadden, 'She was very funny, intelligent and talented. She could joke around and both give and take the usual teenage repartee. She was somewhat boyish-looking and her rugged demeanor often caused her to get into verbal battles with others. Some people may have poked fun at her, but she could dish it out herself.'

Another admirer was Mike Howard, who appreciated Janis both for her talent and her sexiness. He and a friend went to Janis's house to make some posters for an upcoming election and ended up playing a game of button poker – the slower version of strip poker. By the end of the game that day, Janis had undone the top three buttons of her shirt and given the boys a good look at her bra. That, according to Mike, was enough to provide 'many fantasy trips for my mind in the days ahead. Hey, this was considered hot stuff in 1959. My friend and I mentioned our button poker with Janis to other friends and I suspect that these little tales degenerated through the high school grapevine until we were buck naked and rolling around in vegetable oil. Of course, my friend and I would certainly not want to squelch any misunderstanding that made us look cool!' When Janis signed Mike's *Yellow Jacket* yearbook that spring, she drew a hand of poker, with three hearts in a row, and congratulated Mike on his raunchy poker playing.

Janis had her heart set on becoming a painter and began to

turn out numerous canvases, though she knew she needed something to fall back on. She intended to become a nurse after graduation and at TJ she was active in the Future Nurses of America. In one class the teacher said, 'In order to determine if a patient has parasites, you secure a specimen.'

'How do you do that?' one of the students asked.

'You shit,' Janis said.

One day, the girls went on a field trip to a hospital in Houston and watched a gallbladder operation. The other students were fainting, but Janis 'was eatin' it up,' says Linda Higginbotham Carroll, one of the twenty-eight girls on the trip. 'They were pulling guts out of him, *eeeuch,* and it looked like spaghetti!' Immediately following the operation, Janis nudged Linda, who had her head between her knees, and said, 'You can look now. They finished sewing 'em. Let's go to the cafeteria and eat!'

That night, the girls decided to slip out of their hotel room for a night on the town. Someone snitched to the chaperone, and they were called on the carpet when they returned to Port Arthur. 'The girls blamed it all on Janis,' Linda says. 'They told the principal, "It was Janis put us up to it." It was a frame-up. The other girls knew they'd believe 'em if they said, "Janis did it." They asked me and I said, "I wanted to go, too. Nobody twisted my arm." I don't know why they didn't suspend me, because I wasn't that popular in school, either. But they suspended Janis.'

In her junior year, 1958 to 1959, Janis fell in with a group of bright, attractive boys who gave her the social life she'd always dreamed of, three of whom were the first to steer her in the direction of becoming a great singing star. Jim Langdon, Dave Moriaty, and Grant Lyons were handsome, intellectual, decent, and musically sophisticated. They were responsible for what may well have been the happiest year of her life.

Jim played trombone, Dave was editor of the school paper, and Grant was a varsity football player. They never had the problems of peer acceptance that Janis had, but they were outsiders all the same, hating the provincialism of Port Arthur. When Janis started begging to be included in their all-male escapades, they were naturally reluctant. She kept calling and finally, as Jim puts it, she 'insinuated' herself into the group. Their affinity was more for drinking, raising hell, and music than sex, but they definitely shared some early sexual explorations together. 'None of us had a romantic attachment to her,' says Jim. 'That's not to say that there might not have been casual sexual encounters, but nonromantic. We were all young and it was a time for experimentation – with myself for certain and maybe a couple of other guys in the group, at one time or another, while partying and just knocking around.'

I wanted to get the football star's perspective on this, and when I visit Grant Lyons in San Antonio, I say, 'I gather a lot of sexual exploration went on.'

'That it did,' says Grant.

Now that she was running with the group, no one in high school dared harass her. Grant somehow manages to look mean and sensitive at the same time and under no circumstances would you want to mess with him. He tries to assure me that the group did not form a protective posse around her, but clearly word would have gotten around that if you fooled with Janis, you might have her new friends to deal with. Discussing Jim, Grant, and Dave later with *Playboy*, Janis said, 'They read books and had ideas, and I started running around with them. We thought of ourselves as intellectuals, and I guess we were in that place.'

One night, they got drunk and climbed to the top of the three-hundred-foot Rainbow Bridge running across the

Sabine River. Says Grant, 'It's an extraordinary bridge, high, steep, and narrow. We used to joke, "That's how you keep the Cajuns in Louisiana." They'd see the Rainbow Bridge and turn around and go back. We drove up to the base of the bridge, parked, and took the walkway to the top. Then we climbed over the railing and went down a little ladder to the girder underneath the bridge. There we were, three hundred feet in the air on these girders and drinking alcohol. Unfortunately, people started dropping bottles and attracted attention below.

'Somebody reported that we were about to commit suicide. When we finished playing around up there, we took the walkway back down. There were – I don't know how many – police cars with their bubbles going, and they took reports but didn't do anything to us. I believe Janis was the one who threw the can of beer down and hit a boat.'

When I visit Dave Moriaty in Austin, he shows me the green canoe they used to take out on the Sabine. 'It's the last major unindustrialized body of water in the United States,' Dave says. 'The Civil War pilings are still there. At one time, you could get a steamboat all the way up to Denton. One time, a bunch of us took a three-day trip all the way down the Sabine to Deweyville.' They were all drinking and didn't notice that a storm was gathering; eventually, they had to be hauled in by the Coast Guard. That happened more than once, Dave says.

Janis once said she became a singer because Grant Lyons loaned her his Bessie Smith and Leadbelly records.

Ten years later, Janis was hailed as the premier blues singer of her time. She paid tribute to Bessie by buying a headstone for her unmarked grave. Born April 15, 1894, in Chattanooga, Tennessee, Bessie Smith began singing in honky-tonks, minstral shows, carnivals, and cabarets. Columbia Records discovered her in a club in Selma,

Alabama, and by the end of the following year, Bessie had sold 2 million records.

Before singing, Bessie always demanded a drink, and she would empty a pint of straight gin, taking it in one gulp. During her set, she kept a burning cigarette between her lips. 'I never heard anything like the torture and torment she put into the music of her people,' said her pianist Clarence Williams.

Offstage, Bessie Smith would continue her drinking, partying until she passed out. Drunk, she'd do anything to get attention, including fighting, throwing her money around, and screaming. By 1927, she was pretty much burned out, and she died from injuries sustained in a car accident on September 26, 1937. Refused admission to a white southern hospital, she bled to death while being transferred to another facility.

The critic George Avakian called Bessie the 'mistress of vocal inflection,' citing her 'huge sweeping voice which combined strength and even harshness with irresistible natural beauty.' She became for Janis Joplin not only a musical inspiration but a personal role model. 'She showed me the air and taught me how to fill it,' said Janis. 'She's the reason I started singing, really.'

Janis learned to sing the blues by listening to Bessie for hours and then imitating her. 'We'd pile as many in the car as we could,' Grant says, 'and we'd make "the triangle" – go to Beaumont and Orange and then back. One time, Janis was in the rear seat and we were all singing an Odetta song. She made some kind of noise of disdain about the way we were singing it and let out a sound that was so powerful and thrilling that it silenced us and we didn't sing anymore.'

Though rock 'n' roll was in the air in 1957, Janis's inspiration came from the blues. She bought an Odetta record and related to the gutsy, masculine sounds of folk and blues.

She liked Odetta's recording of 'Muleskinner Blues,' which also would have a profound influence on Bob Dylan. Odetta's blend of popular ballads and the blues paved the way for Dylan's famous mid-1960s fusion of folk and rock and later to Janis's explosive mix of blues and rock. She listened to the Odetta record repeatedly, memorizing not only the words to the songs but Odetta's style of delivery.

Janis was partying at a house on the beach at Sabine Pass with Moriaty, Langdon, and Lyons, talking and drinking beer, when they decided to go all the way to the top of the Coast Guard shack. They looked out on sea and marsh from solid glass walls on all sides of the room. Janis lighted a candle, James Langdon brought out a bottle of Jim Beam, and David Moriaty popped open some Cokes. After a while, Grant observed how nice it would be if they'd brought along a phonograph. Suddenly, Janis burst into an Odetta song, stunning everyone with the volume, authority, and melodiousness of her voice. After a big, thrilling finish, she looked around the room, taking in the awestruck faces of her first fans. When they praised her, she was both pleased and embarrassed and told them to get fucked.

Grant Lyons has kept in shape and still has an athlete's build and nimble stance. In his wool pullover and soft buff-colored corduroy trousers, he has a retro Ivy League or Ralph Lauren look today, but he tells me that in his football days at TJ, 'I wore my father's old clothes, which looked absolutely ridiculous, I'm now told. Big, boxy pleated pants. He didn't wear them anymore, so I wore them. Janis wore pretty much what we wore, and no makeup. For a girl with a mind of her own and a lot of creative juices flowing, that environment was absolutely poison. I remember my own high school years as being at the outset very lonely. I was very much isolated; I didn't have any friends at all, either jocks or nonjocks. I wasn't dating. My social life was nil. I didn't buy a class ring and doubt that Janis did, either. I couldn't get away from TJ fast enough. It was a conformist, narrow-minded, anti-intellectual, dim-witted place – hick is not quite the right word, but it certainly was not a sophisticated community.

'There were girlfriends attached to the group – Patricia Denton – Dave's girlfriend – Ollie Thompson, Glenda Burke, but none of them had the status that Janis eventually had. Janis was one of the boys, and we were the only beatniks in Port Arthur.' Frequently, they'd go across the river into Louisiana and party at the dives in Vinton, Starks, and Toomy. Once they went to a shrimp festival, leaving the highway at Lake Charles and dipping far down into Cajun country. Janis got drunk in a very tough bar in Cameron and was fooling around with the 'coon-asses,' as Cajuns are sometimes called, and soon one of them came around to the boys and tried to buy her. Janis went along with the idea and a price was discussed.

'How much will you give me for her?' Grant asked, meaning it as a joke. They were deep into negotiations until it dawned on them that the Cajuns were dead serious. 'Janis seemed to be pretty much unconcerned with it,' Grant recalls. 'It didn't cause her to change her style, which was flamboyant and flashy sexy. We were trying on the one hand to get her to tone down and we were trying to convince these guys that it was all a joke and we weren't serious, without getting them mad. Nothing finally came of it, but we did make a hasty exit.'

One day, Janis decided she wanted to go to New Orleans for the bars and music. When her mother refused her permission, she stole the family car, a Willis, sold one of her paintings to Cammie Oliver for pocket money, and got Langdon and some of the guys to go with her to help pay for gas. They stayed up all night in the French Quarter and didn't start for home until dawn broke over Bourbon Street.

'The guy who was driving was a hotshot race car driver,' Jim recalls. 'Around Kenner, it was raining. A car stopped for a light in front of us and the driver hit his brakes. It was an old Willis and the brakes locked and he slid right into the rear of the car in front of us at the light.' No one was hurt, but the front end of the little Willis was so damaged that it was useless. The police and the wrecker arrived, and the cops checked everyone's IDs and driver's licenses and noted that they were all from out of state.

They were hauled in to the police station. On the way, Janis was 'pretty lippy,' and the police found out their ages. Three males in the car were eighteen and Janis was under eighteen. 'We were trying to be cool,' Jim says, 'but they started talking about booking us on the Mann Act. Scared the living shit out of us. When they got to the station, the police called Janis's parents and her mother said, "No, I know who they are. There are no immoral purposes involved. They're just crazy. We'll wire you the money. You put Janis on a bus. Make sure she gets on a bus with a ticket back to Port Arthur. We don't care what happens to the rest of the guys." '

Jim and the other young men were dropped off on the highway by the police and had to hitchhike back to Texas. They walked across the bridge at Baton Rouge and then managed to get rides.

Jim Langdon and his friends were a class ahead of Janis and when they went away to college in 1959, unfortunately she was left to face the abuse of her classmates alone. She angered a lot of the students when she took a stand against segregation and thereafter was called a 'nigger lover.' When she signed Ronald Colichia's *Yellow Jacket* that year, she scrawled a bold message, cursing the KKK and caricaturing their hoods and burning crosses.

She could have absolved herself in the eyes of Port Arthur

bigots by participating in a local sport called 'nigger knocking,' but she declined. 'A bunch of kids get in a car with a long two-by-four and go driving, fast,' Janis said. 'When they see a spade on a bicycle or walking, they stick the two-by-four out the car window and knock him over.'

Her enemies threw pennies at her in the hallway between classes. 'They were saying she needed the money and didn't think much of her,' says her classmate Michelle Sorenson. 'They were calling her a cheap whore.' They wrote PIG underneath a banner she had laboriously lettered for a football game, and when she wore black leotards to school one day, a smart aleck said, 'You know, Janis, one of these days you're going to be in show business.' Janis smiled and said, 'You really think so?' 'Yeah,' he replied. '*Side*show.'

'Students would spit on her in the halls at school,' says Jim Salling of Beaumont. 'During lunch, we went to my car and drank some whiskey.' Linda R. Pulliam says, 'I remember vividly the girls in the P.E. locker room glancing or sneaking a peek in her direction to see if she was any different or "could you tell" that she was doing it with the team.' Bill Hada says, 'Some guys pointed her out to me as a girl who liked to fuck, a Port Arthur shooting iron.'

'They put me down, man, those square people in Port Arthur,' Janis later told *Playboy,* confirming that rocks had been thrown at her during class and that many fellow students had called her a slut. They were punishing her, she said, for refusing to conform and for asserting her freedom.

The one bright spot in her senior year was a big guy named William McDuffie. No one threw rocks at her when he was around. They dated for three months during their senior year. 'I had my eye on her for some time,' says McDuffie. 'It could have been her friendly nature, or her personality, or a lustful eye on her body – who knows for sure after thirty years? I always thought Janis was good-looking back in those days. I know she filled out a pair of blue jeans just right. She was fun to be with, although she had very serious moods.'

They went across the state line into Louisiana several times dancing – to two very well-known beer joints called LuAnn's and Buster's. 'After a couple of beers,' McDuffie recalls, 'she would loosen up and become giddy. She never flirted around with others when she was my date, although it was told to me that she did. I got slapped the first time I got overly aggressive with her on a date, and told right up front that she wasn't "that kind of a girl." This, of course, could have been a diversion, but I don't think so. She seemed to dance to her own drumbeat and was more of a loner and kept to herself. We didn't communicate well with our parents and viewed all adults as "square."

'She would sing the current pop hits while we did the drag around town and said she liked the ones with "a blues beat." We went to Pleasure Island and drank beer and smoked cigarettes until one or two in the morning. We did some light-hearted petting and kissing. She talked of becoming a nurse someday, but she often said that she felt mixed up inside and didn't really know what she wanted out of life.'

Janis's first homosexual experience occurred during her senior year, and it must have taken great courage for her to explore the lesbian side of her nature, considering the homophobic environment she lived in. A classmate named Frank Andrews tells me about the first girl Janis was involved with but asks me to protect her name. 'She was a freshman when Janis was a senior,' says Frank. 'She looked a little bit masculine and word got out that they were lovers.'

Equally brave was Janis's identification with the beatniks. When Pasea's, a Beat coffeehouse, opened in Port Arthur, Frank's brother Louis Andrews remembers complimenting her on her paintings, which were hung there, and listening to her sing one day and telling her that she could be a star.

'Then we went out and shot some pool for love and kisses,' he recalls. They'd gone to school together since the eighth grade. V. J. Harper remembers seeing Janis at the Keyhole, a pool hall owned by James and Harry Monseur. 'Janis hung out there,' V.J. says, 'though it was an all-male club.'

Billie Jean Chandler heard Janis read some of her own poetry at the coffeehouse and says, 'She was into Jack Kerouac before he was "in." ' Billie Jean and Janis double-dated once, and Billie Jean fixed her up with a Texas A&M 'Aggie,' Dudley Wysong, who later became a professional golfer. 'My parents thought Janis was great,' says Billie Jean, 'and my mother framed her paintings. Janis would sketch pastels and give them as gifts. She didn't even sign them.'

Wanda Dionne remembers that Janis was wearing all black to school, including black stockings, in the beatnik fashion. Another classmate, who asks not to be identified, says for days on end Janis would wear the same thing – 'tennis shoes, her daddy's white shirt with a black belt, and leotards.' As Janis once put it, her only ambition was to live the Beat life as defined by Jack Kerouac – make the scene, meet the hipsters, smoke dope, drink cheap wine, go to the poetry readings, and get laid every night.

Since Jim Langdon was going to college in nearby Beaumont, she still managed to see him regularly. When I ask Jim whether there is any truth to the charge of a previous biographer that he sometimes used Janis to freak people out, he says, 'There were certainly more than a few occasions like that. We'd go into a setting where there was a lot of pretension and unleash the secret weapon – Janis. It was so much more effective coming from her than it would have been from a male.'

One night, they went to a party given by a Beaumont socialite who was in Jim's writing class at Lamar University. 'All her straight Beaumont society friends were there,' he says, 'dressed in evening attire.' Janis came in with bottles under each arm and told the hostess, 'Cut this bullshit.' Says Jim, 'Her language just blew them out of the water. There were a lot of white faces. Myra Friedman [author of *Buried Alive*, a biography of Janis] interpreted that cynically, as if we were using Janis, manipulating her, but we were all in this together, for a lark; we were saboteurs.'

Many of Janis's classmates tell me that she showed up drunk at graduation. Pat Flowers, who'd been in school with Janis since the seventh grade, even says that she came to baccalaureate practice in the school auditorium not only 'drunk but sunburned and wearing a bikini bathing suit.' Where fact stops and legend begins is anyone's guess, but I'm going to trust the account given to me on October 10, 1990, by a man named George Arena, Jr., of Richardson, Texas.

A highly articulate and responsible-sounding man, George Arena, Jr., went on after graduating in Janis's class to attend Texas A&M University, became a commissioned officer in Vietnam, and today runs his own contracting business. He recalls that graduation ceremonies for the large class of five hundred were held in the stadium and everyone had to walk across the field and go up on stage as names were called out. It was a typical graduation, with everyone in gowns and mortarboards, and Elgar's 'Pomp and Circumstance' was played.

'Janis got up when her name was called and was obviously four sheets to the wind,' George recalls. 'She staggered across the field and then walked across the stage drunk in front of half of Port Arthur. She broke all the rules in a redneck town.'

What drove her, she later explained, was her rage over rejection. 'Every time one of my overtures would be refused,' she said, 'it would hurt.'

Grant Lyons, the football player, got amorous with her the

summer after graduation. He came home from Tulane University looking blonder, bigger, and better than ever. Now, away from the group, he and Janis were able to express their desire for each other. 'Janis and I had some close brushes,' Grant tells me. 'We fooled around quite a bit. We were in someone's backyard one night, and I remember the moonlight and getting pretty romantic.'

Dave Moriaty managed to escape Port Arthur, going to the University of Texas in Austin, but Jim Langdon had to go to Lamar University, an obscure Beaumont school, as did Janis. Grant Lyons, who managed to get to Tulane on a football scholarship, calls Lamar 'just a university extension of TJ High or Beaumont High or South Procter High or Port Neches/Groves High – they're all just alike. And you take all of those little high schools and you just roll a lasso around them and pull it tight and you have Lamar Tech. And that was one thing I knew I didn't want. That will give you an insight into the world in which Janis Joplin was trying to express herself.'

Enrolling at Lamar in mid-July 1960, Janis proceeded to scandalize the campus, showing up in the student center wearing nothing but a 'sheer bathrobe,' posing nude for an art class, and sitting on the dorm window ledge in baby-doll pajamas as she sang and played the ukulele in clear view of the boys' dorm. Even more shocking to her Lamar classmates were her efforts on behalf of some Puerto Rican victims of racial discrimination. One of Janis's dorm mates thought that she was holding a sing-along until, on closer inspection, she discovered Janis was conducting a sit-in, the first such protest held on the campus.

In the fall of 1960, Janis dropped out and ran away to Houston, where she discovered the Purple Onion, a folkie club. She was too petrified to sing and drowned her nervousness in heavy drinking. Soon her alcoholism led to a breakdown. When she consulted Dr. Edmund Rothschild much later in the 1960s, she told him that she had been treated for alcoholism when she was seventeen.

Mostly during this period, she was searching for herself, a roving member of the 'rucksack revolution' that Jack Kerouac had predicted back in the 1950s, hitchhiking, drifting through the towns of southeast Texas and Louisiana, panhandling, dreaming, reading poetry and novels, shooting pool for beers, and trying to seduce barflies. She learned to be grateful if someone just took pity and offered their couch or floor for the night. Looking in the mirror, she had to admit she'd never be considered a femme fatale: She was homely and pudgy. But she also knew she had compensating qualities. Bright and ambitious, she was cut out for something better than the job she landed upon her return to Port Arthur – slinging hash in a bowling alley.

Until the summer of 1961, Janis was in and out of Port Arthur. The city was undergoing radical changes. The state attorney general shut down the gambling dives and whorehouses and Marcella was dragged on TV in scintillating public hearings. Though the madams acted smug on camera, as if they were just biding their time till the trouble blew over, things were never to be the same again in Port Arthur and Galveston. 'Everyone was caught with their pants down,' George Arena, Jr., tells me. The wild days were over and although Galveston would survive as a popular resort, Port Arthur dried up forever and all but blew away. Janis's only thought was 'Got to get outta Texas.'

Her former TJ classmate James Ray Guidry had taken a job as disc jockey, working nights at radio station KOLE. He remembers seeing her at a diner on Procter when he got off work at 5:30 A.M. 'Janis always came in with two or three guys. It looked like they'd been up all night.'

She was losing heart as a graphic artist and finally went to a painter she respected, Steve Hodges, and asked him to critique her work. They were sitting in the coffeehouse on Gulfway Drive, where some of her paintings were being displayed, and Steve told her that she 'had heart and passion but no skill. I tried to talk to her about this, telling her that her painting was on the sentimental side and why that was maybe not so good. She listened thoughtfully and said I was an older and more experienced artist and she was glad to get the criticism. She took it very well.'

Nonetheless, she gave up painting, realizing that she was never going to be great – and greatness was her goal in whatever she undertook. The golden mean was not for her, then or ever. The accomplished paintings of friends, such as Tommy Stopher, made it painfully clear to Janis that she just didn't measure up as an artist.

One night when she was partying across the river at the Big Oak, she ran into Frank Andrews. 'She was with two of her girlfriends,' says Frank, 'and they got into a fight.' Following a drunken melee, Janis was left alone in Louisiana, without a ride home. Frank, who was with three guys, gave Janis a ride, and they sat in the backseat, 'smooching up a storm.' When they returned to Port Arthur, Frank dropped his buddies off and then drove his 1951 Chevrolet to the high school parking lot. 'We climbed in back,' he says, and they resumed their 'heavy petting.'

After a while, Janis said, 'This seat here is kinda rough.' They got down on the rear floorboard, which had been hand-carpeted by Frank himself, using the thick gray carpet from the jewelry store where he worked. Police showed up with flashlights but then moved on when they saw it was only two kids making out. 'Oh, baby, I wish I had a pad,' Janis said. Then, according to Frank, 'she put her tongue in my ear and got the wax out.' Thirty years later Frank recalls the episode as 'a nice evening, a nice one-night stand. Janis was very affectionate. I thought it was shitty that someone would leave her in another state.'

In the summer of 1961, Janis's behavior became increasingly erratic. She enrolled in Port Arthur College in March and dropped out in July. Then, according to her father, 'She ran away.' After her death in 1970, he said that she'd been willful in her youth and wild as an adult; wide open to experience, she'd sampled every pleasure life had to offer, but to him, her foul mouth and gung ho licentiousness were but a front for a vulnerable, loving soul. Though Mr. Joplin preferred that she remain at home, he realized that she was killing herself in Texas and hoped she'd find herself in a more interesting place such as Los Angeles. When she left home, it was with her parents' blessing and money.

In a Morris Minor convertible she'd picked up somewhere along the line, she drove to Los Angeles, lived with her Aunt Barbara, and worked for the telephone company. However, it didn't take her long to discover that the action around LA at that time was in Venice, the beatnik enclave on the beach near Santa Monica. Dubbed a 'jerry-built slum by the sea' by Laurence Lipton, author of *The Holy Barbarians,* Venice in the early sixties was a sleazy section of muddy canals, derelict bars, and sinister alleyways. When I go there in 1991, I find it still funky but undergoing rapid gentrification by refugees from West Hollywood. Actor Tony Bill runs an upscale restaurant, and writers, agents, and models are buying chic condos with surreal facades featuring giant clowns. But when Janis hit Venice, it was a grim scene of urban blight and decay, where crumbling houses condemned for demolition awaited the wrecking ball. Even the beatniks and the folksingers had moved on, leaving it to disreputable drifters and druggers.

She found a garage apartment near Speedway Alley, just a stone's throw from the beach, and got a job working at Bank of America. Evenings, she went outside and followed the crowd to the Venice West Café, ending up at Angelo's Pizza for a late-night snack. 'She had a reputation of being really smart and really nice,' says Anna Hull, who today lives in North Hollywood but knew Janis when she and her sister, Rossie Stewart, both aspiring writers, lived in Venice. 'We thought of her as benignly bisexual – she had both a girlfriend and a boyfriend.'

Janis's boyfriend, says Anna, 'ran away from Texas at fourteen. He was upwardly mobile, liked well-educated girls. Janis wore khaki pants or jeans and a plaid shirt, was a little bit overweight, and always seemed rather quiet. Everybody liked her. It never occurred to me that she was a singer, though she'd sing along with Bessie Smith and Bo Diddley records.'

Like most people who came to Venice in search of the beatniks, Janis was disappointed and soon returned to Texas. During the Christmas holidays of 1961, she at last made her singing debut, an inauspicious one, at a club in Beaumont where a friend of Jim Langdon's was playing. Jim talked his friend Jimmy Simmons into letting her sing a song. 'She wasn't what anyone around there was used to, and she didn't go over well at all. She was gutsy and bluesy and that scared them to death. Simmons is head of the music department at Lamar now, and I saw him a couple of years ago and reminded him that he got her off the set. He wouldn't let her do more than one song. Their reaction was against the force and strength of Janis. They were expecting a June Christie, a jazz singer of that era. Instead, they got something stronger and more blues-oriented.'

With the rednecks at the low-life dives across the river in Louisiana, says Jim, Janis was behaving 'increasingly not well. It got to the point where it was dangerous to go over there with her unless we were in a pretty big group.'

Jim was with such a group one night when Janis almost got them killed. 'She incited a riot,' he says. 'She and the other girl with us were very bad. They were coming on to rednecks, playing the pool tables, and when it came time to leave, things got a little hairy.'

At three in the morning, everyone in the party but the girls wanted to go home. When the guys refused to buy them any more drinks, they started hustling the locals for beer. The whole place was about to explode in major trouble when the guys managed to hustle the girls out to the car. They sped down the highway. 'I was riding shotgun,' Jim recalls, 'and I was sitting there watching the driver striking matches to see how fast he was going, because his dashboard light was burned out.

'He was cussin' like hell because the car was supposed to go a hundred and forty miles an hour, but although he had it floorboarded, he couldn't get the speedometer needle past a hundred. He felt cheated. Of course, what he was really upset about was that the girls had been acting like whores at the bar, coming on to the rednecks.'

Something happened and the car flipped off the road and started rolling over and over. 'When you were going that fast, it's incredible to come out of it alive,' Jim says. 'I've thought about it a lot. Seven people in the car might have helped us – we were all absorbing shock from each other's bodies. Another thing, everybody was drunk. The car was a heavy four-door Oldsmobile, and we didn't hit anything that wouldn't move. We knocked down the railing and just took it on out. But we didn't hit a tree or anything like that, so we really just rolled until we came to a stop. Fortunately, none of the doors blew off, so we all stayed in the car. Nobody went through the windshield, though the windshield was cracked.

Three or four of the tires blew out and the front end was smashed in. We just kept rolling and sliding until we ran out of steam and came to a stop. Nobody was scratched.'

The car looked as if a train had hit it, but seven people crawled out of the wreck without so much as a bruised pinky. Says Jim, 'The closest thing anybody came to getting hurt was drowning in all those spilled drinks. Everybody had brought a "roadie" from the bar.' Jim and another one of the guys hitchhiked into Beaumont and called Jim's wife and she brought the car and picked everybody up. They left the wrecked car sitting there beside the road, and the following day, after the driver had slept it off, he came back to Louisiana and had it towed to Port Arthur.

I point out to Jim that a previous biographer said that while the car was rolling over, one of its occupants thought he heard someone say, 'I hope we'll all be killed.'

'That's bullshit,' Jim says. 'I certainly didn't hear it.'

Janis Joplin was not suicidal. She loved life so much that she never wanted the party to end. She was learning that even a plain girl, if she defied convention and threw herself headlong at life, could have it all. And regardless of how much hell she raised, she seemed blessed with flawless luck, like walking out of cars that had rolled over at 120 mph. She was right about all of it except one thing: She wasn't lucky at all.

Long familiar to American drifters as the only Texas city on the beatnik map, Austin is the state capital as well as the home of the University of Texas. In the early 1960s, it had a big crowd of party-loving, folksinging, hard-drinking students who were open-minded, tolerant, and willing to try anything new. Janis's old friends Jim Langdon and Dave Moriaty were there, and Jim told her, 'It's Nirvana compared to Port Arthur. Austin is the best-kept secret in America – a little center of enlightenment in the vast primitive waste of Texas.'

Janis was still working as a waitress at a bowling alley restaurant in Port Arthur and wondering what to do with her life. One day in the spring of 1962, Tommy Stopher, a caterer, invited her to come to Austin, where he was going to visit his brother, Wali, a poet and student at UT. Once there, Janis immediately gravitated to the Student Union Building, where the hip students converged on the Chuck Wagon Cafeteria. She cruised the freaky-looking folkies – and Boz Scaggs – and hooked up with Powell St. John, a short, sinewy harmonica player; Lanny Wiggins, who knew all the songs by the Weavers and Woody Guthrie; and Travis Rivers, an intellectual who looked like a lumberjack. Like many of the beatniks in Austin, they lived at the Ghetto, a World War II army barracks now used as an apartment house, located at 2812½ Nueces. Janis ended up bunking there on the floor of a musical wunderkind named John Clay.

She enrolled at the university as a freshman majoring in art for the summer and fall semesters of 1962 and quickly made an impression on the 20,287 student body. A feature writer on the student newspaper, *The Summer Texan,* wrote, 'She goes barefooted when she likes it, wears Levi's to class because they're more comfortable, and carries her Autoharp [a zitherlike instrument] with her everywhere she goes so that in case she gets the urge to break into song it will be handy.'

Powell St. John found Janis exotic and alluring. 'She was dressed in all black,' he says, 'and I'd read *The Village Voice,* so I knew what *that* meant.' The *Voice* featured Jules Feiffer's cartoon strip 'Sick Sick Sick,' and the 'Feiffer girl,' a strange wild creature in black, was sexually liberated. Powell was impressed that Janis had been to California and wanted to know all about it. 'Aw, man,' she said, smiling, 'it ain't nothin' you can put into words. They ball a lot there. You guys have got to get looser around here.'

One night at the Ghetto, she asked Powell straight out to

go to bed with her. 'People in Austin are just too hung up,' she said. 'We ought to get people ballin' more.' It was about two in the morning and they'd been playing music and getting loaded all night and Powell didn't feel like going home. He was too shy to make love to Janis, who was already in bed, so he stretched out on the floor. Says Powell today, 'We were at John Clay's place, but he was still out. I never have been one to make the first move, so she made it.'

'Hey, man,' she said. 'Come get in bed here.'

'Yeah?' Powell said. 'Why should I do that?'

'Well, 'cause John will be up here in a minute. If you're not in here, he'll get in here, and, man, that's just nowhere!'

Powell says he and Janis were lovers 'for maybe a couple of weeks, and then she drifted off and found someone else. That was cool. Broke my heart, but that was cool.'

'Were you really heartbroken?' I ask. 'Shattered?'

'Oh, I loved Janis,' he says. 'I always did and I always will. The fact she went off with somebody else didn't change that. It was just bound to happen; I didn't see any chance of anything going any further than where it went. For a couple of weeks there, it was pretty steamy. Janis was very uninhibited that way. That was another one of her things. It got intense, but she wasn't ready for any kind of commitment and neither was I.'

When I ask Powell whether Janis was carrying on a straight and gay life simultaneously at the Ghetto, he says, 'Oh, yes! Janis and her girlfriend went from dude to dude. Her girlfriend was a real tough person. Really sweet, though – I always loved her. She and Janis were stormy and tempestuous. She drank way too much – a whole lot more than Janis. They'd both get loaded and begin to scream at one another.' According to Jim Langdon, Janis and her girlfriend spent a lot of time 'rolling around together on the floor at the Ghetto.'

Powell and Lanny Wiggins invited Janis to join their bluegrass duo, the Waller Creek Boys, and they started jamming together, singing folk, country, and blues. 'Sometimes she seemed to be making up songs as she went along,' says Travis Rivers, who saw her perform at the hootenannies in the Student Union Building. 'She never thought that she was a songwriter. People would urge her to put songs down and of course she eventually did on a couple of occasions and they were pretty good songs.'

The hoots soon became so popular that street people and dopers overran the Chuck Wagon Cafeteria. 'We were booted out of the Student Union and went to Threadgill's,' says Jack Jackson, who today is a Texas historian. Threadgill's was a former filling station and now it became an Austin musical mecca. Janis sang there often, passing the tambourine among the crowd of two hundred for dimes and quarters. Jackson taped her both at Threadgill's and the Ghetto.

'One time at the Ghetto, we stayed up most of the night,' Jackson recalls, 'talking, smoking dope, drinking wine. Janis was a slug physically, with rolls of fat concealed by her sweatshirts. But her energy, infectious laughter, and wild enthusiasm made her appealing. When everyone left or passed out, she sang "I'll Drown in My Own Tears" and I got it on tape. It came out later on the LP *Janis*, but they dubbed in a cabaret setting and applause to filter out the background noise on my tape, and in the process they edited out her laughter and her banter after each song.'

At Threadgill's one night Janis got into a dispute with some 'frat rats.' 'She put them down quite well,' Dave Moriaty recalls. 'Their retribution was to nominate her for the Ugliest Man on Campus contest.' Janis pulled so many votes that the *Daily Texan* did a story. 'She thought it was funny and gloried in the notoriety,' Moriaty says. 'Were they calling her a dyke?' I ask. 'Perhaps,' he replies, 'but she was proud to be a dyke, so she wasn't real upset by it.' Other classmates tell a different story. 'She was devastated,' says Powell St. John. 'These redneck guys, we used to walk down the street, they'd drive by and hoot and yell things at her. It just blew all over her.' Another friend, Pat Brown, says, 'She was hurt but she had so much bravado that she didn't show it.'

Though Travis Rivers, a hairy beatnik student, was married, he and Janis became close friends. She appealed to him, Travis says, because she wasn't like other girls of the 1950s and early 1960s, many of whom, in his experience, 'required some elaborate mating game, which I was not at that point perfectly adroit at. I could talk to her like another person, instead of through some filter of civility. Janis dealt with people in a very straightforward fashion, right in your face; she'd talk to you in normal conversation right away, as if she'd known you forever. I knew that she had a girlfriend, and I would visit them.'

Janis and her girlfriend decided to take in Mardi Gras in New Orleans. They drove in her friend's car and when they got to New Orleans, they headed straight for the French Quarter, got drunk, and started fighting. 'I was thrown out of the moving car,' Janis related later to Travis, 'but my purse was still in it.' Penniless, she became a prostitute in order to put together bus fare home. When she got back to Texas, she called Travis from the bus station, and though it was the middle of the night, he came to pick her up. As they drove back to the Ghetto, he asked, 'What happened? How come you're not still in New Orleans?'

'We had a fight,' Janis said. 'I was pushed out of the car without any money or anything.'

'Well,' Travis said, 'how did you get back?'

'I did what any girl would do,' she replied. 'I turned two tricks.'

A few weeks later, Travis received another nocturnal call

from Janis. 'What are you doing staying up this late?' she asked.

'I'm just studying,' Travis said.

'Well, will you come over to the Ghetto and do something without asking any questions?'

'Sure,' Travis said. He drove over, bounded up the steps, and found Janis in a bull session with two fraternity boys. 'What's up?' Travis asked.

'See that sand bucket?'

'Yeah.'

'Piss in it.'

'Okay.' Travis peed in the bucket, zipped up, and looked at Janis.

'Is that it?'

'That's it,' she said. 'See you later.'

When Travis ran into her at the Student Union the next day, he said, 'What was *that* all about?'

'We were having an argument about being uptight,' she explained. 'I made the point that there were folks out there who weren't uptight about much of *any*thing and this was an example.'

After that, Janis nicknamed him 'Travis T-Hip.'

Dave Moriaty recalls taking in the tough Louisiana bars with Janis and her new college friends. Unfortunately, they weren't as skillful as Langdon and Lyons at extricating her from the crises she always seemed to ignite. One night at LuAnn's, says Dave, 'Janis was acting like she was available, and Winn Pratt went to her defense. The Cajuns decided he was a wimp and started pushing him around. Winn decked two of them and started taking all comers. Me and a couple of guys in our party made it out to the parking lot, and when everybody else was in the car they came after us and the car got rammed as we tried to escape. Janis was howling in the backseat, enjoying it all, but everyone was pissed off at her.'

Especially Johnny Moyer, who, according to Jim Langdon, got his jaw broken. 'They got their butts kicked something awful,' says Jim.

On a trip to Louisiana in 1990, I find LuAnn's closed but one of the bartenders, now working in a club called the Liquor Store, regards me wearily when I mention Janis. 'She came into LuAnn's drunk,' she says, 'and she was thrown out drunk.'

As the Waller Creek Boys, Janis, Powell, and Lanny performed for a graduate students' picnic and Powell recalls, 'They didn't know what we were doing at all. They just sat there and looked puzzled. We had fans, though. Hangers-on made themselves attractive by carrying us back and forth to our gigs, just to be around us. We were notorious around Austin. We could always get a ride with Julie Paul. She was usually around, and she could squeeze us into her Triumph.'

They decided to enter the Zilker Park talent contest for best vocal group, sponsored by the Austin Parks and Recreation Department. The day of the finals was scorchingly hot in Austin, but it was pleasant in the park, a leafy oasis extending along the river. As the Waller Creek Boys started to perform, a few people were still splashing in Barton Springs, a delightful swimming hole with artesian-well water bubbling out of the ground.

Janis sang Woody Guthrie's 'This Land Is Your Land,' and, according to Powell, 'she really belted it out. We won, too.' Janis had had plenty of practice singing it, having once done a television commercial, substituting some lyrics penned by Jim Langdon: 'This bank is your bank, this bank is my bank/From Nacogdoches to the Gulf Coast waters/Sixty years of savings, sixty years of earnings/This bank was made for you and me.'

Other songs in Janis's repertoire with the Waller Creek Boys included 'Out on Black Mountain,' 'Careless Love,' and 'Nobody Knows You When You're Down and Out.' Says

Powell, 'She sang blues better than any white girl I ever heard. All Lanny and I had to do was put some kind of musical accompaniment under her voice that was as unobtrusive as possible.'

At Threadgill's, Janis often sang for her beer money, and she loved to hear Ken Threadgill when he'd come out from behind the bar and yodel Jimmy Rodgers songs. 'It was an open mike,' says Powell. 'Everybody played when they wanted to, solo or together, and if you came with an instrument or just wanted to do your thing, you did it.' Janis at the time 'was moving into a pretty butch lesbian scene,' he says, and she drew many other lesbians to Threadgill's. Powell was surprised to see them enjoying themselves in such 'a rednecky bar,' but believes that 'Ken and the regulars accepted Janis because of her music. Kenneth just said, "She's got something." He was a great talent in his own right and he could see that in Janis. Think of "Cheers" with people who played music, and Ken was the singing bartender – and you've got Threadgill's.'

One of the regulars there, and at the Ghetto, was a tall beatnik poet named Chet Helms. He had been hitchhiking all over the country and knew everything about the folk scene from San Francisco to Cambridge. Janis wanted to make it with him. Chet treated her like a lady. Telling her about San Francisco, he said, 'Everybody is supposedly searching for musical roots, but they're all very polished and slick, like the New Christy Minstrels and the Kingston Trio. When I heard you and Lanny and Powell and John Clay, I thought, *This* is roots.'

'We're good, huh?'

'Listen, Janis. If people on the West Coast could hear you, it would knock them on their ass. They've never heard anything this raw, and that's what they're looking for.'

2

The Anxious Asp:
1963–1965

'People always ask if I'm Bobby McGee, knowing I hitch-hiked across the country with Janis Joplin,' says Chet Helms. As in the Kris Kristofferson song, which would one day be Janis's greatest hit, she spent many nights on the road snuggling up to Chet's tall, lean body, and they were busted flat just about everywhere from Austin to San Francisco. They shared dreams, meals, sleeping bags, and the greasy passenger seat in a dozen diesel tractor-trailers.

After they'd known each other a while in Austin, Chet told Janis, 'I think you should come out to San Francisco at some point.' Janis always acknowledged that Chet discovered her, quoting Chet's words: 'That girl's good.' Though she wanted to 'get the fuck' out of Texas, she lacked the courage to leave home by herself. When Chet told her he needed someone to 'help him get rides,' she was ready to go.

She dropped out of college the next day. They traveled light, Janis carrying a small cloth bag with a change of clothes and a toothbrush. Someone took them to the Austin city limits and they set out on the first leg of their journey, hoping to get as far as Chet's family in Fort Worth before nightfall. An eighteen-wheeler stopped for them, and Chet helped Janis scramble into the tall cab. As Kerouac put it in *On the Road*, 'Everybody's going to Frisco.'

Janis had always struck Chet as macho in Austin, but suddenly she turned very feminine, clinging to him. 'She put me between her and the driver and snuggled against me,' Chet says. 'I liked her that way – being cute, coy, cuddly, tender, and cooperative rather than when she'd affected bravado at the university. On the road, in stark contrast, she was like having a girlfriend on my arm.'

It took them longer to hitch to Fort Worth than they'd planned, and after a day on the road, they arrived at Chet's home, 3510 Avenue D, on the east side of Fort Worth. A Christian, teetotaling schoolteacher, Chet's mother was appalled when Janis came stomping into her house in funky blue jeans, the first three buttons of her blue work shirt undone, and wearing no bra. Says Chet, 'Janis sat around swearing like a trooper right in front of my mother. Then she jumped up and said, "Hey, let's go get some beer and party!" '

After dinner, Chet's mom pointedly inquired about sleeping arrangements. 'Mom,' Chet replied, 'Janis and I are not sleeping together. Janis is my friend. We need someplace to stay tonight so we can start out early in the morning. Can we stay here?'

'No, you're not staying here.'

There were screams and tears, and then Chet's brother John drove them to the outskirts of Fort Worth, where they stood under a streetlamp and stuck out their thumbs. Fortunately, they scored a series of rides with 'truckdrivers that were driving straight through – Wichita Falls, Amarillo, Albuquerque, Phoenix. That's how we made a lot of time.'

Chet had been a preacher when he was a fourteen-year-old growing up in Missouri, and they had long talks about religion. 'We both knew religion was the opiate of the people, the way they were induced to conform and fight wars. We were both in rebellion against the restraints of religion and particularly the sexual and physical and antipleasure aspects of it. We were trying to avow sexuality as a positive thing instead of a sinful thing.'

Another long-haul truck carried them across the northern edge of Los Angeles and up Highway 101 to Santa Maria, where Chet's aunt was living. Though it's very close to the ocean, this is ranch country, and sturdy black cattle graze on emerald green mountainsides. Chet's Santa Maria relatives ran a grocery store, and they were far more liberal and broad-minded than the Texas branch of the family. He and Janis spent the night and then proceeded north on the last 150-mile lap, over the great mountains around San Luis Obispo and down into the Salinas Valley.

They arrived in San Francisco at noon and stayed with Chet's friend David Freiberg, who'd soon be a bass player for Quicksilver Messenger Service and later Jefferson Airplane/Starship. That evening, Chet took Janis to an old beatnik coffee shop on Grant Avenue in North Beach. Formerly called the Fox and Hound, it was now known as Coffee and Confusion and was run by a woman named Sylvia. Chet's pitch was simple and to the point: 'Janis Joplin is *fabulous.*' 'Well,' Sylvia said, 'this is a nonstop hootenanny and we don't pay the entertainers. Also, you can't pass the hat. You've got to sign up and be approved to play up there.'

Chet convinced her to let Janis go on that night. 'All right,' said Sylvia, 'but remember, no passing the hat. Nobody gets paid.' Janis stood up, struck a few chords on her autoharp, and sang 'Stealin'.' 'It was primarily an a cappella performance,' Chet recalls. 'She sang four or five country gospel songs, and she got a total standing ovation. People were leaping on the tables and screaming and throwing their hats in the air.'

'Pass the hat, after all!' Sylvia said. Janis made fifty to sixty dollars that night, 'which doesn't seem like a lot now,' Chet says, 'but we were flat broke and, considering the sixties, multiply that four or five times and that was a pretty good little take.'

That night, at David Freiberg's, Janis and Chet slept together on a couch, petting, but only lightly. Having taken her out of college and away from home, he felt responsible for her, but after a few days in San Francisco, she drifted off on her own. At the Anxious Asp, a bar in North Beach frequented by lesbians, she connected with an African-American girl whom she would continue to see off and on. Hooking up with Chet again, they stayed in Haight-Ashbury at 1090 Page Street, an old Victorian rooming house largely populated by San Francisco State College students. 'It was a pretty rowdy crowd,' Chet says, 'a lot of speed freaks and drifters crashing on the floor. To quieten down the racket, the landlord busted out into the hallway with a shotgun and fired a few blasts into the closet.'

Janis sang at Coffee and Confusion for about a week, then switched to the Coffee Gallery at 1353 Grant Avenue. The bartender was a tall young man named Howard Hesseman, who decades later would emerge as a television star on the sitcoms 'WKRP' and 'Head of the Class.' Janis was too young to work there and Howard told her to come back when she was twenty-one. He finally risked his job, and the bar's liquor license, to give Janis a break. Again she was a crowd-pleaser and took her place among the Coffee Gallery's folkies, including David Crosby, David Freiberg, Martin Balin, Nick Gravenites, Bobby Neuwirth, James Gurley, Dino Valenti, Lisa Kindred, and Tim Hardin.

Janis attracted the attention of one of the most powerful men on the folk scene, a man famous for his spectacular sexual endowment. Few women in North Beach ever refused him. Janis was to be the exception. Despite his impressive credentials, Janis was so obsessed in those days with the black girl from the Anxious Asp that when he came on to her, she retorted, 'Are you kidding, man? Get fucked by somebody else.'

He stalked over to the bar and told Howard, 'This chick doesn't come in. I never want to see her around here again.' From then on, during Janis's performances, when Howard saw him enter the bar, he'd yell, 'Get out, Janis! He's coming!' Even if she was in the middle of a song, she'd scurry out the back way before the man saw her.

Chet found more singing jobs for her, in clubs down the peninsula, such as St. Michael's Alley and Catalyst, where she met Jerry Garcia, Jorma Kaukonen and Phil Lesh, but most of the time she was broke and hungry.

On February 2, 1963, Janis was busted for shoplifting in Berkeley. In her mug shot, number 19433, Janis is glaring defiantly at the camera, proud and unrepentant. Chet was unaware of her arrest and is quick to defend her when I show him a copy of the picture. 'Getting busted was like earning your stripes,' he says, shrugging. 'We all stole steaks from Safeway when we didn't have any money, or we went to Chinatown at four o'clock in the morning and stole barrels of salt mackerel. It was part of the beatnik ethos, the drug ethos, an adolescent rite of passage, a way to prove yourself a part of the scene: They fucked us over, so whatever we do is fair – that's the way we thought at the time. Maybe Janis was hungry, maybe she wanted to get speed, maybe she wanted to get heroin.'

Six or eight weeks after their arrival in San Francisco, Chet and Janis went their separate ways. Looking back, Chet sees several reasons for their parting. He was still 'in a Texas male mode,' trying to chaperone her, and she wanted freedom. Says Chet, 'She started hanging out with a very speedy, kinda heroin crowd, and though I'd been into this myself, I was beginning to break loose from those drugs. She'd developed a hanger-on crowd that would give her speed or heroin when she sang.'

Another reason Janis and Chet drifted apart was that she was spending more time with her lesbian friends, and that drew her away from him. After they left David Freiberg's, Janis moved in with a girlfriend. 'That had a lot to do with Janis and I drifting apart,' he says.

Janis's lesbian affairs never interfered with a rampant sex life with straight males. One of her ideal beaux was a romantic beatnik named Patrick Cassidy. According to his ex-wife, Linda Gravenites, 'Janis used to make pilgrimages over to Patrick's, just to hang out and watch him and drool. He would definitely show you a good time.'

Janis referred to Patrick Cassidy as one of her 'mythic men,' and Neal Cassady, Kerouac's friend and hero, was another.

The Coffee Gallery had an earthy, hip-swinging waitress named Sunshine, who was half Menominee Indian, and she became a close friend. Her real name is Pat Nichols. She lives in Aptos, California, today, and she's still an attractive, vibrant woman with a direct, friendly gaze and a practical, no-nonsense manner. When she arrives for our lunch at Palapas, the local Mexican restaurant, she is wearing a dramatic serape and high leather boots. Over four large tumblers of white wine, she recalls her waitressing days at the Coffee Gallery: 'When I was talking to someone in the back room, Janis would take my tray and wait on tables, and when I came back, she'd say, "Hey, I got a tip!" '

After hours, they'd shoot pool at Tony's Pool Hall in North Beach or hang out a few doors down at the Jazz Workshop bar. They read and discussed Gurdjieff, Kerouac, Ginsberg, e.e. cummings, Gregory Corso, and Gary Snyder. Janis was hooked on methamphetamine, 'speed,' which was still legal, and she shot it intravenously. Though speed makes the user feel like Superman, it leaves a very evil hangover – a grinding feeling of being twisted and shrunken.

Sunshine had grown up in Pasadena and given birth to a son when she was thirteen years old. In school, like Janis, she was abused by the other students, who threw pennies at her, an odious practice that meant the same thing in California as it meant in Texas: 'You're a whore.' She left home, hit the streets, and frequented Barney's Beanery in West Hollywood.

One night in Barney's, she spotted the most beautiful man she'd ever seen, and when she overheard him say he was going to San Francisco, she made up her mind to follow him there. His name was George Hunter and he was the founder of the Charlatans, the first psychedelic rock band. 'We had this off-and-on scene for several years,' says Sunshine. 'He'd come to the Coffee Gallery and grab me out of the bar and we'd go off in the alley. I loved to make love to that gorgeous man!'

Janis felt the same way, but George showed little interest in her. They met when Janis fell in with George's friend Michael Pritchard, the caretaker at a hip antique store near Divisidero called the Magic Theater for Madmen Only. The nucleus of the future San Francisco music scene convened there, including Chet, Peter Vandergelder of the Great Society, and Bill Hamm, the light-show artist. 'The original counterculture was about fifty people,' George Hunter says. 'They were all entangled with the Beat Generation – Neal Cassady, Ken Kesey, a character from *On the Road* named Turk. That is the scene Janis Joplin was part of at this time. An artist named Michael Ferguson, who later played piano for the Fugs, owned the Magic Theater store, where everyone came to make connections. Remember, this is pre-Psychedelic Shop, so the Magic Theater was the beginning of the sixties counterculture.'

Janis's affair with Michael Pritchard was short and remarkably concentrated. Today a bearded middle-aged hippie driving a van in LA that says MARKETABLE PRODUCTS on the side, he meets me at Barney's Beanery for lunch. 'Janis and I didn't separate from each other for six days,' he says. 'Twenty-four hours a day, real intense. She was crashing in a tiny place in a basement north of the Haight, across the Panhandle. I was twenty-four and she had the blues, but I didn't. She was drinking, and amphetamine was legal. She was wired. Most people were laid-back, but she was very forward and full of vitality. She wore thrift-store clothes, beads, and funny little glasses from Goodwill. She was exploring and the exploration had taken her over.'

Through Michael, she met George Hunter, who was just beginning to think about forming the Charlatans. 'I was living on Downey Street,' Hunter says, 'and Janis came over with Michael. This is 1964, her first trip to San Francisco. I had no idea she was a singer. At some point, she mentioned she was singing down at the Coffee Gallery, but I never caught her act. We'd both come to San Francisco to be part of the Beat Generation, but there were no more Beats, so we had no identity. We all read William Burroughs's *Naked Lunch* and started emulating the life he described. Janis would come by my apartment on Downey Street to score. I found her to be an outrageous character. She was into heavy sex the same way I was. Not necessarily with each other, though we'd make it later on. She wasn't in real good shape, and the term *speed freak is* pretty accurate in her case. She had a real problem with it. We were IV users. It's amazing that she managed to pull herself out of that. You might say heroin saved her, ironically. The New York people in the crowd brought in heroin – poor-quality stuff, came up from Mexico.

'There was always a little bit of resentment there, because

knowing her the way I did, I couldn't see integrating her into my band, because she was such a mess at the time. But she had indicated that she would like to get involved. Twenty-twenty hindsight tells me that would probably have been a real smart move. We were much more into playing the kind of music she liked than Big Brother and the Holding Company was. But who knows?'

Janis herself claimed that George had talked to her 'about putting me in a rock 'n' roll band, and he had this poster, the first rock 'n' roll poster. George Hunter drew it; it said, "The Amazing Charlatans." I used to have it on my wall and go, "Far out. What have these crazy boys done now?" '

When George failed to make Janis the Charlatans' lead singer, he was not the only one in 1964 to let the future rock star slip through his fingers. Recording companies were aware of her, sending A&R emissaries to search her out, but she was not always easy to find. Sometimes she would wake up from an alcoholic blackout in Memphis or New York's Lower East Side, wondering how she'd made it across the country, and with whom.

The summer of 1964, Janis spent in New York, zonked out on speed. She rarely went outdoors but occasionally was seen in Tompkins Square on the Lower East Side or singing in Slugs, a club frequented by the last of the folkies. Janis's folk songs in those days were tinted by her own style of blues, and amazingly, considering her addictions and deteriorating health, she was in good voice.

In the fall, she was once again living in San Francisco and running around with a man known only as Kenai, who lived across the street from the Coffee Gallery at 1436 Grant, over the Capri bar. Kenai's apartment, which was once featured as a bachelor pad in *Playboy,* became a kind of headquarters for Janis and her circle. 'Kenai had hair to his waist,' says Sunshine, 'and he was one of Janis's favorite friends.'

Kenai had been a student at the University of Southern California in Los Angeles when he'd gone to San Francisco on vacation in 1956. It was the height of the Beat era, and Kenai liked North Beach so much, he stayed. When he met Janis in the early sixties, she was living with Linda Wauldron 'and about ten people' on Scott Street in the Fillmore district, north of Haight. Linda Wauldron had a job working as a ticket-taker at a movie house on Greene Street.

Kenai says Janis and the African-American girl were still lovers, but Janis was also part of a lesbian-bisexual set that often had communal sex with men, including, on at least one occasion, Mike Bloomfield. 'This was the era of free love,' says Kenai. 'There was no AIDS then.' Janis and four other girls got a crush on a male pop singer and they all went to bed and became so excited and acrobatic that one of the girls fell out and broke her arm.

Dino Valenti, later of Quicksilver Messenger Service, and David Crosby were always around, as well. Folkies like Dino, David, and Janis would sing in about three places every evening, passing the hat. Kenai worked with Howard Hesseman as a bartender at the Coffee Gallery, and when Janis sang there, Kenai passed the hat for her, collecting about eight dollars and divvying it up between singer and musicians. Sometimes there'd be only enough for bus fare home, but often they'd all go out to eat, usually at Woe Loey Goey, a basement restaurant on Jackson Street, just west of Grant Avenue.

At Woe Loey Goey, five people could eat for three or four dollars. The bars closed at 2:00 A.M., and they'd go in when the restaurant was packed and one waitress was trying to handle twenty tables. Everyone knew everyone else, and when the waitress wasn't looking, someone would slip into the kitchen and grab leftovers from the bowls lined up at the dishwasher. When the waitress finally came around, they'd have finished eating the leftovers and the waitress would assume the table hadn't been cleared yet from the previous customers. Janis and her friends would then just order tea. 'We'd do anything for survival,' Kenai says. 'Sometimes we carried plastic bags and would dump leftovers in the bag to take home.'

One day, Janis and the crowd at Kenai's apartment decided to dye their hair. They managed to slop black and red dyes all over Kenai's expensive rug, and they also flooded the bathroom. When the same crowd showed up the following day, Kenai went to Woolworth's and bought several containers of paints. 'Here,' he told the stoned bunch back at his pad. 'Pretend you're Jackson Pollock. I want to see every inch of that carpet drip-painted.' Kenai claims the results were highly decorative.

When Howard Hesseman was busted for dealing grass, paranoia swept through the coffeehouse community. 'I got popped for dealing an ounce,' Howard says. 'It was decent weed, but I wasn't a dealer, man. If I got hold of a kilo for a decent price, yeah, I would sell most of it to friends and I would hold two or three cans for myself. I was just tired of this asshole pestering me. Finally, I said, "Yeah, I can sell you a lid or two." And he wanted to talk pounds and kilos and I said, "Yeah, I could possibly do that. I don't know what it would cost. Maybe a hundred and fifty a kilo. I could check it for you." And a month later, here's this guy in my face again and I'm saying, "You know, man, I'm not really in this business." "Well, then," he said, "come with me." I thought it was a joke, but he was a fed.'

Kenai grew grass in his apartment, on the sun deck, and one day Janis screamed, 'There's a helicopter hovering overhead! Get these fuckin' plants inside.' It was a complicated process, because Christmas tree balls were hanging from the plants. 'Shit,' Janis said when she showed up the next day. 'We might as well move the plants back out. That wasn't the pigs, after all. Clint Eastwood's making a movie over in Washington Square Park.'

Janis was having such a good time that she forgot her primary purpose in coming to San Francisco had been to make it as a singer. She came to resent singing gigs if they interrupted her partying. 'The girls started on grass,' Kenai tells me, 'then went to cocaine or speed and then heroin to come down.' Janis was now dealing speed and hash, cruising the streets most of the day, looking for customers or a one-night stand. Often penniless, she knew that she could always sing a few songs to cover her bar tab.

Representatives of record companies regularly showed up at her gigs and spoke of signing her, and she'd have won a recording contract at this time had it not been for a series of violent incidents. 'She had two really good opportunities,' Chet says. 'Record people came in from LA, heard her, and said, "Oh, she's fabulous." One was from RCA Victor, and Janis was on the verge of a big deal that would have transformed her, monetarywise and careerwise. Then she had an accident on her Vespa and totaled it and ended up in the hospital. The deal just went away during the course of her recovery.

'The other time, again she was on the brink of a major record deal and she walked out of the Anxious Asp when it closed one night and there stood a bunch of bikers. She noticed the rednecks staring at her and gave them some lip back and they beat the shit out of her on the street. They broke a bottle over her head. She was pretty fucked up by it. This was at a juncture where her career was fixing to take off. Each time she arrived at a crucial point, something would happen to thwart her. Something underlying in Janis put her in destructive situations – she had to back up the machismo she affected by taking unnecessary risks. I think she was afraid of success, felt in some deep way that she didn't deserve it.'

Janis bought speed at a place known as the Hot Dog Palace or, to the drug crowd, the Amp Palace on Grant and Columbus. It was open twenty-four hours a day, and every morning the area was littered with broken two-and-a-half-inch amphetamine ampules. 'Janis would shoot speed right there,' Kenai says, 'or pour the liquid speed into her coffee.'

She was also using heroin, and her favorite hangout after shooting up was the Kearny steps between Valejo and Broadway, which was too steep for cars to drive up. There was a dirty bookshop nearby that was open all night and she'd go there to buy liquor in the back. 'A junkie's favorite nutrition on heroin is candy bars,' Kenai says. 'Janis's routine was to go by the dirty bookstore, get a cheap bottle of wine, which was illegal after two in the morning, stroll past Banducci's sidewalk café and up the Kearny steps, sharing her candy bars and wine with other junkies.'

She was hitting a spectacular bottom. All she wanted to do was to wallow in dope – any kind she could get – 'smoke dope, take dope, lick dope, suck dope, fuck dope.' Her obsession with drugs had become so total – scoring, using, and crashing – that she lost interest in everything else, including singing.

Sometimes she could afford an eight-dollar-a-night room at one of the Broadway hotels, but it was no big deal when she couldn't. There were places for street people to go, like Washington Square Park, site of St. Peter and Paul Catholic Church. 'Janis often lived in the park,' Kenai recalls, 'or she'd take her guitar and party there.' People were living in the bushes bordering the park and cooking their meals in little clearings inside the hedges. It was clean and sanitary, because the public toilet was only yards away. Someone always had a fire going, and there were plenty of extra blankets for sleeping or making love on. The bushes were shoulder-high, and the clearings inside were big enough to accommodate five or six people. 'You'd pass by and there'd be the aroma of grass,' Kenai says. Janis's philosophy for living on the street was simplicity itself: 'When you're tired, you rest. When you're hungry, you eat. When you're horny, you ball the next available buddy.' In the bushes, she'd found her true home – a place she could go where all her needs were met. She had become a street person at last.

'She liked to pick up wounded animals,' recalls Jim Brennan, one of the strays she befriended. At that time, Brennan suffered from such a pronounced stutter that he'd decided to become a mute, and when she started talking to him one day on the N Judah streetcar, he gave her his full attention but said not a word. Janis kept chattering, musing on philosophy, music, and Zelda Fitzgerald, talking a mile a minute. If she noticed that her interlocutor was a mute, she made no mention of it, and Brennan remembers that their connection was intimate and highly charged. She'd planned to debark at the DuBose Triangle but was rapping so madly, she missed her stop. 'Oh well,' she said, 'I guess I'll go to the beach.' She told him she was 'living in the bushes and out of garbage cans.'

'Janis's fiancé was an asshole,' Sunshine says, referring to the man Janis became betrothed to in 1965, helping to make it the darkest year of her life. 'Speed just about did her in. That whole two years was a very sad situation, the whole sequence of events – coming out to San Francisco, then going to New York, then coming back, and then meeting her fiancé, leaving San Francisco, going to Seattle, flipping out and going to Texas because this man was going to marry her – to Janis marriage was the answer to all her prayers.'

After living on the bum, sleeping in the park or cheap

North Beach hotels, Janis moved into an apartment on Baker Street, but it was too late to save her health. She was slowly dying. Chet describes her physical condition as 'emaciated,' and others say her weight was down to eighty-eight pounds. At one point, she tried to commit herself to San Francisco General Hospital but was rejected as a derelict trying to freeload.

She hit bottom one day sitting in a bar. Life, she realized in a flash, was a big gyp. In her embattled adolescence, her only consolation had been the conviction that things were going to get better when she grew up. But now she was an adult and worse off than ever. She wrote to her father a long *cri de coeur*, begging moral support and confessing that she'd lost faith in God and considered life a bad joke. Seth Joplin was the last person to go to if you were looking for hope. A pessimist, he exposed Janis to the cynical philosophy of his only friend in Port Arthur, a man who told her that life was nothing but a swindle – the 'Saturday Night Swindle,' he called it.

Considering her condition, it's a wonder that when she did work in 1963 to 1965, her performances were so moving. At last laying claim to her right to sing the blues, she overcame an old theory of hers that the blues belonged exclusively to African-Americans. As a middle-class white girl whose parents had been able to send her to college, she'd never felt entitled to call herself a blues singer. Now, somehow she managed to transform her pessimism, her certainty that life sets us up only to shoot us down, into art, inventing her own brand of blues, which she called the Kozmic Blues.

In 1965, she made a tape with the Dick Oxtot Jazz Band in San Francisco, and it is a rare and precious relic of an otherwise-disastrous period. 'I'm goin' down to the River Jordan,' Janis sings, accompanied by Dixieland jazzmen. 'I'm going to find that bless't salvation. I'm going to walk and talk with Jesus, walk and talk with Jesus one of these days.' In this gospel song, her countrified voice sounds clear and pure, and her loving caress of the word *Jesus* suggests vestiges of a spiritual life had survived even her darkest days of drugging.

In 'Mary Jane,' she's reminiscent of Bessie Smith, and again Janis has a Dixieland backup. In 'Walk Right In,' her voice flares into thrilling falsetto at the end of this delightful standard. She's equally riveting in 'Black Mountain Blues.'

These performances, which can be heard on the double Columbia album *Janis,* make it clear that, had she not been so ill, Janis might have taken her place alongside Dylan, Judy Collins, and Joan Baez as one of the era's significant folk-singers. There was a raw edge to her voice at this time, a quality that also characterized Dylan's, and she would temper it when she returned to the country/folk genre at the end of her career in 'Me and Bobby McGee' and 'Mercedes Benz.'

Suddenly, a young man – her future fiancé – came into Janis's life and offered a way out, or seemed to. Though Chet Helms didn't care for him, Chet qualifies, 'I give him credit. He was the guy who just felt it was out of control and he couldn't handle her and couldn't help her. The only thing he could think of to do was marshal everybody's efforts to send her back to her parents in Port Arthur. We had this big party, we raised the money, her ticket was bought, and she was to go back to Texas.'

Everyone who knew Janis, says Chet, 'even those of us who were doing speed at the time,' became very concerned about her obvious downfall. She was skeletal and strung out, or, as Chet puts it, 'so far gone on speed in particular and some heroin that she was visibly, graphically out of it.'

Her going-away party was held at Minna Alley, and everyone who came contributed some money for her airfare or bus fare out of town. Chet remembers that it turned into a wild all-night soiree. Afterward, Chet was under the impression that she returned to Port Arthur. Sunshine says it didn't happen quite that way: 'When she got involved with him, she left her Baker Street apartment completely furnished and went to Seattle with him. Linda Wauldron and I went by and cleaned Janis's apartment out. We had to get her stuff because she said she wasn't coming back. She left her apartment with food on the table.'

According to Sunshine, Janis 'flipped out' in Seattle. Her boyfriend wasn't much better off. He was having hallucinations and had to be taken to the hospital. 'Just completely freaked out,' Sunshine says. 'She went home to Port Arthur, and he stayed in Seattle and then came down to Texas and asked Seth Joplin for Janis's hand in marriage.'

The wedding was planned and Janis's mother started making a bridal dress, but unfortunately the groom never made it to the ceremony. 'He stood her up,' Sunshine says, 'and I think that's what changed her life right there. She tried to go straight after that, but she never could, because she was who she was.'

Thanks to the loving care of her family, Janis began to put on weight and regain her health. She teased her hair into a Jackie Kennedy bouffant crown, put together a conservative wardrobe, enrolled at Lamar for the summer and fall semesters of 1965 and the spring of 1966, and grimly confronted a future in southeast Texas. One of her classmates says, 'She sat behind me in a couple of classes at Lamar. She was obnoxious, rude, and she insulted the teacher. I think she was asked not to return to class.'

Charles Williams was in the Student Union when she came in one day. Looking forlorn, she sat down by herself, and the other people in the lounge stared at her and whispered. Charles told her that he was majoring in mechanical engineering and Janis said, 'Well, I'm just passing through.' She identified herself as 'a successful singer.' 'But she didn't come across to me that way,' Charles says.

Gradually, word spread that she was back in town and her old group rallied around. Says Jim Langdon, 'She came back from California weighing about ninety-seven pounds and wearing long-sleeved dresses buttoned to here because she had needle tracks up and down her arms. She'd been involved with some other woman out there and they were both speed freaks. She almost killed herself. She was totally fucked up. She said she'd been out there trying to make it as a coffeehouse single, doing folk songs for the tourists.'

Grant Lyons had a wife now, Bonnie, and they went over to Port Arthur to see her. 'She had her hair pulled back in a bun, and she had on makeup for the first time I recall, and she was playing canasta with these very, very dull people that I myself would not have spent a moment with, typical Port Arthur types,' says Grant. 'She was clearly trying to become something she wasn't. She seemed very repressed and almost shattered, and I remember when she smoked, her hand shook. She wouldn't look up at me.'

Grant told her he had gone to Northwestern for a year on his Woodrow Wilson fellowship but hadn't liked it and 'bailed out and went tramping around Europe.' Dave Moriaty had also been bumming around overseas, attending the University of Munich and doing anything he could to maintain his student-deferment draft status. On a trip to Port Arthur in the fall of 1965, he ran into Janis at a party and found her 'very thin but enthusiastic about going straight and learning how to keypunch. I already knew how to run a keypunch and I knew that would be certain death for Janis. She gave me all this propaganda about going to college and becoming a secretary, going straight and never again trying to be a beatnik.'

One woman, who was in four of Janis's classes, tells me, 'Janis sat in typing class in a beehive hairdo, a sad and lost-looking person. I offered to help her but got a blank stare. "No," was all she said. One girl told me, "That's Mrs. Joplin's daughter. She wanted Janis to come to school here because she flunked out of the University of Texas." She just sat there seven hours a day, her hands folded, staring straight ahead, not even smiling. For some reason, I liked her and felt a kinship. Though she was hurting, she was never unkind to anyone else. You have to understand that, in a refinery town like Port Arthur, if you're different, you never get in with the group.'

Eventually, Janis returned to the coffeehouses in Beaumont and Austin, hustling rides from Port Arthur friends. Powell St. John says she was a completely different person from the hell-raiser he'd known at the University of Texas. 'She was very uptight,' Powell says, 'dressed straight, acted straight. She was very constrained. Whatever had happened in San Francisco scared her nearly to death. She felt she'd gone over the edge but somehow come back, determined to reform. She wasn't singing when she came up to Austin that first time; she was just very severe and withdrawn and contained.'

Jim Langdon now had a wife and two children and was writing for the *Austin Statesman*. He remembers Janis 'sitting in front of the fireplace with her guitar, singing to my young daughter in our house on the hill off Bee Cave Road.' When Jim urged Janis to let him book her as a single folkblues act at the Eleventh Door, an Austin club, she told him that she was afraid of getting back on drugs.

'You know, it doesn't have to be that way,' he said.

'I'm afraid, Jim. I know what it did to me before.'

'Singing and drugs don't have to go hand in hand.'

Her mother, once asked why *she* hadn't pursued a singing career, said she didn't care for 'the scene.' Janis, too, feared the music scene, and unconsciously she may have linked singing with the surgical disaster that had befallen her mother.

Janis attempted to stop drinking but received little encouragement in Port Arthur. Instead of supporting her efforts to combat alcoholism, some people actually criticized her for being boring when she didn't drink. She became such a teetotaler, one of them grumped, that old friends shunned her. Janis had come to the wrong place to recover from drug addiction and alcoholism. She had returned to the garden from which she'd originally sprung, a twisted and poisoned flower, and the most she would achieve was a short-lived sobriety. One of her most frequently heard grievances at this time was that she hadn't had sexual intercourse in a year and that no one in Port Arthur would touch her. 'I was down there trying to kick,' she told David Dalton, 'not getting fucked, trying to get through college, because my mother wanted me to.'

She went to a local therapist, who told her she didn't belong in Port Arthur and surely would find someone in Austin or San Francisco who could help her. Though she often turned to medicine and psychiatry for help, they had none to offer, and it was only a matter of time until the next slip.

After about six months, Langdon finally convinced Janis to sing at a benefit at the Eleventh Door for a blind fiddler named Teola Jackson. She got a ride from Port Arthur to Austin that day from Cliff Hodges, who'd been three classes behind her at TJ and had always wanted to make it with her. In the car, she told Cliff that she was thinking about going back to California. 'I don't have anything lined up, nothing to do there,' she said. 'I just want to get out of Port Arthur. I figure I can get something going, singing in California.'

Langdon introduced Janis that night, and Grant Lyons was

in the audience. It was the first time that Grant had heard her onstage and when Janis finished and the audience broke into applause, he gave Langdon the high sign. Langdon wrote her performance up in the *Austin Statesman,* calling her 'the greatest white blues female singer in America.' He received letters to the editor saying, 'How can you call a total unknown that?' Says Langdon today, 'I wasn't playing booster to a personal friend or hometown girl. I really believed it. I thought she had something unique as a talent. She had the most versatile voice I've ever heard, from Odetta-type huskiness to Jean Ritchie falsetto. Later on, her mother commented on how sad it was to hear Janis's records because Janis could sing so pretty if she wanted to. And she could.'

She possessed three distinct voices, Janis once said: the screamer; the deep, emotional voice; and the shrill Jean Ritchie lament. Her mother preferred her rich, emotional voice and begged her to stop yelling and utilize this 'pretty voice.' That, quipped Janis, was the voice she'd use if she ever ended up in Vegas.

Dorothy Joplin got extremely angry with Jim Langdon when she saw his review in the *Statesman* and, according to Langdon, said, '*Stop encouraging her.* That's not doing her any good. That's doing her harm, writing things about her.' Her mother had wanted her back in Port Arthur, Jim tells me, 'back to school, to do this stenography. She did not want her to get back into singing because of the drug associations. Can't really blame her, I suppose.'

Powell St. John remembers seeing Janis at the Eleventh Door 'about six months after she got back to Texas. She had loosened up a little bit, just enough to be able to perform. She played guitar and performed in a very serious manner.' She didn't sing with Powell and the Waller Creek Boys again, because she was now a solo act and, besides, Lanny Wiggins had gone his own way and the duo had dissolved. Powell remembers talking with Janis about the decline of the sixties folk scene. She'd heard the new electric sounds and found them exciting. When Dylan went from acoustic guitar to electric at the Newport Folk Festival, backed by the Paul Butterfield Blues Band, he created a schism among the folkies. Neither Janis nor Powell was among the die-hard purists who denounced Dylan. They both welcomed the fusion of folk and rock, and Janis would shortly be instrumental in the fusion of blues and rock.

When she performed, Powell says, 'She wore women's business suits, stockings and heels, and high necklines all the way up to her Adam's apple and she had a serious demeanor onstage when she sang the blues – and it *worked*. All this power was coming out; she was singing great and playing guitar, not a lot of guitar, but she was very tasty with what she played.'

Janis surprised an audience one night by suddenly departing from her raw, powerhouse voice to sing a ballad in a smooth melodic alto. When the audience cried for more of the same, she said, 'Thank you, but I can't do much of that because I have to think of my image.'

She carefully studied the proto-hard rock style of Roky Erickson of the 13th Floor Elevators. This band was on the same bill with Janis at the Teola Jackson benefit, and she met them that night, performing with them at a later date. One of the first rockers to advocate drugs, Roky, who had curly hair and a baby face, was riding the crest of his short-lived fame with the most popular band in Texas during the early sixties. Says Chet Helms, 'Roky's influence on her in terms of stage delivery is pretty clear. Roky had been exposed to Little Richard and had that screaming style when you thought you were going to get hit with a tonsil at three hundred yards. Janis's style is basically Little Richard translated through Roky Erickson.' Unfortunately, Roky had used too much

LSD and underwent shock treatments, spending three years in Rusk State Hospital, a mental institution, and his band never broke nationally.

Having again tasted the headiness of singing before an audience, Janis told Langdon on May 10, 1966, that she wanted to move to Austin and join the 13th Floor Elevators. 'Please get me some more bookings,' she begged him. 'I want to work some more at the Eleventh Door. Can you fix it?'

Ever the dutiful friend, Langdon called all his contacts, including Bill Simonton at the Eleventh Door. 'I stuck my neck out for her,' he says. 'I had a reputation around there as being professional, but Janis asked me to help her and I tried to do that.' Soon he was able to call Janis with the good news that he'd gotten her into the Eleventh Door. At last, she was back on the folk circuit.

3

Big Brother and the
Holding Company: 1966

College Station, home of Texas A&M, is as bleak as a Texas town can get. Janis played there one night in May 1966, and a young man came up to her and said, 'You're really good. I know a guy who could get you a job with a rock 'n' roll band in San Francisco.'

'I've already made that scene, man. Thanks, anyway.'

'This is for real. Look, why don't we go get a beer, and I'll tell you about it.'

They ended up at his place at one in the morning, and after a while, Janis got ready to leave. 'No,' he said, 'why don't you stay overnight? I'd really like to make it with you in the morning.'

She needed to start home, but he kept talking about someone from San Francisco who'd been around Austin, looking for her. 'He says a Bay Area band is auditioning for girl singers.'

Janis suspected she was being conned, that he just wanted to get her in bed, but she went along with the game. 'What's the cat's name?' she asked.

'I'm sleepy now. Look, let's go to bed, and I'll go to Austin and help you find him in the morning.'

Finally, he told her the man's name was Travis Rivers. Suddenly, she knew it was all on the level. She liked and trusted Travis, and she didn't rest until she found him. Says Travis today, 'She ended up on my doorstep, pounding on the door at six or seven in the morning and yelling, "It's Janis." I said, "Goddamn! What are you doing here?" ' Travis, a tall, rugged he-man, dragged himself out of bed, tiptoed into the kitchen, and put on a pot of coffee.

'Now what's this band you have?' Janis demanded.

'Janis, it's not me,' he said. 'It's Chet. How did you find all this out?'

'I have my ways,' she said.

'Has Chet called you? I'm going back out there. I'll certainly take you, if you want to go, and look after all the details. Besides that, I'd love to travel across America with you, darlin'.'

Over coffee, Travis explained that Chet had become a very important promoter of rock dances at the Avalon Ballroom and was managing one of the Bay Area's most popular bands, Big Brother and the Holding Company. Everyone in the band felt they needed more of a vocal element, and two of the musicians, Peter Albin and James Gurley, had heard Janis sing at the Coffee Gallery. When Chet had suggested Janis as a vocalist, the response was, 'Oh, yeah. We know her. She's good but she's weird. It will give too strange an aura to the band.' After auditioning fifty to sixty vocalists of all kinds, 'Male, female, and everything in between,' Chet had said, 'Well, come on. Let's give Janis a chance.'

Since Travis was going back to Texas, Chet asked him to pass along the job offer if he saw Janis. At last, luck and timing were on her side. When Travis outlined the deal to her, she said, 'I don't know, man. Things are pretty steady in my life right now. I don't know if I can handle San Francisco. What if I go back and become a speed freak again?'

'Look, it's happening out there,' Travis said. 'You'd be in on the ground floor of something new.'

Travis says they talked for the next fourteen hours, but Janis said they did more than talk. 'This cat came in and *scooped* me right up, man, it was Travis. Travis just came and threw me onto the bed. He just fucked the livin' shit out of me all night long! Fucked me all night long! Fucked me all morning.'

Langdon confirms that 'Janis said Travis was a good ball.' When I'm talking with Travis in 1991 and press him for details, he begins to cry and says, 'I *loved* her, man. I was so happy to be with her. We were nose-to-nose.'

Janis's feelings for Travis ran no deeper than lust. Later, she'd tell Kenai that when she needed help from men for dope or money, she often ended up with the 'Travis Rivers/lumberjack type.' Sex was her payment to them for favors given, but her true sexual taste, in men at any rate, ran toward pretty boys. 'When she picked up someone,' Kenai says, 'it was a punk, an alcoholic-looking man or a speed freak.'

Travis had been working in a bookstore on Haight Street, and in order to finance the Texas trip, he'd invited a guy named Mark to come along and help pay for the gas. Mark also provided the car, which Travis described as 'a '53 Chevrolet two-door Bel-Air, tan, with a loden green roof and metal-fleck stripe.'

On arriving in Austin, Travis had heard reports about Janis that made him reluctant to suggest any change in her life. 'I heard she'd had nothing to drink in over a year,' he says, 'and was in therapy, making A's at the university. I didn't want to be the person who'd put her in harm's way.' He made an appointment with her psychologist, who confirmed that Janis was indeed doing well. Travis told the psychologist about the job offer, assuming the man would pass it along to Janis at their next session, but after a few days, Travis still had heard nothing from him. Not until the kid at College

Station mentioned Travis's name did Janis rush to Austin to find Travis.

On their first evening together, around 9:00 P.M., Travis took Janis out to a rock 'n' roll bar called Fred. 'New York has Arthur, we have Fred,' Travis said. 'You've never sung in front of a rock 'n' roll band, just acoustic. Listen to these guys.'

Says Travis today, 'We sat down and listened to – I think it was Boz Scaggs – and Janis turned to me and her eyes were dilated and shining. "Yes," she said. "It's what I want to do." ' Though Janis was ready to leave for San Francisco, Travis was anxious for her to consider all the angles and burn no bridges behind her. He advised her it would be wise to 'check out her home relationships. Maybe we ought to go down and talk to your parents, go about this in a logical way.'

They drove to Port Arthur, and Travis remained in the car while Janis went in the house. 'I felt I shouldn't be in the conversation, that it should be between daughter and parents, considering the shape she'd returned in from San Francisco. Janis's sister, Laura, said "This weird guy sat in the car." Well, when I started letting my hair grow long in '63, I said, "I'm not going to get my hair cut till we're out of Vietnam."

'It didn't go perfectly well with Janis inside the house. They came out. I assured them if it didn't work out, she'd be back in time for the next semester.'

At the Lamar campus in Beaumont, Janis spoke with her counselor. Again, Travis stayed in the car, and this time he waited two hours. 'The counselor agreed if she kept her head about herself, she could handle it,' Travis says. Back in Austin, they went to the house of a friend named Houston White. 'I needed a phone and he had one,' Travis recalls. He called Chet in San Francisco and reported, 'I have Janis and she'd be interested in coming out and auditioning, given the following provisions.' The gist of it was that Chet agreed to give her a bus ticket back in time for the next semester if it didn't work out.

'I basically told her what was up,' Chet says. The whiskey clubs wouldn't hire the longhairs, so Chet created his own venue, the Avalon Ballroom, for his band, Big Brother and the Holding Company, to play in. They were the Avalon's house band and just beginning to receive national publicity. The name of the band had come from a long list of suggestions, the final two being 'Big Brother' and 'The Holding Company.' Unable to decide between the two, the band chose both. 'Big Brother' came from George Orwell's novel *1984* and 'The Holding Company' was derived from the current vernacular denoting marijuana possession.

If Janis was concerned about 'the drug thing,' Chet assured her that the junkies and alcoholics had cleaned up through the psychedelic process, substituting LSD for booze, speed, and heroin. 'People here are in a positive frame of mind,' he said. 'They're beginning to make it, at least locally if not nationally, beginning to get some attention and money beyond playing a wedding party or a birthday party.' He promised to pay her rent out-of-pocket for the first five or six months. 'She knew that she could survive,' Chet says, 'that she'd have a roof over her head.'

She decided to take the plunge. Before leaving, she paid a visit to Powell St. John, telling him, 'I'm going back to San Francisco, man. I've got contacts out there now. I won't fall into the same trap as before. They told me I could come out and make my music.' He sang a song he'd just written, 'Bye, Bye Baby,' and she said, 'I like it. I want to learn it.' Powell taught her the chords and she wrote down the lyrics. 'Janis had been known for folk music,' says Powell, 'so "Bye, Bye Baby" was a good song for her, because it was for older folkies and rock 'n' roll, as well. I told her that once I was through with Austin, I would either go to New York or San Francisco.'

Janis, Travis, and Mark prepared to return to San Francisco. Though she traveled light, Janis brought along two books, including *The Ten Commandments*. A quarter of a century later, I hold this book in my hands as I stand in the Nob Hill apartment of Janis's friend Richard Hundgen. It's a foggy, melancholy day in late January and I can just make out the Golden Gate Bridge and Alcatraz from Richard's big picture window. Through all the permutations of Janis's life, *The Ten Commandments* somehow survived. 'It could have been a childhood sentimental thing, reminding her of home,' Richard says, watching me as I turn the yellowing pages. 'It was one of the only things I ever recognized from a long time in her background, that and her high school graduation picture and her little-girl picture that she gave to Pattycakes Josephson. I got *The Ten Commandments* at Janis's house, and she'd taken it from her junior high school library in Port Arthur. She always kept it on her bookshelf, anywhere she lived, from Haight-Ashbury to Marin County.'

'Was she religious?' I ask.

'No, no,' he replies. 'Nobody was religious in an ecclesiastical way, but everybody was spiritual. The Billie Holiday biography was her bible.' Billie Holiday's *Lady Sings the Blues* was the other book Janis took to San Francisco and kept all her life. Billie opened her life story with the announcement, 'Mom and Pop were just a couple of kids when they got married. He was eighteen, she was sixteen, and I was three.' Coincidentally, both Billie and Janis were summoned to California to punch up bands. Artie Shaw, writes Billie, 'thought he needed something sensational to give his new band a shove. "Something sensational? That's easy," I told him. "Hire a good Negro singer." ' Chet was hoping Janis would put Big Brother in the same league with the Jefferson Airplane, which was poised on the brink of its first smash LP.

On her way out of Austin, Janis remembered to contact Jim Langdon, who'd gone to considerable effort to get her some bookings at the Eleventh Door, putting his own reputation on the line for her. Says Langdon, 'Then she very abruptly decided to leave town, and of course I wasn't happy to see her run out on those commitments, but there wasn't anything I could do. I didn't think it was real responsible toward me, considering she'd asked me to help her and I'd tried to do that and then she kind of made me look bad. I wasn't thrilled with that, but I wasn't angry with her.'

At the time, Langdon told her, 'I think you should seriously consider staying and fulfilling the booking commitments. Then, if you still want to go to San Francisco after that—' But she'd made up her mind, and there was no turning back.

As she stuffed the books in her knapsack, kicked the dust of Texas from her feet, and set out for San Francisco one more time, she may have noticed the lines printed on the cover of *The Ten Commandments*: 'I am the Lord thy God, which have brought thee out of the land of Egypt, out of the house of bondage.'

Leaving Austin on May 30, 1966, they drove through the Texas hill country, passing the LBJ Ranch on the Pedernales River, and then began the long trek to Fort Stockton, over three hundred miles of endless mesas and plateaus. They started having flat tires as soon as they entered this austere and pristine wilderness. They laughed at the first blowout, but the next time, it was scary; they nearly ran off the highway.

When they reached El Paso, they decided to duck across the border into Mexico. After drinking tequila in Juarez dives, they looked up college friends who were serving out drug sentences in a Mexican jail. Recrossing the Rio Grande, they left El Paso and headed into New Mexico. Janis once said, 'Halfway through New Mexico, I realized I'd been conned into being in the rock business by this guy that was such a good ball. I was fucked into being in Big Brother.'

Asked to explain this statement, Travis says, 'Her "I got fucked into it" story was done as a favor to me. She said it during an interview in New York years later, and when she got back to San Francisco, I ran into her at the Avalon Ballroom. She saw me and bounded across the lobby and jumped on me and threw both legs around me. "I fixed you up, honey," she said. "Anytime you go to New York now, there won't be a single girl who won't go to bed with you." '

Somewhere around Truth or Consequences, New Mexico, they decided to go exploring and left the highway, following two-lane blacktops wherever they led. 'We stopped at a lake,' Travis recalls. 'It was surreal – big stones, crystal blue water, but not a tree in sight.' At just about every stop, they made love. In the middle of New Mexico, they came to a fork in the road and realized they were hopelessly lost. They spotted an Indian up on a mesa, skinning what looked like a deer. 'We're wondering which way to go,' Travis hollered.

'Take the one to the right,' the Indian said.

'Does it go to Golden?'

'I don't know. But the other one has quicksand. See the top of that car over there? That was a priest. He took the left turn.'

Approaching Golden, a ghost town on a hill, they had their sixth blowout. An old man at the service station offered to go to Albuquerque and get a 'boot,' promising to come back the following day to fix their tire. Since it was a ghost town, they had their pick of buildings to stay in. Mark wandered off somewhere, and Travis and Janis climbed to the third floor of a ramshackle building that was flooded by sunlight from big windows on all sides. 'We could see forever in all directions,' Travis says. 'We stayed up there a long time.' The service station owner returned the next day, fixed their tire, and they were soon back on the road again.

Two days later, they arrived in San Francisco without having arranged for a place to stay. Travis had a cabin in Big Sur and had planned to return there, but now he was in love with Janis and felt he should settle down in San Francisco. They found an apartment at 1947 Pine Street for thirty-five dollars a month. That night, Janis cuddled up to Travis and told him she wanted him to 'travel with the band' in some capacity. He kissed her and said, 'Thanks, li'l darlin', but I don't want anything.' Says Travis today, 'In the back of my mind, I'd been thinking about putting together a band for Powell St. John, so it was good to be able to stick around and see how to operate a successful rock 'n' roll band.' Chet handled the rent for both of them.

On the following day, Janis auditioned for Big Brother and the Holding Company at a rehearsal on Henry Street. 'It was an old horse-driven fire-buggy firehouse built in 1888,' recalls the poster artist Stanley Mouse, who had a studio upstairs and watched the audition. Janis was terribly nervous and frightened. Usually accompanied by acoustic guitar, she felt completely unqualified to sing with drums and electric instruments. A girl named Susie was also present and later recalled, 'She didn't know anyone there and she seemed so scared, trying to please, wanting so much to belong.' James Gurley, the lead guitar player, recalls, 'Janis came in wearing Levi's, Mexican sandals, and a torn sweatshirt. Her hair was funky, long and pinned up. She had real bad acne and was a bit overweight. Not promising material, I thought. I'd seen her before, of course, and knew what she looked like. You know, we were nothing to look at ourselves at that time. I'd been working with a daredevil show and had had all my front teeth knocked out. Janis and I were a couple of desperadoes. We were feeling it out to see if it would work.'

After the audition, one of the band members asked Stanley Mouse, 'Is she any good?'

'She's either great or really awful,' he replied.

As far as Chet was concerned, the audition was strictly a formality. He'd always known she'd be perfect for the band. 'Sure she was strange and weird and off-the-wall and she raised the hair on the back of your neck,' he says, 'but so did the band. There had never been any question in my mind that it would work. It was just that early in the game I had gotten a lot of resistance from the band.'

Sam Andrew, the bass player, says that the band was very aware that female singers had worked out well with three other Bay Area groups – Grace Slick with the Great Society, Signe Toly Anderson with the Jefferson Airplane, and Linda Tillery with the Loading Zone. At first, he says, Janis's voice was 'like a tape on fast forward. It was as if she had caught hold of a passing freight train barreling through the night and was not sure if she could hold on.'

For Janis herself, the audition was a baptism by fire that transformed her into a rock 'n' roll singer. The band started up behind her and the avalanche of volume and rhythm engulfed her, body and soul. In the past, she'd just sat still while singing the blues, but now the bass seemed to penetrate all the way to her bone marrow and suddenly she was set free, as if by an IV dope rush. She'd never sung or moved her body with such abandon. She strained to hear her voice over the band, but everything was drowned out by the onslaught of electric guitars. Determined to be heard, she pushed on to another decibel and started screaming, still in perfect pitch.

Though Mouse recalls that Janis 'was all bright-eyed and excited, and everybody was real up,' he took a dour view. 'Big Brother was much more exciting without Janis,' he says.

'There was a Detroit entourage that followed them around, and when she came along, the band changed to support her trip. They had been a real wild, raunchy rock band, but now they modulated themselves to accompany her.' That night, after everyone had departed, two policemen showed up at the firehouse and said, 'We have a report of a woman screaming in here.'

'Oh, no,' Mouse said. 'That was no woman. That was Janis Joplin.'

After the audition, Janis and Big Brother's drummer, David Getz, went to North Beach and dined at the Spaghetti Factory, where Getz worked part-time. The photographer Bob Seidemann was there and says that Janis talked in a whiny, rasping voice that reminded him of a buzz saw (*'Rearrow-rearrow-rearrow!'*) 'She had an irritating manner about her, but somehow she was charming,' Seidemann remembers. He asked her to pose for a poster and they made a date for a photo session. Meanwhile, she wrote to friends at home that she was probably going to be the first counter-culture pinup girl. Seidemann's poster of James Gurley in western garb and sporting an Indian feather had already had a nationwide impact on the style and behavior of the younger generation, and Seidemann's nude poster of Janis would also create a sensation.

Asked to describe the scene in his studio the day Janis arrived to pose for the nude poster, Seidemann says that originally the plan was for her to be bare only from the waist up, except for a cape and some beads. He shot several rolls of black and white 35 mm film of Janis with a nipple peaking through the beads. 'After I'd gotten what I wanted that day,' he says, 'Janis said, "Oh motherfucker! I want to take my fuckin' clothes off." '

' "Janis," I said, "don't take your fuckin' clothes off!" It was too late. Her pants were off and suddenly we were taking pictures. That's the way she was. She wanted to take her clothes off real bad. After the photo shoot, she got dressed and I drove her to her apartment.' The complete nude shot of Janis was far too controversial to use and did not appear until about five years later, when it showed up in *Rolling Stone*. 'Her panty line is clearly discernible in the photo,' Bob says. 'Usually in taking nudes, I have the model take off her panties in plenty of time for the panty line to disappear. But Janis took off her clothes unexpectedly and we went right to work, and that's why you can see her panty line in the photograph.' The seminude poster, showing Janis in beads with one breast exposed, was a hit when it was distributed.

About a year after the nude picture session, Bob and Janis went to bed together. 'Hey,' he said, 'let's get it on.'

Janis replied, 'I wondered when you were going to ask me.'

Sex with Janis was 'ferocious,' he said. 'We were just ships passing in the night, all night, every night, night after night. She was hungry and insatiable. And desperate. "All of it. Everything. I need it now." '

When I observe, 'That doesn't sound like very comfortable sex,' Bob replies, 'It depends on the mood you're in.' After reflecting a moment, he adds, 'It was a little bit scary, actually, to have someone come at you. She made love to men and women with equal aplomb and frequently at the same time. There wasn't any aspect of outrageous that she left uncovered. I liked her. You had to hand it to her. She was just trying to have a good fucking time as hard as she could. I don't know how she lasted for more than a week.'

Big Brother did a sound check with Janis at the Avalon Ballroom and then Chet told her they'd try her out in front of an audience on June 10, 1966. They rehearsed all week and

worked up an arrangement of an old gospel song, 'Down on Me,' which she wanted to open with. Recalling their first performance together, Sam Andrew says the band came on before she did and played their usual 'insane, free-jazz, speedy clash jam. It is difficult to exaggerate how fast we played then. It was faster than the punk rockers who came later. Maybe it was Charlie Parker tempo, around two hundred and eighty-five quarter notes per minute . . . prestissimo!'

When Janis came on, she was wearing her drab, beatnik college gear – jeans and a blue work shirt. One of the musicians announced her, and with the first blast of rock from Big Brother, she went wild, possessed by the same ecstasy she'd felt at the audition. The Avalon regulars, who usually stood around in the back, drinking and talking and looking blasé, put aside their libations and surged toward the stage. After the set, Janis turned to the band and told them she'd decided to keep the job. 'She was a knockout,' Chet says. Travis adds, 'Word spread like wildfire that Janis was back – everyone on Grant and Green remembered her, and all her old friends from North Beach started showing up at the Avalon.'

Sunshine caught her act one night in June and says that Janis was wearing a muumuu and 'really screaming.' Many fans came up to Gurley after Janis's debut and said, 'Get rid of her! She's terrible. All she can do is scream.' Before Janis joined the band, Gurley had been Big Brother's main attraction. Today, his voice still retains an edge of resentment when he speaks of her. 'People think she discovered us, but the opposite is true. We took her when nobody would have given two cents for her, to look at her. We kept at it, changed the focus, and people began to see and hear what we heard, which was the incredible voice.'

Mark Braunstein, later Big Brother's roadie but at the time still a freshman at San Francisco State College, says, 'She was not well liked when she got to town. I remember being pissed off. I went to the Avalon to hear Big Brother and here's this chick singer, screaming. I came to hear James Gurley's erratic, loud, passionate guitar playing, which made me feel exhilarated and free.'

The hippie dances at the Avalon were something new in American nightlife. The separation between performers and audience was abolished. The band was on a low platform, and when things got going, band and audience were part of one big happening. Instead of spotlights on the performers, psychedelic light shows and strobes strafed the whole scene, melting them together in an experience without precedent. Neal Cassady 'would get up and rap and the band would stop sometimes for an hour,' Gurley remembers, adding, 'If I felt like playing my guitar for forty-five minutes, high on LSD and going wherever it led me, I'd do it.' Janis dazzled everyone nightly with vocal feats that seemed to defy the laws of nature. She appeared to be able to harmonize with herself, and one awestruck reviewer said, 'Her voice stretched past the breaking point without ever snapping.' Janis said, 'That forty or fifty minutes I'm out there, that's when it happens for me. It's like a hundred orgasms with somebody you love.'

For many people in San Francisco at the time, going to the Avalon became a way of life. 'I went dancing six or seven nights a week, from eight o'clock until midnight every night nonstop,' says Mouse. 'Everybody just got out there and boogied their bottoms off.' Occasionally, everyone on the dance floor would become aware of an eerie presence among them and stop in their tracks. It was Augustus Stanley Owsley III, the short, dark-haired manufacturer of the best LSD in the world. Dancers parted like a wave in front of him. He always got the musicians high on his latest brand of acid and passed out Blue Dots or other varieties of LSD to people on the dance floor.

Some nights, the band played venues other than the Avalon. Journalist Tom Wolfe saw Janis at a loft called the Berkeley Club, which charged two dollars admission. 'I had never heard such a voice or seen such a presentation,' he said. 'She was riveting.'

Janis soon became a familiar figure in the Haight, but her earnings were meager and she had to live frugally. In 1966, the band made about $250 a week, which gave each of them $50. 'She was living in this flophouse in Pine Street,' says Jim Langdon, who came out from Texas that summer to visit her. Travis speaks more fondly of the Pine Street apartment, where he was very happy as Janis's lover. David Getz, Big Brother's drummer, calls it 'a one-room apartment – a bedroom with a sink.'

The apartment on Pine Street was in an old Victorian house, and in order to live rent-free, most of the tenants subdivided their apartments and rented out rooms. Janis and Travis, for instance, occupied the rear end of a floor-through apartment leased by Motorcycle Richie, who acted in Michael McClure's play *The Beard*.

Janis's favorite member of Big Brother was the muscular, compact drummer, David Getz, who was good about giving her rides. They'd gotten as far as necking. 'We would make out like teenagers,' Dave recalls. 'We all lived this real free life; none of us had anything besides some clothes, draperies, maybe a few pictures. Bill Graham wouldn't hire us in those days, but we played the Avalon for Chet and there were enough other places to play, and we were performing every weekend, two or three times a week.'

Dave was still a waiter at the Spaghetti Factory, and one night he and Janis had some drinks there, then went down the street to the Anxious Asp. A black lesbian was playing pool, and Dave remembers how beautiful she was. 'There were definitely vibes between Janis and the black,' Dave says. 'As soon as we left, Janis said, "Boy, am I turned on by her. I'd love to ball her." '

'What?' Dave asked. 'What did you say? *"Her"*?' He'd never expected this and was shocked. 'After that,' Dave says, 'we were like brother and sister.' Janis's affection for Dave was both personal and professional. In her estimation, Dave Getz was the classiest guy in the band. She respected him for his equanimity and integrity and said she could always depend on him to do the right thing.

When Dave drove her home one day after rehearsal, she said, 'It's just a temporary thing with me and Travis. I don't plan to stay with him, but he's a good fuck and a good person and it's very convenient.' From time to time, she and Travis would split up and then come back together. She was grateful to him for bringing her to San Francisco and tried to return the favor, forever telling people how he'd revitalized the *Texas Ranger* in their Austin days, putting the paper on sound financial footing. Soon her promotional efforts on Travis's behalf bore fruit. 'I credit Janis with getting me on *The City of San Francisco Oracle*,' Travis says. Again his publishing and advertising acumen paid off and the underground newspaper went from zero circulation to 100,000 in six issues.

The most charismatic member of Big Brother was lead guitar player James Gurley. He already had a large following when Janis joined the band and many looked on him as a spiritual leader. Gigantic god's eyes (yarn wrapped around sticks to form a triangle) were draped from the amps at Big Brother concerts, symbolizing the third eye of spiritual understanding, and Jim was referred to as the one-eyed guitar player (though he has two perfectly healthy, functioning eyes). Many regarded him as the archetypal rock 'n' roll guitar player –

Janis had a bracelet tattooed on her wrist. She made her necklaces on a loom, using antique beads and knotted leather. (*David Gahr*)

The house in Griffing Park, Port Arthur, that Janis moved to as a small child and where she grew up. (*V. J. Harper II*)

Janis was baptized in 1954 in First Christian Church. (*V. J. Harper II*)

Woodrow Wilson Junior High, where Janis completed grades 7–9. (*V. J. Harper II*)

The "old" Thomas Jefferson High School, where Janis attended grades 10–11. (*V. J. Harper II*)

She broke the rules in a redneck town and paid the price. Janis felt the edge of the universe came up as far as the Port Arthur city limits and abruptly stopped. (*V. J. Harper II*)

Janis as a sophomore in 1958. She tried to use outrageousness as a means of gaining popularity in high school; she failed.

Janis as a senior in the "new" Thomas Jefferson High School, 1960.

In her junior year of high school Janis fell in with a group of bright, attractive boys who were Port Arthur's first beatniks. James Langdon was their leader.

Grant Lyons, the high school varsity football guard who got Janis interested in singing.

Like Janis, David Moriarty, editor of the high school newspaper, would go to San Francisco and become a "hippie capitalist," running the Rip-Off Press.

Janis first performed in this coffeehouse in Port Arthur, and she also hung some of her paintings here. The building still stands on Gulfway Drive. (V. J. Harper II)

Chet Helms (*left*) hitchhiked to San Francisco with Janis in 1963. He helped found Big Brother and the Holding Company, whose main attraction, before Janis, was a romantic, mystical guitar player from Detroit named James Gurley (*right*). (*Herb Greene*)

Travis Rivers fell in love with Janis while bringing her back to San Francisco in 1966 to be Big Brother's "chick singer." She turned down his marriage proposal. (*Señor McGuire*)

Big Brother and the Holding Company, Golden Gate Park, 1966. *Left to right*, Sam Andrew, David Getz, Janis, James Gurley, and Peter Albin. Janis and James were in love, and he left his wife for two weeks to live with Janis. (*Herb Greene*)

Photographer Bob Seidemann didn't want Janis to take all her clothes off but she stripped anyway. (*Bob Seidemann*)

Tyrannical Bill Graham refused to book Janis until she became an international star in '67. When she finally played the Fillmore, she violated his rule against pot-smoking backstage, and he threw her bodily out of the theater. (*Herb Greene*)

ethereal, mystic, and aloof. Says Richard Hundgen, the Avalon's mescaline tester and later Big Brother's road manager, 'James liked to play guitar constantly, all day long, sitting on his chair, watching television without the sound on. People would come and go and he would never stop. He was stoned, and people would come in and leave him some pot. While he was transfixed, glued to the soundless TV, playing the guitar, his entourage would sit at his feet. James was very highly thought of, a mystical leader.'

I like James Gurley when I meet him in Palm Desert, California, for an interview. Time has not dimmed his alluring aura. We dine at TGI Fridays and right away he leans across the table and starts talking like an old friend. His face radiates a punk nobility, with high, savage cheekbones and a merry blue-eyed smile, and his body is lean but very strong and broad-shouldered. His laugh is early Eddie Murphy mule bray (*honk honk honk*), but it is soft and endearing.

In the early sixties, Howard Hesseman had met him in the Coffee Gallery and gone over to Gurley's apartment to listen to him play guitar for hours at a time. 'Nobody played guitar like Jim Gurley,' Howard says. 'It was more like a sitar – he had so many different weird kinds of sounds, blues runs going on, country and western licks, jazz. He was the first fusionist that I heard playing before it became an over-used and overrated term.'

Gurley was pure catnip to Janis, but his beautiful wife, Nancy, had her climbing the walls. In a bare-breasted photograph owned by Richard Hundgen, Nancy has all the earthy vitality and exotic appeal of a gypsy flamenco dancer. Nancy and James lived in a house on Oak Street, and Janis was always welcome there. Though it was perfectly clear to Nancy that Janis desired her husband, she tried to avoid jealousy and anger. She loved Janis as a kindred spirit and sympathized with her when she was lonely and depressed.

During my Palm Desert visit with Gurley, I show him a Herb Greene photograph in which Janis is gazing at him lovingly and ask him to comment. 'She's looking at me because that's when we were in love,' he says. 'That's when my teeth were out. I ain't got no front teeth. That's the way she looked when she first joined the band [like a poor beatnik chick in sandals].'

'How,' I ask, 'did your wife, Nancy, tolerate your relationship with Janis?' He smiles and shrugs, saying nothing. 'Her love could encompass . . . even that?' I venture. Again he smiles faintly but remains silent. After a while, he says, 'Not long after Janis got to San Francisco, I left Nancy and lived with Janis for two weeks.'

In coming between the Gurleys, Janis betrayed her best woman friend and jeopardized her own professional future, as well as Gurley's. When she spoke of her relationship with Jim, she tried to minimize it by referring to it as a mini affair, but at the same time she admitted that it nearly destroyed the band. Even several years later, she still grew rapturous when she referred to Jim, extolling his physical beauty, spirituality, and kindness. She loved him with a passion she'd never known before, sleeping with him every chance she got, completely disregarding the fact that Jim and Nancy were married and responsible for a young son, Hongo (pronounced with a silent *H*). Says Sam Andrew, 'I remember hearing Janis and James making love, because I was living in the same house, in the back, with Rita, and I was quite impressed. Janis was expressing herself as well that way as she did when she was singing. It was great, but Nancy reasserted herself. She and James had been together for a long time and there was the baby, Hongo, to take care of.'

The inevitable explosion occurred one day when Nancy burst in on Janis and Gurley in bed. 'What an embarrassing situation,' Janis later said to Langdon, who was visiting San

Francisco. 'His old lady come marching into my bedroom with the kid and the dog and confronts us.'

Recalling the ruckus, Sam says, 'Nancy was yelling around the place, whereas James was reticent. Nancy was very upset and she expressed just what she felt like all the time, in loud and raucous language. She was very unhappy about it.'

Janis invited James Langdon to catch her set at the Avalon, and later he told her that he was very impressed with her singing. The band, he didn't care for. 'Maybe there was something about dope-driven energy that captured the spirit of the times better than some of her later groups,' he says, 'but musically, I did not think they were proficient.'

As to the condition he found Janis in, he says, 'I thought she was probably back into drugs. It just seemed to go with the territory. Travis Rivers was living in a closet out in the hall. I think it was a junkie palace. There were a lot of hard-core junkies living in the building.' Dave Getz also noticed the druggie character of the building, calling it a 'speed-freak house.'

Janis was getting ready to go to Canada for the Vancouver Trips Festival, and she let Langdon use her apartment while she was away. Gurley's face cracks into a wide smile when he recalls this period. Despite his mixed feelings about Janis, he speaks of this time with obvious warmth. 'All's we had was money to get to Seattle,' he says. 'We took a plane to Seattle and then walked from the airport to the freeway and hitch-hiked to Vancouver, with all our equipment. Janis carried a bunch of drums and I had a guitar and amplifiers. Guys picked us up, and when we got to Vancouver, we slept on the floor, all of us in one room.'

'Was that fun?' I ask.

'Yeah! That was great! In fact, the best years were before we made it. She used to hang out in pool halls and bars.

Texas girl, you know – she'd do anything. So what? She was right there, where a lot of women wouldn't have done that. They wouldn't have been sleepin' on the floor and hitchhikin' and carryin' a guy's drums. Those were the best years to me because that's when we were all together. We were all united in our quest, you know.'

Janis shared Gurley's love of the band's early days. Once again, she was a lone woman in a pack of rough-and-ready men, just as she'd been in Texas. Four abreast, Janis, Gurley, Getz, and Andrew ambled down Haight Street, swigging from a bottle of Ripple, acknowledging greetings from adoring groupies, and sizing up potential bedmates for the night. Truly, she'd never had it so good.

This was the era of communes, and the band now started talking about taking a big house and all living together in the country. 'It was the thing to do,' Dave Getz says, 'to get out of the city, live communally, and play music together every day.' The Grateful Dead were all living together in a house in Marin, as were Quicksilver Messenger Service. Janis decided that if she went to live with the band, she'd split up with Travis Rivers. Says Dave Getz, 'She always said that it was a temporary thing. To me, he didn't have a whole lot to offer as a personality or a talent. To Janis, he had some talent, which was that he was a great fuck. That's what she said. He looked like Clark Kent, strong but mild-mannered. It was a comfortable arrangement, but they had no strings on each other, and she liked it that way. He was romantically attached to her, but it would never work at all for her because she was just coming into her own as a singer.'

In July 1966, Travis, who'd always been an ardent lover, became even more passionate. 'In a misty-eyed moment, I asked her to marry me,' he says. Janis eyed him coldly for a moment and said, 'No.' Then she stood there waiting for him to react, and when he didn't, she became agitated, lighting a cigarette and swaggering around the room. 'She got mad because I didn't pursue it,' Travis explains. Finally, he grabbed her and said, 'What's the matter?'

'If you really loved me, you'd want to know why.'

'Why?'

'I know that I'm going to be really big,' she said. 'Really, really big. This will be the only time in my life I'll be able to have any boy over the age of fourteen I want and I don't intend to miss the opportunity.'

Knowing Janis as he did, Travis was not surprised by her reaction. The only thing that was hard for him to understand was the edge to her voice, which seemed uncalled for, under the circumstances. But he was willing to drop the subject without further comment. Not Janis. In a loud voice, she said, 'After I've said something like that to you, you would have to beat me up if you'd really loved me.'

'No,' Travis replied, 'it's not what I would have done.'

She stormed out of the apartment. 'It was a complicated moment for her,' Travis says. 'She went and looked at the place in Lagunitas that very day. That evening, she came back to Pine Street and said, "They took the place. I'm moving." And by the following week, she was up there, living in a commune with the band. We didn't speak for a while, and it was a bit awkward. After she left the apartment that day, Motorcycle Richie's girl came in and said, "I overheard the entire conversation and I just want you to know I think you just got a raw deal. But here's the good news. My boyfriend and I are moving to Mexico and you can have the whole floor for a hundred dollars a month." '

Travis could now live there for free by renting out the other end of the floor-through. It was small consolation, though. Today, twenty-five years later, he still speaks of Janis with hurt and love in his voice.

During my visit with Sunshine in Aptos, I ask, 'How could someone who bitched as much as Janis about not getting laid turn down a guy like Travis?'

'Travis was gorgeous,' Sunshine observes, 'no doubt about it. But having a honey like him on the one hand and being faced with stardom on the other – I wouldn't have married him, either. I would have said, "Hey, man, down the line. Check it out later." She wasn't ready to give up the opportunity to be famous.'

'I don't buy that,' I say. 'Marriage and fame are not mutually exclusive, especially where Travis was concerned. After Janis, he managed and lived with Tracy Nelson for years. Isn't the truth simply that Janis was a lesbian?'

'Janis didn't care for labels,' Sunshine says. 'You're talking about somebody who drank a lot and blacked out. We used drugs, very often didn't know what was happening. Although she could drive across town and act like she was completely sober, she couldn't remember the next day who it was she'd been with. She just fell into what was happening.'

In July 1966, together with the other members of Big Brother, Janis moved to Lagunitas ('little lakes'), a former logging camp in the redwoods, just over the Golden Gate Bridge. It was one of the first of the sixties communes, part of a Utopian movement that would briefly flourish before dying out in the early seventies. 'All the bands who could were moving to the country that year,' Sam recalls. 'It was the hippie version of getting a little money and going to the suburbs.' Sam lived in a small cabin behind the main house with his girlfriend, Speedfreak Rita. 'We would make love for hours,' he recalls, but for Sam, country life soon palled and he longed to return to his urban roots.

The isolation of the country was anathema to Janis, who was now cut off from lesbian bars and jive-punk lovers. Her room in the big, rambling main house was upstairs next to

Peter and Cindy Albin's, and it was spacious and bright, with a view of the redwoods. While everyone else in the band had a spouse or lover, except for Dave Getz – and shortly he would, too – Janis sat at her bead loom, stringing beads for hours on end. She made a beaded string to hang from the head of her guitar, a Gibson Hummingbird. Eventually, Sam inherited the guitar and today still praises its 'lovely singing tone in the treble and the big and resonant bass.' Being the sole single in a houseful of couples became 'a big hassle' for Janis, says Sam, and he found her loneliness 'very poignant. Rita and I often thought of her sitting in that room by herself. She was convinced that her bad skin scared off lovers, but I didn't notice that it was that bad, myself.'

On the professional and artistic level, the commune succeeded brilliantly. Thrown together in close quarters, the band honed itself into the pile-driving juggernaut that shot to fame the following year at the Monterey Pop Festival. To compare their sloppy, amateurish performance of 'Ball and Chain' at California Hall on July 28, 1966, with the 1967 version in the film *Monterey Pop* is to realize the miracle that was achieved through long hours of rehearsal during the months at Lagunitas.

And while the band improved, Janis and Sam were busy composing original songs that would form their concert repertoire as well as the basis for their hit singles and albums. Sam wrote his beautiful ballad 'Call on Me' – 'to Rita and for Janis' – and he and Janis together wrote 'I Need a Man to Love,' which evolved from a backstage warm-up session before a performance one night. Sam wrote 'Combination of the Two,' which would be the opening cut on their second LP, *Cheap Thrills,* and would also be on the sound track behind the credits in *Monterey Pop*. The title 'Combination of the Two' refers to Chet and Bill Graham, the two guiding lights of the San Francisco music scene. 'It's about the Avalon and the Fillmore,' says Sam. 'Chet is the spiritual side of life and Graham is the aggressive, hard, money side. I was wrestling with the idea at the time – you need both those things in life, the combination of the two. You have to be warm and sensitive and tuned in to the spirit, like Chet, while keeping it together on a physical level, like Bill.'

Sam and Janis also wrote 'Flower in the Sun,' which ended up on *Greatest Hits*. As a composer, Sam faced many obstacles with the band. 'I'd work on a song in the little cabin out back and then bring it to rehearsal. I'd pass it out, with all the music written down, and nobody would play it the way I'd written it.'

'Didn't they read music?' I ask.

'Oh, no. It surprises me that you would even ask. Very few of those people were professional musicians. The whole hippie thing was aprofessional. It was about having fun.'

'Janis didn't read music?'

'No! Heaven forbid. Are you kidding? It was hard, especially with the band, because not only did they not read music, there was a resistance to learning anything period. What everybody wanted to do in those days was play real hard and fast for a long time and then whatever came out of that improvisation, you'd work on that. There's nothing wrong with that – Mozart and Beethoven were both extremely great improvisers who'd play for hours, endlessly improvising; that's the way they composed.

'What I'm saying is that it was hard for me to come in and say, "Could you play C-sharp minor?" I had to do it real underhanded, come in real timidly and say, "Well, would you try this? Just put your fingers here for this chord." I had to overcome the hippie prejudice against formal structure; it was a constant battle. James is completely instinctive and at one time that was his great strength and that is what he brought to the band and it was beautiful and it was his great weakness, too, because he couldn't adapt and learn anything new.'

'How about Janis?' I ask.

'That's different. As a singer, she didn't have to learn anything; she could be more instinctive. She'd just have to see the words and the background was provided by the band. But to learn how to play the song, there's some formal learning that has to take place.'

I tell Sam that I've always been impressed with Big Brother's contribution to Janis's development as an artist. Though her early Texas tapes are impressive, not until she joined Big Brother did she become a star. 'We allowed her to be herself, to flower,' Sam explains. 'We stayed out of her way. That might have been our greatest virtue. Maybe there was something in our organization, the level of mentality, that just let her develop. A lot of groups would have channeled her. If she had hooked up with John Phillips, for example, who has a real structured scene, she would have had to fit right in. She would have loved big-time professional LA, but she'd have been limited by it, too. Just the fact that we were amateurs and let her go and stayed out of her way was important to her.'

At Lagunitas, the Gurleys – Nancy, James, and baby Hongo – lived in the main house, as did Dave Getz, whose quarters behind the kitchen became a social center for the whole band. When I ask Dave, 'How could Nancy endure living under the same roof with Janis after Janis tried to steal her husband?' he replies, 'There was a little altercation, but Nancy was a paradigm of the hippie ethic of freedom and "everybody has to do their own thing." She was an earth mother, and her attitude was, "love is beautiful and I can love you and you can love me and let the world run free and let the dogs run all over the place and don't clean house and if the kid wants to shit on your bed, it's beautiful." She knew what had gone down with James and Janis but she played it real cool and loved Janis. In fact, she loved Janis as much as anybody. They were very close.'

Nancy Gurley and Janis had something besides their passion for James in common: speed, which they began injecting intravenously. Janis developed a needle fetish. 'She was a maniac with needles,' says Dave. 'She loved to do other people up, loved the thrill of hitting somebody, shooting them up intravenously and getting them off and being the one who did it. And she wanted you to get really off. There's nothing worse than doing that and not getting off, like not enough.'

One day, Nancy Gurley and Janis were lounging in Dave's room behind the kitchen, and they all snorted some crystal meth. 'They knew I'd never shot anything,' Dave recalls, 'and I expressed the desire to try it.' The girls got into a big argument over who would get the honor to do Dave up on Methedrine.

'Oh, let me do it,' said Nancy. 'No,' said Janis, 'let me do it!' Dave can't remember who finally injected him, but he vividly recalls what he accomplished as the drug's serene and superhuman energy took possession of him. He re-covered his drums, using the leather binding from his copy of the Torah. 'It was like a scroll and I covered my bass drum with my Torah and lacquered it. Then I covered another drum with a tiger hide, and then I covered another drum with something else. They were Levy drums, the rarest, the most collectible, and I used them for years, finally giving them to a fledgling rocker.'

Dave loved to listen to Janis when she sang at Lagunitas with her seldom-used 'Joan Baez voice.' 'She did a song called "Pathways," which was never recorded, and it was a very mystical minor-key tune and she sang in a high, smooth, eerie lyrical soprano – her mysterioso folk voice – and it was gorgeous.'

They regularly went in to town to play at the Avalon and rapidly established themselves as the band to see in San Francisco. This was accomplished entirely by word of mouth and through brilliant poster art. The local press remained oblivious to the rock renaissance occurring under their nose. Chet's Herculean efforts to browbeat Ralph Gleason, a *San Francisco Chronicle* critic, into reviewing Janis proved unfruitful. Amazingly, though the *Chronicle* ignored all of Janis Joplin's June 1966 performances at the Avalon, Mimi Farina, Joan Baez's younger sister, received a good review for her Fillmore debut as a rock singer the same month from critic John L. Wasserman.

The crowds at the Avalon were there largely because of Chet's innovative psychedelic posters and the hours he spent telephoning hundreds of personal friends, telling them, 'Be there or be square.' The ultimate expression of the new hip sensibility, the posters' swirling, turbulently alive script, listing times and dates of dances, was indecipherable unless you were stoned. The Mouse/Kelley poster for Big Brother's June 24 to 25 Avalon gig, featuring the pirate on Zig-Zag rolling papers, became an instant classic, ending up on the walls of half the crash pads in the Haight.

Janis's personal popularity grew so fast that other bands tried to steal her from Big Brother. Taj Mahal was the lead singer in the Rising Sons, and when they played the Avalon with Big Brother, their manager, Paul Rothchild, an up-and-coming producer who was just getting involved with the Doors, saw the potential in Janis. Says Dave, 'Rothchild approached her about forming a band with her, Taj Mahal, a guitarist named Steve Mann, and Barry Goldberg from the Police Project playing organ – an all-star LA band with all of the best musicians – and Paul was going to put it all together. Janis was real thrilled and didn't know whether to stay with Big Brother or not.'

Sam also recalls that 'Taj Mahal made a strong play for her and promised her the world and she was very confused about what to do. The band was apprehensive and it was an unpleasant time.'

Chet called the musicians together and said, 'I've booked you into Mother Blues in Chicago. Janis is easily seduced by flattery and offers, whether they're sound or not. If she's this disloyal, if she wants to leave you, if she's that ruthless and ambitious, fuck it, let her go. You guys were a good band before Janis came along. You had national publicity and there's no reason that you can't make it on your own.' But the band was not so sure. Janis had been undermining their confidence. When Elektra Records made her an offer, the band had thought it included them, but Janis returned from a meeting boasting that Elektra only wanted her and were promising the moon. She was already envisaging a Mercedes and a big house in Hollywood. People were telling her that she didn't need Big Brother and deserved professional musicians.

When the press finally discovered Janis and Big Brother, most reviewers doggedly pecked at all the members of the group except Janis, who they raved about. Says Bob Seidemann, 'James Gurley took a beating not only from the critics but from Janis herself.'

'What did she beat on Jim for?' I ask. 'I thought they were sleeping together.'

'The black widow syndrome. Eat the mate. She was very cruel to him. She told him he was a lousy fuckin' guitar player. And she never stopped saying it to him, and he became a lousy fucking guitar player. Critics said it and she said it, everybody said it so often that he believed it and got to be bad, but for a brief moment, a period of a year and a half or so, James Gurley was probably the most dynamic, the best guitar player in the history of rock 'n' roll, up there with Jimi Hendrix. Listen to his opening guitar licks on the records – gut-wrenching, emotion-packed guitar playing.'

Mickey Hart of the Grateful Dead caught Big Brother at the Matrix, a club Martin Balin had started, and he found Gurley overwhelming. 'James Gurley picked up his guitar and he raped it,' says Mickey. 'I'd never seen anything like it. It was magnificent, the best solo I'd ever heard. That amplifier was just pulsing on the floor.'

Many heads would fall in the career of Janis Joplin, and if Gurley's was the first, the second belonged to the man most responsible for her emergence from total obscurity, Chet. Though mild-mannered and gracious, Chet is not a yes-man, and when he declined to concur with Janis that the band was nothing without her, she turned on him and urged his dismissal as their manager, completely disregarding all he'd done for her.

When Sam tried to reason with her, bringing up moral issues such as gratitude and loyalty, she snapped, 'Don't bandy words with me.' Reminiscing today, Sam good-naturedly says, 'There was always that schoolmarmish quality to Janis, that old-timey Texas uppityness, that I loved and responded to – Aunt Polly scolding Tom Sawyer.' Not everyone was so indulgent, especially when she threatened, 'I'll kill anyone who stands in my way.' James Gurley assures me that she meant it.

As she grew more confident with success, a voracious exhibitionism manifested itself in her social behavior. She demanded the spotlight everywhere she went and would stand in the middle of a party and address fifty people, shooting one-liners at everyone in range. 'It was stunning but also frightening,' says an acquaintance, Bill Perez, 'like she could consume you.' Says Hundgen, 'After she recognized her potential for stardom, she played it to the max. She was always the center of attention, trying to monopolize large groups of people. Bob Dylan once walked out of a party, saying, "I'm not putting up with this." Around the scene in San Francisco, it was accepted as part of her hard-drinking, hard-living ethos – but elsewhere, her loud, vulgar, raunchy, Hell's Angels, stoned, fuck-the-world, listen-to-me attitude just looked like egomania.'

The band's first record deal began to take shape in 1966. A man from Chicago named Bobby Shad, who owned a label called Mainstream Records, auditioned Big Brother on a visit to San Francisco and wanted to sign them up immediately. After the audition, says Chet, Shad turned to him and outlined 'how he and I are going to get together and we're gonna lock this band down totally.' Chet didn't like the deal because it didn't seem fair to the band. 'I went in and pulled the plug and said, "We're leaving." The band was shocked.'

Now everyone was mad at Chet. The boys in the band naïvely believed that a record contract would prevent Janis from leaving them. 'If you guys expect to keep me,' she had said, 'you'd better come up with something better than what's being thrown at me – and quick.' Says Dave, 'We thought if we signed a record contract, that would end other people coming along and trying to steal her. This could keep us together as a band.'

At that point, Janis and the band decided to fire Chet. The 'principal communicator' of the news, says Chet, was Peter Albin. He may have been accompanied by Dave or James, but 'it was left to Peter as the leader of the band, the one who always signed the contracts for gigs, and because we were close friends. The objection was twofold – one, they wanted to get a record deal and felt I was an obstacle to that, and the other stated reason was they felt I was giving all my attention to the Ballroom and they were suffering. I feel some irony in that because the raison d'être for the Ballroom was as a venue and as a vehicle for them. In fairness, though, a lot of my attention was being called on by the Ballroom.'

Though Chet was shaken, he didn't see any point in trying to cling to Big Brother. Nor did he want to foster any animosities. 'I just said, "Okay." We should have had contracts, but a piece of paper wouldn't have made much difference except to restore to me the money they owed me, about seven thousand dollars – money that I had put out-of-pocket into various things for the band. But they didn't have it then. They were starving and I was starving. A contract might have given me a claim against future earnings, but I just let all of that go.'

Today when he speaks of Big Brother, he betrays no resentment. 'Did Janis ever tell you face-to-face or ever feel that she owed you any kind of explanation?' I ask. 'No, no,' he replies. 'She never spoke to me about it.' He thinks of the band as his children and says, 'A parent might be disappointed in a child but never stops loving them.'

A few days before Big Brother were due in Chicago to fulfill the Mother Blues engagement, another crisis arose. Janis and the band were all out on the sun deck at Lagunitas when she dropped a bombshell. 'I don't know whether I can go to Chicago,' she said. 'I've been approached with this thing—'

'Look,' Peter Albin said, 'you have to make this decision right now. Either you're with us or you're not, because we got to go to Chicago and we're going to do this gig. If you're not going to do it, you're out right now. We'll get another singer.'

She felt a stab of terror and quickly said, 'Okay, I'm going to stay with the band.' Says Dave, 'She blew off this other thing.' Unity restored, for the present at least, they set out for Chicago, vulnerable and without proper representation. They hired Jim Kalarney, but their situation didn't improve. And since they still had no roadie, they had to move all their equipment themselves.

They flew into O'Hare Airport without hotel reservations and ended up, says Dave, 'wheeling our amps and drums around the streets, looking for a motel. We were pretty damned scared. People were eyeing us like they were going to beat us up. Nobody had yet seen real long hair like we had. In hotels, they looked at our hair, our amplifiers sitting out on the street, and figured we were on drugs. "Forget it," they said. "We got no rooms." We were out on the street, desperate.'

Nick Gravenites, who was playing a blues club called the Burning Bush, saw them around the Loop and thought they were scary-looking. Janis was wearing too much patchouli, she had on a madras garment, and her face had broken out. The band were equally wary of Nick, who had short hair and a thuggish facade that concealed his sensitive nature. When they realized he wasn't a gangster, they stopped and talked. Janis was lonely and Nick decided it was because she was so bizarre, taking the blues further than they'd ever been taken before, screaming and tearing at herself, exposing her guts to the world. Who would approach such a creature?

Fortunately, one of the musicians had relatives in suburban Glenview who agreed to put them up, all except for Sam, who took his girl Speedfreak Rita and moved in with some hippies they'd met in Old Town. When Big Brother opened at Mother Blues, the audience was flabbergasted. This was their first exposure to the counterculture's avant-garde. The Jefferson Airplane had been there, but they still looked like folkies. When Janis came on, a vision in sackcloth, and let out a sound that was grittier than Louis Armstrong's, the audience sat and gawked, wondering whether it was possible to dance to such visceral croakings. Finally, one brave soul ventured onto the dance floor and went into something resembling a seizure. But the band was not without Chicago supporters; Howlin' Wolf came to hear them and told Sam, 'You've got more soul than I have on my shoe.'

Always heavy drinkers, in Chicago the band members fell in with some alcoholic hipsters and learned to drink even harder. Peter Albin was a notable exception. 'It was Peter's straightness,' Richard Hundgen says, 'that in a lot of ways pushed Janis to the other extreme. She was always deeply close to Sam and James in a very stoned way and to Dave Getz in a different way. They were the stoners. Peter was superstraight, living his peace-and-love hippie life with his hippie wife and two kids. He didn't want to get too far out; he wanted to be cool in a straight way. It offended Janis to the nth.' In Janis's estimation, Peter was 'more crazy than he thinks he is; he thinks he is very middle class and he just went a little gooney, but he is really gooney, man.' To prove her point, she quoted some wacky lyrics from his song 'Caterpillar,' concerning the love life of pterodactyls.

Gurley maintains that everyone in the band drank. 'I used to get quite drunk for performances,' he says. 'We'd be down on the Southern Comfort, you know, backstage. I was very shy and repressed, brought up in the Catholic boys' school tradition. I was very screwed up by it, actually, for years, and, in fact, I'm still trying to work it out. I'm a recovering Catholic. I had so much stage fright, and in order to get onstage, I had to get drunk. It's weird that I wanted to do it at all, but I loved it at the same time, like a moth to the flame. I think we all had a bit of stage fright.'

'Everyone in Big Brother?' I inquire.

'Yeah,' Jim replies. 'I think we all needed a couple of shots to get out there and work.'

Janis and Gurley resumed their sexual involvement in Chicago. 'Nancy wasn't around,' says Dave, 'and James got drunk enough to where Janis could basically rape him, dragging him home one night when they got so bombed. We carried him in and threw him in a room and Janis went in there and all of these sounds started coming out. It was all Janis, sounds of Janis getting off. Incredible sounds, like she was having hour-long multiple orgasms. We were all kind of looking at each other, like how can this be? I mean, this guy was dead, virtually passed out. What was she doing? It happened two or three times.'

Janis may have been on the powerful drug DMT, which had been slipped to her by a fan who was a drug dealer and the leader of a band of roving hippies. When they heard that Big Brother was playing in Chicago, they traveled halfway across the continent to see them. After the show, Janis invited them back to the house in Glenview to party. Janis had an intense affair with the leader and he laid a quantity of DMT on her. Later, he became quite successful, making a fortune as a dealer. Says Dave, 'The DMT looked like pot but had been soaked in some killer chemical. You took just a pinch of it and put it in a pipe and took one puff, held it in, and KA-BOOM! Like a rocket to that place where acid takes you. It was pretty scary, because acid sort of came on; this was like you were just right there—'

'Instant infinity?'

'Right! We probably killed a few zillion brain cells with that stuff.'

When I ask Gurley to describe his experiences with Janis in Chicago, he says, 'Me and Janis were together that time. We were sleeping together in Chicago. She had a waist bracelet. She used to wear it around her waist. It was like a gold chain, which she wore when she was nude. A lot of girls used to do that. She made it with just about everybody. She'd take on all comers. And I was certainly doing a lot of it myself.'

The Mother Blues gig went from bad to worse. 'They got fucked,' Nick Gravenites recalls. 'Attendance was poor and they didn't get paid, and since they'd fired Chet, they had no one to fight for their money.' One night, a record producer caught the act and told Nick, 'Gee, they're nice; it's too bad no one will pick them up.' The problem, Nick explains, was that Big Brother was 'too outrageous for any sane, thinking person even to consider recording or getting involved with at that level.'

'We were playing to empty houses,' Dave says. 'The owner was paying us a thousand dollars a week, and we were playing six, seven nights a week for four weeks. We got paid for the first week, we got paid for the second week, and somewhere in the third week we knew he had no money to pay us.'

Chet had several deals going with the owner of Mother Blues and consequently had the clout to collect Big Brother's money, but since they'd fired him, he wasn't even aware of their plight. 'So they're sittin' in Chicago,' says Chet, 'it's cold, they're starving to death, they're crashin' on people's floors, they didn't have enough money to get any kind of transportation back to the West Coast, the gig had fallen out from under them, and they're playing the last part of the gig against the gate, just whatever came in the door was theirs – and at this point, Bobby Shad comes down to the club and puts the strong arm on them.'

The Mainstream recording deal, consummated at this time, represents the worst business decision of Janis's and Big Brother's lives. Without Chet, whom the band had fired for criticizing Shad, they marched straight into a trap, and it would cost them a fortune later to extricate themselves from it.

With the exception of Peter Albin, who had a ticket back to San Francisco, they couldn't even afford to fly home. At the end of the third week, when Shad reappeared in their lives, they signed with Mainstream Records, mistakenly assuming he'd at least pay them enough money for plane fare. But Shad paid them only two or three hundred dollars each per session, and they completed one four-hour session and one six-hour session. Says Sam, 'For us, it was a losing proposition . . . Bob Shad indulged in, shall we say, some rather sharp business practices. It was almost as if we were held hostage in this harsh and hellish city at the whim of Shad.'

The recording is as smooth as it is because they were getting so much experience playing five sets a night at Mother Blues, the most hectic schedule they'd ever undertake. 'We had ample opportunity to polish our rough sound,' Sam says. 'Janis was in good spirits for the session. She double-tracked her vocals and we were pleased with how that sounded. The sound of the guitars was very elementary and 1950s. We were quite disappointed at the time that we could not make the engineer understand what we wanted. He was afraid of the needle going into the red and that is where we wanted the needle to be all the time. Later engineers would understand that some distortion was built into this kind of music.'

After returning to the West Coast, they went to Hollywood to complete work on this, their first LP, which was simply called *Big Brother and the Holding Company*.

When they were ready to leave Chicago, they pooled their money, rented a rattletrap car and set out for California – James, Janis, Sam, Speedfreak Rita, Dave, a set of drums and two amps. It was yet another Joad-like pilgrimage for Janis. 'I don't know how we did it,' says Dave. 'We had the bass drum on the backseat and two people and then in the front seat were three people, and the whole two thousand miles Rita sat on Sam's lap except when he drove. And I don't know whose lap she sat on then.'

They had just passed through Ogallala, Nebraska, when they were stopped by highway patrolmen. Sam was driving and his license wasn't current. The cops made them come into town and started searching the car. One of the cops looked at the men and said, 'Are you girls?' No one responded, and another cop took up the taunt. 'What are you, girls or what? With that long hair, it's hard to tell. Are you a girl or a boy?'

Janis said, 'Fuck you, man.' Everyone blinked in shock, including the cops. 'She wouldn't take it,' says Dave. 'She was ready to get into a fight with them. The rest of us knew that if we answered back, took the bait, and started getting into some kind of argument or protesting, they would throw us in jail. That's what they wanted to do. Janis was very dangerous that way – she'd get into it with the wrong people and not have any sense of the danger or that she was always endangering the people around her.'

Just as she started cursing the cops again Dave rasped, 'Shut up!' They literally pulled her back from the cops and held their hands over her mouth. They were fined fifty dollars, which was about all the money they had left.

Once they were safely home in Lagunitas, Janis pulled out an ounce of DMT. Seidemann was present the day Janis and Dave smoked the powerful drug in Dave's room behind the kitchen and photographed them just as it hit. 'It's a two-minute psychedelic,' Dave says. 'You smoke it, come down, smoke it again. It's like being high on LSD or mescaline for like ten minutes, and we were smoking it all afternoon.'

Big Brother played the Avalon with Sir Douglas Quintet in October, while over at the Fillmore, Grace Slick made her performance debut with the Jefferson Airplane. Grace had switched from the Great Society to the Airplane when their singer, Signe Toly Anderson, became too pregnant to perform. The Airplane's first LP, *Jefferson Airplane Takes Off*, had come out in September and gone gold.

In order to finish their album, Janis and the band piled

into a 1952 Ford station wagon and drove to the recording studio in Los Angeles. As usual, they arrived without hotel reservations. After half the fleabag motels on the Sunset Strip turned them down, they rented one room with five beds for fourteen dollars a night at the Hollywood Center Motel on Sunset Boulevard.

They worked in LA for two or three days and completed the album. Though they eagerly awaited its release, months passed and they heard nothing more from Mainstream. Finally, it would come out the following year, after Monterey Pop, timed to capitalize on their fame. Listening to this record today, twenty-five years after it was cut, I still enjoy its freshness, wit, and originality. It begins with the song Janis picked up from Powell St. John when she left Austin, 'Bye, Bye Baby.' A carefree salute to the open road, Powell's tune sums up the vagabond spirit of a generation of runaways. Though Janis started building her career on this song, she never paid Powell a penny for it, and he was too nice to complain. He arrived in San Francisco with twenty dollars in his pocket and started struggling to put together a garage band. Says Powell today, 'I heard she was singing my song with a band.'

'Did you go to see her?' I inquire.

'Janis was busy on the next level above me at that point,' he says without any trace of bitterness. 'There were rumors flying about that Big Brother wasn't going to be able to cut it. There was a lot of pressure for her to move on and shuck them off. I liked them. They had a soul, something that happens when a band is formed out of a mutual association, a meeting of minds and lives, like the Grateful Dead, instead of professional musicians.'

When I asked Powell if Janis ever offered to help him, he says, 'No, she never offered me a job. I never asked her. I really didn't want to work with Janis. I knew I would be in her shadow and that would be fine, but I wanted to go ahead and do my own stuff.'

According to Travis, Powell was not paid for his song and collected nothing until years later.

There are other memorable songs on the Mainstream album. 'Call on Me,' a duet by Janis and Sam, evokes the most beautiful thing about being in love: having someone to lean on, in good times and bad. 'Caterpillar' is a charming tune reminiscent of the Beatles, and when Janis harmonizes in her perfect alto, she sounds a bit like Mary Travers.

The Mainstream album also includes 'Down on Me'; Moondog's raga-like 'All Is Loneliness'; and 'Women Is Losers,' notable only for being the first feminist song of the rock era. There were also several forgettable numbers, such as 'Blindman,' Gurley's 'Easy Rider,' Janis's undistinguished 'Intruder,' and Peter Albin's muddled and pretentious 'Light Is Faster Than Sound.'

Big Brother's first single came from this album – 'Down on Me' on one side and 'Call on Me' on the other. Years later, 'Call on Me' turned up in the film *Coming Home* in a love scene between Jane Fonda and Jon Voight that was so steamy that it was cut from the version shown on television.

Though they now had a new manager, Julius Karpen, their problems with management continued. 'He was known as Green Julius,' says Seidemann. 'He wouldn't do any business with anyone unless they got high with him on marijuana or whatever he happened to think they should get high with him on. So that put a real curb in his negotiating style. Who's going to get high with some guy they're going to do a contract with?'

By September 1966, Haight-Ashbury was swarming with dropouts and drifters. Almost every weekend there were free concerts in the Panhandle, an extension of Golden Gate Park, and Big Brother played from atop flatbed trucks. On October 6, 1966, Janis sang in the Panhandle at the Love Pageant Rally, a 'happening' that marked the birth of the 'love generation' and set the style for the mammoth be-ins of the following year. The Love Pageant was staged as a peaceful protest against the new law making LSD illegal. As Janis sang, Richard Alpert, standing among the happy people in their Indian headdresses, Old Glory capes, and top hats, referred to 'humans being,' which was later coined as 'be-in.' Ken Kesey, who'd been hiding out in Mexico after his drug bust, made a surprise appearance and managed to escape without being caught. Torn Wolfe described the Love Pageant as 'a freaking mind-blower, thousands of high-loving heads out there messing up the minds of the cops and everybody else in a fiesta of love and euphoria.'

The next night, Big Brother played the Avalon on a bill with the Jim Kweskin Jug Band and the Electric Train. In November, they went into the Matrix, a nonalcoholic cabaret on the border of the Marina district, for a week. One night at the Matrix, Janis met Kim Chappell, a blonde, athletic-looking young woman who appealed to her immediately. Kim was sitting at a table with some friends, and after the set, she asked Janis to join them. The other girls at the table were Teda Bracci, who was later in *Hair* and made a couple of films with Joe Namath; an African-American girl named Barbara Montgomery, and Nancy Carlen. Janis sat down with them, and right away Kim said, 'You were magnificent.' Recalls Kim, 'She looked at me as if no one had ever told her she was any good. "Really?" she said. *"Really?"* She was so powerful. The band wasn't great. Sam Andrew couldn't play guitar, but he was so good-looking. I guess that's why they kept him around. Janis had so much inside and I loved the way she could reach in and give it out with her music.'

Janis couldn't take her eyes off the dazzling Kim and boldly asked her, 'Are you involved with anyone now?'

'I'm not monogamous, if that's what you mean,' Kim said. 'But I live with a terrific woman. Her name is Peggy Caserta. I want you to meet her.' Janis didn't take that to mean no, and she continued to pursue Kim.

Janis was not the first star of the folk-rock era to be smitten by Kim Chappell. As Janis and Kim got to know each other, Kim's extraordinary story came tumbling out. Joan Baez had fallen in love with her right after Kim had graduated from Carmel High School earlier in the sixties. 'Joan Baez was my first lover and brought me out and I still haven't recovered from that woman,' says Kim today.

In 1962, Baez had retreated to Carmel to recover from the pressures of being the queen of the folk movement. One day, wrote Baez in her autobiography *And a Voice to Sing With*, Kim 'blew in, fresh, tan, skittery, ragged, shy, rebellious,' and Joan became obsessed with her. When they made love, Baez found the experience to be 'superb and utterly natural . . . There are pools which run deep, bathing pools for ladies only.'

Besotted with 'the divine softness of Kim,' Baez gave her a motorcycle and they both bought Doberman pinschers. Baez's dog was sickly but Kim's 'was a stud.' They rented a house and though they appeared together in public, they pretended they were just heterosexual friends. Baez bought Kim an Austin Healey, and Kim looked after her 'records and receipts' and went on tour with her. But when Baez fancied a biker with a sidecar, Kim retaliated by trashing the bedroom. Shortly thereafter Baez slapped her and told her the affair was over.

Kim drifted to Cambridge, where Baez had previously introduced her to some interesting people in the folkie crowd. Two of them, John Cooke and Bobby Neuwirth, would later figure prominently in Janis's life. Kim next turned up in

Mexico with a crew of divers but got 'strung out on Mexican pharmaceuticals.' When she returned to the Monterey Peninsula, she stayed in Nancy Carlen's house in Big Sur and tried to kick her barbiturate addiction, but no sooner was she off downs than she became an acidhead. In the middle of a party with Jerry Garcia and Pigpen, she grabbed an ax, climbed to the roof, and started chopping the house in two. Then she jumped into the Austin Healey Baez had given her and drove at 120 mph to Baez's house in Carmel Valley. She walked through Baez's plate-glass window and passed out on her Persian rug.

Baez and Kim's mother deposited her at the Langley Porter Neuropsychiatric Institute in the Haight. A male nurse there turned Kim on to heroin, and shortly thereafter, in the summer or fall of 1966, Nancy Carlen introduced Kim to Peggy Caserta, who became Kim's lover.

Peggy lived at 635 Ashbury in an apartment over the clothing store she owned and ran. Says Kim today, 'Peggy was just madly in love with me.' Peggy objected strenuously to Kim's heroin use. Peggy and a previous girlfriend had done heroin in New York, before Peggy had moved to San Francisco, and the girl had almost died. By the time Peggy and Kim met, Peggy was dead set against the drug.

All that shortly changed. Says Kim, 'Peggy started ranting and raving and that's why I started using regularly. Once she found out I was using it, she started using it with me for spite, because she had told me not to. Her attitude was, "Okay, well, fuck you then, I'm going to do it, too, and I'm going to do it right! I'm going to do it until we're dead." It was a payback, and it mushroomed on us and got out of control. She became enslaved to the drug.'

The day following Janis and Kim's meeting in November, Kim decided to go back to the Matrix and see Janis again. Inviting Peggy to accompany her, Kim suggested they get stoned before the show and she lighted a joint.

At the Matrix that night, there were about fifteen people in the audience, including Nancy Gurley and Mimi Farina. Big Brother started their set, and Peggy was awestruck by Janis's singing, though, like Kim, she deplored the band. Janis's outfit was Salvation Army chic – an antique top over jeans secured by a Peter Max necktie.

During intermission, Peggy, Kim, Nancy Gurley, and Janis sat at a table, chatting. Peggy asked Janis how much she was paid, and Janis told her about four dollars, plus beer on the house. Over the weekend, Peggy and Kim caught all of Janis's shows, and about a month later, Janis visited Peggy's boutique. As they stood talking, Janis took Peggy's hands and held them. Though surprised by the familiarity, Peggy realized that Janis was starved for affection and did nothing to discourage her advances. When Janis admired a pair of jeans in the store, mentioning she couldn't afford them, Peggy gave them to her.

Today, looking back on Janis's relationship with Peggy, Sunshine says, 'She idolized Peggy because Peggy owned a store in Haight-Ashbury and she had a gorgeous lover, Kimmie, and it was almost as if Kimmie was more important because she had been Joan Baez's lover. When Janis described Peggy to me, the first thing she said was, "Well, Peggy's lover was involved with Joan Baez." I said, "Well, why is that so important?" '

A southern belle in a Peck & Peck suit, Peggy Caserta was born in Covington, Kentucky, where her father, a gambler, lost all his money when she was three or four and the family had to move to a run-down neighborhood. Popular as a child, at twelve she was elected Queen of the May Festival. At Perkinston Junior College in Mississippi, she began her first lesbian relationship, with a girl named Pat Napier, who was the head cheerleader, and it continued when they both became Delta Air Line stewardesses in New Orleans, where a contingent of gay stewardesses ran together in the French Quarter. Peggy opened her boutique in Haight-Ashbury in April 1965 in the middle of a chaotic affair with a woman named Carole Smith, who killed herself with a pistol while tripping on acid.

Gradually, Janis was drawn into a relationship with the volatile Peggy Caserta. In an article in *Ms.* magazine, Dave Getz stated, 'She and Janis became friends and, later, shooting partners and sometime lovers. Peggy is an unattractive character, constantly crazed with lust and bursting with vanity and self-congratulation.'

'Crazed with lust' also describes Janis, so in that respect at least, theirs was a marriage made in heaven. Off and on for the next few years, their lovemaking and drugging would provide spectacular and dangerous adventures for both of them. Violence, bloodshed, and broken bones would also come into the picture, because, while involved with Janis, Peggy chose to continue her relationship with Kim. At the same time, Peggy was frantically pursuing Janis's guitar player Sam Andrew. Though Sam admits that he enjoyed Peggy as a dope-shooting partner, he says, 'She was fixated on me, which was masochistic of her, since I wasn't attracted physically to her. She was fixated on a lot of people that way; she was very into unrequited love.'

According to Kim, 'Peggy fucked Sam and tried to keep it on the sly. I wish she'd have been more open about it. Then she wouldn't have given me so much lip when I wanted to see one of my old boyfriends, just to affirm my supposed bisexuality joke.'

'Is bisexuality a joke?' I ask Kim.

'Yes, although I can have orgasms with both men and women, and I used to like to sleep with men. But it was an act and I would rather have been sleeping with a woman.'

'Was Janis's real preference for women, too?'

'God, I don't know. She sure did like guys.'

Peggy, too, liked men, and among her conquests were Marty Balin of the Jefferson Airplane and the poster artist Wes Wilson. With almost identical sexual drives, Janis and Peggy would prove compatible not only as lovers but as hunting partners when they went out cruising for men.

'Janis thought Peggy was gorgeous,' says Linda Gravenites, who'd later be Janis's roommate.

'Well, *was* she?' I ask.

'She had a nice body.' Kim Chappell agrees, adding, 'She has the tits of life and a great sense of humor.'

To celebrate the 1966 Christmas holidays, Big Brother threw a huge party at their house in Lagunitas that was attended by the reigning royalty of the new San Francisco rock scene. The Grateful Dead and the Quicksilver Messenger Service, both of whom lived within two miles of Big Brother's house, were there, as were Country Joe and the Fish. 'We cooked up a mess of food,' Dave says, 'bought a few cases of cheap wine, and rolled a hundred joints from a big pile of grass that had been found growing in Nebraska.'

'We played far into the night around our giant Christmas tree,' Sam recalls. Half a dozen guitars were going at once during this jam. People kept arriving all night long and well into the morning hours, some two hundred in all. 'Pigpen of the Dead partied heavily with Janis,' Hundgen says. 'She hated everyone in the Dead at first and then decided she liked Owsley, Pigpen, and Rock Scully. Owsley was part of the Grateful Dead family. He had laboratories making the purest LSD and would mix it with other drugs, giving you dual highs, such as LSD and heroin, which can be nice because it mellows you out when you withdraw. Owsley recorded many of Janis's shows but was so spaced out on

acid that he confused the dials and messed a lot of them up.
Janis could get down with Pigpen because he was into drugs
other than strictly psychedelics. Later, she would come to
appreciate Jerry Garcia as a spiritual leader of the whole
generation.'

By dawn, says Dave, guests were lying all over the place,
'coming down from this, waking up from that.' Someone had
brought a goat and it 'had shit all over the house and it had
eaten half my bedspread.' When Janis saw Powell St. John,
she said, 'Aw, man! How are you?' She didn't mention having
recorded his song 'Bye, Bye Baby' or that she was using it in
her act without paying him. Nor did Powell object, since he
liked her so much. No matter how successful she became,
she never condescended to her old colleague from the Waller
Creek Boys. Says Powell, 'That's something that I really
appreciate, too. I have an enormous inferiority complex
anyway and always have had. If she'd put me down, I would
have remembered it to this very day. But it was never that
way. She never changed. She was genuine straight up-front
and very friendly always to me. That's another thing that I
really love her for. It could have gone to her head if she
hadn't been Janis.'

Powell remembers the party for its 'good food, booze, and
a lot of weed. We laughed, recalling that she'd given me my
first joint back in Texas. I got pretty stoned at Lagunitas.'
Janis's only complaint to Powell was that she'd recently had
some bad trips on DMT. 'She was kind of reckless. "Do it
because it feels good" – that was her motto. She felt
invincible, like, "It won't happen to me," but at the same
time, she knew it *could* – and that was part of the appeal of
drugs. The possibility of death makes it even more exciting.
She didn't hesitate to go too far, always. She liked to push it.
She told me that. She liked to see how high she could get. She
liked playing Russian roulette.'

'When she said that, was she referring to alcohol or heroin?' I ask.

'She was speaking of heroin,' Powell replies. 'She used to talk to me about it once in a while, not often, because she knew it gave me the willies. Someone had told her, "Don't bum trip yourself, Janis," but she did with the DMT. "I don't like that stuff," she told me. "Give me downers anytime. Heroin really lights my fire." I told her, "That's the one thing I'm just not going to do, but there's a lot of other things I'll try, like acid." Looking back, acid was crazy, too; it's one thing to risk your life on heroin and another to become a bloomin' idiot on LSD.'

Despite good times like the Christmas party, there were too many conflicts in the band for the commune to survive. Peter and Cindy were good housekeepers, ate at regular times, and liked an organized life. Nancy Gurley and Janis got stoned and never went to bed, stringing beads, fixing drugs, rapping madly as Nancy plotted the downfall of the Establishment. Completing the chaos at Lagunitas was a wretched German shepherd named Mishka, who belonged to the Gurleys. A neurotic wreck, Mishka never stopped barking and whining and went chasing after everyone who came near the house.

Finally, Julius Karpen said it was essential for the band to relocate in San Francisco and give up the whole commune idea. They all moved back into town, Janis taking an apartment on Lyon Street. She hinted to her parents that the perfect Christmas present for her in 1966 would be a comprehensive cookbook. *Betty Crocker* or *Better Homes* would do.

In the new year 1967, Janis would celebrate her twenty-fourth birthday. Janis and Nancy Gurley grew closer than ever, and under Nancy's tutelage, the transformation of the eyesore of Port Arthur into the clotheshorse of the Haight began. Janis relinquished her butch, rough-hewn look and acquired a measure of elegance. 'My wife inspired Janis to become a fancy dresser,' Gurley says. Nancy evolved and developed many of the hippie styles, and Janis admired her flair and copied her attitudes. Beads, lace, shawls, mantillas – Nancy introduced all these into the Haight, and she was an inspiration to the women in Janis's circle. Hundgen remembers the impression Nancy made at the Avalon, spinning in circles around the dance floor, barefooted, wearing a floor-length slip and a nineteenth-century shawl with strands of sterling silver in it and stretching her arms heavenward as Janis sang 'Oh, Sweet Mary.' 'Nancy created a shimmering psychedelic effect,' Hundgen says, calling it 'art that was equal to what was happening onstage. She was an essential part of the Big Brother act.'

Having survived their competition over James Gurley, Nancy and Janis were like blood sisters. Nancy initiated Janis into the rites of the Aquarian Age, telling her, 'The Piscean Age of the leader hero is over. No more Christs! No more Napoleons! No more Mick Jaggers! The Aquarian Age is about the equality of all peoples, all races, all sexes, all creeds. All religions are based in the same truth and they're just different manifestations of different cultures.'

Together, Nancy and James introduced Janis to tarot readings, crystals, and ecological principles years before they were popularized as New Age concepts. 'Here's what I believe in politically and philosophically,' Nancy told Janis, 'the total destruction of all outmoded political systems and ecclesiastical constraints and religious differences.'

Nancy's influence also had a negative impact. Like Janis, she loved to inject both methamphetamine and heroin. After shooting up meth, Janis and Nancy used the flood of drug energy to string beads together. During my visits with

Hundgen, he shows me many strands of beads that Nancy and Janis had strung on tough, knotted lengths of leather. They bear no resemblance to the little hippie love beads I remember from the sixties. These are made of antique cut glass, crystals, and Tiffany tubes, and they have a rough beauty. Some are fragments from long ropes that had hung around Janis's bed. 'They could easily be tied at the end and worn as a necklace,' Hundgen says. 'Janis wore dozens of them. Janis and Nancy were stoned out of their minds, beading all night long.'

These speed binges turned them into nervous wrecks, and then they would smooth out their jittery ganglia with a shot of heroin. 'They all did heavy-duty drugs,' says Hundgen, referring to Janis's early entourage of women, among them Nancy Gurley and Sunshine.

Though I find much about Nancy Gurley admirable, she also seems to have had a creepy streak. Some of her jewelry is witchy-looking, such as a necklace she made out of goat's teeth, ivory, carnelian, and eight-pointed Stars of Solomon and six-pointed Stars of David and triangles. Says Hundgen, 'She had altars in every house in which she ever lived, magical altars from the Detroit wizard Martoon. She made an altar at the top of a flight of stairs on Oak Street with hundreds of votive candles surrounding a six-foot blue Virgin Mary statue, and bouquets of dead flowers were all around.'

'*Dead,* you say?'

'All of the junkies loved dead flowers. Janis's girlfriends would staple live roses to the ceiling upside down so they'd dry in perfect color and position. Every now and then, a dead rose petal would flutter to the floor. The girls always had huge bouquets of dead flowers, mostly carnations and roses.'

'But I still don't understand why they liked *dead* flowers.'

'Because they just *did,*' Hundgen huffs. 'They were beautiful! They were like the essential oils.' Searching through a box of mementos, he brings out a bottle and says, 'Here is the potpourri made from all of Janis's and Nancy's flower arrangements. Dead flowers became potpourri.' Janis and Nancy also loved to watch Boris Karloff movies, which they claimed were loaded with secret heroin symbolism.

At 2:00 P.M. on January 1, 1967, Janis sang at a big Hell's Angels bash in the Panhandle. Called the New Year's Wail/Whale, it was a thank-you party for the hippies who'd sprung some Hell's Angels from jail. Janis's relationship with the gang would bring her both joy and pain. When I ask Linda Gravenites, 'Is it true that you and Janis went out with bikers?' she replies, 'Yes, it's true. I had some very good friends who were in the Angels, and Janis had a little thing with Freewheelin' Frank, whose old lady from those days I just saw last December [1990]. Lady Jo, they called her.'

'Did she mind Janis sleeping with Freewheelin' Frank?'

'Those old ladies don't mind anything. Talk about macho bullshit! Those guys just did straight what they wanted to do and their old ladies better like it!'

'Did you have a special one?'

'Ummmm. Well, Sweet William was a real wonderful friend of mine for a long time. And Hank, who later showed up in a photo of Irving Penn's in *Look* magazine, in their spread on the San Francisco scene, which included a photo of Janis and Big Brother.'

Freewheelin' Frank was one of Ken Kesey's special pets, and Tom Wolfe, the Merry Pranksters' Boswell, described Frank as 'a wiry little guy who looks like a pirate with long black hair combed back Tarzan-style, and a mustache, and a gold ring through his left earlobe.' When the Pranksters fed Freewheelin' Frank acid, he said, 'Fuck God,' and 'climbed a redwood and was nestled up against a loudspeaker in a tree grooving off the sounds and vibrations of Bob Dylan singing "Subterranean Homesick Blues." '

Janis loved flying up and down the hills on the back of Freewheelin' Frank's Harley, his silky hair whipping against her face. When she held on to a guy on a bike, it was more like a hug or a massage, so that giving her a ride became an erotic experience alfresco. The fact that Frank had a girlfriend never bothered her. According to Travis Rivers, 'Freewheelin' Frank was the Hell's Angels' PR man. Handsome, charming, a silver-tongued devil, he made out with Janis.'

'Janis was a heavy-duty personality,' says Hundgen. He reaches into a box of Janis's keepsakes and brings out *Hell's Angel Book,* signed 'S.K.' 'These are pornographic drawings that illustrate the poems and fantasies of a stoned Hell's Angel,' he says. 'It's like something out of hell and total stonedness, and it was presented to Janis when she was photographed with Freewheelin' Frank, the secretary of the Angels. Many of the San Francisco Angels knew and partied with Janis. She was used to the mentality of the bikers who would slit your throat and kill you for nothing. She could handle them. She played pool with them, challenged them to games, and they'd play for drinks and get totally fucked up. I was there on a number of occasions when she beat the ass off all the Hell's Angels at pool. That's how tough she was.

'The San Francisco Angels were hip and mellow, but then it spread to her knowing the Oakland Angels and they didn't give a shit about anything and were just dopers and murderers. But the San Francisco Angels admired her and followed her as an entourage and hung out at her house and probably fucked her dog Thurber.'

Janis's tolerance of the Angels' virulent male chauvinism is surprising in view of the groundwork she was laying for women's liberation as the first woman lead singer in the previously male-dominated world of rock. Referring to women, a Hell's Angel once said, 'They're all sleazes, but at least we get the nice-looking sleazes.' Janis probably tolerated such bigotry in the Angels because, as Hundgen notes, 'the San Francisco Angels were one of Janis's drug connections.'

'Individually, I would trust them with my life,' Linda Gravenites says. 'As a group I would never expect them to act other than for the group. They will lay their life down for their brother. And you may be their best friend, but if you are opposed to what their brothers are doing, you lose.'

After the Wail/Whale, according to Hundgen, 'the Grateful Dead and Janis and Big Brother became the Hell's Angels bands. They hung out onstage, backstage, they got the bands high, they brought their motorcycles in and anything they wanted to do, they did.' On one occasion, Janis and the band performed at a Hell's Angel's funeral and Janis managed to upstage the corpse by baring her breasts in public. She later explained that she'd accidentally dropped ice cream on her freshly laundered T-shirt and took it off only long enough to turn it inside out.

On the afternoon of January 14, 1967, in the polo grounds at Golden Gate Park, Janis sang at the Human Be-In, the first of the massive counterculture convocations. Twenty to fifty thousand people were expected, and the purpose of the be-in was to usher in 'the epoch of liberation, love, peace, compassion, and unity of mankind.' Rick Griffin's poster featured an American Indian mounted on a horse and holding a guitar. It read:

POW-WOW: A GATHERING OF THE TRIBES FOR HUMAN BE-IN. Timothy Leary, Richard Alpert, Dick Gregory, Lenore Kandel, Jerry Rubin, All San Francisco Rock Bands, Allen Ginsberg, Lawrence Ferlinghetti, Gary Snyder, Michael McClure, Robert Baker, Buddha. Bring the color gold. Bring photos of personal saints and gurus and heroes of the underground. Bring children, flowers, flutes, drums, feathers, bands, beads, banners, flags, tangerines, incense, chimes, gongs, cymbals, joy.

January 14 dawned a clear, crisp winter day, and by 1:00 P.M., it was sunny and mild in the polo fields. As people made their way through the meadows and dells and around the lake, the path to the be-in was marked with wind chimes. They carried god's eyes on towering poles, flags, and flowers. Gary Snyder launched the festivities by blowing on a conch shell while Allen Ginsberg chanted, 'We are one! We are all one!' The crowd seemed to extend to the curvature of the earth, and everyone shared joints, wine, bread, and cookies. Some people shed their clothes and danced nude.

Janis always psyched herself before a performance, rapping to herself and shaking out her tensions. 'Come on, honey,' she said, 'ooh, baby, come on come on come on try try try try try try!' By the time she got to the microphone, her blood was going cha-chung cha-chung cha-chung. A rock singer's feelings before a crowd of this size were once described by David Crosby, who said, 'Magic is having a great big love beast crawl out of your amplifiers and eat the audience.' Nick Gravenites says Janis was at her best in the park, 'enthralling thousands.'

Jim Morrison, who'd come up from LA with the Doors to play Winterland that weekend, attended the be-in but was not asked to perform. Furious, he tried to hide his disappointment by bragging that the Doors were too satanic for the flower children. Hearing Janis sing the jet black 'Ball and Chain,' however, he could hardly have escaped the realization that Big Brother was every bit as dark as the Doors.

On January 24, 1967, Big Brother and the Holding Company began a three-night gig at the Soul City Club in Dallas, opening for Chuck Berry. Unlikely as it seems that anyone could shock Berry, who went to prison after being found guilty of transporting a minor across state lines for immoral purposes, Janis managed to. 'She was not well known to me then,' says Chuck, 'and I thought she was rather bold to appear onstage with a drink in her hand and sing so well.' When he went on next, Chuck fell off the stage backward, though he swears it was an accident and he wasn't trying to upstage Janis.

In February, back home in San Francisco, she started an affair with Country Joe McDonald. Like Janis, he was a Capricorn, born January 1, 1942, in El Monte, California. He'd gone into the navy when he was seventeen and then attended Los Angeles City College before settling in Berkeley and becoming active in radical politics. He served as musical director of the October 1965 Berkeley Vietnam Day Committee demonstration, standing on the back of a truck and entertaining fourteen thousand people who'd come from all over the western United States to protest the war.

Joe and guitarist Barry Melton played together in the Instant Action Jug Band and in 1965 founded Country Joe and the Fish, famous principally for the 'F-U-C-K' cheer from their anti-Vietnam War shuffle song, 'Feel-Like-I'm-Fixin'-to-Die Rag.' The band's name refers to Mao Tse-tung's requirement that a revolutionist must 'move among the people like a fish in water.'

'Janis and Joe's relationship was very short-lived,' Sam Andrew says. 'I couldn't imagine two people less likely to be together, for a lot of reasons. You could go down a list of his qualities and they would be Janis's opposite in every respect. Joe is a real political person and he's opinionated and sarcastic. He just didn't make people comfortable.'

They met on February 10 when they played a concert at the Golden Sheaf Bakery in Berkeley. He found her lively and compatible, though he was tripping acid and very subdued and quiet, whereas Janis, who was drinking, was over-amping as usual. Her intelligence and sense of humor appealed to him, and it must have thrilled her when he said she was pretty, something she'd previously heard only from her mother.

Joe lived in a commune with his band, which was directly across the street from Peggy Caserta's store in Haight-Ashbury, and soon Peggy noticed that Janis and Joe were living together off and on.

Ultimately, Joe proved to be incapable of accepting Janis as she was, and he'd later confess his behavior at the time was 'pretty insane.' He considered himself to be political because he'd appeared at large rallies and announced, 'The revolution is now. It's happening on the streets.' Janis, he felt, wasn't political, nor, he complained, was she an acidhead. Actually, when Janis was with a congenial partner, she didn't hesitate to drop acid. Both Milan Melvin, later one of her loves, and Dave Richards, Big Brother's equipment manager (roadie), had thoroughly enjoyable acid trips with Janis. 'It was east of San Anselmo, up in the foothills,' Dave recalls. 'The band went up there and played one night and then just hung out in the mountains and camped in the woods. Janis told me she wanted to take acid, so she and I dropped some tabs and went down by a lake. It was kind of a sweet afternoon. She had a good time and it was just us two friends, walking around on a gentle afternoon.'

According to Peggy Caserta, Janis's relationship with Joe turned into a painful and unfortunate experience. Janis couldn't count on having Joe in her bed more than two or three nights at a time. Career issues may have been preoccupying Joe, whose band had split up every year since 1965. Peggy used to go over to Joe's commune to have sex with a randy teenager who occupied the front room. As she passed Janis and Joe's room, she looked in on a scene less than rollicking: Janis was restlessly puffing a Marlboro and Country Joe was snoozing. Janis begged Peggy to stick around and keep her company, but Peggy rushed on to her date.

One day, Joe failed to keep an appointment with Janis and she ran to Peggy and Kim for solace. They dined at the Golden Cast restaurant, but Janis ate little of her meal, constantly running to the pay phone, still trying to locate Joe.

Dave Richards observed Janis during her affair with Country Joe. 'She was living on Lyon Street, and then she was living with Country Joe for a while,' he says. 'She may have been with him right when I was first with the band, and then they split up. He tends to be a very self-righteous guy. Joe is a very strange person.'

When the end came, Joe pointed out that they were no longer simpatico and Janis agreed with him wholeheartedly. When he announced he was thinking of leaving, she didn't try to stop him.

Jack Jackson, an Austin acquaintance, had moved to San Francisco and was now working with the Family Dog, Chet's entrepreneurial commune. 'Joe dumped Janis and it hurt her,' says Jackson. 'She was vulnerable and it really fucked her head up.' About a month after they parted, Janis asked Joe to write a song about their time together. The result, which he entitled 'Janis,' is a perfunctory ditty, full of tired love-song phrases, but Joe felt it was 'a really pretty song.' When Janis chose not to incorporate it in her repertoire, Joe blamed the band, saying Big Brother was strictly hard rock. On the contrary, Janis and Big Brother's haunting rendition of Gershwin's lullaby 'Summertime' was anything but hard rock. 'Janis' just isn't a very good song.

*

A much cozier boyfriend from this period was Mark Braunstein, a cheery, blue-eyed San Francisco State student Janis met while walking her dog George one afternoon on Stanyan Street. Mark was emerging from Golden Gate Park, a baseball glove hitched to his belt, and his dog, Shana, half German shepherd and half wolf, was trotting along beside him. Janis must have still been seeing Joe occasionally, because she pointed to Mark's baseball glove and told him, 'My boyfriend Joe is Country Joe and we play baseball.'

They began a relationship that went through many stages, starting platonically, going through a sexual phase, and finally evolving into a professional association in 1967, when the band hired Mark as a roadie. On Stanyan that day, Mark told her he worked in the Psychedelic Shop and invited her to drop by. When Janis went in the following evening, she joined him behind the counter and they spent several hours listening to records, drinking coffee, and chatting with mutual friends. After that, the Psychedelic Shop became one of her regular stops. Much more than a head shop, it was a community center and a sanctuary for students of psychedelia. Over half the space in the store was devoted to a meditation tent. 'There wasn't anyone nodding or sleeping off a drug in the tent,' Mark says, 'and Janis and I liked hanging out in there.'

They started going to Japanese movies together and they borrowed each other's books. One of Janis's favorites was Thomas Hardy's *Jude the Obscure*, but she also read current bestsellers. Mark was living on Page Street in a top-floor apartment that had no water pressure, and he began to take his showers in Janis's apartment. Soon he was staying to watch TV or have supper with her. Mark was, and remains, an exceedingly attractive guy with a lustrous mane of thick brown hair. One day, in Janis's steamy bathroom, their friendship suddenly turned erotic. 'It was fun,' Mark said. 'It wasn't like a groupie fucking a star. We were friends and neighbors having a good time.'

When Peggy Caserta wrote her book about her affair with Janis, *Going Down with Janis,* the opening line became an instant camp classic: 'I was stark naked, stoned out of my mind on heroin, and the girl lying between my legs giving me head was Janis Joplin.' Nonetheless, David Getz, Janis's drummer, said in *Ms.* magazine that Peggy's book contained 'a trashy truth about Janis that [Myra] Friedman's more serious book [*Buried Alive*] misses.'

On the first night Janis and Peggy made love, Janis revealed herself to be both insecure and a powerful sexual manipulator. She initiated elaborate games, cleverly maneuvering Peggy, who wasn't even sure she wanted to be unfaithful to Kim, into the role of aggressor. Then she turned coy, forcing Peggy to court and coax her, and she required a long seduction scene followed by extensive foreplay.

Janis reached her climax, or appeared to, in less than ten minutes, and it was an authentic orgasm, she assured Peggy, unlike the bogus displays she frequently staged with men. Peggy wasn't entirely convinced. Some days later, when they made love again, Peggy noticed that Janis took much longer to achieve orgasm, and she decided that Janis had been acting that first time. On subsequent occasions, however, it was clear to Peggy that Janis's orgasms were genuine. Equally real were many of the climaxes Janis reached with male lovers. The men I interviewed left no doubt about Janis's sexual competence.

From Peggy's account and my own research among men and women who made love with Janis, it is possible to understand her at a deeper level than heretofore. With men, she was ferocious and insatiable, as if trying to prove she was a woman. With women, she was tentative and hesitant and seemed truer to her feelings, putting emotional reinforcement above physical release. She looked to women for love, but because of her feelings of unworthiness and her fear of disgrace if exposed as a lesbian, she had to be drunk or very close to it to admit that side of her nature. Like a child, she received her pleasure and reassurance from Peggy that first time without making any effort to return the love she'd been given.

Having conquered the formidable Peggy, Janis now set her sights on Peggy's lover, Kim Chappell. 'Janis asked me to sleep with her a couple of months after she and Peggy started their affair,' says Kim. 'Janis wasn't much to look at when she first arrived in San Francisco this time. She was overweight, she had bumps on her face because of bad diet, and she was puffy from drinking. She had a lot of trouble getting laid. I responded, however, to her terrific magnetism, and I wanted to go to bed with her. She asked me to come over to her apartment, but I couldn't figure out a way to do it without Peggy finding out. Janis was hurt, looking like it was one rejection too many.'

No doubt Janis's pain was assuaged by the 'good-looking, short-haired black girl' Kim saw Janis with on the street one night shortly thereafter. 'They were having an affair,' Kim says.

The questionable judgment Janis showed in poaching on established relationships such as the Gurleys and Kim and Peggy would soon come home to haunt her. The air around her grew thick with intrigue and resentment. While Peggy claims that Kim objected to her spending so much time with Janis, Peggy seems completely unaware that Janis was simultaneously trying to seduce Kim. Peggy continued to obsess over Sam Andrew and give him priority over Janis. Janis, in turn, blew up at Peggy, cursing and scolding her for spending time with Sam when she could be with Janis instead. Though Peggy maintains that Sam was in love with Janis and used her to get into Janis's good graces, Sam pooh-poohs this notion when I present it to him. He insists that he never loved Janis romantically, though he admits to having had sex with her.

On one occasion when Peggy was spending the night with Janis, Kim caught on to their affair and confronted Peggy, reducing her to tears. Janis advised her to leave Kim at once if Kim wouldn't allow her the latitude to have sex with people outside the relationship, but Peggy loved Kim too much even to entertain the idea. Kim today categorically denies ever having been jealous of Peggy's and Janis's intimacies and insists that she would have preferred an open relationship with Peggy. It was Peggy, she stresses, who was the possessive one.

Somehow Janis, Kim, Sam, and Peggy, despite their tangled relations, all managed to remain friends, for the present at least.

4

Down in Monterey:
1967

Janis had met John Phillips, the driving force behind
Monterey Pop, when he'd played San Francisco with his
group, the Mamas and the Papas. Later she'd attended a
party at his house in LA, just a few weeks before Monterey.
John and Michelle Phillips owned the old Jeanette
MacDonald estate at 783 Bel Air Road, and Janis was
impressed by the grand Tudor-style country home, which
looked like a fairy castle perched on a cliff in the midst of
spacious grounds. The living room, big as a baseball
diamond, was full of people such as Warren Beatty, Candice
Bergen, the Beach Boys, and Jane Fonda. While guiding Janis
on a tour of the stables, pool, and guesthouses, Phillips
noticed that she was drinking Southern Comfort from a
bottle and asked her for some of it. Explaining that the bottle
was full of codeine cough syrup, she confessed she'd been
guzzling codeine all day.

When the bill was put together for Monterey Pop, Janis
and Big Brother were slotted into a Saturday concert. In June,
a few days before the festival, Mark Braunstein went by her
apartment to take a shower. When he finished bathing and
stood drying off and chatting with her, she told him about
Monterey Pop. 'Hey, Redding's gonna be there, man. You
oughta come. Be my old man.'

Mark was tempted, but he already had a girlfriend, Mary, who'd gone to the Midwest to visit her family. 'Won't you please be my old man?' Janis persisted. 'Would you come to Monterey with me? Please?'

'No,' Mark said. 'I'm really with Mary. No.' She took out a bottle of Southern Comfort and drank from the bottle cap. 'With me, she drank like a lady,' Mark says, 'always from the cap. There was no way I wanted to be Janis's old man. She was not a stable person, and I was from a slightly upper-middle-class background, pretty well educated, was fairly stable and had common sense.' Janis started talking about Joe McDonald, telling Mark that she missed him and was unhappy their on-again, off-again affair was over and that Joe had said, 'This isn't working out. I want out of this. Let's not do it anymore.'

Says Mark today, 'She felt rejected by Joe and was falling apart. Their relationship was kind of a tenuous thing and Joe was a pretty big star, pretty established, so there were those dynamics taking place. She and I were sympathetic and liked each other, and she just couldn't face being alone. She wanted an old man. It could have been me; it could have been someone else. But I had a girl and told her so.'

A few nights later, Mark went over to Janis's to watch TV, and again she urged him to accompany her. 'Come on down and be our guest,' she said. 'Be my old man – just for Monterey.' They made love and Mark told her, 'Okay, I'll come with you, but where will I stay?'

'With me and the band,' she said, 'where else?'

Mark drove his parents' car down the peninsula and camped in Big Brother's hotel room, sometimes sleeping on the floor and sometimes in the bed with Janis, depending on who else was in the room at the time. 'They had taken whole motels,' Mark says, 'and ours had a big U-shaped driveway and there were separate cabins. Country Joe and Quicksilver

Messenger Service were in the same motel as us. Janis and half the band slept in the same suite, and her room was like a little adjunct.'

Monterey Pop originated in Los Angeles and was designed as a platform for the Mamas and the Papas. Says Sam, 'We felt LA was trying to capitalize on the San Francisco sound. LA always seemed rosy, superficial, and plastic to us. Monterey Pop was the Mamas and the Papas's party and then we, Otis Redding, and Jimi Hendrix walked off with it.' Linda Gravenites says she didn't even bother to go because she thought, 'Oh, those *LA* people!' David Crosby of LA's Byrds accused the San Francisco bands of having a 'hipper than thou' attitude. He was right, and, as Monterey Pop would demonstrate, so were they.

Two important hit records of 1967 drew thousands of people from all over the world to Monterey. The Beatles' LP *Sgt. Pepper's Lonely Hearts Club Band,* released in June, urged everyone to congregate in large groups. To Peter Fonda, who viewed Monterey Pop as a direct outgrowth of *Sgt. Pepper,* the album's message was: 'If only we could all be together and share the same attitude.'

John Phillips wrote 'San Francisco (Be Sure to Wear Some Flowers in Your Hair)' a short time before the festival. Sung with plaintive appeal by Scott McKenzie, 'San Francisco' became a megahit, soaring into the Top 5 on release. 'The song was written as a message,' says Phillips. 'It was to be a nonviolent festival celebrating peace and love.' Partly as a result of the song's popularity, four of Monterey Pop's five concerts completely sold out.

Janis and Big Brother were initially given short shrift, slotted into Saturday afternoon's concert instead of one of the evening shows. The big three closing acts at Monterey were Simon and Garfunkel, Friday night; Otis Redding, Saturday night; and the Mamas and the Papas on Sunday night. Some of the other acts on the main Saturday- and Sunday-night shows included Jimi Hendrix, the Jefferson Airplane, and the Who. The committee that chose the bands was composed of Phillips, Paul McCartney, Terry Melcher, Lou Adler, Paul Simon, and Cass Elliott.

The complete bill, consisting of thirty acts, was hailed by the local paper, the *Monterey Peninsula Herald,* as 'the most outstanding assemblage of popular music groups ever brought together in one place.' Three hundred members of the press converged on the town, including reporters from *Life, Look, Esquire,* and the (London) *Times.* One hundred and twenty-eight musicians performed.

Clive Davis, Columbia Records' aggressive new president, came to the festival to sign up new acts. Fusty Columbia, known for their Broadway show albums, had only two rock artists, Bob Dylan and the Byrds. As the festival opened on Friday evening, Davis and his wife, Janet, were among the 50,000 people swarming to the Fairground, though the occupant load within the Horseshow Arena, where the concerts were to be held, was only 7,200. Despite this, observers agree that it was the most orderly, harmonious crowd they'd ever seen. 'I just can't believe it,' said a helmeted Monterey policeman. 'Hell, I've seen more trouble than this at PTA meetings.'

At the last moment, the Fairground was thrown open for camping. Hippie artisans set up booths outside the arena, and the place looked like a Renaissance fair, with colorful displays of handmade leather and jewelry, silk flowers, tattoo artists, head-shop paraphernalia, and candles. At his booth, Stanley Mouse 'was busy airbrushing mandalas on big pieces of material.' Among the crowd were Victorian dandies in lace trim and people with bells tied to their knees or wearing face paint. Writer Ellen Sander remembers seeing silly grins on people's faces as everyone felt 'a sense of internal connection

. . . close to the divinity within each one.' Monterey she saw as 'the culmination of the dropout society that began earlier that year at the Human Be-In.'

Owsley, the acid king, prowled around in his short leather jacket, both pockets full of purple acid. Though he didn't perform, Brian Jones of the Rolling Stones was backstage, looking stoned. David Crosby, a self-professed 'closet junk taker,' there to sing with the Byrds, mixed with the audience in his fur cossack hat.

At 9:00 P.M., just as the show got under way, a bone-chilling fog descended on the Fairground. Eric Burdon and the Animals, who'd had a number-one hit in 1964 with 'The House of the Rising Sun,' were in the featured spot, with the Association as the opener. According to Dave Getz, 'The Animals didn't do shit at Monterey.' Eric sang his salute to the hippie capital, 'San Franciscan Nights,' which was charming despite its very British, highly uncolloquial reference to '*warm* San Franciscan nights' (who has ever experienced one?), and later he would write the nostalgic 'Down in Monterey,' proclaiming that a new religion had been born at the festival.

The Association came on, singing 'Cherish,' 'Along Comes Mary,' 'Windy,' and 'Poison Ivy.' Dave Getz says Janis and many in the San Francisco contingent 'felt these people from LA were plastic and phony. The Association were real clean and wore suits. I would see those guys and puke, and the audience felt the same way. We considered ourselves to be on some higher level of truth, out there a little further, you know, and more real, more willing to take risks. Compared to them, we were the avant-garde. It's funny, because I rather like the Association today.'

The Paupers came on next. They were a highly touted band managed by Albert Grossman, 'but they went over like a lead balloon,' Dave says. 'Laura Nyro was a real dud on Saturday.

She was the most phony, trite, awful thing they'd ever seen. Her presentation did so much to kill her that no one was paying any attention to what she was singing. She came on with two black chicks and it was almost a slick New York nightclub act. I listen to her now and love her music, but she bombed at Monterey. She was almost booed off the stage. The audience didn't like a presentation that was old hat or folky.'

Evenings after the concerts, the Monterey Peninsula College football field was used to provide accommodations, and almost three thousand fans slept on the field. Thousands more slept at the Fairground itself, in buildings and on the grass. Many others used an area next to Uncle John's Pancake House.

For years, Monterey Pop has been lauded as a model rock festival, but the city of Monterey hated it so much that when John Phillips tried to stage another festival there the following year, the city refused permission. Local residents complained of noise that went on all night and drugged-out fans who turned their streets and private lawns into toilets.

'People were getting stoned and making love on the grass,' John Phillips said. They were also fornicating in the horse stalls, said an irate William R. Lewis, a Monterey doctor who was vexed by the inordinate number of pregnant women who sought assistance from the Salvation Army in the weeks and months immediately following the festival. Dr. Lewis revealed in a letter to the *Herald* that many young people who came from out of state ended up on the missing-persons list. A policeman believed they were summarily 'buried in shallow graves in Big Sur.'

No deaths were officially reported, but misery and psychic trauma were all too common at Monterey Pop. John Phillips admits that the 'bummer tent' was packed with kids on nightmarish acid trips.

By Saturday morning, estimates of the number of people flooding into the city ran as high as 72,000. Dressed as pioneers, Civil War characters, Arabs, cowboys, and drum majorettes, they jammed into the Fairground, clogging the grassy corridors between the merchandise booths. Miraculously, no one appeared to be impatient or angry, and the hippie merchants did a brisk business in pottery, metalwork, posters, and buttons with slogans such as BAN THE BRA and MARINE CORPS BUILDS OSWALDS. The air was fragrant with the odor of marijuana smoke, incense, and frangipani oil, which blended with the familiar carnival aroma of popcorn, hot dogs, and beer.

'Almost every rock star in the world was there,' says Paul Kantner of the Jefferson Airplane. 'It was the first and finest rock festival. Playing at Monterey Pop was like playing in a bubble. Like all the people from our culture were all beamed to another place.'

Saturday was a big day for the San Francisco musicians. The 1:30 P.M. matinee included Big Brother, Electric Flag (with Mike Bloomfield, Buddy Miles, and Nick Gravenites), the Paul Butterfield Blues Band, Canned Heat, Country Joe and the Fish, the Steve Miller Blues Band, and Quicksilver Messenger Service.

'We love you all, man,' yelled a jubilant Bloomfield. 'This is our generation. Dig yourselves. It's very groovy.' The Electric Flag's 'A Long Time Comin' ' heralded an era of change and growth. Says Dave Getz, 'The Electric Flag, who are not in the movie, were an incredible success at Monterey. Bloomfield and Buddy Miles blew people over. What you don't get when you see the film *Monterey Pop* is what a triumph the festival was for the San Francisco bands. The audience was blah during the Mamas and the Papas, but you wouldn't know that from the film. Since it was made by John Phillips, he puts the Mamas and the Papas in a prominent place and they performed twice at the festival and they were very visible, but the audience, while appreciative, made it clear that they just weren't there to hear that kind of music.

'The festival came alive when the bands from San Francisco came out with this raw "this is what we are" attitude, the tradition that has now found its way into punk. Everything looks equal in the film, but at the actual festival itself, the thing that knocked people over was the San Francisco bands, particularly Janis and Big Brother.'

Far more typical of Monterey Pop than its peace-and-love facade were the cutthroat business negotiations going on backstage between the promoters and the artists over the movie that was being shot of the festival. 'They sold tickets and took in money, but none of the performers got paid,' Dave Getz says. 'Airfare was paid, hotels were paid, and there was a lavish spread of food and an open bar backstage. It was wonderfully put together. But Lou Adler and John Phillips waited until they got everybody together there and did this very clever thing – they threw this contract in front of all the acts. The contract basically said: We are going to film you for a TV movie and we want you to sign this and if you allow us to film you, we get all the rights to your performance.

'Our manager, Julius Karpen, was a very good friend of Quicksilver Messenger Service's manager, and they were close to the managers of the Grateful Dead, Danny Rifkin and Rock Scully. They all got together and said, "We're not signing." '

The film rights alone brought in $250,000, so it seems clear that the promoters were less than fair in their dealings with the artists. Albert Grossman, the large, bearlike manager from New York who handled Bob Dylan, Peter, Paul and Mary, and the Band, confronted John Phillips in his office and announced that Janis, the Grateful Dead, Quicksilver, and the Jefferson Airplane were boycotting the movie.

Phillips in effect told him to go to hell and take his two-bit San Francisco acts with him. He wasn't about to let Grossman order him around. Albert refused to budge, and when Janis and Big Brother went on Saturday afternoon, they were not filmed. No visual record exists of the Saturday matinee, which was the performance that propelled her to stardom. Clive Davis was in the audience and rushed backstage afterward to offer Janis a recording contract. In view of the complications with Mainstream, who held an option on the next record, Karpen advised Davis to contact Big Brother's attorney. Davis then invited Karpen and the attorney to Columbia's sales convention in Miami in August, offering them $75,000 for Big Brother. Usually, Davis offered far less, around ten thousand dollars, for new artists, but he suspected that Big Brother were going to have to buy their way out of the Mainstream deal and wanted to provide the means for them to do so.

Another backstage visitor was Kim Chappell, who introduced Janis to Albert Grossman. Albert explained he was at the festival to plug into the San Francisco sound, and, though Janis was represented by Julius Karpen, she and Albert immediately started talking business.

Recognizing that Janis had suddenly become the biggest star on the program, John Phillips went directly to her and promised to let her sing again if she'd override Grossman's veto. She gave Phillips a hit from her booze bottle and thanked him.

According to James Gurley, Phillips told him, 'Listen, you guys are blowin' it by not bein' in this movie.'

'Okay,' Gurley said, 'we *want* to be filmed.' Phillips told him to get ready to go on Sunday night, when they'd be filmed for a TV special. Dave Getz recalls Lou Adler and John Phillips coming up to him and saying, 'Look, if you guys sign this, you can go on again. You guys are so great, we really want you to be in the movie.'

Big Brother agreed to break away from the other San Francisco groups protesting the movie. Janis and the band then got into a fight over Karpen, who was still urging them to hold out for artistic control of their segment. 'No,' Janis said. 'Nobody else is; everybody's doin' it for free. It's just a TV movie, it's not going to make any money.' According to Gurley, Karpen held firm. 'We wanted to be in the film,' says Gurley, 'but Julius wouldn't let us.'

In desperation, Janis turned to Albert, who advised, 'Don't give up no rights to that kind of shit in no form letter. They want the rights to record this stuff and put it in a film. You sit down and you make a deal with me about it.'

That evening, Janis, in tears, went to Phillips and told him that Grossman was refusing to let her go on. 'He says I'll get overexposed,' she said, sobbing. 'He told me you had to pay me for the evening performance.'

Phillips counseled her to get rid of Grossman, sue him, or browbeat him into submission. According to Nick Gravenites, Janis 'insisted that Albert sign the agreement and Albert said he would. Albert never signed an agreement for Electric Flag to be filmed and that's why we got left out of the film *Monterey Pop*. He didn't feel that it was a good deal, and we didn't insist that it be done. He just didn't feel that the deals he was gettin' from Lou Adler [at Monterey] and Michael Lang [at Woodstock] were good deals for his artists. He wasn't used to giving that shit away – even though they were historic documents or whatever. He didn't give a fuck about the surge of the moment; he was a levelheaded businessman.'

As time for the Sunday show approached, Phillips still had no release to film Janis. Running out of patience, he threw scalding coffee on Grossman and threatened to drag him into court for ruining Janis's career and falsely posing as her agent. Burned and beaten, Grossman caved in at last, and when Janis heard the news, she said to Mark Braunstein, 'Julius Karpen doesn't know it yet, but he just lost Big Brother and the Holding Company.'

When it was almost time for the Sunday performance, in the midst of all this intrigue, Janis somehow found time to help Helen Richards, Dave's wife, who was freaking out on acid. 'Janis was drinkin' and it was right before she was to go onstage,' Helen recalls. 'She saw me come across the room and took me under her wing. "I just feel like killin' myself," I said. "What's the matter?" she asked, and I told her David and I were screwed up. Janis was so kindhearted – she put her arms around me and started walking me around. She was real sweet and spent a long time talking to me. She bought me a corn dog, made me eat it, like bringing me back into reality. It was beautiful, and I was always real fond of Janis. A few months later, she came on to me, but it wasn't my thing. I was real fond of her, though. She was a sweet lady.'

If the Saturday matinee had made Janis a rock star, Sunday night's performance made her a movie star. When the film *Monterey Pop* was released, she completely dominated it. D. A. Pennebaker and his crew, which included John Cooke and Bob Neuwirth, pioneered the art of filming rock festivals that weekend. The 8:00 P.M. show was the highlight of the festival, including Hugh Masekela, Janis, the Byrds, the Jefferson Airplane, Moby Grape, and Otis Redding.

Fortunately, the Pennebaker movie has preserved the glory of Janis's evening performance. From the first ominous phrases of 'Ball and Chain,' she gives a new meaning to the blues. The power of romantic passion to turn human beings into hostages has rarely been so starkly or poignantly evoked. Sam Andrew, who was onstage with her, playing guitar, says, 'I looked down and saw Mama Cass in the front row and her mouth dropped open and she said, "Wow!" '

As if to herald the birth of blues-driven rock at Monterey, a huge fire broke out at 242 Cannery Row, turning the night sky to livid red. Enterprise Packing, one of the last sardine canneries to go up in 1945, burned for forty-five minutes, and flames were visible across the bay. 'It was the largest fire we'd had in ten years,' said Monterey fire chief Clifford Hebrard, who estimated damage at $150,000.

Janis once told Richard Goldstein that 'Ball and Chain' was the most difficult song she'd ever sung. 'There's this big hole in the song that's mine and I've got to fill it with something. So I do. And it really tires me out.' It was the song that best demonstrated her ability to go further into the violent heart of blues than perhaps anyone else ever had, and it earned her the rank of diseuse, an actress-singer in the same league with Edith Piaf and Billie Holiday.

Not all of Monterey's bands fared as well as Big Brother. 'There were a lot of acts that just did terribly,' Dave Getz says, 'like Hugh Masekela. Half the audience walked out. They were bored with that kind of jazz. It just didn't mean anything to them anymore. Quicksilver didn't make a big impression, but Steve Miller did really well. He had a powerful band in those days – a lot different from what he became.'

Despite her two show-stopping Monterey performances, the local press consistently failed to spot Janis as the star of the festival. At last, on June 19, an anonymous caption writer singled her out under a photograph appearing on page five of the *Herald*: 'Belting It Out With Gusto: One of the biggest hits of the Festival was big-voiced Janis Joplin with Big Brother. She sang at the Saturday afternoon session, and was recalled to sing.'

Mark Braunstein and Janis were together in the audience when Otis Redding, the only soul singer at Monterey, went on at 1:00 A.M. Sunday. 'This is the love crowd, right?' Otis yelled. 'We all love each other, right?' The crowd roared in agreement. He opened with 'Shake,' and Robert Christgau of *Esquire,* standing near Brian Jones, noticed that the Rolling Stone had tears in his eyes. With Booker T. and the MGs & the Mar-Keys backing Otis up, and Head Lights providing the light show, Otis launched into his 1965 hit, 'I've Been Loving You Too Long (to Stop Now).' By the time he sang 'Respect,' Janis and Mark were standing on their chairs.

Just as Janis had walked off with Saturday's concert, Sunday belonged to Jimi Hendrix. Dressed in swashbuckling freak clothes and sporting a plumed purple hat, Hendrix had only a small underground following in the United States, though he was already celebrated in England. The chemistry between Jimi and Janis was immediately apparent when they met at Monterey, and after the festival she would become erotically involved with him as well as with another member of his group, the Jimi Hendrix Experience. 'I was with Jimi backstage at Monterey,' Sam recalls, 'and he was throwing little white pellets in his mouth. There were a lot of them. I thought they were Tic Tacs but later discovered they were LSD.'

Says Dave Getz, 'I was sitting on the stage when Hendrix played and also for the Who. A lot of performers sat on the stage or on the edge, off the side. Jimi and the Who were doing what we wanted to do – going out there as far as you could, with energy and outrageousness.' Also sitting on stage were David Crosby, Paul Kantner, and David Freiberg. Crosby had watched Hendrix take Purple Haze before the set and saw him come on to the acid as he played. When he was peaking on the drug, he played his guitar with his teeth and made it sing as never before.

Hendrix managed to upstage the Who, who'd demolished their instruments during their set, by spraying his guitar with lighter fluid and setting it on fire. 'Finally he smashed it,' wrote the *Herald* reviewer, 'and lovingly tossed the pieces to the vibrating audience.' Christgau, unimpressed, denounced Hendrix in *Esquire* as a 'psychedelic Uncle Tom.'

If Janis needed any verification of her triumph, she received it when the national media reviewed Monterey Pop. On June 30, *Time*'s critic singled her out from the 128 other performers, writing, 'When soul took over last week, the festival took off. Among the high points: Janis Joplin, backed by a San Francisco group called Big Brother and the Holding Company, belting out a biting alto and stamping her feet like a flamenco dancer.'

She saw Hendrix again shortly after Monterey and began an affair with him. Hendrix had been in London during its years as the rock capital, and then, says Dave Getz, 'right after Monterey, he came to San Francisco. He knew it was now the place to be. We opened for him at the Fillmore.'

Mark Braunstein remembers meeting Hendrix in Janis's dressing room one night. Mark had come to enlist Hendrix's help with a Haight-Ashbury civic project. The so-called Summer of Love was drawing unmanageable crowds to the Haight, and the residents of the small community were protesting. Mark and some friends had come up with a peaceful solution, staging free concerts in the Panhandle as a way of diverting tourists from the congested streets to the park.

Janis turned to Hendrix and said, 'Hey, anything Mark wants, I recommend. He's on the level. You'll have a great time. This is not a bunch of bullshit. We have to get everybody off the fuckin' street and down to the Panhandle so the tour buses won't have anything to stare at.'

Asked to enumerate Janis's lovers during this period, Dave Richards says, 'She made it with Country Joe, Jimi Hendrix, and Jim Morrison. She and Hendrix would make it after a gig. Right after Monterey, we were on the same bill with Hendrix [at the Fillmore West], and they'd go back to his motel.' Both Janis and Hendrix needed to decompress after a performance, and the quantum sex they were capable of offered a convenient way. Beyond their mutual affinities for the blues and heroin, perhaps his strongest attraction for Janis was the color of his skin. Having sex with a black stud represented the ultimate finger flip at the 'nigger knockers' of Texas.

For rock audiences, a large part of Hendrix's appeal was the age-old myth of African sexual supremacy, and many fans became extremely agitated when he rubbed his guitar against his crotch. As Eric Clapton put it, 'Everybody and his brother in England still sort of think that spades have big dicks. And Jimi came over and exploited that to the limit . . . and everybody fell for it.' Graphic evidence concerning the dimensions of Hendrix's penis was provided by a pale, overweight Chicago groupie known as Cynthia Plaster Caster. This otherwise-shy girl performed oral sex on Hendrix, and while his penis was still erect, she plunged it into a bucket containing a slick, soft solution called alginate, having first applied baby oil to his pubic hair to keep it from getting stuck. His penis was withdrawn as detumescence set in, and plaster was poured into the hole. Later, when the alginate was peeled away from the hardened plaster, the finished product clearly revealed that Hendrix was only somewhat on the plus side of average.

At concerts, Hendrix frequently leaned over the stage and flicked his tongue at female fans, an obvious invitation to cunnilingus, which at the time was considered to be a depraved act. 'Janis had never known the experience of being high until she got with Jimi Hendrix,' says Linda Higginbotham Carroll, a girlhood friend Janis still kept in touch with. 'She told me she was in love with Jimi and they were doing heroin together. She said her parents wouldn't approve of her being in love with him because he was black. I don't think she ruined her life until she met Jimi Hendrix.'

Hendrix was violent with women, which ultimately drove Janis away from him. He was so dangerous that he put one woman in the hospital and later had to pay her ten thousand dollars to prevent a lawsuit. Though Janis felt a frisson of fear added piquancy to lovemaking and sometimes provoked her partners to harsher intercourse than they cared to perform, she was furious when a man beat her up in bed one time and never allowed him to get near her again.

With Jimi and his band, Janis was like a kid in a candy store. She got a crush on his roadie, Gerry Stickells, who'd been a car mechanic until Noel Redding had recruited him for the Experience. Hendrix's drummer, John (Mitch) Mitchell, noticed that Janis was so excited over Stickells that she couldn't stand still. 'I remember her clearly jumping up and down on a hotel room bed, her dog in one arm and a bottle of Southern Comfort in the other,' Mitchell said.

Jim Morrison was another rough character who came into her life in 1967. From the beginning, their bands had been linked in people's minds. The Doors were known around San Francisco as 'Hollywood's version of Big Brother,' and in LA, Janis was referred to as 'the female Jim Morrison.'

'The Doors came north and we went south,' Sam says. Big Brother started gigging at LA's Whiskey-A-Go-Go and the Golden Bear Club in Huntington Beach, and the Doors came up the coast regularly to play the Matrix and Winterland. Says Sam, 'They were a slithery crew even then. We were playing the Matrix one weekend when we heard about the Doors coming to town. This was when we first met all of them. They were in an incubation period just as we were, still sweet and innocent.'

James Gurley, recalling the night he and Janis first saw the Doors, takes a more acerbic view. 'Janis and Morrison were two big egos clashing in the night,' he says. 'They never got along from the first time we saw the Doors at the Matrix. She didn't like Jim Morrison and he didn't like her. They were too much alike – two monstrous egos.'

In January 1967, the Doors were playing Winterland, and Paul Kantner of the Jefferson Airplane told them they should catch Janis's act at the Avalon between their sets. The Doors complained that the Avalon was two miles across town, but John Densmore would never regret the trip. Said John, 'The female lead singer was so good, we were told, it would be worth the hassle of getting back for our last set. I remember thinking that a girl who called herself "Big Brother" must be kind of butch.'

Robby Krieger and Densmore arrived 'in the middle of a torching rendition of "Down on Me" ' and later went backstage to tell Janis how sensational she was. Said Densmore, 'She thanked me kindly and offered me a slug of her gallon of rotgut wine. Seeing Janis Joplin up close wasn't as appealing as from a distance, but she was warm and friendly, and that deep, husky voice kept reminding me how powerfully she could belt the blues.'

In June 1967, Jim Morrison was in New York, complaining bitterly that he had not been invited to participate at Monterey Pop. The weekend of the festival was practically a national holiday in the rock world, and the Scene, the hip club in Manhattan where the Doors usually played, closed so that everyone could go to California. The Doors were reduced to playing dumpy little clubs in Philadelphia and Long Island, and Morrison began to nurse a grudge against the San Francisco bands. 'My flower-child half strongly wanted to be tripping and dancing at the Festival,' said the Doors's Densmore, 'but I was in the demon Doors.'

145

'Morrison took it personally,' according to his biographers, feeling he was being discriminated against because of his identity as an LA rocker. By the time Janis and Morrison got together after Monterey, she'd returned to Haight-Ashbury a star. *Rolling Stone*, which started publishing in 1967, called her 'the major female voice of her generation,' and Ralph Gleason said she was 'easily the most exciting singer of her race to appear in a decade or more.' Alternately happy and puzzled by the big splash she'd made, she said she was enjoying fame but was acutely mindful that 'before this, nobody ever cared whether I lived.' A social outcast since puberty, she was bewildered by the world's sudden adulation and frankly didn't know what to do with it. But there was one aspect of fame that she embraced instantly and wholeheartedly: It was an aphrodisiac. Some of the most attractive men of her time were now available to her.

Jim Morrison was in her apartment one night with a group that included Dave Richards, Sam Andrew, Morrison's girl, Pamela Courson, and his tailor. 'When I got there, Morrison was already there with some hippie guy who was his clothing designer and traveled all around with him, making Morrison's leather pants,' says Dave Richards. 'Morrison was very drunk. We all were. Sam was, I was, Janis was. Only Morrison's girlfriend wasn't drunk. She was a little uptight, actually. She didn't much want to be there. Both Sam and I had designs on her. The only other woman there was Janis and we both knew that Janis had designs on Jim Morrison.'

Morrison had met Pamela Courson upon returning to LA in the summer of 1967, immediately following the Doors's gigs at the Scene in New York. Pamela had reddish golden hair, porcelain skin, and lavender eyes. Their sex life was weird. Pam could take his tying her up and beating her, but what she really minded was Jim's penchant for anal intercourse. In retaliation, she scrawled *FAGGOT* across the back of his favorite vest.

At Janis's apartment that night in San Francisco, Janis went over to Dave Richards after a while and whispered, 'I'm going to go in there in my bedroom. Why don't you tell Jim to come in there? I want to talk to him for a minute.'

'Oh,' Dave said, 'okay.' Then he went over to Morrison and said, 'Hey, Jim.' Morrison glanced up drunkenly and said, 'Yeah?'

'Janis wants to talk to you for a minute.'

Morrison got up and walked into the bedroom. Says Dave, 'The door closed and I heard it lock – clank! And that was that. The girlfriend sat there and sat there. Hours passed.'

Janis's boudoir was a soft and seductive seraglio, with velvet, satin, lace, and silk everywhere. Bob Seidemann's nude poster of her adorned one wall, and there were incense, lubricating lotions, booze, dope, water pipes, and needles.

Morrison may well have struck her as the ultimate catch. Writers of the sixties outdid themselves attempting to capture his sensuality. Biographers noted that in black leather he 'looked like a naked body dipped in India ink.' Journalists referred to him as a 'surf-born Dionysus' and a 'hippie Adonis.' Rock critic Lillian Roxon wrote adulatingly, 'The Doors are unendurable pleasure prolonged.' Richard Goldstein lionized him as 'a sexual shaman' and a 'street punk gone to heaven and reincarnated as a choir boy.'

Describing a typical Jim Morrison sexual encounter – this one at the Alta Cienega Motel in West Hollywood – his biographers Jerry Hopkins and Danny Sugerman revealed that he first elicited the girl's life story and then 'butt-fucked' her. If Morrison got as far as Janis's life story that night in her bedroom, he learned that they had much in common. Jim wanted to be a writer, and Janis, too, intended to write a book, according to Sam. They were both avid readers and both had been Venice, California, beatniks because of *On the Road*. Both read Nietzsche, Ferlinghetti, McClure, and Corso, and if Janis wasn't the expert on Plutarch, Baudelaire, and Norman O. Brown that Jim was, she could readily discuss Gurdjieff, Wilfred Owen, and F. Scott Fitzgerald, not to mention *The Sensuous Woman*.

Jim and Janis remained cloistered in her room for hours, while Sam, Dave Richards, and Pam waited just outside the door. Says Dave, 'Finally, I said to Pam, "You know, if you're waiting for him to come out of there, he's probably not going to be out of there until tomorrow. He's not coming out."

' "Oh, yes he will!" she said.

'She was pretty young. "No," I said. "He's not coming out." Sam and I had ulterior motives, anyway. Finally, she got really mad, and she said, "Call a cab." I called her a cab and later, as I was walking her down to the street, I opened the door of the cab for her and she got in and Sam went in right past me, pulled the door shut, and the cab went off with both of them in it. I told Sam later, "You son of a bitch!" He said, "You got to be quick." Sam slithered right in there. Sam had this myth in his mind about the equipment men: "Goddamn, you guys get all the women because you always get to town first." Since he was a star and making more money than us, he'd invested the oppressed workers with great sexual prowess. That's what was in his head.'

Sam confirms Dave's account, saying, 'Yes, it's true. The equipment men arrive first at a gig and get all the girls. At last, with Pam, I could challenge the typical proletarian myth about the potency of the working class.'

Sometime after Janis's night with Morrison, she told her friend Henry Carr, 'I don't like Jim Morrison. He was okay in bed, but when we got up the next morning, he asked for a shot of sloe gin.' By Janis's standards, sloe gin was a sissy drink.

Pamela Courson, though hurt when Jim slept around, went along with the Lizard King's peccadillos. Given her choice, Pam would have preferred a 'more traditional' relationship. She was living with Jim at this time at 1812 Rothdell Trail in LA's Laurel Canyon and they were already playing the dangerous games that would eventually kill them both, drugging, scaring each other with spiders and black magic, getting high on acid, and driving down Mulholland with their eyes closed.

Around the time that Jim was sleeping with Janis, Pamela got even by making it with handsome young actors such as John Phillip Law and Tom Baker. Later, Tom Baker fell in with Andy Warhol's crowd in New York and starred in *I, a Man,* one of Warhol's pornographic epics. Ironically, when Pam broke off with Baker and went back to Morrison, the two men became close friends and drinking buddies, and Baker became one of Janis's lovers. He lived at the Casa Real near the Chateau Marmont with two other young men, and the three of them became known as 'the boys who fuck famous women.'

Baker, who'd appeared nude in the Warhol film, told Morrison he was nothing but a 'prick tease' and challenged him to 'let it all hang out' at a rock concert. Eventually, Morrison did exactly that, in Miami, and the resultant legal complications drove him to a nervous breakdown. Baker perhaps also goaded Janis to some of the extremes, including exposure, that came to typify her later concerts.

One day in late June, shortly after Monterey Pop, Janis was scheduled to sing in Golden Gate Park as part of the summer solstice be-in. It was a perfect San Francisco day, mild and sunny, and she decided to take her dog George out walking before the concert. Janis and Sunshine were very close at this time, so she picked up Sunshine and *'sashayed'* through

Haight-Ashbury, stopping at a liquor store to buy some Ripple. They ran into Freewheelin' Frank and he joined them on their stroll to the park.

At the end of Haight, they crossed Stanyan and entered the cavernous, shadowy park. At Hippie Hill, they came out into the sunshine again and then headed on into the deeper recesses of the park. Janis and Big Brother performed that day from the back of a flatbed truck, and Quicksilver Messenger Service and the Grateful Dead also played, using equipment that had been borrowed from Monterey Pop. Nimble as a panther, Jimi Hendrix scrambled up on the back of Big Brother's sound truck and started snapping pictures with his Instamatic camera. As Janis sang from the flatbed, someone leaned over the edge of the platform and passed out marijauna joints to everyone present.

At these great 1960s celebrations of life and love, she was as close as she'd ever be to perfect happiness. After the performance, she was too elated to go home and spent the rest of the day loitering in front of a big 1940s car, smoking a fat cigar and taking swigs of booze straight from the bottle. The next day, she was exhausted, confused, and drinking more than ever. Her friends feared the excitement of her career breakthrough at Monterey would prove to be more than she could handle. When Peggy offered her the use of her house in Stinson Beach, Janis left for a few days' rest.

She went barhopping around Marin County the first day of her vacation and well into the evening. Coming home drunk that night, she nearly crashed her car through the front gate. The next day, she was sunbathing nude on the deck when Peggy arrived unexpectedly. Undressing, Peggy joined her, and soon they were massaging each other's breasts with suntan oil. Janis commented on the stupendous proportions of Peggy's breasts, revealing an insecurity about the size of her own. She very likely found the reassurance she needed in the passionate love they made that day in the open air, completely indifferent to gawking neighbors. Kim somehow learned of their escapade and, on the following weekend, she confronted Peggy, asking her point-blank whether she was sleeping with Janis. Peggy admitted she was.

Although Kim denies being jealous, she says that she assaulted Peggy, breaking her nose. 'Peggy and I used to fight like cats and dogs,' she says. 'I took the aerial off the Shelby on Van Ness Street one time and ran after her with it, beating on her car. She made me mad many times. I put my fist through many windows. I threw stereo stuff out of second-story apartment windows.'

'Was it over her running around with Janis?' I ask.

'No, no. I was never jealous of Janis. I was tired of Peggy's obsessive ways, but there wasn't much I could do about it. I was strung out and we had everything together and I didn't know any other life or business. We had our home, our business, our dogs, our people, everything.

'We were out at Stinson one night, and I guess we didn't have enough dope, or she wouldn't have been on the rag. We had a little bit, but she started nagging one afternoon.' Tired of fighting with Peggy, Kim tried to make peace by keeping the conversation positive and pleasant. She was determined that nothing Peggy said would 'push her buttons' and make her react. Peggy 'ranted and raved, picked, and bitched for fourteen hours,' Kim says, but Kim maintained total silence, refraining even from facial expressions. They fell asleep for a while and when they woke up, Kim said it was time to return to the city. On the way back in the Porsche, they took the winding, narrow road over Mt. Tamalpais. Kim admits, 'I'm not a slow driver,' and when they got to a curve and Peggy told her to slow down, Kim 'just kind of snapped.'

'I had my right hand on the wheel,' she recalls, 'and I reached over with my left and I went *Thunk! Pow!* right into 'her cheek and it broke her nose. She was so mad. I didn't say anything. I drove her directly fifteen minutes from there to the Marin General Hospital and waited for her, and she was still ranting and raving to the doctor. She was just on a trip, but she really had a case now because she had to wear this great big X on her face, a big adhesive white X right across her nose up to her forehead and down her cheek, and if she didn't look a sight!'

Peggy took revenge by carrying on her affair with Janis more brazenly than ever. Lying to Kim, Peggy would tell her she was going on a buying trip for the boutique, but she and Janis would meet at a hotel or Janis's apartment. They made love so feverishly that they forgot to take breaks for meals or sleep and became dizzy. Some of these sessions took place in dirty hotel rooms they rented for as little as ten dollars a night.

Peggy stated in her book that when she and Kim made love, the experience was somehow more definitive – akin to a man-woman relationship. With Janis, it was more like the secret lesbian garden that Joan Baez described, something only two women could know. Though there was more physical attraction with Kim, Janis was just as essential in Peggy's emotional life.

Though Janis put considerable pressure on Peggy to leave Kim and move in with her, Peggy declined, fearing that she'd become another sycophant in Janis's entourage.

One result of Janis's growing national fame was the reversal of the Fillmore auditorium's long-standing policy against her. Suddenly, after Monterey Pop, she was welcome in Bill Graham's legendary rock palace. As a rule, Chet Helms discovered the talent and Bill Graham exploited it, or, as Janis herself put it, Graham sucked up to anyone who'd 'made it.' Her relationship with Graham, a hotheaded egomaniac, had always been tempestuous. From the start, Graham had resented her association with Chet, his archrival at the Avalon Ballroom. Chet and Bill had started out together, producing dances at the Fillmore on alternate weekends. The partnership flourished, giving San Francisco good live entertainment for the first time since the fifties heyday of the jazz and folk clubs.

Graham had never heard of the Paul Butterfield Blues Band, who were playing to empty clubs in Southern California when Chet and his partner, John Carpenter, discovered them. They had to fight with Bill to get Butterfield into the Fillmore, finally issuing an ultimatum: 'It's our show. Let us do it.' Chet and John then got on the phone to everyone they knew and hounded them into coming to the Fillmore that weekend. Butterfield was a smashing success, playing to some 7,500 people. When Graham saw the record crowd, he woke up early the next morning and called Albert Grossman in New York, buying all the potential bookings for the next two years for the Butterfield Blues Band in California and paying Albert a large lump sum.

Says Chet, 'I had an option on Butterfield's next appearance, but Graham misrepresented the situation to Grossman, presenting it as if it was his show as opposed to a Family Dog Productions show. Graham was getting ten percent of the gate, and I was pretty naïve in thinking that since he had a fiduciary relationship to us and we were partners, he should not be stabbing us in the back.'

Graham eventually threw Chet out of the Fillmore, and Chet opened the Avalon, which went on to become more important in the development of the San Francisco sound than the Fillmore. Poet Michael McClure says the Avalon helped give spiritual birth to the entire sixties counterculture.

In 1966, when Janis and Big Brother attempted to attend a show at the Fillmore, Graham refused to let them in. She assumed Graham thought she was still being managed by Chet, but even after she explained to Graham that she'd fired Chet, he still blocked her way. With typical Graham cruelty, he lashed into her, saying he couldn't stand her because she was totally devoid of talent. The real reason, says Dave Getz, was that Janis had recently criticized the Fillmore in print. In an underground newsletter called *Mojo Navigator,* an interviewer asked Janis which of San Francisco's premier ballrooms she preferred, the Avalon or the Fillmore. Go to the Avalon for the music, she said, and go to the Fillmore to pick up a sailor.

When Graham saw the article, he ran amok, says Dave, attacking Janis 'just as she was coming in up the front stairs. She was wired and was taken completely by surprise. It was a scene, both she and Graham screaming and cursing each other at top volume. Janis always started screaming when she was taken off guard.'

Janis wasn't the first member of Big Brother to clash with the pugnacious Graham. 'I struck sparks with him right away,' says Sam. In early 1966, several months before Janis joined Big Brother, Graham was controlling a crowd trying to get into the Trips Festival. 'He seemed like some kind of monster to me,' Sam recalls. 'He was yelling and screaming and generally terrorizing everyone . . . The fact that he let me in but not our drummer Chuck Jones seemed to me to be an unconscionable breach of Aquarian ethics. I whispered into his ear that he was a motherfucker. Why he didn't annihilate me on the spot, I don't know, but he definitely vocalized a lot. We finally had to call the gentle and affable Chet Helms to calm everyone down.'

Even after Janis became a star attraction at the Fillmore, she and Graham frequently squared off. When he posted a rule against pot smoking backstage, 'Janis wasn't havin' any of that shit,' says Nick Gravenites. 'Janis was gonna smoke a joint in the middle of her rock 'n' roll empire whenever she wanted.' One night while she was onstage, Graham hid in the wardrobe in her dressing room. After the show, she returned to her room and lighted up a doobie. As soon as the smoke wafted over to the wardrobe, Bill came bursting out and threw one of his rabid fits, shouting, '*I said there was no fucking dope being smoked in this place!*' Seizing her by the back of her neck, he marched her publicly through the Fillmore, threw her down the stairs and out onto the street.

Janis was crying when she confided her humiliation to Nick Gravenites. Though Nick is a gentle man, he looks like a killer. 'Bill Graham knew that if he ever attacked her again, I'd kill him,' he says. Graham left Janis alone after that, but he avenged himself on Nick, refusing to book him into the Fillmore.

'It was an antagonistic relationship,' says Chet. 'Graham represented to Janis the kind of male machismo that she was very much in conflict with always. They were both very determined, very vicious Capricorns and they locked horns.'

Janis's sudden fame also emboldened Mainstream Records at last to release the LP *Big Brother and the Holding Company*, and it stalled at number sixty on the *Billboard* chart. Critic Ralph Gleason called it 'a bad representation of what the band did,' and when Janis saw him at the Avalon, she seemed to agree, saying, 'Hey, man, thanks for what you said about our shitty record.' I have a higher opinion of it myself. Though the mechanical quality of the recording may be substandard, the tunes are catchy and both Janis and the band are loaded with wit and originality.

In the autumn of 1967, Linda Gravenites became Janis's roommate. Linda had been married to Nick and they'd had a son, but when Nick's career had taken him back to Chicago in the early sixties, Linda had said, 'Have a good time! I'm staying here and doing what I started.' Now Linda would provide one of the few continuing relationships in Janis's life, becoming her dress designer, best friend, and confidante. Today, Linda lives deep in the redwood wilderness near the Russian River, a few hours' drive north of San Francisco. She strikes me as a beatnik Sophia Loren, voluptuous, intelligent, and warmhearted. She wears comfortable soft jeans, a dark cotton turtleneck, and suede fruit boots. Standing in her sunny kitchen, she grinds her own Italian coffee and serves it in big steaming mugs, with real milk. When we settle in the living room, which has a wood-burning stove, her dog Sidney, an ardent Lhasa apso, a Tibetan terrier, sits at my feet, gazing at me with intelligent eyes.

After spending some time with Linda, I can see why she was Janis's roommate. She's an up-front, no-bullshit lady who's at once earthy, witty, and sexual. I can as easily imagine her dancing on tabletops in North Beach coffeehouses, which she assures me she did, or as a pioneer woman on a wagon train heading west. Today, she makes her living by creating stained glass on commission, and she's currently working on a huge window for the local church. It will be installed over the altar, and it shows a towering cross shining through a forest of giant redwoods, complete with squirrels and woodpeckers.

At one point in our visit, I get an eerie déjà vu sensation that Linda is Janis Joplin reincarnated. One of us says something funny and she throws her whole body into a roar of laughter that comes out in several stages and lasts for almost a minute. First, she rolls onto her back, letting out screams and guffaws. Then she sticks her long legs into the air and thrashes them as she cackles, yelps, and hollers. Totally uninhibited, she wrings the last ounce of joy out of the moment before sitting up and wiping her eyes. Outside, a sleek silver cat jumps on the windowsill to see what all the commotion's about. 'That's Pearl,' Linda says. It takes me a moment to realize that Linda has named her cat after Janis, who came to prefer the name Pearl.

It was in 1967 that Janis first heard of Linda through Sam Andrew. One day, Janis complimented Sam on one of his shirts and he told her that Linda had designed it. 'Go over to the Grateful Dead's house on Ashbury Street,' he said. 'There's a chick there makes them for me.'

When Janis called on Linda, they discussed a costume for Janis's appearance at the Monterey Jazz Festival, which was to be held in September, a couple of months after Monterey Pop. 'We sat around and talked and I drew up what I thought would be something right for her and she liked it,' says Linda. When Janis asked her what she was doing in the Dead's house, Linda said, 'The guys are on the road and all the old ladies took off for New Mexico. They're going to buy some land out there, so they left me here as their house sitter.'

As they talked that day, Linda revealed that she'd once been married to a legendary beatnik named Patrick Cassidy. Janis was so impressed, she yelped and said, 'He's one of my mythic men!' Linda is convinced that Janis was attracted to her primarily out of curiosity about Patrick. Says Linda, 'Like, if I'd been married to Patrick, I must have something going for myself. So she was interested in finding out who I was. I wasn't just somebody to make her a garment.'

Janis agreed with Linda's theory about clothes, which Linda sums up as: 'No matter what it looks like, it has to be at least as comfortable as jeans and a T-shirt. You have to be able to forget it the minute it's on. It has to move and just be able to be forgotten. Because you can't afford to be self-conscious and do whatever it is you're supposed to do.'

She envisaged Janis as a 'pirate chick' whom she'd dress in velvet vests, pants, chiffon blouses with huge full sleeves, lace

.unics, and spectacular beaded and sequined capes. With Linda, Janis's transformation into a chic, sexy hippie would soon be under way.

While Linda was still working on Janis's costume for the Monterey Jazz Festival, the Grateful Dead returned to their house in Ashbury Street and Linda was suddenly homeless. 'Can I stay on your couch to finish your outfit?' she asked, and Janis agreed. When the costume was finished, Linda told Sam she was moving to Marin, adding, 'I think I might be in the way at Janis's.'

'Listen, has Janis said anything about your being in the way?' Sam asked. 'She's the most up-front chick in the world. If you were in the way, she'd have told you. At rehearsal, she's saying she really likes having you there. So why don't you stay?'

One day shortly thereafter, Janis stood looking at the dirty dishes in the kitchen sink and said with a sigh, 'I need a mother.'

'I could do that,' Linda said. She moved in and 'did everything Janis didn't want to do before she knew she wanted it done.' That amounted to running the household and grooming Janis to the point that she was sought by Avedon for *Vogue* and Scavullo for *Harper's Bazaar*.

At the Monterey Jazz Festival, Janis was intimidated by the prospect of appearing on the same stage with traditional blues singers such as B. B. King, T-Bone Walker, Clara Ward, and Big Joe Turner, and before an older audience who disapproved of rock and electric instruments. After hyping herself, she stomped onstage, said, 'Shit,' and started to scream the blues. The audience sat in shock, then jumped up, cheered, and started snake-dancing around the Horse Arena. 'Nothing like it had ever happened before in the Festival's ten years,' wrote Ralph J. Gleason in *Rolling Stone,* 'and nothing like it has happened since.'

Gleason was there making a film for educational television, and Janis was quivering when she came offstage and asked him, 'Did you film it?'

'No,' Gleason said, explaining that 'in a burst of paranoia still to be equaled' her manager 'had refused to OK our filming Janis's performance.' She was disappointed as she absorbed the news that no record would exist of what Gleason called 'that incredible performance. It was Janis's day, no doubt about it. She turned them on like they had not been turned on in years. Old and young, long hair or short, black or white, they reacted like somebody had stuck a hot wire in their ass.'

Back in San Francisco, Janis settled into an apartment that was at last in order, thanks to Linda. Linda Gravenites was a Southern California girl who'd been adopted as a baby and grown up near Palm Springs, on the edge of the desert, in a town called Banning. In 1959, unhappy and rebellious at home, she traveled to San Francisco on a bus, with only the clothes she was wearing, and settled in North Beach.

Around the mid-1960s, Linda moved to North Point Street, where two of her neighbors were Carl Gottlieb and Milan Melvin. 'Linda was a fox,' says Carl. 'Milan and I would wake up at ten or eleven o'clock and see if Linda and her roommate were awake, and the four of us would walk across the street to Ghiradelli Square, to the top level, overlooking the Bay. There was a little coffeehouse called Portofino, so we'd all have some coffee and read the paper, watch the boats on the Bay, smell the chocolate from the factory, and smoke a joint. It was idyllic; there are certain times in your life when you can say, "Okay, if you can freeze it just like that." We all stayed friends, and I knew that Linda went on to do a lot of stuff for Janis, like seamstressing.'

Besides Linda and Sunshine, Janis's growing circle of women friends now included the poet Lenore Kandel. *Love*

Book, Lenore's collection of poems, including the erotic 'To Fuck with Love: Phase One,' had created a sensation back in 1966, when the Psychedelic Shop was busted for selling it.

Janis and her girlfriends were known around the Haight as 'the Capricorn ladies.' Says Linda, 'We four Capricorn ladies included Suzy Perry – Stanley Mouse's little lady – Sunshine, me, and Janis, and we'd walk down Haight Street, raucously laughing and carrying our Rainier Ale in paper bags. We called Rainier Ale "Green Death." It's a little stronger than beer and a little more flavorful.'

Adds Richard Hundgen, 'When the Capricorn ladies walked down the street, they'd knock anyone out of their way.' Janis wore her hip-hugger jeans and a T-shirt and her favorite thrift-store jacket, which was made of black velveteen with regimental-color sleeves. 'Sunshine sashayed better than anybody in the world,' Linda says, 'and Suzy Perry was lovely.'

At home, Janis shared the cooking chores and often prepared her favorite dish, spaghetti with pesto sauce. The recipe had been given to her by a bartender at Gino and Carlo's, the longshoremen's bar in North Beach, where she liked to shoot pool.

One day, Sweet William, Linda's favorite Hell's Angel, brought Linda a lace tablecloth he'd picked up at the Free Store. 'Here, make yourself something out of this,' he said. Linda fashioned a saucy and provocative lace blouse, and when Janis saw it, she said, 'Hey, make me something out of lace.'

'Well,' Linda replied, 'bring me a tablecloth and I'll make you one.' It was the late summer or early fall of 1967 and Big Brother was playing a gig in Salt Lake City. At a party after the show, Janis spotted an elegant lace tablecloth on the buffet table. Sidling up to the hostess, who'd been fulsome in her praise of Janis's performance, Janis said, 'Oh! I've been wanting a lace tablecloth just like that.'

The hostess said, 'This is the first time I've ever had it out and I hate it.'

'You do?'

'Yes. You can have it if you want.'

Janis immediately started shifting dishes and bottles to another table and carried the tablecloth under her arm for the rest of the night. When she returned to San Francisco, Linda created a delightful outfit from the tablecloth. 'The pants were hip-huggers,' Linda notes, 'and I left a little triangle of skin showing. The top was see-through, but not the pants, which were lined in purple lightweight cotton-Dacron.'

'Where-all did she wear it?' I ask.

'She wore it to shreds!' Linda says.

Janis always enjoyed going to see *The Committee*, an improvisational satirical review in San Francisco that was closely aligned with the counterculture. She became romantically involved with some of the actors and crew, including Howard Hesseman, who was now acting in the show. He and Janis renewed their friendship at a party, and Hesseman told her he had just separated from his second wife. 'I was totally stoned and stunned,' he says. 'She came home with me that night. I had a great little place on Telegraph Hill, and she was the first woman to spend a night with me when I moved into that house. She had a beautiful body. I always thought that. She had a mole on one breast that was almost like an extra nipple. Like all of us, she could look less than terrific, but then there were times when she just looked sensational. It definitely was not a body to sneeze at. She could get heavy, like we all do; she could let herself go and look really bad. But when she looked good, there were few who could touch her, in my book. That night, she looked wonderful and we were really smokin'.'

She began an intense affair with Milan Melvin, who shared an apartment on North Point with Carl Gottlieb, another *Committee* actor. Milan is a tall, rangy man who resembles James Taylor from some angles and Christopher Walken from others, and he used to walk around the Haight in a purple cape, carrying a violin case, which he used as his briefcase. At radio station KMPX, he worked from six to midnight with Tom Donahue, who was one of the first DJ's to broadcast rock 'n' roll on FM.

'I can't remember if I met her at the Coffee Gallery, through Linda Gravenites, or around *The Committee*,' Milan says. 'I just remember Janis and I coming together like crazed wildcats in heat, just kicking and biting and scratching and fucking one another to death and then gettin' up and takin' some more drugs and doin' it some more. But I don't remember somebody sayin', "Milan, this is Janis." '

They began to see each other on an exclusive basis, though they always maintained separate apartments. 'It was night after night after night,' he says, 'at her place or mine.' Besides wild sex, what he loved most about her was her sensitivity and the fact that she was totally open and up-front with him from the first moment. Those traits had a downside, as well. 'Her nerves were nearer the skin,' he says, 'and nobody broke like Janis, nobody seemed to reach the depths of disappointment or to take hurt so heavy.'

Often, Janis would go over to the station and wait for him to get off work. Sometimes they'd go up on the roof and trip acid. 'I took LSD with Janis a couple of times,' he says, 'and mescaline a couple of times. We lay up on the roof at KMPX one time in August of '67 when there was a blood red eclipse and that was *somethin'*. She kept saying, "We're in the bottom end of a microscope, man. And that's God's bloodshot eye up there lookin' down at us." And you could really see it.'

One evening, Milan gave her a ride to a gig at the Fillmore in his Volkswagen bus, and when they arrived at the auditorium, Janis left her dog George in the van, as usual. During the show, a burglar broke into the van, and while he was robbing it, the dog jumped out and ran away. Janis went on the radio, pleaded with the people of San Francisco to help her find her dog, and eventually got George back.

Another time, they hopped on Milan's Harley and vroomed up to the Nevada desert, where they stopped at an Indian reservation. 'There was a pretty big peyote scene at the time and people were eating a lot of cactus and goin' into tepees and observing the Native American church rituals,' he recalls. 'Janis and I sat in a tepee with members of the tribe and took mescaline. The Indians led us through the psychedelic trip with velvet gloves. Everyone sat around the tepee and a staff and a rattle were passed from person to person, and you got your turn to sing your song or to explain to people why you were there or to ask for help, like "I got sickness in the family," "I'm broke, guys," whatever. Or if you said, "My paranoia is kicking in," someone would say, "Shake that rattle!" It was a refined ritual of some twenty-five centuries, and they had it right down to takin' a piss. We called them pee sticks – elaborately beaded sticks that were stuck between the canvas and the tepee pole. That means that there's only two people that can leave the meeting at a time to go outside to take a pee.

'You go outside and take this long piss and all of a sudden you've messed up your psychedelicized trip. You realize just how unbelievably beautiful nature is, right? And these clouds going over and everything and eventually your focus would come back to this brightly beaded thing out there in nature and it would remind you, Go *back to the meeting. Maybe somebody else has got to pee.*'

After they came down from the psychedelic, they splashed

around in the hot springs. 'Man, psychedelics and the city just don't mix,' Janis said.

'That's what's good about Nevada,' Milan said. 'You have space to fuck up. We're so surrounded by nature that we can't have a bad trip.'

Milan attributes their happiness to the fact they always kept their relationship completely separate from her career, which was really zooming at this point. 'I hate the backstage life,' he says. 'I just stayed away from that like a plague. I didn't like the groupieness, the power trips goin' on with the managers and producers, the sycophancy, the hanging around with other stars, so I never went into a dressing room with Janis – or anyone else, for that matter.

'When I was with her, we would be at my place or hers, or the desert, or we'd be on a motorcycle takin' a ride somewhere away from the scene. Except for when she was actually singing, she didn't like the music scene that much, either. What really began to grind her down was hanging out backstage for interminable periods before she got to go on. It was an ugly scene.'

Despite the band's breakthrough at Monterey, their business affairs were in a shambles and nothing had been resolved in their ongoing conflict with their manager, Karpen. Due to drugs and alcohol, a potential multimillion-dollar act was headed for destruction. Janis, James, and Sam were hooked on heroin. 'Big Brother and the Holding Company used to refer to themselves as an *alcodelic* band, as a joke,' says Dave Richards. 'I was their equipment manager and I was drinkin' a lot, and, in fact, the whole band was drinkin' a lot. Julius Karpen, their manager, was a heavy-duty dope smoker.'

According to Linda, 'Janis and Julius fought like mad. Basically, they just couldn't work together. After Monterey, they got too big too fast for Julius to be comfortable coping with it.'

The band attempted a semblance of order by scheduling regular meetings where they'd hash out what was bothering them. 'They talked about what they were mad about, what their plans were, what they had to do,' says Dave Richards. 'Most of the ones I went to were at Peter Albin's flat on Haight.'

Rehearsals were held in a big second-floor warehouse on Golden Gate near Van Ness. Dave Getz lived there with his wife, Nancy, and Dave Richards lived downstairs in the garage, taking most of his meals at the Doggie Diner nearby.

Janis and the band were excited in late 1967 when Bill Graham asked them and the Grateful Dead to play at a Hollywood Bowl concert headlined by the Jefferson Airplane. 'Julius Karpen didn't want us to do it,' says Dave Getz, 'because we were opening and he felt we should be headlining.' Graham started telephoning all the members of the band individually and telling them to get rid of Julius because he was a problem for him.

Albert Grossman had been expressing interest in managing them ever since Monterey. 'Hey, he was Bobby Dylan's manager,' Dave Getz says. 'We couldn't do better than that, so finally we decided, Why not?'

Janis came running to Linda for advice – and to everyone else, for that matter. 'She wanted everybody to be totally involved in Janis,' Linda says. 'She was definitely the center of her world, but most obsessional people are very self-centered. She was going around asking all of us, "Who should we get for a manager?" Finally, I told her, "If you want to just stay in San Francisco and play around and have a good time – anybody. But if you want to be an international star – Albert Grossman. You've got to figure out if that's what you really want to do. If it's Janis, the international star, it's Albert." '

One day, Janis told Dave Getz that she was calling Albert.

'So that was it,' Dave Getz says. Dave Richards remembers the day it happened: 'Julius kept threatening them, saying he was going to quit, and he'd walk out of meetings. And we had a meeting up at the warehouse one night and Julius said, "If you don't do it my way, I'm going to walk out"; and he jumped up and walked out. People used to call him back or run down the street after him. "Come on, Julius! Come on back!" But this time, everybody just sat still. Nobody moved. He just walked out and was gone.'

Fat and unkempt, Albert flew out to San Francisco when Janis summoned him. He had olive skin, two double chins, and jowls, and there was a monkish look to his rotund face. He often wore Wrangler jeans and a dark blue crewneck sweater over a substantial paunch, and his ponytail was secured by a rubber band.

When the band put Albert on the spot, demanding to know exactly what he could do for them, he cleverly turned the tables and challenged them to define their expectations. Says Dave Richards, who was present as Big Brother's roadie, 'They didn't know what they wanted, so Albert said, "If you want to make a lot of money and tour a lot and be really rich and famous, I'll make you really rich and famous. If you want just to tour once in a while – I'm also managing Richie Havens, and Richie likes to go out and do a few gigs a year and just make enough money to get by and not have a high profile – well, I can do that – it's up to you. You can do whatever you want." They were very impressed. Albert was so low-key.'

Janis and the band opted for rich and famous. They wanted to work enough to clear $75,000 to $100,000 a year, and that meant working four to six nights a week for almost two years, risking early burnout. With all the money coming in, says Dave Richards, soon his salary was increased from $25 a week to $125.

Albert struck Linda as 'one of the funniest people in the world. He spoke in a low monotone and everybody took it straight, but there were always three other meanings, all of them hilarious. Everyone took him seriously except for Emmett Grogan and me. While they would be saying, "Oh yes, Albert!" Emmett and I would be rolling on the floor. To Janis, he was like Uncle Albert, the absolute authority who took care of everything, and she respected him tremendously.'

Though it has often been written that Albert forbade the band to use heroin, Gurley says, 'There was never any condition about that. He just said he didn't like it, didn't approve of it, but there were no restrictions about us doing it.' When asked whether band members were doing it anyway, Gurley replies, 'Oh, yeah!' Hungden confirms this, adding, 'At the Avalon, fans thought Janis and Big Brother were always running backstage to adjust the amplifiers, but they were vomiting. They had a bucket back there especially to puke in. When you do heroin, you vomit a lot.'

Sam believes that 'drugs destroyed the musicality of the band.' Unlike Gurley, he maintains that Albert did in fact warn them against using heroin. 'Obviously, he'd had some personal experience with the drug that was painful to him,' Sam says. 'We said, "Okay," but sure enough we got involved with it to one degree or another.'

Though Janis thought she was doing herself a favor by signing with Albert, she was moving into treacherous territory where she would be viewed as a piece of meat, at best. Albert looked Janis in the eye at their first business meeting and warned her that he was untrustworthy. Unfortunately, she thought he was kidding. Mary Travers of Peter, Paul and Mary sized him up as a 'flesh peddler. Albert wasn't a very nice man, but I loved him dearly. As a manager, he was notoriously evasive.' Mary added that he rarely spoke to his artists. Dylan fired him – some say over money matters. To record producer David Geffen, Albert was 'reprehensible. Albert Grossman always looked after himself.' Robert Spitz, Dylan's biographer, calls Albert 'cryptic, arrogant, condescending, shrewd, underhanded, cutthroat, even diabolical to some people.' Dave Van Ronk says Albert was 'an astute but very cruel man – extraordinarily cruel in a very cold and calculated way.' Albert claimed he never took more than 20 percent of his artists' earnings, but in fact he was siphoning 25 percent off the gross income on recordings.

Born in Chicago and raised on the tough, working-class North Side, Albert managed an all-African American public housing project until he was fired for 'gross irregularities.' After that, he opened the Gate of Horn nightclub, which pioneered the folk revival around 1950. In 1961, he came to New York, scoured the streets of Greenwich Village for folkies, and discovered Dylan, whose career provided the base for Albert's music empire.

When he signed Janis, according to Nick Gravenites, 'The first thing Albert told her was to get rid of Big Brother. Instead of splitting the money five ways, he and Janis could work out the percentages between the two of them. Janis felt a deep loyalty and love for the guys in the band and didn't want to lose them. But Albert kept applying the pressure. He came at her with a record deal and said, "I can get you a quarter of a million dollars, but it's strictly for you. The deal doesn't include Big Brother. Think it over." '

Albert introduced them to John Simon, their new record producer. When Simon attended a band rehearsal and tried to teach them how to be professional musicians, he met with resentment and solid resistance. 'Simon liked them as people,' says Dave Richards, 'but hated them as musicians, 'cause he's a perfectionist.' Sam was disappointed when Simon rejected his idea of Janis and Big Brother cutting their own version of 'The Star-Spangled Banner.' Says Sam, 'A year or so later, Jimi Hendrix did an instrumental version, but how much more revolutionary would Janis's singing of this song have been a year earlier.'

Janis offered Mark Braunstein a job as a roadie in the winter of 1967. 'We're gettin' ready to go on tour,' she said. 'We may be needing another equipment manager, someone to drive the truck and set up the band's equipment.' Mark started during the band's Winterland gig and then went to LA with them when they played the Whiskey-A-Go-Go. Among the band members, Mark came to be regarded as 'the kid.' Dave Richards, the senior roadie, recalls, 'He was a very naïve flower child, only eighteen or nineteen, but with a deep voice and a gigantic Afro haircut. He didn't quite realize that people with long hair and velvet bell-bottoms and beads were not particularly welcome, and we were going all over the country in a truck carrying six thousand pounds of band equipment.'

In LA, after they checked into a motel on Santa Monica Boulevard, John and Michelle Phillips invited them up to their home to view the film *Monterey Pop*. They all tramped up to the attic recording studio, where there were large speakers and a 16 mm projector. 'We were smoking joints in Jeanette MacDonald's old attic and watching raw footage of Big Brother at Monterey,' says Mark. 'I said, "Yes! This is for me!" and that's when I knew I'd really taken the job. I officially started working for them in February 1968, when we went to New York.'

Janis discovered she was pregnant around Christmas 1967, and there are various theories pertaining to the father of her child. Gurley says, 'I think that might have been one of the Hell's Angels she was messing around with.' Speculating on why she didn't have the baby, he says, 'It would have interfered with her career. She was right at the peak of her thing, and she wasn't going to give it up to go have a kid.'

Dave Richards says the father 'could have been any one of a number of men. I don't think she wanted to be a mother, though she might have eventually. The only serious ambition she ever told me about was to open a bar. She said, "When I get old, I can sit around and get drunk and play the piano and sing." That's when I gave her the name Pearl, as a gag. I was in a health-food store and I saw the name pearl barley. I made a joke about pearl barley and that's where the Pearl thing started.'

She spent Christmas in Port Arthur with her family, saw old friends at a party in Beaumont, and, in January 1968, she celebrated her twenty-fifth birthday by getting a Mexican abortion. Too late, she grew remorseful and wished she had never done it.

5

Sex, Dope, and
Cheap Thrills: 1968

In February 1968, Janis and the band flew to New York for their most important gig since Monterey Pop. The entire rock press was expected to attend their eastern debut, which was set for the seventeenth at the Anderson Theater on Second Avenue. By this time, they were getting $4,500 per performance, which, equally divided, came to $900 each.

When they arrived in New York, they went directly to the Chelsea Hotel, the venerable redbrick building on West Twenty-third Street that has hosted a clientele over the years as diverse as Thomas Wolfe, Edie Sedgwick, Arthur C. Clarke, Dylan Thomas, and Sid Vicious, the punk rocker who killed himself in one of the Chelsea's rooms.

'Janis Joplin was a very sexual woman,' Stanley Bard, the general manager, tells me when I visit him in his office just off the lobby. 'Over her bed in her room, she had written in lipstick *The world's greatest sex object.*' I brought it to her attention and said, "Janis, what are you doing?"

' "Well," she said, "it's true." Sometimes, when the parties in her room got too noisy and other guests complained, I told her she had to respect the other person's need for peace and quiet, and sometimes she agreed and other times she resented it. But after we talked, she always learned to calm herself somewhat.'

Proudly ticking off the other rockers who've stayed at the hotel – Dylan, the Jefferson Airplane, the Grateful Dead, the Mamas and the Papas, Simon and Garfunkel, and John Lennon – Stanley says, 'Albert Grossman stayed here when he would come into the city from Bearsville, and we got a lot of his clients, like Bobby Dylan, who had a baby here. A lot of uptown hotels at that time wouldn't even take them. Janis told me the Plaza wouldn't take her, and I was surprised, because I thought her hippie regalia was very pretty. She was exotic and beautiful. She was also very bright, very verbal, said she'd almost been a schoolteacher. She would come in the office when she needed money, and she'd sign a voucher against her account. Bills were always paid by either their record companies or their managers.'

The first time Janis and the band checked into the Chelsea, there was a mix-up about the rooms, with the roadies getting a spacious suite and Janis and the musicians consigned to the Chelsea's grim singles. Mark and Dave Richards luxuriated in their suite, assuming everyone else had similar accommodations. When they all met down in the El Quijote bar for drinks, one of the musicians complained that none of the rooms was large enough for a band meeting. 'Oh, you can meet in our suite,' said Mark. 'There's plenty of room.'

When Janis got a look at the roadies' relatively plush layout, she said, 'What is this crap?' Dave Richards, who was one of the few people she respected and always listened to, said, 'Right, Janis. We're just workers, and you're the star—'

'Aw, fuck you, man,' Janis said, stomping out. The roadies continued to live in their spacious suite, at least for that trip. Mark also recalled the band's triumphant entrance into Max's Kansas City that night.

By this point in the sixties' the denizens of Max's thought they'd seen everything – Eric Emerson had exposed his penis in the back room, Andrea Feldman had bared her breasts, and the customers routinely shot up coke and speedballs at their tables. 'Max's was packed,' Mark recalls. 'We entered all in a line, having a great time, and Albert or someone had arranged for a tape of Joe McDonald's "Janis" to be played. Everything stopped; not a word was spoken as we walked the length of the bar, all the way to the back room, and sat down at a big round table. Max's immediately became our New York home.'

Regulars at Max's included Bobby Neuwirth and Michael J. Pollard, who became Janis's friends. Mark remembers Neuwirth as 'a smart-ass young guy, a school chum of Janis's road manager John Cooke. Neuwirth worked for Albert in New York and was always around on tour.' Neuwirth had recently survived a melodramatic love affair with Edie Sedgwick, the Andy Warhol superstar who claimed she was Neuwirth's 'sex slave,' capable of making love to him 'for forty-eight hours without getting tired.'

In New York, Janis became a regular at another club, the Scene, often getting up and jamming with whoever was playing there. Edie Sedgwick was also frequently at the Scene, fiddling with her hypodermic needle. One night while Jimi Hendrix was performing, Jim Morrison got carried away, opened Hendrix's fly, and started sucking on his penis. Already annoyed over Morrison's having clumsily upset her table, spilling drinks all over her, Janis rushed to the stage and wrestled Morrison to the floor. They each landed several punches before they were pulled apart.

Albert was at the center of the action in New York. 'Janis wanted to fuck Albert,' says James Gurley. On subsequent New York trips, she would do so, ensconced with him in his Gramercy Park house. She had always dreamed of having a brilliant peer as a drinking buddy, and though Albert logged in numerous hours with her, ultimately he did not turn into the father figure of her dreams, or even the manager she deserved.

When she and the band came to his office to see him, one of his assistants asked how they wanted to be promoted. At first, it seemed an odd question, since she'd already established herself at Monterey Pop as the biggest sexual provocateur since Mae West. Trying to wring something useful out of such meetings, Janis later inquired at a Columbia Records conference whether anyone could coach her on the proper response should a reporter call her a dope fiend.

Dave Getz regards the meeting in the Grossman office as the beginning of the end for the band. 'We didn't know what they were talking about when they asked, "How shall we present you?" What they were trying to get at was, We're going to promote Janis instead of the band.' Within a few months, the billing would go from 'Big Brother and the Holding Company' to 'Big Brother and the Holding Company with Janis Joplin' to 'Janis Joplin.' Dave maintains that in the Grossman organization's press kits and overall marketing plans, 'they acted like the band didn't even exist.'

Preparing for the Anderson gig, they rehearsed in a loft in the East Village. 'Everything in New York was new to us,' Sam remembers, 'the snow, sending out for regular coffee and tea during rehearsal, the coats and hats necessary in the northern weather. The East Village was the equivalent of Haight-Ashbury, with Ukrainians and Jews from East Europe and Russia. After rehearsal, we'd stuff ourselves into the old Checker cabs, laughing and joking, making friends with the driver, who was usually somewhat wary at first, and go driving off, a party on wheels.'

A man named Neil Louison, who'd booked them into the Anderson, was concerned when he realized that the band only had two rehearsals in New York. Neither Janis nor the musicians seemed to care about the opening – Janis went shopping and the band took the day off. On opening night, Linda Eastman, who'd later marry Paul McCartney, entered the dressing room to take pictures for *Creem* magazine. Sam flirted with her and made a date for after the show.

Janis and the band received a standing ovation that night, but Columbia Records executives and engineers who'd come to appraise them were concerned. Elliot Mazer, who'd been asked by John Simon to work on their first album for Columbia, says, 'I was amazed at her, but there were problems with the band.' Backstage after the show, as newsmen crowded into the dressing room, Janis took a swig from her bottle. Reporters couldn't believe their eyes; celebrities usually concealed their drinking, and surely imbibing straight from the bottle was something only derelicts did. Noticing their reaction, Janis told them to feel free to refer to her as a 'juicer.'

Outside, in the lobby, *New York Times* critic Robert Shelton was trying to secure a picture of Janis. Albert's assistant seemed flustered and admitted she didn't have one. Linda Eastman tried to help, but her shot of Janis was too dark for good reproduction.

There was supposed to be a rehearsal after the show for the Columbia album. One of the boys in the band disappeared into the night – and so did everyone else once the rehearsal was officially called off. Alone, angry, and feeling the usual letdown after giving her all, Janis wandered alone on Second Avenue, a stone's throw from the Bowery, one of the seediest areas in the world. She went into the R.O.K. bar and sat down with half a dozen Ukrainians. Louison came in and joined her for a drink, and she told him the musicians were fuckoffs. She kept ordering drinks and harping on the subject, calling them incorrigible. She was furious at them for skipping rehearsal.

Louison told her the band knew Grossman was going to ax

them and they'd lost their motivation. Bored, Louison started staring at her skin and noticing that she had acne. He had a chilling thought: She was doomed, lost.

Back at the Chelsea, Sam was frolicking with worshipful groupies. Regarding his relationship with Linda Eastman, he says, 'We made love a couple of times. It was nice. Later, she brought me things to my room to make me comfortable, like a radio. I was amazed when Paul McCartney decided to marry her. It made me think about him in a different way. There may be untold depths to her that I don't know about.'

Monday's *New York Times* carried a two-column, top-of-the-page photo of Janis and a rave review. Shelton had used a group shot from which every member of the band except Janis had been carefully cropped. Under the headline JANIS JOPLIN IS CLIMBING FAST IN THE HEADY ROCK FIRMAMENT, Shelton wrote: 'The lines can start forming now, for Miss Joplin is as remarkable a new pop-music talent as has surfaced in years. Only her remaining in San Francisco and a singularly unrepresentative first recording kept her from national prominence months ago.'

While in New York, Janis and the band signed their recording contract at Columbia Records's 'Black Rock' skyscraper on Sixth Avenue. After they'd finished, without any explanation, the boys shocked Davis by taking off all their clothes. 'We were running late for a press conference uptown and our clothes were downtown at the hotel,' Gurley explains. 'We were halfway at Columbia, so we sent our roadie downtown to the hotel to get our clothes. He brought them to Clive's office and we all just changed right there, in front of Clive. The way it came out in *Rolling Stone,* they said I jumped up on Clive's desk to open my raincoat and was stark naked underneath and screamed, "Can you dig it?" That just shows you the kind of yellow journalism bullshit that *Rolling Stone is* always dishing out. Just complete lies and fabrications. Now I wish I had done it.'

After Columbia paid a large lump sum to Mainstream to release Big Brother, very little money was left over for Janis and the band to split. Still, Janis felt like celebrating and offered to seal the record deal by going to bed with Clive Davis. 'For her, it was the event of a lifetime, the culmination of her professional dream,' says Davis. 'For a mere signature to be taking place between the two of us seemed an inadequate expression of the event.' Davis was content to commemorate the occasion with a kiss.

Away from all her San Francisco boyfriends, Janis was lonely on the road, and her demands made life difficult for the men in the band. Says Gurley, 'As she got famous, she got separated from us emotionally, but, at the same time, everyone who worked for her, musician or roadie, had to be at her beck and call totally. It was a very corrupt use of power, abusive to herself and everyone around her. I have to admit, I was doing the same thing myself, of course.'

One night, they went down to the Village for dinner at an Italian restaurant. Most of the band had picked up young girls and had them hanging on their arms. Janis was feeling lonesome and said, 'Goddamn, you guys have all these groupies and I don't have anybody.'

Turning to Mark, the youngest person in the crowd, she ordered, 'Go out on the street there and find the first pretty boy you see and bring him on in to me.'

'Aw, I dunno,' Mark said.

'Go ahead,' Janis said.

After a while, Mark returned with a handsome, long-haired youth with a British accent. He was wearing a floor-length embroidered afghan wool coat. Looking him over, Janis nodded approvingly and said, 'He's cute, Mark!' Turning to the young man, she said, 'Well! Hi, honey! Sit down! My name's Janis Joplin. Have you ever heard of me?'

'Yeah,' he said. 'I've heard of you.'

'Oh,' she said. 'What's your name?'

'Eric Clapton,' he said. According to Dave Richards, Janis had nothing to complain about for the rest of that evening.

Sometimes, says Sam, if nothing better was around, Janis would sleep with the 'soft little boys' who were always hanging around backstage waiting for her to hit on them. 'Naturally, the way life works, she liked another kind of man altogether,' Sam notes, 'the Grizzly Adams type. That sort of man rarely attends rock concerts. They're out making log cabins somewhere. Every now and then, one of that kind would come around and that would be nice for Janis. Mostly, though, it was the androgynous sort – pretty boys.'

After New York, the band went on tour. In February 1968, *Rolling Stone*'s reviewer caught their Boston show and said, 'They were messy and a general musical disgrace.' Dave Getz admits that they 'were a hit-or-miss kind of band,' and Sam says, 'We couldn't keep up with Janis and the reason was drugs.' In March, they attempted to do some live recording for their album in Detroit's Grande Ballroom, but the results were so wretched that their producers, John Simon and Elliot Mazer, asked that their names be deleted from the LP's credits.

Mazer went to dinner with the band in a Detroit coffee shop, and when they all got up to leave, 'a nickel bag of heroin fell out of one of the guys' pockets,' Mazer says. The situation was reported to Albert, who brought everyone to Woodstock and, according to Mazer, 'really gave it to them. Janis and the entire band went to Woodstock, but I don't know that talking to a junkie is going to change him or her.'

They returned to New York two and a half weeks later and began to record in the studio. Again they clashed with John Simon. 'One couldn't have found someone more unsympathetic to what we were trying to do,' says Sam. Janis was bitterly complaining about the band and informed Sam she was going to leave Big Brother. 'Sam wrote some great songs,' she told a reporter, quickly adding that she and the band were no longer capable of performing them. All they could manage now were simple, quick tunes.

To Sam, she said, 'I want to play with horns, do something different. I want to sell out. Just show me where I can sign. I want to be rich, and I want you to come along with me.' 'Oh, great,' Sam replied. Obviously, Big Brother's days were numbered.

They raked in $22,325 at the Fillmore East. After deducting Albert's commission, that came to about $3,500 each. Despite the money, everyone was noticing the friction between Janis and the band. The boys complained of being treated like backup musicians instead of partners.

On April 20, they played a trendy club in Greenwich Village, and Peggy was in the audience. She was staying with Sam at the Chelsea. One morning, Janis walked in on them just as Sam was stepping out of the shower. Janis scolded Peggy for not spending the night with her instead of Sam, and she reminded Sam that he was due at rehearsal. When questioned today about his alleged romantic imbroglio with Janis and Peggy, Sam laughs it off as fiction. 'Peggy had it built up in her mind that she was torn between Janis and me and I was in love with Janis,' he states. 'That's completely untrue. Peggy wasn't really that close to Janis or me. The connection was very tenuous. She made it out to be more than it was.'

'Myra Friedman, author of *Buried Alive,* says Peggy exaggerated her role in Janis's life,' I point out.

'That's funny,' says Sam, 'because that's just what Myra did.' Returning to Peggy, he says, 'She would come and stay in the lobby of the Chelsea for days; she'd just show up unannounced and wait for Janis or me, whoever would come in first. She was halfway between a groupie and a friend – halfway, not totally one or the other.'

Whatever his relations with Peggy, Sam remained so close with Janis that when she eventually left the band, he would be the only member of Big Brother invited to join her next group.

In April 1968, Janis and Big Brother continued working on their album in New York and they also fulfilled engagements in nearby cities. In Philadelphia they played the Electric Factory, and backstage before the show the musicians drank beer and argued with their road manager, John Cooke. Janis was drinking tea and Southern Comfort. She never drank iced liquor because extreme temperatures, either cold or hot, affect the voice. During a performance, she drank a pint and a half of booze, and she'd have drunk more but for the danger of passing out.

Richard Goldstein was in the audience that night, and his description of her performance is a classic: 'To hear Janis sing "Ball and Chain" just once is to have been laid, lovingly and well.'

Halfway through the set, she got everyone out of their seats, turning the concert into a gigantic dance. Between sets, she mingled with the crowd, looking in vain for someone to dance with her. The room was packed with ruttish males, all scrupulously avoiding eye contact with her. At last, she stomped up to one and demanded that he dance with her. A perfectly normal-looking Ivy Leaguer, he turned into a spastic automaton the moment he started to dance. Later, when she asked John Cooke why she always ended up so disappointed, he suggested it was because she looked so weird. The part of her that liked being queen of the freaks was flattered, but there was a part of her that wanted to be debutante of the year, just as she'd once longed to be a Red Hussar in school.

They returned to the Chelsea and went back to work on

their LP, which was now tentatively titled *Sex, Dope, and Cheap Thrills*. At the hotel, she'd often go down to the roadies' suite to 'frizz' her hair. 'Mark, turn the oven on,' she'd say. 'I've got to dry my hair.' She'd open the oven door and sit in front of the stove, shaking and drying her hair until she had it 'snarly,' the way she liked it. Mark and Dave kept some food in the suite and cooked a few meals in. 'Janis liked stuff you couldn't get in restaurants,' Mark says, 'like underdone vegetables and brown rice.'

Shortly before they returned to California, Janis was drinking with Dave Richards in the El Quijote when she got into a fight with a kid from another rock group who referred to Ray Charles as a 'blind nigger.' She threw a drink in his face. Richards recalls that Janis often said, 'Racism is bullshit. They called me a nigger lover in Texas.'

Back in California, they checked into the Landmark Motor Hotel (now renamed the Highland Gardens Hotel) in Hollywood and went daily to the Columbia Recording Studio on Sunset Strip to finish the album. Eric Clapton was often around and sometimes jammed with them at the studio. Mazer says that Janis was 'a hard-working perfectionist. If we decided to work from ten to four in the morning, she was into it. She was there, constantly giving ideas, criticism, and help – much more than the rest of the band, who were there some of the time, but they were not interested. The band would trail in late but Janis was always on time. She was impatient, but she would sit there and work on her beads, stringing them.'

Howard Hesseman and Garry Goodrow, who had come to LA with *The Committee* for an extended run at the Tiffany Theater, visited the studio and contributed some bar-room babble during the cutting of Janis's boozy song 'Turtle Blues.' Some of the other cuts included 'Combination of the Two,' which was introduced by Bill Graham announcing, 'Ladies and gentlemen, Big Brother and the Holding Company,' and 'Summertime,' sung by Janis in a hoarse, raspy voice as Sam strummed 'a classical Bach invention done at half the speed.' 'Piece of My Heart,' which would become a hit single, had first been brought to the band's attention by Jack Casady, Jefferson Airplane's bass guitarist, who'd heard Aretha Franklin's sister, Erma, sing a very mellow version of it.

While staying at the Landmark, Janis encountered Hesseman in the hallway. He explained that a rock group had checked out early and left him the key to their room. He'd been living in his dressing room at the Tiffany and was glad to be able to take showers again. Janis started visiting him at *The Committee* and soon was going onstage, improvising with the actors. Howard recalls one night when she and Neuwirth, 'both plowed, came onstage, and Janis was carrying an armful of calla lilies. She hopped right into this improvised song we were doing, like she'd been in *The Committee* forever.'

One day, Hesseman invited her to a party that a girlfriend of his was giving at John Davidson's house in Hidden Valley. About midway through the party, someone told Hesseman, 'Jim Morrison just smashed open the liquor cabinet to get at the hard liquor.' Guests had brought their own beer and wine, and the contents of the liquor cabinet belonged to Davidson and were strictly off limits. When Hesseman went to investigate, he found that Morrison had vomited most of his intake for the party on a huge cowhide rug. Minutes before Hesseman had entered the room, guests told him, Morrison and Janis had gotten into an argument and he'd reached across the coffee table and grabbed her by her hair and slammed her head down onto the coffee table. Janis had then locked herself in the bathroom and was now crying and refusing to come out.

'I vaguely remember saying a couple of words to her through the bathroom door,' Hesseman says. 'I told her that I had to leave because I had a show to do that night. Who knows how much of that Wild Turkey she was putting down in the bathroom? After all, the cat had bounced her face several times on the coffee table.'

Hesseman left and another guest tried to coax Janis from the bathroom, saying, 'It's cool, it's okay, you can come out now. Morrison is leaving.' Suddenly, Janis ripped the door open, came flying out of the bathroom, and ran outside. She caught up with Morrison in the driveway and, in front of a large number of guests enjoying a backyard barbecue at Don Drysdale's house next door, she nearly coldcocked him with her bottle. According to reports that reached Hesseman the following day, she then cackled over Morrison's prostrate body, returned to the party, and had a good time. 'I'd left,' says Hesseman, 'so I didn't see the bounce and I didn't see the whiskey kiss.'

In New York, Columbia had enough orders to ship half a million copies of *Cheap Thrills,* as the LP was now called, but there was so much trouble at the studio in LA that John Simon finally walked out. His associate Elliot Mazer says, 'I worked on it for two months in LA, added some voices and did some mixing and some guitar bits and cleaning, mopping up stuff.' Mazer says Clive Davis called one day and asked to speak to Janis.

'I want her to keep working,' Mazer protested. 'What do you want to say to her?' Columbia was allegedly declaring that *Cheap Thrills* was shipping gold (500,000 units). 'That's the *last* thing I'd ever want to say to a band trying to finish a record,' Mazer replied. He and Davis argued and Mazer finally said, 'Call Albert.' Mazer's recollection is that Davis then said, 'I'm sure we'll just hold it quiet and call Albert and let Albert deal with it.'

Albert bought the producer some more time. 'They can't bully the producer into releasing that record,' Albert assured Mazer. 'I've made a commitment on behalf of the band.' When I interview Clive Davis, he says he has no recollection of any question about the album's release. 'It was fully approved,' he says. 'I can't imagine anyone saying it wasn't ready. The album was ready for release. She was there; she approved it.'

Janis and Gurley received engineering credit on the jacket, but Sam claims that he also contributed heavily. 'Janis and I and an engineer from Columbia spent thirty-six hours doing the final mix,' Sam says. 'A day and a half with no sleep and very little to eat.' When it was all over, they stepped out onto Sunset Boulevard at dawn and then went to the Landmark to celebrate. 'We felt like we had something,' Sam recalls. 'We thought there was a good chance it would be well received.'

The next day, Hesseman took her to lunch at a restaurant on Fairfax. 'We were sitting at the counter,' he recalls, 'and the waiter refused to serve her because of her hair. He wanted her to put on a hair net and was refusing to serve her until she did. She gave him an earful and we split.'

In June, Janis and the band were back in New York, posing for the album cover. Bob Cato, Columbia's art director, wanted a shot of Janis and the band in bed together in a hippie crash pad. When they arrived on the set, what they saw was Madison Avenue's idea of radical chic, a Peter Max fantasy in pink and ruffles. Janis let out a cackle and started clapping her hands and stomping her foot. 'Let's trash it, boys,' she said. They set about demolishing the set, ripping down the froth and replacing it with props they found around the studio. Says Sam, 'Then we took off all our clothes, jumped in bed, and smiled for the camera. It was a very merry morning.'

Hundgen adds, 'Peter Albin remained in his long johns. If

you look at the picture carefully, you will see Janis's bottle of Southern Comfort, her box of Marlboros, a guitar, and the candle for cooking heroin in a spoon.' The photo didn't make it onto the cover of the LP because it was too daring for Madison Avenue, circa 1968.

The original title of the LP was to be an old phrase Sam used frequently – 'sex, dope, and cheap thrills' – which came from the ads for the anti-marijuana movie *Reefer Madness*. 'We looked on it as an antidote to being overly serious about our music and what the movement was doing,' he comments. 'It was a way of saying lighten up, of being tongue-in-cheek about the whole thing.' Columbia Records didn't agree; they were nervous about sex and dope, but since cheap thrills didn't threaten them, that became the LP's title. At the band's request, the Hell's Angels imprimatur, a skull and wings, appeared in the lower-right corner of the jacket, with the words APPROVED BY HELL'S ANGELS FRISCO.

The final cover art came about as a result of a meeting between Dave Richards and R. Crumb, the great *Zap Comix* cartoonist. Dave's job as the band's roadie was to drive their truck, loaded with all their equipment, from gig to gig and then to make sure everything was set up properly before a performance. One day, Crumb told Richards that he'd love to meet Janis Joplin, and when Janis heard this, she said, 'Wow! The "Keep on Fuckin" guy! I'd love to know him.' Dave Getz became enthusiastic, too, and said, 'How about getting R. Crumb to do an album cover for us?' Dave Richards promised to discuss it with Crumb.

By this time, R. Crumb, a homely guy with thick bifocals, was a minor cult hero. He'd left San Francisco in 1967, when his wife had tried to kill him by dropping thirty sleeping pills in his soup. He'd wandered around the country and ended up in New York, where his off-beat cartoons at last found acceptance in the *East Village Other*. Returning to San

Francisco, he contributed to the first number of *Zap Comix* and immediately became an undergound sensation. When Richards offered him the *Cheap Thrills* jacket, he said, 'Yeah, I'll do your album cover, but the only thing is, when I meet Janis, I want to be able to pinch her tit.'

'Why, I don't know about that,' Dave said, but several months later, after the album came out, they ran into Crumb at a party. When Dave Richards introduced Janis to Crumb, 'he grabbed her tit,' says Dave. 'She just looked at him and said, "Oh, honey!" and R. Crumb was delighted.' The following year, at the opening of the New Comix Show in Berkeley, Janis and R. Crumb posed for photographers, kissing each other passionately. The woman on the *Cheap Thrills* jacket is Crumb's idealization of Janis as the ultimate hippie chick, with proud, ripe buttocks and jutting nipples. Crumb also caricatured other members of the band, studying them as they played at a gig one night, and his impressions originally were planned for the back of the album. A high school yearbook layout was to appear on the front, 'but the flavor of it just wasn't right,' Sam recalls. 'The back of the album was superb, though, so we just put it in front and it worked.'

At some point in 1968, Janis and Linda Gravenites moved into a new apartment on Noe Street in San Francisco – four rooms in a large white Victorian building atop a hill in the Mission district. Janis's room looked like something out of *Topkapi*, with tie-dyed satin sheets, velvets, furs, and Indian canopies. Scattered about were articles of Victoriana. The most prominent objet d'art was a three-foot-high statue of a penis, which Janis had named Gabriel. A Siamese fighting fish darted about inside a squat wine bottle, and her dog George romped around on the Oriental rugs. Purple floral arrangements served as shades for naked light bulbs, casting a lurid brothel glow

Janis was using heroin 'frequently,' says Linda, who hated the stuff. Dr. Edmund Rothschild, who eventually put Janis on methadone, said she sometimes shot up as many as three times a day, though not necessarily every day. Most of her intimates, including Sam, Sunshine, and Milan, were also injecting heroin.

By 1968, Milan had moved to radio station KSAN, where he was working as a disc jockey. Asked to describe a heroin high, Milan says, 'Dreamlike, warm, and secure. Never felt as cozy, as protected, as enveloped, as mothered, as surrounded with comfort as on heroin. I'm describing the first time you take it in the right amount. When you continue to use, you don't feel like that anymore. The only reason you take it is not to feel bad. That's the problem with heroin. Opium is a better way to get those feelings than smack. Opium, you can't overdose on; Janis and I *did* overdose on heroin. The problem with heroin is that you can screw up too easily – whether it's cut or uncut. It has to be tested. You can't be impatient. Janis always wanted to plunge right in.'

Carl Gottlieb, Milan's roommate, describes a typical night in their apartment when Janis stayed over. 'It was sex, drugs, and rock 'n' roll all night long. We had a loft apartment and my bedroom was just a little closed-off area with no door and an American flag draped over the doorway. After Janis and Milan went to bed, it became pretty clear to me what was goin' on in the next room. I was in bed with my date, and the timing was such that as my girl and I would be resting between orgasms, Milan and Janis would be building. Then they'd climax and kind of cool off, but listening to them would get us going, so we would start again. It alternated like that all night long.

'I knew that there was a possibility of switching girls, that all that needed to happen was for one person to make the

move and everything would fall into line. I remember thinking to myself, I don't want to trade my date for Janis. I was
perfectly satisfied with my girl. I never found Janis sexually
attractive, but a lot of people did. The next morning over
breakfast, which was communal, we were sitting around and
someone said, "Gee, it was pretty sexy listening to each other
last night."

' "Yeah," someone else said, "we were thinking of
switching."

' "Yeah," another one said, "but we didn't." '

Milan was the perfect man for Janis because he filled all the
requirements for a lover that she listed once in a conversation
with Bonnie Bramlett. She was sick of brown-nosing star-
fuckers and looking for someone 'ballsier than me.' Though
the fans who haunted her dressing room sufficed for one-
night stands, the real men, she said, would never stoop to
being acolytes. Her type lived in the wilds, cultivating
marijuana crops. Trouble was, they didn't attend rock
concerts, so she never met them.

When Milan stood Janis up one night, she got so mad, she
nearly drove him away from her. She assumed the worst,
thinking he no longer cared for her, and never gave him a
chance to explain. 'I don't know that anybody could have
given Janis what she wanted,' Milan says. They'd had a date
to go to the Fillmore, where she was performing. Milan had
said he'd come by her place and pick her up on the Harley,
but he forgot their date. 'I had taken some mescaline,' he
explains, 'and it got late, and by the time I went over to her
house, she was gone.' When he arrived at the Fillmore, she
was onstage, singing 'Piece of My Heart.' The lyrics describe
a woman who loves a man so desperately that she tells him to
break her heart, if that's how he gets his kicks. Janis pitched
the song directly at Milan, her eyes full of hurt and
accusation.

'I'm about as loaded as I have ever been on mescaline,' Milan recalls, 'and to this day when I hear her voice, I just shiver. There were a lot of emotions mixed up in that moment for me. I feel that I'd let her down somehow. Not just that evening, but the incident typified my sadness toward her. I don't remember ever hurting her deliberately. I'd just goofed, but, wow, did she get hurt. It was like I drove a stake in her heart. It was a minor fuckup but she took it as though I'd left her and I was goin' with somebody else.'

Though his relationship with Janis would continue intermittently, Milan says, 'There was some sort of a break for a while between us. I guess it was when I was getting married and being with Mimi Farina or something.'

Mimi Farina, Joan Baez's younger sister, came to San Francisco following the death of her husband, Richard. As a young girl, Mimi had left her Boston home to marry Richard, a writer and folksinger described by Baez as 'a mystical child of darkness – blatantly ambitious, lovable, impossible, charming, obnoxious, tirelessly active – a bright, talented, sheepish, tricky, curly-haired, man-child of darkness.' When Richard was killed on his motorcycle en route to the publication party for his first novel, *Been Down So Long It Looks Like Up to Me*, Mimi was devastated. Not only had she and Richard established a career together as folksingers and recording artists, she had lived completely in his shadow, letting him make all her decisions for her. After his death, Mimi struck Joan Baez as being perpetually on the brink of suicide, waking up in the middle of the night screaming for help and banging on the floor with her shoe until neighbors came to her aid.

In San Francisco, Mimi met and fell in love with Milan. She started writing new songs, and soon her depression began to lift. 'Mimi gave me the nicest verbal valentine once,' says Linda Gravenites. 'I'd just brought her a blouse of ecru-colored silk crepe-backed satin, embroidered with antique red glass beads. She put it on, looked in the mirror, and said, "Oh, Linda, it's me as I've always dreamed of being!" '

When Mimi and Milan decided to get married, Mimi went to Linda Gravenites and asked her to design and make her wedding dress. Mimi had also become friendly with another of Janis's friends, Linda Wauldron, who'd roomed with Janis back in 1963 to 1964. It must have seemed to Janis that Mimi Farina was appropriating not only her lover but all her girlfriends, as well.

'Janis and Linda Wauldron were very tight friends and continued close all the way through,' Linda Gravenites says. 'Around this time, Linda Wauldron came back from Hawaii and was living in Santa Cruz. She and Janis were hanging out together when I was working on Mimi Farina's dress, which, by the way, was appliquéd lace, with a beaded lace train. When Janis heard that Mimi and Milan Melvin were getting married, she yelled, *"Marry my boyfriend ??!! And Linda Wauldron, humph, some friend! Hanging out with Mimi Farina! And you – doing her wedding dress!"* '

At the wedding, which was held during the Big Sur Folk Festival, Milan wore a velvet suit, his long, lustrous black hair cascading over his shoulders, and Mimi, lovely in her white Linda Gravenites, wore a crown of daisies. The sight of the bridal pair inspired 'Sweet Sir Galahad,' the first song Joan Baez composed.

While Janis nursed a broken heart, Milan and Mimi moved into his apartment atop Telegraph Hill. Mimi began to grow as a person in ways that she had never been able to with the willful Richard Farina. She learned to drive a car, got involved in *The Committee,* and, as Baez put it, 'since she didn't have much of an identity outside of Dick and me, and then Milan, she began to create one.' However, the marriage ended in divorce after three years, and Milan was soon back in Janis's life, though not as before. They were occasional lovers, nothing more.

One night shortly after Janis moved to Noe, she lay on the floor, dying from an overdose. It was one of the six overdoses, according to Dr. Rothschild, that she suffered between July 1968 and December 1969, when she first consulted him about her drug use. 'I was in my room and I heard this little sound, *"Oooo,"* ' Linda Gravenites recalls, 'and I thought something might be really wrong, so I went into her room and she was on the floor, purple. She wasn't breathing. Since she was dying, there wasn't time to take her to the hospital. Sunshine was there and knew what to do, and together we got Janis in the bathtub and turned the cold water on and she started to recover. "Oh, man," she said, "what happened?" I made that woman walk for hours up and down those hills, kept her moving. I was so furious with her. I mean, you don't do that to friends. I hated that shit.'

If Sunshine was part of the solution, she was more frequently part of the problem. 'Janis and I were very co-dependent,' she says. 'All we had to do was look at each other and we got a twinkle in our eye and that was it! We didn't even want it, but that's what happens when you're together – you look at each other and go, Hey! It becomes a peer pressure kind of thing whether you're trying to go in the opposite direction or not.'

Sunshine was working seven nights a week at bars and clubs like the Coffee Gallery and the Matrix, and for a long time she lived upstairs over the Coffee Gallery. Janis would drive up in her car and get out and throw rocks up at her window. When Sunshine leaned out, Janis would yell, 'Don't you want to come out and play?' Then they'd round up Linda Gravenites and a few other Capricorn ladies and go to the Fillmore.

'We all had huge purses for our Southern Comfort and whatever,' says Sunshine. 'Janis was great to drink with – she expected everyone to take care of themselves and have a good time, but if you blacked out, she'd take over. I blacked out at the Fillmore and she carried me home. I woke up and wondered how I got there. She was such a great driver that she could drive in a blackout.'

In attempting to understand the allure of heroin, I look into one of the books that Sam Andrew says helped him kick the drug. Aleister Crowley's *Diary of a Drug Fiend* offers this description of a heroin high: 'We felt crowned with colossal calm. Our happiness was so huge that we could not bear it. When we went downstairs, we felt like gods descending upon the earth, immeasurably beyond mortality.' Paradoxically, heroin also destroys everything in its path. Though Sam and Janis had written some good songs together, heroin put an end to that, killing their creative urge. As Crowley wrote, 'With heroin, the feeling of mastery increases to such a point that nothing matters at all.'

At Noe Street, Linda's room offered a startling contrast to Janis's. 'Mine had beaded curtains in the windows to catch light and the whole morning sun came into the room,' Linda says. 'I had my little narrow bed and my work space. It was like a studio; I slept in the corner. When Sam saw it, he just laughed and said, "God! You're so different." '

In the year since the Summer of Love, the Haight had been plundered by tourism and raped by drug dealers. Everyone but diehards like Janis fled to the country. She still loved walking its streets and sitting on car fenders with her bottle of Ripple. When Dave Moriaty came to see her, he was told at her building that she had gone to the Laundromat. Sure enough, when he found her, she was folding her clothes and holding forth in front of a gaggle of fans. Glad to see Dave again, she jumped all over him, kissing him and asking about Langdon and Lyons. He noticed that she kept an eye on the fans and continued to talk loudly enough to hold their attention.

'Janis was really a part of the city when she was home,' wrote Ralph Gleason. 'You'd see her anywhere, likely to pop up at a flick, in the park, at Enrico's – anywhere. She dug it, and the city, with its tradition of eccentrics back to Emperor Norton, dug her.' Gleason found her to be 'impulsive, generous, softhearted, shy, and determined. She had style and class, and in a way, she didn't believe it. It was all there for her but something that she knew wasn't fated to happen.'

The downfall of the Haight reflected the drama of the nation at large, which in 1968 was reeling under the impact of war, assassination, and street riots. When Senator Robert F. Kennedy visited San Francisco to campaign for the Democratic presidential nomination, Janis and Linda Gravenites went to hear him. 'Janis really wasn't political,' Linda says. 'Dope, sex, cheap thrills, and rock 'n' roll forever – that's what she stood for. But she was registered with the Peace and Freedom Party, and Kennedy was making street-corner speeches, so we went down to the Castro to hear him.'

They were caught in a mob, literally lifted off their feet and carried by the movement of the crowd, which was surging toward Kennedy. 'It was frightening,' says Linda, 'but *she* found it exciting.' Kennedy was being mauled. 'Look at that smile plastered on his face!' Janis said. The Secret Service men were holding him in the car, and the crowd was trying to pull him out of it. 'The poor man's being dismembered,' Janis said. 'I swear he's in pain.'

'How could anyone choose such a life?' Linda asked. 'He must be mad.'

'It's so bizarre,' Janis said. As they talked, they were being swept along by the mob. Linda remembers that her shoes 'were back there, fifteen or twenty yards'; she walked home in her stocking feet.

In June came the news that RFK had been shot and killed in Los Angeles by Sirhan Sirhan. 'We all talked about it,' Linda says. John Cooke made plans to leave the band to do something useful for the country. 'He didn't really want to have anything more to do with road managing,' says Sam. 'I think he wanted to go and work politically or maybe he just didn't want to be in the public eye anymore. He went and talked to Janis about it and told her that he wanted out at that point, and I guess she talked him into staying. He was with her to the end.'

Linda's husband, Nick Gravenites, was close to Janis and sometimes saw to it that she did not go to bed lonely and alone. 'We'd flip a coin to see who'd fuck her,' Nick says. Adds James Gurley, 'Janis was in love with everybody. She wanted to fuck everybody she knew, especially when we were out on the road.' She once asked Nick to marry her, and he said, 'I can't. I'm married to your roommate.' Linda and Nick were married from 1962 to 1972, though Nick had returned to Chicago in 1964. They have one son. When Janis and Linda roomed together, Nick lived in San Francisco with Ron Polte, manager of Quicksilver Messenger Service. Nick sang and played rhythm guitar with the Electric Flag, Mike Bloomfield's band.

Janis was so possessive about Linda that she didn't want her making clothes for anyone else. After they'd lived together a short while, Linda realized she could never work for Janis in any conventional sense. 'She was such a bitch and people who worked for her really caught it,' says Linda. 'I couldn't take that, so the only thing keeping me there was me *wanting* to be there. When she realized I was not going to be an employee, she became thoughtful, kind, and nice. It became a buddy and friend relationship, somebody to go out and play with when she wanted to.'

One morning after a night on the town with Linda, Janis came in to breakfast and said, 'How the hell did we get home?' Linda told her they'd driven. 'That woman had radar,' Linda says. 'She'd be blind and still she wouldn't waver an inch going down the road.' At this time, Janis was driving an Austin convertible, and Stanley Mouse had painted some stripes on it for her. When she was ready to buy her Porsche, she offered to give the Austin to Linda, but 'being penniless,' Linda says, 'I couldn't even take the insurance on it.'

When Janis received an invitation to play at the Newport Folk Festival in the summer of 1968, she considered it an honor. In the early sixties she'd begged people to hitchhike to Newport with her, but no one had been willing. Turning to Linda for a costume, she asked, 'What can I wear that would really knock them dead?' Linda created a shocking dress by attaching a skirt to a 'push-'em-up' bra, and Janis sewed on some beaded daisies to cover her nipples. When she appeared on the cover of *Time,* she was wearing her minimal push-'em-up bra dress.

At Newport, according to James Gurley, she acted like a 'star bitch' at the sound check, giving the technicians a hard time. 'Just sing a little bit,' the sound man begged. 'I have to hear you sing so I can get it right. Everyone's going through this. It's routine.'

'I'm not going to sing until you've got your act together,' Janis said. 'I can't let anybody hear me sing like this.' She was cranky, demanding, and unprofessional. 'She didn't trust anybody anymore,' says Gurley. 'She was drinking a lot, doing heroin, cocaine, whatever she could get her hands on.'

The real action for Janis at Newport that year began when she got a look at the young assistant who'd come to the festival with Danny Fields of Elektra Records. Janis took him to her bedroom at the Viking, where he became her paramour for the weekend. When Danny went looking for him, he found the door to Janis's room wide open. Inside, Janis and the young man were in the throes of coitus. After an appropriate interval, Danny told him, 'You have to be backstage at six-thirty.'

'Yeah,' he said, getting up.

'I'm going to close the door, okay?'

According to Danny, while this exchange was taking place, 'Janis turned her head to the side in modesty.' When the assistant left, Danny himself took over as her escort. Over drinks with Danny, Janis said, 'Man, is that kid really a press agent?'

'Well,' Danny said, 'not for much longer, unless you let him do some work.'

'Oh,' Janis said, 'I don't want to get him in trouble, but he's so cute!'

Critic Jon Landau lambasted her performance at Newport, calling her overwrought and the band woefully inept. At the after-concert party, Janis chatted with Richard Goldstein, who asked her to describe the feeling that came over her after giving a really great show. 'Like a great lay after not getting fucked for half a year,' she replied.

When she played the Fillmore East on August 3, *The New Yorker* called her 'exalting' and noted that she was called back for four encores. On August 23, they played the Singer Bowl in New York. While they were staying at the Chelsea, Janis again told Sam that she was leaving the band, and he agreed to help her put together a new group, suggesting Jerry Miller of Moby Grape as a guitar player. 'We put in a call to him in Santa Cruz, California,' Sam says, 'but he was too busy wrestling with his own private demons to consider our proposition. Janis appreciated the fact that I wasn't antagonistic to her plans, even though they did not include me at that point.'

Her determination to break away from Big Brother saddened her, because she loved the musicians more than anyone she'd ever known. But in order to grow as an artist, she longed for the support of serious, professional instrumentalists. She and Big Brother had been working almost every night since 1966 and, in her view, they were tired and burned out. She wanted to perform at the emotional pitch of Tina Turner and Otis Redding, but now all she and the band could do was go through the motions, and her work had become meaningless to her. The band had not yet seen it, but, to her, the handwriting was on the wall.

Cheap Thrills was shipped in August and shot to number one on the best-seller charts. *The New York Times* splashed Janis across the top of their Recordings Section with the caption, 'Janis Joplin, currently riding the crest of popularity, belts out a music that helps fulfill the deep inner needs of youth.' *Billboard* statistics show that the album debuted on the charts on September 14, 1968, held the number-one position for eight weeks, and remained in the Top 40 for nine months. 'Piece of My Heart,' the LP's hit single, went on the charts on September 28, rose to number twelve, and remained in the Top 40 for eight weeks. Eventually, the album sold more than a million copies. 'At that time, it was wonderful,' says Clive Davis.

Janis was on the phone regularly to Davis, checking up on sales. 'She was competitive,' says Davis. 'She wanted her records to be number one. She was eager for success and the accoutrements of it, though she couldn't appear to be concerned about money, preferring to be known for her role in the counterculture and for artistic integrity.'

In 1968, she made a clean sweep of *Jazz and Pop* magazine's awards, winning the International Critics Poll for

Best Female Vocal Album and Best Female Pop Singer, as well as the magazine's Readers' Poll for Best Female Pop Singer.

Janis and Big Brother were in New York, at the Chelsea, when she called them to her room one day. It was a sunny afternoon, and they stood facing each other on the eighth floor, overlooking Twenty-third Street. 'I'm leaving Big Brother and the Holding Company,' she announced.

'The band was outraged,' Sam recalls. 'Peter started screaming. James didn't say a word and I just stood there, because I already knew.' Dave Getz had long seen it coming and felt no surprise. 'She'd been banging her head against some of the limitations of the people in Big Brother,' Dave says. 'Also, Aretha Franklin and Tina Turner had come along and they had all that brass. She figured she could just put another band together and go anywhere she wanted to. As it turned out, she couldn't.'

As they filed out of the room, she asked Sam to remain behind. 'I've decided that I'm not going to take you, either,' she said. 'I'm just going to go ahead and start brand-new.' Sam told her he understood and was still willing to help her find musicians for her new group. When he got back to his room, the phone was ringing. It was Dave, who wanted to set up a meeting. Says Dave today, 'Sam, Peter, Jim, and I got together and started planning a whole new life for the band.' But Janis had second thoughts about Sam, deciding she needed to retain a link to the past. When she invited him to join her new band, he accepted. Inevitably, he ran into Dave in the elevator at the Chelsea and broke the news. 'Oh, by the way,' he said, 'I'm going to be joining Janis's band.'

Dave felt betrayed. 'What?' he said. 'Thanks for telling me, Sam. Why are we sitting around making plans about what we're going to do? That's the end, if you're going to go. That makes it impossible.'

Says Dave today, 'If at that moment Sam had stayed with

us and made that commitment, we could have made a lot of money. As it was, Peter and I got together and jammed for a while and tried to put something together, but it didn't happen. Finally, in the beginning of 1969, Country Joe asked Peter and me to join his band, which had split up, and we did.'

Hundgen believes that Janis's leaving Big Brother was a 'cop-out,' because she 'still partied and had sex with Big Brother after she left to sing with the hired band.' Jim Langdon, hearing that Janis was looking for horns, hoped that she'd remember him and offer him a job. 'Why don't you call Jim Langdon?' a mutual Texas friend suggested to her. 'He plays great jazz trombone. You ever thought about gettin' Jim in the band?'

'Aw, man, I don't think he'd dig the scene,' she said. Jim is convinced that she didn't want anyone around her who wasn't doing heroin. 'She knew how I felt about drugs,' he says, 'but in light of what I'd done to help her, I thought it would have been a nice gesture if she'd at least offered.'

Despite fame and money, Janis was still unhappy. She allowed Grossman to put her on a three-hundred-dollar weekly allowance and then complained that she felt poorer than when she'd been jobless and on the dole. The only substantial way her life had changed was that she had substituted one set of worries for another. Once she'd longed for affluent leisure, but now that it was hers, it terrified her. Offstage, she couldn't escape the truth that she was emotionally and spiritually bankrupt. Her only solace lay in yet another addiction – compulsive overwork – which in the long run would prove as destructive as any other bad habit. Without the clarity of a sober mind, she was powerless to change her life for the better, and her misery had the unfortunate effect of making her insensitive to the feelings of others. She became abusive in her personal and professional relationships. Deciding she needed a fur coat, she hatched a scheme to extort one from the Southern Comfort distillery, browbeating a Grossman assistant into collecting and photocopying numerous newspaper photographs of her drinking Southern Comfort. When the distillery received these clippings, they demonstrated their gratitude by bestowing on her enough money to purchase a lynx coat. 'Best hustle I ever pulled,' she bragged.

She was not above hooking her friends on heroin as a way of keeping them in her power. Peggy contends that Janis seduced her into shooting up as they lay nude in a motel room in Hollywood. Another friend, who was trying to stay clean, finally gave into her relentless nagging and grabbed her syringe, jabbing the needle into his leg. 'Hey, you muscled it through your jeans,' she said, impressed. 'That's the hippest thing I ever heard of. From now on, I'm callin' you "Mr. Hip." '

Terence Hallinan, who today is a high city official in San Francisco, almost died of an overdose in her Noe Street apartment. Hallinan had started dating Peggy in late 1968, and when the relationship turned sexual, Janis felt threatened. Revenge may have been an unconscious motive the night she nearly killed him. Linda Gravenites, one of the few nonaddicts in her milieu, says, 'I was pissed at Peggy Caserta and Janis for getting stoned and I left the room. They were with Terry Hallinan.'

Hallinan had never done heroin before, and when Janis injected him, his eyes rolled toward the top of his head and he slumped to the floor in a coma. Certain that he was dying, Peggy was frantic. Janis seemed unconcerned, making love to Peggy while Hallinan lay unconscious on the floor.

The girls were so full of heroin that orgasms were out of the question, but they continued to make love for an hour, drenched in sweat. Having a third party in the room, one who might be expiring, added a touch of novelty and suspense to their pleasure.

When they finally decided to get up and do something about Hallinan, Peggy noticed that his face was green. All efforts to revive him failed until Peggy started getting amorous, which promptly brought him around. Hallinan angrily accused Janis of overdosing him, but she lied, telling him that he'd fallen asleep. He calmed down then, blaming his own body chemistry for his adverse reaction to the drug.

In November, Janis went to Minneapolis for one of her last appearances with Big Brother, who still had to fulfill commitments made before the breakup. They were awkward and tense with each other and tired from five straight days on the road, but Janis became playful when she got backstage at the Tyrone Guthrie Theater and discovered some Elizabethan costumes and props left over from a Shakespearean production. Grabbing a cape and sword, she jokingly ordered her minions to bring her a dozen hot teenyboppers and lay them end to end.

Her mood changed when a reporter from a local magazine approached her. Having exhausted her supply of wisecracks in hundreds of previous interviews, she begged off and told him to talk to the band. Such condescension did not sit well with her musicians. When the hapless reporter started quizzing them about Janis, they snarled, 'Ask *her*.'

Everyone's nerves were taut by the time they got onstage, and a fight broke out between Janis and Peter Albin, her least favorite member of the band. Peter had long resented what he called her 'star trip,' ignoring the band and playing to the audience as if she was a solo act. After she finished 'Piece of My Heart,' she was exhausted and started gasping into the microphone. Peter made the mistake of quipping, 'Now we're doing an imitation of Lassie.' The audience heard him and roared. Looking daggers at Peter, she mumbled inaudibly but controlled her anger, deciding to get even with him later.

After the set, she read the riot act to John Cooke: Peter had as much as called her a bitch, she wasn't taking any more of his crap, and what was Cooke going to do about it? Cooke, the son of British-born TV commentator Alistair Cooke, seemed out of place among these jejune squabblers. He was a Harvard graduate and former Cambridge, Massachusetts, folksinger. When Janis's mother had first been told of his hiring by the band, and learned he'd been a Spanish major in college, she'd demanded to know why Albert hadn't hired a sociology major, someone better qualified to care for her emotionally disturbed daughter. Actually, Albert could hardly have found anyone, by all accounts, more exacting and authoritative than Cooke. 'He was good,' says Gurley. 'He did his job.'

During the Minneapolis fracas, Cooke set about the task of restoring sufficient order for the show to go on. When he went to Peter's dressing room, Peter proved intractable, charging that Janis had humiliated *him*. Cooke then returned to Janis's dressing room, where he informed her that she and Peter were making much ado about nothing. The audience had found their exchange amusing.

The volatile situation at last began to cool down when Janis spotted her fifth of Southern Comfort on her dressing room table and ordered someone to pour her a cup of whiskey. After the intermission, she let the band walk back onstage without her. Growing restive, the audience started yelling for her, but she tarried backstage, permitting the crowd to make it unmistakably clear whom they'd come to see. Finally, she ambled on, turned her back to Peter, and put on a tremendous show. People were beginning to notice a nervous mannerism she'd developed – scratching her head while singing. Hundgen explains it as a drug reaction. 'A lot of heroin and speed use will give you a bad complexion. You're always itching when you're withdrawing, scratching the skin a lot.'

After the show, there was no longer the old camaraderie that had once existed between Janis and the band. 'Even being in the same room was a total stone drag,' Peter Albin said. Her only experience of love was giving herself to an audience, and once the show was over, she felt isolated and without personal support of any kind. She may at this time have been having second thoughts about casting off Big Brother. Emotionally, she could ill afford to lose them, for they had given her the warmest unconditional love she'd known since the Langdon clique in Texas. But there was no turning back; she was already locked in a pattern of throwing people out of her life rather than learning how to live with them.

When they returned to the hotel in Minneapolis that night, a groupie who'd been tailing them in a Volkswagen hit on Sam. Everyone in the band decided to go to a party with the groupie, but Janis sullenly repaired to her room.

In November, they also played the Aragon and Cheetah in Chicago, Hunter College Auditorium in New York, and performed in Vancouver, Canada. During the Hunter engagement, the derelictions of the Grossman office became glaringly apparent. Janis was expected to get around Manhattan's busy streets without a limousine or driver, and as a result, she almost missed her concert. Why her manager would have assumed she'd be able to find taxicabs during New York's frenetic theater rush hour boggles the mind. At one point, a Grossman assistant obediently complied when Janis asked her to go out and fetch some barbiturates, evidently unaware that she was harming Janis by doing so. The assistant had a prescription filled for two Seconals.

Danny Fields saw Janis alone in Max's Kansas City in a

pitiful state. She was drunk and her feathers were in disarray. He had never seen anyone so forlorn and hopeless, and he tried to talk to her and get her into a taxi. 'There was no help you could think of to give her,' says Fields, 'except to let your love be there for her.' Others evidently felt they were helping by becoming drinking buddies. Mike Klenfner, who went from the Fillmore East's stage crew to vice president of Atlantic Records, says he and Janis got so drunk, they 'couldn't stand up.'

Janis and the band returned to San Francisco to play their last show together on December 1. Appropriately, it was a benefit for the Family Dog, Chet's organization. They were back where they'd begun, returning in victory as recording artists with a hit album.

Calling on her in Noe Street, Chet found her surrounded by books and eager for intellectual companionship. 'It was a side of Janis not everyone saw,' says Chet. To him the bravado, swearing, and swaggering she affected were but a protective shell; underneath, he found her to be intelligent, literate, and a pleasure to be with. Both at home and on the road, she haunted bookstores and became a passionate collector and a voracious reader. Her large and impressive library included numerous volumes of F. Scott Fitzgerald, including his collected letters, *Tender Is the Night,* and *The Crack-Up;* Nancy Milford's biography of Zelda Fitzgerald, *Zelda;* and Thomas Wolfe's *Look Homeward, Angel.* 'We discussed everything from politics and art to philosophy and psychology,' says Chet. 'She was politically sophisticated and capable of carrying on a well-informed conversation on any subject under the sun.'

The schism between Janis's polished intellect and hoydenish behavior was nothing compared to the schizoid signs she was beginning to show in her sex life. After becoming a public figure, she would sometimes stop in the middle of making love to ask, 'Do I ball like I sing? Is it really me? Or am I putting on a show?' Asked to comment on the meaning of these curious questions, two men who made love to her agree that she was experiencing an identity crisis. 'When she was in college, her sense of self was so identical to her stage self that she made love with abandon and beauty,' says Travis Rivers. 'But after fame, her sense of self was equated with what the public saw, and she got image and reality completely confused.'

Sam Andrew says, 'She was wrestling with her identity all the time. She felt the hippie part of her was sincere; the professional was an act – and she couldn't resolve the contradiction. She felt real when she was a part of the Big Brother commune, but afterward she was tortured by the notion that she'd sold out by becoming famous. She once said the Grateful Dead embodied the hippie spirit but that she was going in the opposite direction, couldn't wait to sell out. She never stopped struggling with the question of how much was genuine and how much was putting on an act.'

Having fired Big Brother, she was now a singer without a band and she didn't know how to form a new one, especially a large soul band with horns and keyboards. The soul sound she was after obviously required African-American expertise, but Albert inexplicably assigned an all-white team, composed of Michael Bloomfield and Nick Gravenites, to advise her.

Nick's group, the Electric Flag, had just disbanded, and shortly he would replace Janis as lead singer in one of Big Brother's short-lived and largely unsuccessful reincarnations. Janis's new goal, she told Nick and Mike, was to attain the same high level of professionalism as the reigning soul singers, especially Aretha Franklin. Bloomfield, a heroin addict from a rich Chicago restaurant-supply family, had provided the great electric-guitar sound on Bob Dylan's 'Like a Rolling Stone,' but his collaboration with Janis would prove less fruitful. 'Mike and I tried to help her with her arrangements,' Nick told Ben Fong-Torres of *Rolling Stone,* 'but we couldn't get too far . . . Michael was so head-strong . . . and it just conflicted too much with Janis's ego.'

Nick was invaluable during auditions, showing Janis how to spot exceptional musicians. It was a grueling process, because each time a new applicant came in, Janis had to perform in front of him in order to judge whether he was right.

Almost from the start, Sam, the only holdover from Big Brother, regretted having joined the new band. No longer an equal partner as he'd been in Big Brother, he faced a gross cut in salary as well as in prestige, and he would never adjust to his diminished status. On his birthday, December 18, 1968, the newly named Kozmic Blues Band (also known as Main Squeeze) rehearsed for the first time. 'Janis stood to one side,' Sam recalls, 'a little bemused at what was happening. The horn section was the real reason for the new band and they were marvelous, especially Luis Gasca, on trumpet, who'd later play Camegie Hall with Ray Charles, and Snooky Flowers on baritone saxophone.' Snooky was the only African-American in Janis's honky soul band, and Sam calls him 'a force of nature from Lake Charles, Louisiana, just across the border from Port Arthur and Beaumont – incredible, volcanic and Dionysian.'

Snooky tried to warn Janis and Sam about the perils of heroin. 'He talked seriously to Janis and me when we were near the bottom,' Sam says. 'He would speak in a soothing voice, telling us of good friends he had who had died from overindulgence. He was like a preacher, the only voice of moderation with any authority to it that I heard at that time. I still think of things he told me when he was trying to show us we were on a collision course.'

Elliot Mazer came to San Francisco for a couple of months to help Nick and Michael rehearse the new band. Ironically, after all of Janis's talk about horns, Mazer 'preferred the guitar stuff to the horns. I didn't like what they did a lot.' He noticed that Janis 'flirted all the time, with everybody. She wanted to feel attractive to men. She had a gorgeous smile, really pretty eyes, and she looked great onstage. I'm sure she was attractive to a lot of men, but not to me personally.'

The year 1968 ended in disaster for Janis because of a major miscalculation on Albert's part. His decision to debut the new band at the high-profile Memphis Stax/Volt 'Yuletide Thing,' on a bill with professional African-American rhythm and blues bands, led to critical slaughter. 'It was sheer insanity,' says Sam. 'Janis wanted to emulate Aretha and Otis, but before we even had the repertoire down, we were going to play in front of one of the most demanding audiences in the country, our heroes from Stax/Volt.'

Decked out in a glamorous cerise jersey pantsuit with cerise feathers at the cuffs, Janis opened with 'Raise Your Hand,' followed by the Bee Gees's 'To Love Somebody.' It was painfully obvious to the largely African-American audience in the Mid-South Coliseum that Janis's band couldn't play blues, at least not like the hard-core soul acts they were accustomed to. 'It was intimidating, playing blues for black people,' says Sam. 'They invented the blues, and how dare we get up there and play their music? Naturally, we were kind of nervous. We just blew it.' Janis said she was 'scared to death' and, as she later confided to Peggy, she was also drunk.

For the first time in years, she received almost no applause, and no one called for an encore. Backstage, she and the band stared at one another, slack-jawed and dazed. The only relief she felt was that the audience had somehow restrained itself from pelting them with tomatoes. Later, her anger, and a dormant racist streak, surfaced when she characterized the African-American audience as a 'boogaloo' bunch who were simply not her kind of people. She would have done well to heed the counsel of a Memphis blues musician who observed that her new band should do their homework in some local dives and learn to play the blues.

Janis compounded her Memphis losses by engaging in a war with *Rolling Stone*. When their reporter asked her for an interview, she flew into a rage, cursing the magazine's staff as self-righteous 'shits' and San Francisco hicks. Though *Rolling Stone* would later relocate in New York, at the time it was still in San Francisco, and she felt the editors had taken it personally when she'd fired Big Brother, considering it a slap at Bay Area bands. *Rolling Stone* replied, with Stanley Booth writing, 'Janis Joplin died in Memphis, but it wasn't her fault.' Booth blamed Michael Bloomfield for being unable to pull Janis's band together, but Janis was apoplectic when she read the review.

Both *Rolling Stone* and *Playboy* seemed unduly eager to bury her, but Janis valiantly told the press that news of her demise was premature. Granting that her new band was flawed, she intended to prove that she could make it without Big Brother. Maybe they weren't as hot as Santana, she admitted, but, after all, they'd 'only fucking been together two months!'

But the press jackals scented blood and shortly moved in for the kill. In his book-length study of *Rolling Stone,* Robert Sam Anson censures the magazine for its inability to recognize new talent, singling out the relentless snubbing of Janis as one of its most obvious 'critical lapses.'

6

Queen and Consorts:
1969–1970

'Just as Janis had feared, without Big Brother thundering along behind her, she was lost. Though Janis wanted to do new material, fans demanded her familiar hits. But when the Kozmic Blues Band attempted a tour de force like 'Ball and Chain,' the results were ludicrous. Without Gurley's savage guitar, Janis was out there by herself, squealing like a stuck pig. As Gurley's son Hongo says, 'If you want to see who she should have stayed with, listen to the Kozmic Blues's version of "Ball and Chain" and then listen to Big Brother's. Kozmic Blues's is a complete joke.' Though her ballads wouldn't suffer as critically from the change of bands, the Faulknerian resonance was gone forever from 'Ball and Chain,' her trademark song.

After bombing in Memphis, two of her musicians, Marcus Doubleday and Bill King, dropped out and were replaced by Terry Hensley on trumpet and Richard Kermode on keyboard. The personnel situation continued to be highly unstable, with frequent changes. But for Janis, there was at least one advantageous side effect. The first time she laid eyes on the princely keyboard player, she turned to Mark Braunstein and said, 'God! That Richie Kermode! He's *cute!*' He was young and had a rich black beard and long dark hair.

'They had an affair,' says Mark, 'but it was all a little

awkward. Janis was having a hard time as a boss, defining her role. She had gone from being a chick singer and an equal with the band to being the one who was ultimately responsible for everybody. Most of all, she didn't want to be alone, and she didn't have any real friends. At this time, she and Sam were both junkies and that tends to drive you within yourself and apart from other people. She turned to Richie, and it was like sex and escape.'

On heroin, her sexual requirements were prodigious, as Kermode soon discovered. Heavily drugged, she was more intent on prolonged, harsh, cauterizing intercourse than she was on reaching orgasm. She liked pain and sought it, but Kermode, repelled by her efforts to turn him into an abusive stud, ended the affair.

She and her roadie Dave Richards made love together only once, and they were both so loaded that it turned into a case of coitus interruptus. Tall and powerfully muscular, Dave was also a carpenter and a biker, and while treating Janis to some erotic gymnastics, he fell out of the bed. According to Dave, she never stopped kidding him about it.

Though Dave would continue indefinitely in her employ, working as a painter and carpenter, he resigned as the band's equipment manager in 1969. 'I had a girlfriend at the time and she was traveling around with us in the truck on the East Coast and she and Mark didn't get along,' Dave explains. 'Also, I'd been on the road for a couple of years and it's basically lonesome. You hung out in motels and chased after women, but the success rate is exaggerated. Maybe for rock 'n' roll stars, but for roadies—'

His departure was a blow to Janis. He'd always been a stablilizing influence as one of the few persons who could cut through her rationalizations and speak the truth. 'Stop feeling sorry for yourself,' he'd say. 'Don't give me that self-pity bullshit. Come on, Janis, you can't fool me. And stop trying to fool yourself. That ain't gonna work.' Says Mark, 'He had a good bullshit detector, and they were very close friends.'

When she bought a pale gray used Porsche, she commissioned Dave to paint it for her, instructing him to 'do whatever you want to.' She let him drive the car to LA, where he was living in his parents' house in the San Fernando Valley. 'It took me about a month or so, just messin' with it,' Dave recalls. He painted the car blue, yellow, and red, putting Janis's portrait on a front fender, a landscape on one side, and mushrooms and butterflies on the other. In Southern California, the Porsche has the status of a religious icon, and the first to view Dave's handiwork considered it a desecration. Delivering the car to Janis, Dave drove it from LA to San Francisco, and an outraged motorist on 101 yelled, 'How could you do that to a *Porsche?*' When he pulled up in front of the Avalon, where Janis was playing, she came down to the curb and pronounced, 'Now *that's* a paint job!'

Though Dave had covered almost the entire body with psychedelic pictures and designs, Janis said, 'Can't you get some more stuff on it? What about the dash?' Dave remained in San Francisco and continued embellishing the Porsche. 'She kept buggin' me about it,' he remembers, 'and she looked at this guy I'd painted on the dash screamin' and said, "That must be you, because I've been botherin' you so much." I was wanting to get back to LA, but she kept saying, "Oh, I want some more on this! It's not finished yet." '

Soon after New Year's 1969, Janis and the Kozmic Blues Band started preparing for their opening on February 11 at the Fillmore East in New York. She and the band met at a bar for drinks before rehearsal and she proudly recounted the great sex she'd had the previous night. It had been her twenty-sixth birthday and she and a girlfriend had frolicked for two solid days with two supermen. It was the most libidinous party of her life to date, she said.

Janis was now earning $50,000 a year (about $200,000 in 1992 dollars). The whole point of living, she said, was drugging and partying. When assailed by fear or worry, which was often the case, she'd just 'juice up real good.' Her alcoholism and drug addiction were beginning to affect her body and her mind. She'd gone to a doctor and he'd told her to slow down. Her liver was shot – 'a little big, swollen, y'know,' she told a reporter. The doctor couldn't believe a woman in her twenties could have done so much damage to her body. Why would an intelligent, gifted young person such as Janis want to destroy herself? he'd asked. Irate, she vowed never to go back to the doctor again. She'd prefer a decade of 'superhypermost' rampages to seventy years as a couch potato rotting in front of a boob tube. To her alcoholic mind, nothing existed but the extremes of excitement and boredom.

Though a long vacation would have restored her health, she had never been able to step out of her addictions – work, sex, drink, and drugs – long enough for a true rest. After several months on the road, she tried taking a holiday but 'just about went out of my head.' If true rest was impossible for her driven spirit, so was the simple joy of work. She looked to her career to provide the thrills and high drama that she felt were missing in her personal life. She turned her upcoming Fillmore East debut with the Kozmic Blues Band into a crisis, convinced that her entire professional life depended on a single gig. 'But I gotta risk it,' she said. 'I never hold back, man. I'm always on the outer limits of probability.'

She was still sipping her afternoon breakfast of vermouth when rehearsal time for the Fillmore East opening came and passed. Although the band was standing around waiting for her, she decided to stay and shoot a game of pool with a tattooed lounge lizard. When she was about to make a difficult shot, a kibitzer tried to show her the safe way to do it, but she told him he lacked nerve and slammed the ball into the pocket with great force and precision, winning the game. She wasn't known in New York as the poolroom wizard of the Lower East Side for nothing, she said gloatingly.

She finally left for rehearsal, but she was in no condition to work. The alcohol she'd consumed had sapped her energy and dimmed her mental acuity. In the cold warehouse attic, she became testy and abusive, stopping in the middle of a song and scolding the musicians for chatting while she was trying to perform. Efforts to pacify her only sparked further abrasiveness, until she was pulling rank and reminding them that they were only hired help. Only the drummer stood up to her, miming a grade-schooler promising teacher to be quiet from now on. That brought her to her senses and she apologized for being conceited.

Three weeks before their New York premiere, they went on the road, playing Rindge, New Hampshire, and Boston in order to burnish their act. Though they'd improved since Memphis, reviews were mixed when they opened in New York to four sold-out houses.

Janis was the hottest ticket in town, if not the world. By 1969, she had gone beyond rock stardom into the realm of folk legend. The opening was a major media event with television cameramen from the networks and critics from *Time, Life, Look,* and *Newsweek* all braving the freezing cold. Paul Nelson, the *Rolling Stone* critic, resented the way the press had been handled, with the slick establishment periodicals getting most of the seats, while gonzo rock critics were consigned to standing room only. Evidently, the Grossman office hadn't been romancing *Rolling Stone,* the key player in the rock press, and, as a consequence, Janis would suffer both emotionally and professionally.

The Grateful Dead opened for her, and during their set one of Janis's impatient fans said he'd been nursing a hard-on all day, waiting for her. She was the first star to incite the male rock audience to the same fever pitch that Elvis and the Beatles evoked from girl teenyboppers. She came onstage, danced around in a wild cape-gown, and then threw it off, revealing a shoulder-strap pantsuit. The young men in the audience sent up a randy roar.

When she started singing, however, the band couldn't keep up with her. Hard-core Big Brother fans started yelling, *'Where's Peter Albin?'* In frustration, she reached for her bottle, which was sitting on an amplifier. Clearly, the Kozmic Blues had not come up with their own distinctive style. 'The audience didn't stone us, anyway,' says Sam Andrew. Frank Zappa came backstage after the performance and got into a conversation with Sam, who said, 'We're changing things – we still do not have quite the right sound.' Zappa reassured him, saying, 'The band will loosen up in a while.'

Benny Goodman and his wife also appeared backstage and congratulated Janis. On a sudden inspiration, Sam said, 'Hey, why don't you sit in with us on "Summertime"?' Sam mentioned the Gershwin tune because it was from the Goodman era 'and it would be an excellent opportunity for him and us to bridge the generation gap through music.' Unfortunately, no one had the gumption to recognize that Sam's suggestion – a Joplin-Goodman duet – made perfect sense.

Though the audience reaction had been mixed, Janis was so full of herself that she went around after the show telling everyone how great she'd been. *Rolling Stone*'s Paul Nelson was as intolerant of her innocent, naïve narcissism as the ignoramuses of Port Arthur had been, and he hurt her just as callously, headlining his pan, JANIS: THE JUDY GARLAND OF ROCK AND ROLL? He quoted her ill-advised self-congratulatory remarks at length, such as, 'Hey, I've never sung so great. Don't you think I'm singing better? Well, Jesus fucking Christ, I'm really better, believe me.'

Equally mindless were her gauche jabs at her new band, which were delivered in front of reporters. 'I just wish the band would push as hard as I am,' she harped. She sounded just as ungracious when she jabbed at former colleagues in Big Brother. 'We were lying,' she told *Newsweek*. 'We were repeating ourselves, not creating.'

TV's 'Sixty Minutes' lined her up for a segment, and during her preliminary meeting with Mike Wallace, she told him to scream 'Fuck' every time she made a faux pas and she'd do the same thing should he – which would be the editor's signal to begin cutting. Once the cameras started rolling, Wallace asked her how it was possible for a Caucasian to sing African-American music. Janis looked at the camera, said, 'Fuck!' and lapsed into an alcoholic blackout. Later, she admitted she couldn't remember a word she'd said.

The New York Times gave her a rave, as usual: 'Miss Joplin has never been better. Even though her new group sounds as if it were just getting to work well together, it still is very good.' *Newsweek* said, 'With a voice like a nutcracker she fragments the syllables, looking for the kernel of sound within.' While in New York, she met the *Newsweek* critic Hubert Saal, who praised her 'attractively open face' but grimaced at what she was drinking for breakfast: 'an unlovely concoction apparently made of wood alcohol and chocolate syrup.' She wore a sheepskin coat and her Harold Lloyd spectacles had no lenses. 'I'm just learning my trade,' she told Saal. 'I want to be more of a singer and less of an entertainer. And when I can't sing anymore, I'll have babies.'

After the Fillmore East gig, Janis and the Kozmic Blues Band flew to Ann Arbor to play the huge University of Michigan gymnasium. They used the locker room to change into their stage clothes, and the air stank of jockstraps. Says Sam today, 'Janis and I often talked about silly things she wouldn't discuss with anyone else. That night, she was concerned whether it was sexier for her panties to show through her silk slacks or if she should wear nothing at all under her clothes.'

Following some discussion, she decided in favor of keeping her panties on. As dark-skinned Snooky Flowers stood in his shorts, getting ready to step into snazzy bellbottoms, two priests entered the room and made solicitous inquiries. Previous celebrity visitors to the campus may have asked for a word of prayer before going on. Janis, who was trying to chew a reluctant cork out of a bottle of B&B, looked up and noticed that one of the clerics had a balloon-shaped Afro haircut. Blinking incredulously, she pointed at the ordained freak and let out a barrage of cackles. After he beat a hasty retreat she asked whether priests could have sex. Yes, she was told, provided they were Episcopalians. She then indicated her readiness to accept an alternative to prayer should the hippie priest reappear.

Cooke warned her that the audience was full of students and she couldn't swear during the set. She replied that she'd say anything she damn well pleased. By now, she was gulping the B&B and sighing as contentment radiated from her stomach. Seconds before showtime, Sam started playing 'a Bach guitar piece,' and Janis fondled Richard Kermode's neck, looking dotingly at his wavy hair and thick beard. When she finished rubbing him, he reciprocated by giving her a vigorous neck massage. Every time someone came in the locker room, they could hear the crowd roaring out front.

Soon Cooke burst in like a drill sergeant and ordered them to go onstage. Everyone shifted into character and shot out of the dressing room as if they were already on and performing. They plowed through a heavy contingent of security men lining the hallway and jumped up onto the flimsy makeshift stage.

The spotlights weren't in operation yet, and the band started tuning up, taking their time. Finally, the stage was drenched in violet light and Janis took her place at the microphone, poised like a Wild West gunslinger. When she started to sing, an uninhibited male jumped into the aisle and put on a dance exhibition. She nodded in approval and soaked up the magic rapport that existed between her and the audience. Here were all the warmth and affection she craved and had never found elsewhere. A young man with a deep macho voice suddenly called out, 'Oh, fuck me, Janis, fuck me!' She had them where she wanted them.

At the close of the first set, as the audience screamed for encores, she appeared to be addled. Those in the front rows recognized her indisposition and tried to bolster her by shouting compliments. Reviving from her momentary blackout, she started groping her way across the stage, seized a Styrofoam cup from atop the organ, and drained it.

When she sang 'Piece of My Heart,' the lyrics masochistically inviting a lover to dismember and cannibalize her, the exhibitionistic dancer fell on his back and began to kick his legs in the air. The concert had exceeded its prescribed length, but Janis and the crowd had become inseparable. Finally, the only thing that broke them up was a stagehand throwing the light switch. Backstage, she protested that she hadn't been ready to end the show and cursed the crew.

For Janis, an inveterate night owl, a new day was just dawning, and she was off to a Detroit bar to hear her friend Jeff Karp play harmonica and direct his group. At one point in the evening, the owner asked her to sing, but when she got up to the bandstand, she discovered that none of the musicians knew her songs. Leaving the club at 4:30 A.M., she confronted the owner. 'Just getting me up there was all you cared about,' she said. 'Low-class-ass thing to do, man, and you can go to hell.'

She drove back to her Ann Arbor motel with Karp and writer John Bowers, who was interviewing her for *Playboy*. Karp endeavored to interest her in his career, hoping for some advice from the established star, saying, 'Man, I am ready!' Just twenty years old, he'd arrived in Detroit the day before with a dollar to his name. Anxious to keep the spotlight on herself, she pulled out her Sony and played a tape of the performance she'd just given at Ann Arbor. In her estimation, even her gaffes merited their attention. 'I blew this note here,' she pointed out. 'Listen to it.'

'One of these days, *I'm* going to be discovered,' Karp persisted, but she was intent on locating the place on the tape where the kid in the audience had asked her to fuck him. 'Hey, *listen,*' she said, 'listen to what some guy is yelling in the audience. *Man, too much!*' Despite her overweening self-centeredness, Bowers liked her so much that when he turned in his *Playboy* piece, he refrained from mentioning the most interesting fact he'd turned up about her – that she was shooting heroin.

Around dawn, she was seen stooping in her motel hallway, poking at leftovers on a dinner tray on the floor. She'd been trying to lose weight and had gone without her evening meal, but now she made a feast out of stale morsels. Finally, she went to bed, though she was due in New York the same day, a Sunday, to appear on the 'Ed Sullivan Show.'

Less than two hours later, she and John Bowers were in a car speeding to the airport. Rationalizing her wan and wired countenance, she said she was going to enjoy freaking out Ed Sullivan with her depraved strumpet look. But all traces of her hangover magically disappeared when she arrived at the Ed Sullivan Theater on Broadway. 'I had seen that show for years and imagined a huge arena where the acrobats and musicians played, something like a circus where Ed was the master of ceremonies,' says Sam. 'Not so. Everything was so small and close. I could almost reach out and touch Mr. Sullivan from where I was playing. It amazed me that all those stupendous events had happened on such a tiny stage area.'

After Janis sang, she sauntered over to Sullivan, expecting to shake his hand, but in a departure from his usual practice of chatting with performers on camera, the straitlaced host turned his back on Janis. His brusque dismissal stung her.

Although she'd only had a couple of hours' sleep in the past two days, she decided to party at Max's Kansas City with the dazzling New York City Ballet dancers who'd just shared the Sullivan bill with her. A connoisseur of pectorals and gluteri maximi, Janis busied herself with the male dancers while Sam chatted up Suzanne Farrell, the prima ballerina, whom he found 'beautiful and graceful. It was magic that night. At Max's, we talked with Rip Torn, Larry Rivers, Bobby Neuwirth, Edie Sedgwick, and Andy Warhol, and our waitress was Debbie Harry. Salvador Dali came out of the crowd and spoke to me for a while. Tiny Tim came through carrying his ukulele in a paper sack.

'Janis was Albert Grossman's date that night. They were real cuddly and she called Albert a big bear. He had a house in Gramercy Park and she went there all the time.'

Back in San Francisco, Janis prepared to face the hometown crowd, many of them still resentful over her treatment of Big Brother. Under the auspices of Bill Graham, she was set to play Winterland and the Fillmore West in March 1969.

Janis's old friend Sunshine had moved into the Noe Street apartment and was now living with Janis and Linda. John Bowers met both Sunshine and Linda when he came to Noe

Street to finish his piece on Janis for *Playboy*. When he arrived, Sunshine and Janis were out grocery shopping. Linda kept him company while they waited for the women to return. Since he worked for *Playboy*, Linda volunteered that she'd once done cheesecake, and Bowers noted her shapely figure.

Janis blasted into the room, juggling bagfuls of groceries and ordering everyone to help her put them away. Sunshine followed her into the room, and Bowers described her as a blonde with educated hips. Trying to size up Janis's girlfriends, Bowers felt that beneath their aggressive exterior they were wounded and suffering. When the article was published, Bowers seemed anxious to assure *Playboy's* straight male audience that Janis wasn't gay, specifying that each of the three roommates slept in their own private quarters within the apartment.

Though the following day was Janis's Winterland debut with her new band, they all went out in the Porsche for a night of boozing, Janis and Linda in front and Sunshine and Bowers crouched behind them. At the controls, Janis gave a new meaning to the term *hell on wheels*. Burning rubber at the intersection, she charged up a hill, stripping gears and briefly going airborne at the crest. Later, zooming through an African-American section, they saw a man making urgent gestures at them. He looked fierce enough to kill, but it turned out that he was a fan and had been throwing Janis only a friendly black-power salute.

As if by osmosis, Janis located a parking space immediately upon skidding into North Beach. After dinner, they found a bar for a game of billiards and endless rounds of drinks. Any tavern Janis entered became an instant party, her presence bestowing status on everyone there. The jukebox jumped with the deafening sound of her hit records, turning the pool hall into a Joplin concert. Bonhomie abounded as friends from as far back as her North Beach speed-freak days gathered around to embrace and reminisce. Sunshine and Janis stayed to drink, but Linda left to visit people she knew in the area, and Bowers reeled off to his room.

'The next day,' says Sunshine, 'I did some heroin, and then we stopped at the connection's on the way to the gig.' Janis wanted it for later. 'She had a thing about never fixing before a performance,' Sunshine explains. 'She knew what she was going to get from an audience.'

On the sidewalk at the Winterland arena, they saw a crowd that emanated an eerie, hostile aura. Hip, slick, and cool, they murmured among themselves, snorting, smoking, or dropping their drugs for the concert. Despite the rain and chill, one kid was half naked, but most wore boots, capes, and beads. Glancing around balefully, they looked as if they'd come to witness an execution instead of a rock show.

Janis and Sunshine went inside. 'Suzy Perry and a bunch of people were sitting around on the concrete floor in the back,' Sunshine says. 'We hadn't seen each other in a long time. Big Brother wasn't there to play and that felt very weird.' Janis peered out of her dressing room and shuddered, sensing the crowd's mood. To her, they were like buzzards, hunched and eager to pick her bones.

She was drinking B&B, greeting her friends and drawing what courage she could from well-wishers. James Gurley arrived and she became emotional, running to him and melting in his arms. He'd been camping in a cave in the wilderness since the breakup, and his body, reassuringly familiar, was firm as a bulwark. 'She was totally isolated and paranoid,' he recalls. He saw her as a victim of 'the New York attitude – "If this band doesn't get a good review, keep changin' bands until you get one that does." As if the whole game was to please the fuckin' pencil pushers at *Rolling Stone*.'

During her performance that night – one of her best ever – the audience remained aloof, and when she finished, few applauded and no one wanted an encore. Stunned and ashen-faced, she fled to her dressing room. To associates, she insisted that it wasn't her fault, that she'd given a great show but the audience hated her for firing Big Brother. Cooke didn't agree. 'Bad set,' he pronounced.

When Janis and Sunshine went to the garage to get the Porsche, the attendant regarded her blankly and said, 'Somebody already come and took it. Said, "I'm pickin' up Miss Joplin's car for her," got in, and drove away.'

Peter Coyote – an actor who'd later make a splash as the scientist who saves the extraterrestrial in the film *E.T.* – gave Janis and Sunshine a ride home. 'Coyote's still one of my favorite men,' says Sunshine. She and Janis used up the supply of heroin and then decided to go out and get some more. Janis was now doing about two hundred dollars' worth of heroin a day. 'Bill Graham loaned her a car,' says Sunshine, 'and we went over to the connection's.'

After she and Sunshine got the heroin that night, they returned to Noe Street. They must have used the heroin, because Janis had depleted her supply by the time she met Peggy the following day in a North Beach bar. She required moral support as she awaited the *Chronicle* review. Janis badly needed a break with the press, because *Rolling Stone* had come out with a cover story on March 15 questioning her status as a rock star.

She bought the *Chronicle* at a stand outside the bar and quickly turned to Ralph Gleason's column. To her horror, it was a scathing diatribe. 'Her new band is a drag,' he wrote, and he advised her to go back to Big Brother, appending a poisonous postscript: 'if they'll have her.'

She'd wandered back into the bar by the time she'd finished reading the review. She threw the *Chronicle* on the floor and stomped on it. Gleason, she wanted to murder or, at the very least, stick his column where the sun don't shine. All she could think of was getting hold of some heroin and shooting it until her rage subsided. If she wasn't so recognizable, she'd score from the first street pusher she came to. Peggy promised to hunt down a connection and call her later.

Meanwhile, the police had found the Porsche. 'One fender had been painted over,' Sunshine recalls. Over in his office on Market Street, Bill Graham saw the Gleason pan and nodded in agreement. He bitched to anyone who'd listen that Janis had been better back in 1966 to 1967 – a rough street girl with an unprofessional acid band. Grumbling that she should stick to the same old tunes – 'Combination of the Two' and 'Ball and Chain' – he opposed her efforts to explore new musical frontiers, both in terms of material and delivery. That she and the new band were not as bad as Graham and Gleason claimed would be amply demonstrated when they cut the LP *I Got Dem Ol' Kozmic Blues Again Mama!* the same year. It includes some brilliant work, such as 'Little Girl Blue,' 'Maybe,' and 'Try.'

Peggy told Janis to meet her at the Fillmore where they'd be able to buy some heroin. She'd located a connection who'd promised to come there with a supply, but she couldn't be absolutely positive he wasn't a mugger. She and Janis cowered in the shadows of the empty Fillmore, kvetching and commiserating with each other. Janis was sorry she wasn't in LA, where her connection always had good uncut heroin.

The pusher finally arrived, Peggy and Janis scored, then drove to Noe Street and shot up. They'd intended to make love but the ecstatic rushes from their near-overdose superseded all thoughts of sex. After a while, Janis started cursing Ralph Gleason again. She said that Gleason's review had driven her to shoot heroin that day, not to mention all the time she'd wasted trying to score it.

The second Winterland show went somewhat better. It was either after this or a subsequent Winterland performance that one of her fondest wet dreams came true. During the set, she'd worked harder than ever to stimulate the crowd, and after the show, she came offstage highly aroused, dying to make love to someone, anyone. Suddenly, a strapping man in a cape enfolded her in a steamy embrace and swept her outside to his Volkswagen bus, where he lifted her into the back. It was Milan Melvin, and while she was still quivering from the intensity of her performance, he made love to her. 'I wanted to prevent that vacuum she felt after giving her all,' Milan recalls. 'The trick was to get the van close enough to Winterland so that we could jump in the minute she came offstage and ride out the storm.'

A few days later, Milan again showed up unexpectedly, this time at Noe Street. 'That's when Janis let me in on the secret,' he says. That day, there were three other women in her living room, and their interest in one another was clearly sexual. Milan had not previously been aware that Janis led a full-fledged lesbian life in addition to her prodigious pursuit of heterosexual males. She looked at Milan and said, 'This is my life now.'

'Cool by me,' he said. 'Hey, I'm lookin' to get it on with you again.' Janis glanced at the girls, said, 'Later,' and led Milan to her bedroom. After they made love, she said, 'Let's go out for a couple of drinks.' They tried to play pool at a lesbian bar on Castro Street, but, says Milan, 'The little bull dyke behind the bar said, "No men on the tables." I said, "Hey. Wait a second. What's the matter? I'm here with Janis. She comes here often. I'm not an asshole. All I want to do is – I mean, where is this equality thing we're talking about here when you're—" She pulled out a gun from behind the bar and repeated, "I said no men on the tables!" '

Milan racked his cue and mumbled, 'Sure. Whatever.' Today he says, 'So that's the point at which I first got on to Janis's scene. From then on, it wasn't anything Janis was hiding.' Milan also knew Peggy Caserta and recalls, 'Peggy and I would get it on in her back room with a couple of the young girls that worked there. The emphasis was more bisexual than pure lesbian. Peggy was pretty good-lookin'. And sexy. Great tits. And really vivacious.'

Her battles with the *Chronicle* and *Rolling Stone* brought Janis perilously close that spring to a mental and emotional collapse. The press assault on her went beyond the parameters of legitimate criticism, she felt, and into the gutter of malice and character assassination. Jann Wenner got his kicks from injuring others, she said, and Ralph Gleason's hatchet job she found unforgivable, calling his suggestion that she go back to Big Brother male-chauvinist 'cunt shit, bitchy-chick shit, she's-gettin'-too-big-for-her-britches shit.' They could all go and fuck themselves, and that's precisely what she told them anytime they called her for an interview.

Rolling Stone continued to go out of its way to knock her even when there was no performance to review. On April 19, 1969, their 'Random Notes' column said, 'The whole Janis Joplin Hype has grown to outrageous proportions.' It was finally Bobby Neuwirth who called off the press hounds. Says Sam, 'Bobby put in a call immediately to Jann Wenner and got a dialogue going. He offered relief by putting all of Janis's subconscious fears out into the open. Most of all, though, he just made her laugh and say to hell with *Rolling Stone*, anyway. Bobby relished this sort of court jester role and he did it quite well.'

'I wish I had some dope,' Janis said. She and Linda were strolling through the streets of Paris, where Janis was playing the Olympia Theater during her European tour in April 1969. Remembering Janis's Noe Street OD, Linda stopped and said, '*No no no no no.*'

'*Yes yes yes yes yes,*' Janis hissed. Completely exasperated, Linda said, 'Janis, do you want me just to shut up?'

'*No,*' she yelped. 'You're my anchor.' She refrained from pressuring Linda to shoot up with her, not only because Linda didn't like heroin but because Janis needed at least one sane person in her life.

From Paris, they went to Frankfurt, Germany, where Janis invited the audience to join her onstage, and a remarkable number of them did. 'More and more people were dancing all around us,' Sam recalls. 'Finally, someone stepped on my guitar cord and pulled it out of the amplifier. I just kept on playing and dancing, since it was the last tune and by this time the audience was the real show.' Thwarted in her efforts to introduce new songs and improve as a singer, Janis had changed her tactics and now was trying to turn every concert into a riot. If she couldn't maintain her stardom through artistic growth, she'd do so through sheer outrageousness.

In London, a reporter from *Melody Maker* presented her with a dummy of her canceled April 7, 1969, *Newsweek* cover, which showed her in Linda's push-'em-up bra with the beaded daisies. The caption read, 'Janis Joplin: Rebirth of the Blues.' When former President Eisenhower died, she'd been yanked from the cover, and a photograph of Ike had been substituted. 'Mother*fucker*,' she yelled. 'Fourteen heart attacks and the son of a bitch has to croak in my week. In *my* week.'

At Albert Hall, Janis had the British roaring from the beginning of the show. 'Eric Clapton and I were going wild with everyone else, clapping, yelling, shaking and stomping,' says Bob Seidemann. 'The band was tight and at last had found the perfect technique and volume for backing her up.'

Bobby Neuwirth had worked his magic with *Rolling Stone* and now they were calling her the greatest thing since the Beatles. Janis was still glacial when their reporter David Dalton approached her in London, but later on, in 1970, she became very friendly with him. She'd snubbed him in London, she said, because the magazine's abuse had reduced her to tears. Janis also admitted to Dalton that she'd been shooting heroin in London, which accounted for her pallor and discomfiture. She'd somehow managed to satisfy her devoted fans, but she lacked the artistry she would display the following year, in Kansas City, during an all-too-brief drug-free interlude.

The British critics gave her rhapsodic reviews. On April 20, Tony Palmer called her 'a hot white soul sister' in *The Observer* and *The Daily Mirror* said she was 'the wildest happening since Elvis.' During an interview, she jolted a *London Evening Standard* reporter, who later wrote, 'I'm a complete stranger and right away she's asking me to massage her neck and kisses me hello with a scorching calf's lick on my right eyebrow.'

She took the trades by storm, Tony Wilson calling her 'sexy' in *Melody Maker* and Nick Logan raving about 'the legend of Janis Joplin' in *The New Musical Express*. As Jonathan Cott and David Dalton wrote in *Rolling Stone*, 'Janis came and London came with her.'

The party she threw in her hotel suite after the concert was attended by Clapton, Seidemann, Mouse, Linda, Sam, and Suzy Creamcheeze. Suzy was a groupie who'd been showing Sam around London, introducing him to roast beef and Yorkshire pudding. Also at the party, according to Mouse, were 'a few teenage boys who looked like they'd come in off the street. It was just bananas.'

Seidemann remembers that 'someone brought in a bunch of heroin. Janis did up and said, "Aw, this is great. I really got off." Sam got off and OD'd. Turned blue. I was sober and had my head on my shoulders and began to clear the room out, got Eric Clapton out first and then the riffraff after that. Then I proceeded to run around the hotel to try to find some antidote to no avail.'

For Linda, it was Noe Street all over again. She recalls, 'Suddenly Janis came out and said, "Linda! Come 'ere! You know what an OD looks like." Sam Andrew had OD'd, and for me it was the last straw. Suzy Creamcheeze, Janis, and I got Sam in the bathtub and that fucker was getting stubborn. We kept saying, "Breathe, Sam, breathe!" And he puffed up like a little kid and said, "I'll hold my breath until you go away!" '

When Seidemann returned, the suite looked like something out of a Heironymus Bosch painting. 'Sam was nude in the bathtub full of cold water and Suzy Creamcheeze had torn her panties off and was sitting astride him with some interesting therapy I'd never seen administered to an OD patient before,' says Seidemann. 'It went on like that until Sam stopped being blue. I don't know why he didn't die. Mouse and I kept ordering peach melbas from room service, and the waiters would show up and serve our dessert while at the other end of the suite a life-and-death struggle was going on. Janis just whined and complained that everyone was shooting up all her dope, and she had a really bad attitude. Mouse and I left at dawn that day, wrung out like a rag, and walked home to a flat that he and I were sharing.'

One reason that Sam's life was falling apart was his demoralization over being treated like a hack musician. 'The guys in Kozmic Blues had come from playing on Broadway,' he says. 'I liked them, but in Big Brother it had never been our goal to be professionals. In the new band, I felt like a nightclub musician and hated it.'

Linda found the crisis at the hotel such 'a nightmare, a

recurring one,' that she couldn't take it any longer. She made up her mind to quit at the end of the tour.

One night before they left London, Janis, Linda, and Albert Grossman were invited to George and Patti Harrison's for dinner. Janis sat next to George on the living room couch, gazing at her favorite Beatle as he expounded on mysticism and meditation. After a while, he turned to Janis for her response.

'Hey, man,' she said, 'I've been wanting to make it with you for years.'

'I don't think I'd be big enough for you,' George said.

Patti burst out laughing. 'All of us just cracked up,' Linda recalls, 'because it was so funny to see two people talking about two completely different ways of life. Janis was the most basic chick in the world.' Smiling warmly at Janis, Patti said, 'I love your purse. It's so original. Please tell me about it.' When Janis explained that Linda had embroidered it, Patti asked Linda to make her one. Then George asked Linda if she'd make him a jacket.

Linda agreed to everything, and George offered to pay her twenty-four dollars a week. It was a ridiculously low sum for an original jacket, but Linda knew that a commission from a Beatle would be a good way to start her new life as a clothes designer in England. A few days later, she turned in her notice to Janis, and Janis returned to America without her.

Linda remained in London from April until late November, working on Harrison's jacket. One day, Janis called her and said, 'I'm getting a house in Larkspur, just over the bridge. Hey, come on back. We'll have a great time in the country.' Explaining that she could no longer stand to see Janis and her friends killing themselves, Linda declined. Then, says Linda, Janis assured her 'she'd do it my way and stay clean and made all these wonderful promises.' Linda made no commitment and returned to embroidering Harrison's jacket, which by now had turned into a spectacular psychedelic design of swirling purples, lavenders, and blues.

Eventually Harrison paid her $250 and said, 'I want you to finish it, but I don't want to give you any more money.'

'Fuck you,' Linda said.

She continued to mull over Janis's promises, but for the present she remained in London.

'It was the dumbest thing I've ever done in my life,' Milan Melvin says. 'Janis hit me and KA-BOOM. Years later, Peggy Caserta told my wife, Georgeanne, that she thought that Janis had killed me. They couldn't get me around at all.'

The three of them – Janis, Milan, and Peggy – were in Janis's room at the Chateau Marmont Hotel in Hollywood, and they were getting off on Janis's killer heroin. She'd acquired the stuff from her LA connection, who always sold her very pure shit.

In June 1969, Janis had gone to LA to record a new LP with the Kozmic Blues Band. Peggy wanted to be with her and lied to Kim, telling her she was going on a buying trip for the store. Then she flew to LA and joined Janis at the Chateau Marmont. They went out for the evening, dining at the Old World Restaurant on Sunset Strip and later going to Barney's Beanery for drinks. An hour or so later, they decided to take in *The Committee,* which had proved so popular in LA that it was still running at the Tiffany.

'I saw the two of them,' Milan says, 'and thought, Yes, man! Here we go!' Janis was thinking the same thing: Nothing could be funkier than a three-ways with Milan and Peggy. They went back to Barney's for drinks, and before they left, Milan was already making love to both of them with his eyes. Janis extolled his virtues as a lover to Peggy, trying to excite her. His sexual dimensions seemed to have been created specifically with a female in mind, Janis said. He was neither too big nor too small.

'We went back to the hotel,' Milan remembers, 'and the idea was, before we got in the sack, everybody wanted to get off.' Janis bound her arm with a scarf, holding one end between clenched teeth, found a vein, and injected herself. Then, as she measured out Milan's dose, Peggy noticed that it was excessive, though not as large as the near-lethal shot that had knocked out Terence Hallinan. Despite her apprehensions, Peggy remained silent. In retrospect, she would state in her autobiography that she'd been too preoccupied with the imminent orgy to warn Milan.

'Janis, I'm clean,' Milan said. 'I don't have a habit. I really want you to go very light on this. Or let me do it myself.' But it was Janis's dope and she was as addicted to power as she was to heroin. Says Milan today, 'She was insisting that she fix me. I never let anybody ever do that in my life. I've always taken care of my own business. But in this case, she really wanted to.' He finally told Janis, 'Okay, but look, I know you've got to have it. I don't. You've got to go real light on this.'

'Aw, come on, man, we're gonna party,' Janis said.

Milan watched her carefully, and it looked as if she was cooking too much. He was worried because he had no idea whether this heroin had been 'hit.' 'Janis!' he said. '*Less!* I'm clean! I know you've been doin' runner for a while.' But it was too late. She jabbed the needle in and started pumping far too strong a dose into him. He stood up, took a few steps, and sank to his knees. As if in slow motion, he settled on the floor, spread out his arms, and lost consciousness.

Though his face was pallid and he could have been dying, Janis was too busy preparing Peggy's heroin, holding it over a flame, to bother with Milan. Peggy warned her that she was fixing an excessive amount. Whispering endearments, Janis assured her that she knew how to measure out heroin.

As soon as Janis shot her up, Peggy slumped to the floor, out cold. Janis started hitting both Milan and Peggy and shrieking in anger, her orgy foiled. When they finally revived the following day, Janis chided them for not being able to keep up with her. Over twenty years later, when Milan Melvin takes me to a biker's bar near Santa Barbara, I observe, 'You could have died. Why didn't anyone call a doctor?'

'Apparently, I was breathing enough that they didn't want to,' he replies. 'I don't believe Janis overdosed me intentionally.' It's clear from his eyes and tender tone that he still loves her.

Gabriel Mekler produced the *Kozmic Blues* album and co-wrote the title song with Janis. Her concept of 'Kozmic Blues' came to her when she was sitting in a bar one day. 'There are blues about losing your job and drinking too much,' says Sam, 'but the Kozmic Blues are the kind you get that there's no name for, anomie, alienation, the worst kind of blues, the blues that has no name, "waking up in the middle of the night" blues – that's what she meant by the Kozmic Blues.'

When Janis composed her blues songs, such as 'Move Over,' 'One Man,' and 'Mercedes Benz,' her creative process was the opposite of Wordsworth's, who defined poetry as 'emotion recollected in tranquility.' Janis had to be in the depths of rejection and heartbreak to put pen to paper. Every song she wrote came out of her despair over a lover's desertion. Understandably, she hated the whole business and would have preferred never to write another lyric rather than undergo the trauma it took to make a song happen.

During the summer of 1969, she continued recording the *Kozmic Blues* album. The most memorable cut, and Janis's own personal favorite of all her recordings, was 'Little Girl Blue.' The Rodgers and Hart ballad was first introduced in the Broadway circus musical *Jumbo* in 1935, and in the 1962 movie version, Doris Day sang it.

The recording sessions were held in Hollywood, and Sam sensed 'a spirit of malaise' in the band. It was as if Janis's ego left no room for anyone else to breathe. He requested a meeting with Grossman, during which he asked whether the band could be cut in for a percentage of the profits on the album. 'The rest of the band looked shocked,' Sam recalls, 'as if I was causing trouble. Albert refused and that was that. We were guns for hire and I could see that it was just a matter of time before we would be traded in for another band.'

Like Janis, Sam in 1969 was hitting repeated bottoms with his heroin addiction. 'I was exhausted, disillusioned, strung out, and helpless to change anything,' he remembers. 'I knew I was going to crash and burn soon and I did. Janis fired me.' One day, she called him and told him to come to her room in the Landmark. He found her in the process of cooking up some heroin, and she offered to share it. After they got off, she said, 'Sam, I have to tell you that your services are no longer required.' He was so numb that he didn't react. 'Well,' she prodded, 'aren't you going to ask me why?'

'It doesn't make much difference,' he said, 'since I'm going.'

'Yeah,' she said, 'I guess you're right.' Sam never learned from Janis why she fired him, assuming 'it was because she needed another change or that she simply didn't care for my guitar playing. I read somewhere that I was stealing her drugs. This is entirely possible, but I do not remember it. I do have a larcenous streak that I have always had to keep under control.'

Whatever the provocation for firing Sam, once she'd done it, she again couldn't bring herself to let go of him. A week later, she asked him to stay with the Kozmic Blues Band, at least until she could replace him. Another motive was her sexual attraction to Sam, which had never been satisfied. She wanted him, but he was always involved with someone else. Still, she had never given up hope and refused to now.

'All of this was happening while we were trying to record the *Kozmic Blues* album,' Sam notes. 'Needless to say, it was difficult to give one's best in the studio with no confidence among the band members. Everyone felt as if tomorrow could be the last day, and it could have been.'

According to Peggy, Sam did not take his firing graciously and called Janis a 'bitch' and an 'egotistical cunt.' Moreover, she says that Sam believed that he, Travis, and Chet had created Janis.

Janis and Peggy were continuing their complicated but sexually turbocharged relationship. With Peggy, Janis had developed into a more giving and resourceful lover; Janis now occasionally took the active, aggressive role. Peggy was still involved with Kim, and sometimes Peggy shot up with Janis several times and then went home and injected heroin again with Kim. None of them seemed to heed the warning implicit in the death of Nancy Gurley, who was only in her twenties when she died of a heroin overdose.

Nancy, James, and their son, Hongo, had been on a camping trip on the Russian River, near Healdsburg, when James and Nancy had decided to use heroin. The shot killed Nancy. 'My whole world was destroyed,' says James Gurley today. 'I was destroyed, everything was leveled. I was with her when she died, and I'd had the heroin, too. I was talking to the police and I was in no condition to conceal anything or to deny anything. I said, "We were doing heroin and she died." It's against the law to use it and I gave them what was left of the heroin, so they had that evidence right there. It took about a year and a half, fighting it with the lawyers. I was convicted and had to do a couple of years on probation.

I forget what else. I stopped using after Nancy died.'

Janis sympathized with Jim for the ordeal he was subjected to, but when she first heard of Nancy's death, she defiantly went out and bought some heroin. Then, like someone who's been thrown from a horse and feels the needs to remount instantly or spend the rest of life in fear, she shot the heroin intravenously.

Chet Helms describes Nancy as 'a fiery spirit and a loving person.' At the time of her death, Richard Hundgen was asked to help the stricken family. 'James and Hongo were totally distraught,' he remembers, 'and I went to the city morgue at Healdsburg to identify Nancy. Hongo was left for a few days as a ward of the court, and then Nancy's relatives got Hongo out.' Shortly before Nancy's death, she'd sent Hundgen a letter saying, 'Please take care of Janis, our canary.' She'd named the bird after Janis, says Hundgen, 'because it sang so well, and Hongo really liked this little bird.' Janis honored Nancy's memory by dedicating the LP she was working on, *Kozmic Blues,* 'to Nancy G. love.'

Some of Janis's friends realized that it was only a matter of time until she, too, died of heroin. Placing her in the same category as all his other junkie pals, Nick Gravenites accepted the fact that she was going to die, so that when it happened, he wouldn't 'get too crazy on it.' Albert Grossman took a hard-boiled approach, making sure he'd profit from her death. In June 1969, he bought a $200,000 life insurance policy on Janis, paying $3,500 in yearly premiums, though Janis was only twenty-six years old. As for Janis, she felt impervious to danger, telling Sam, 'Nothing will ever happen to me because I come from good pioneer stock and I'm strong.' Says Sam today, 'Every alcoholic or junkie who has ever lived feels the same way, but that kind of Superman fantasy is just whistling in the dark.' Janis fully expected to live a long, if not necessarily productive, life. To Albert, she confided that she lived in terror of toppling from the charts and ending up on the Bowery as a bag lady screwing runaways.

She was surrounded by sycophants, mostly indigent junkies, groupies, assorted employees, and avid journalists, and though she was a well-known tightwad, she often picked up the tab for a table of fifteen to twenty musicians and cronies at Max's or Barney's Beanery. Few ever called her generous, and many commented on her meticulously kept checkbook. Even so, she always gave her employees Christmas presents, and one friend, embroiled in a drug bust that included a killing, was the recipient of considerable largesse – she gave him twenty thousand dollars for legal counsel.

Some of her roadies served her sexual needs, and when old ones left, new ones took their place. 'I definitely know that she was involved with quite a few of them at one time or another,' says Sam. 'For one thing, they were probably younger and cuter than we were in the band.' Dave Richards had already gone, and Mark Braunstein quit in June of 1969, because 'I didn't like the Kozmic Blues Band as much as I'd liked Big Brother. I was twenty-two and wanted to travel and it didn't look to me as if the band would be going to Europe again.'

Vince Mitchell, a good-hearted, rustic fellow with a healthy sexual appetite, came on board as the new roadie and fell in love with her. She didn't want a permanent commitment with him, having decided she couldn't trust anyone on her payroll who said they loved her. She didn't hesitate, however, to put Vince under constant pressure to verify that she was lovable and talented. Vince tried to get her to stop using heroin, but she pulled rank and outshouted him.

In June, they went to New York to polish the *Kozmic Blues* album in the Columbia studios and then they played

Newport on June 20. Sam says the band by now was so disenfranchised, 'it was almost like we were servants who should come in the back entrance when we went anywhere.' Says Bob Seidemann, 'I think she always knew the magic was gone once she'd left Big Brother. That nagged at her. All the guys in Big Brother were written out of the book of history, and she always believed that she'd done the wrong thing. It was never the same again.'

They returned to New York and then visited Albert in Woodstock, attending a star-studded dinner party that included the Band, Dylan, Arlo Guthrie, and Neuwirth. The festivities went on so long that Albert asked Janis and the other guests to remain overnight, and they continued to drink and drug until most of them went to sleep. In the end, the only two people still conscious were Janis and a willowy, large-bosomed girl who started caressing Janis's breasts. They found a secluded corner and made love.

While Janis and the band were playing an upstate gig, her long relationship with Sam was at last consummated. 'Something strange happened,' says Sam. 'We were very close, but there was never any question of a sexual relationship aside from a lot of kidding around. Then at the very end of our time together, we made love. She was very soft, intense, but very feminine. This surprised me, but it really shouldn't have. There was this same quality of force and delicacy in her voice and indeed in her whole manner. She made love lightly as a feather on the wind and yet the passionate strength of the wind was there, too. Because of her accent, her attitudes, even her clothes, she was like a sister or cousin to me long before she was a lover. She could have come from my mother's family, who all lived in the same part of Texas that she did.'

At Monterey, Janis had helped launch the era of giant rock festivals, and in 1969, she played most of them, including

Atlanta Pop on July 5. It was here that Michael Lang, a young rock promoter, first got the idea to bring her to Woodstock. On July 18 she appeared on the 'Dick Cavett Show' in New York. 'Dick Cavett was quite taken with her,' says Sam.

Cavett wrote in his autobiography, 'The last time I made moocah, or dug sweet Lucy [smoked marijuana], was with Janis Joplin, who gave me one that must have been rolled by Montezuma himself.' In another context, Cavett said, 'Have a pot orgasm twice a year, would be the limit in my book.'

In July, Janis exposed herself in front of 110,000 fans attending the Atlantic City rock festival. During her ninety-minute set on Saturday night, she'd been unable to stir the crowd, who'd given a cool reception to her new material and called out for her familiar hits. Aware that the scuttlebutt among the fans all day Saturday had been that the festival was bombing, that too many mediocre bands had been booked, Janis decided to give everyone something to talk about.

She began by dancing suggestively with Snooky Flowers, thrusting her pelvis like a stripper, and then, in a display calculated to upstage Morrison's flasher act in Miami, she crouched and opened her legs, revealing all. Some of the young men in the audience stroked themselves erotically. Screaming and cheering went on for minutes as the audience expressed their appreciation for an undeniably stellar moment in an otherwise-lackluster festival.

Janis played Forest Hills Stadium in New York on July 19. It was a cool, breezy night, and in the audience, Albert talked throughout Richie Haven's opening set, disturbing everyone around him. He was with some business associates and was bragging about what an intrepid agent he was. Then he extolled Janis, saying she was probably as bored with Havens as he was and itching to get onstage and steal the show.

Finally, she came on, receiving a tremendous ovation. Grossman observed that although her voice was different that night, she more than made up for it with her bumps and grinds.

Later, when Janis announced the final number, the audience protested so violently that policemen suddenly appeared from nowhere and surrounded the stage. She cursed the cops, ordering them out of her sight. As the police started to move away, she said, 'They got to understand, these pigs, that what's going on here is for *us;* it's not for them!'

This was Sam's last concert with Janis. After she'd fired him, he'd agreed to stay on long enough to train his replacement, John Till. 'I left the stage toward the end of the set,' Sam says, 'and went to put my guitar away. Albert had been backstage and had brought a mammoth bag of pistachio nuts. I scooped up some of these and put them in my guitar case. They were a symbol I was getting something from Albert, after all. I waited for the set to end. Janis came back and wanted to know why I had left the stage, but I think she really knew that my time was up and that I had done the right thing. I cleaned up some odds and ends in New York and left for the West Coast, where I rejoined Big Brother.'

By midsummer, Janis was busy juggling male and female lovers. Though '*Vi*-unce,' as she called Vince Mitchell, was unquestionably as potent and dependable a sex partner as she'd ever had, she missed making love with women and started urging Peggy to come to Woodstock, where Janis was to perform in August. When Peggy consented, Janis tried to break the news to Vince as gently as possible, telling him that she had a lover from San Francisco who'd be arriving any day. In practical terms, he was going to have to vacate her hotel room, where he'd been enjoying star treatment. She deliberately neglected to specify Peggy's gender, uncertain of

Vince's views on women having sex with one another.

Before appearing at Woodstock August 16, Janis caught a few days' vacation in the Virgin Islands, in a house loaned to her by one of the Woodstock production coordinators, John Morris. When she saw Morris later at Woodstock, she said, 'I loved staying in your house.'

'Well,' he said, 'how was it?'

'Oh, like anywhere else. I fucked a lot of strangers.' Morris thought, Uh-oh, we're in trouble. He could see that she was in no condition to perform. 'She had a bottle in each hand and had just gotten totally ripped . . . She was past it. We weren't going to get a great one. And it was an awful performance.'

Michael Lang, who conceived the Woodstock Music and Art Fair, says, 'Janis was not at her best at Woodstock.' Today, he manages Joe Cocker and other artists from his office in the SoHo section of Manhattan. Though Lang is in his forties, he still has the untamed look of a woodland satyr. He is disarmingly mellow, pensive, and friendly. In the sixties, he had a head shop in Florida that served as a counterculture community center and southeastern headquarters for radical movements and ideas. Says Michael, 'One day, I just knew that it was time for us to get together and look at each other and see if all the philosophizing we'd been doing was something we could live with. Music seemed an obvious catalyst.'

He staged the Miami Pop Festival in December 1968, featuring Fleetwood Mac, Richie Havens, and the Grateful Dead. Almost 100,000 attended. 'That was where the idea for Woodstock came to me,' Michael recalls. 'I saw the reaction of the kids there and knew that this was something special. Then I moved from Coconut Grove to Woodstock. The combination of living in Woodstock and having had that experience with large crowds led to the festival.'

A few weeks before Woodstock, Michael had seen Janis at the Atlanta Pop Festival, where she sang before an audience of 100,000. 'I was kind of disappointed in the band,' Michael says. 'I just didn't think they were doing her justice. They seemed thrown together and not as complementary to her as Big Brother had been. I went backstage and met her and she was pretty wasted.'

As Michael was putting together the Woodstock festival, Janis and the band were staying with Albert in Bearsville, nearby. Though Michael hadn't cared for her at Atlanta, he invited her to perform at Woodstock 'because she was an essential part of the music of that era, one of the founders, really.' He paid her ten thousand dollars.

Asked whether the enormous size of the crowd at Woodstock – 500,000 people – had perhaps intimidated Janis, as some writers claim, Michael points out that 'the Atlanta Pop Festival had one hundred thousand kids. So it wasn't half a million, but after the first hundred thousand, what's the difference? So I don't buy that. I think she was a bit out of it, but if the band had been more inspired, she would have been, too. It was really a matter of the music around her. She had trouble getting them going. I saw about half a set, and she was really trying to work them into a groove and it just wasn't happening. She wasn't any more out of it than she had been on many other nights when she'd done wonderful shows. I thought it was unfortunate.'

The film that was made at Woodstock, like *Monterey Pop*, is one of the key social documents of the time. Asked why Janis wasn't in the movie *Woodstock,* Michael replies, 'Albert felt the performance wasn't really up to what he wanted to expose. He held out basically on all of his acts. None of his performers was particularly stellar. The Band was not great that night, Janis wasn't great. Among his clients, Richie Havens was the exception. So it was an artistic decision on

Albert's part. It was never really a business decision.' Nick Gravenites disagrees on this point, stating that Albert told him he didn't care for the movie deals at either Woodstock or Monterey.

Janis's exclusion from *Woodstock* may have been the reason she detested it. She liked some of the music, she said, but as a cinema buff, she felt it lacked structure, ambling along without direction. It was as formless and interminable, she grumbled, as a *Rolling Stone* interview.

Stanley Mouse arrived at Woodstock early and started lettering signs. 'I'd just come back from England,' he says, 'and we did all the signs that were stuck on the trees, like "Go this way to the swimming hole." We were splashing through the mud.'

Like most of the stars at Woodstock, Janis was stranded at the Holiday Inn when it rained before the festival. The San Francisco musicians walked around embracing each other like long-lost relatives; they'd been on the road for several years and many of them had risen from hippie penury to fame and wealth since they'd last seen one another. As the rain continued, someone loaded the jukebox with coins and played 'Hey, Jude' over fifty times. Janis, Country Joe McDonald, Marty Balin, Richie Havens, Tim and Susan Hardin, Jerry Garcia, and Jack Casady led the room in chorus after chorus, linking arms and slowly rocking as they sang. Then, unlike the hungry hordes at the festival site, Janis, Grace Slick, and others feasted on a seven-course expense-account meal that included steak and champagne.

Gradually, people who'd braved it to the festival site began to come back to the motel with incredible stories about the record-shattering size of the crowd. Late Friday afternoon, Country Joe, long considered passe by the music industry, went on and was a surprise hit with his 'FUCK' chant. Says Michael Lang, 'The "Feel-Like-I'm-Fixin'-to-Die Rag" wasn't part of the official set. During one of the rainstorms, we needed someone to fill in and we weren't prepared to let an electric act go on. Joe had an acoustic guitar and could do it without getting fried. It was late Friday afternoon and it was great – he really got the crowd to pulling together.'

Janis didn't have to perform until the next day, so she and Vince went off to her room to make love. Janis warned him that they could be interrupted at any time by the arrival of her lover from San Francisco, though she still had not told him that her lover was a woman. When Peggy called from the Chelsea, Janis invited her to come to Woodstock.

Hours later, Peggy stood knocking on Janis's door at the Holiday Inn. Completely nude, Vince crawled off of Janis and let Peggy in. Looking past him, Peggy saw Janis, lolling in preorgasmic dishabille. Janis explained to Vince that Peggy was her lover, apologizing profusely but reminding him that he'd been forewarned about clearing out as soon as his replacement arrived. Wiggling into his jockey shorts, the complaisant roadie dressed and started to leave. At the door, Janis consoled him with a kiss, caressed his butt, then waved him away, a rock queen in complete control of her consort. Sexually, she'd arrived at the point where she could have anything she wanted – and get away with it. This is true of most rock stars at the apex of their fame. She was no different from Elvis or any one of the Beatles in this respect, except that as a woman she would be judged more harshly than her male counterparts.

Peggy and Janis at last fell asleep well after sunrise. At noon, Janis held a press conference and fondled Peggy's breasts in front of twenty-five reporters. When Peggy attempted to restrain her, Janis pompously proclaimed her immunity from ordinary human constraints. In a sense, she was right. Reporters protected Janis, exposing neither her heroin addiction nor her wide-ranging sexual tastes.

Though Janis was to perform in the afternoon, she was advised that the festival was ten hours behind schedule and she wouldn't be going on until the evening. She stayed high on heroin until a helicopter arrived to transport her to the festival site. When she arrived at her tent, she started drinking tequila and vodka on top of the heroin. Grossman was decked out guru-style in all white. Lurking around behind the scenes, Bill Graham appeared to be baffled that the greatest event in the history of rock had gone on despite, or perhaps because of, his absence at the helm.

Deciding she needed a booster shot of heroin just before her performance, Janis entered a filthy Portosan toilet to fix. Though excrement was piled inches above the toilet seat, she stood in the stinking crapper until she had cooked up her heroin and injected it. Outside, angry people with more pressing needs yelled for her to hurry up and get out of the Portosan.

Just before going onstage, she almost blacked out. In the distance, she could hear the Grateful Dead, who were limping through an uninspired set as a maniac threw bad brown acid from the stage. As a result of the rain and sixty-mile-an-hour wind, the stage was slowly sliding into the mud. Clutching a bottle in each fist, Janis alternated slugs of vodka and tequila until she was so loaded that the only way she could make it to the stage, which had now been secured, was with three people supporting her and then literally shoving her to the microphone.

According to writer Ellen Sander, a great cheer went up for Janis and her new band, which most of the audience were seeing for the first time. The official Woodstock photographer, Henry Diltz, says, 'She was tortured and crying in the microphone. She really screamed in agony in those songs. She really meant it. You could see that in the way she contorted her face and her body.' In one of Diltz's still photographs, she is hanging on to the mike with both hands, her face a waxen junkie's mask, slit-eyed and reptilian. Somehow, she plodded through 'Piece of My Heart,' 'Summertime,' 'Little Girl Blue,' and 'Try.' Says Sander, 'She danced with them as if they were one. They shouted back at her; they wouldn't let her off until they'd drained off every drop of her energy.' At 1:30 A.M. Sunday, Sly and the Family Stone came on and started singing 'I Want to Take You Higher.' Grace Slick and Janis began a joyful dance together, seeming to levitate each time Sly shouted 'higher!'

When Crosby, Stills and Nash made their historic Woodstock debut, Janis was among the stars standing behind them in a semicircle. David Crosby recalls looking around and seeing 'everyone we respected in the whole goddamn music business' – Janis, Grace, Sly, Jimi Hendrix, Robbie Robertson, Levon Helm, the Who, and Paul Kantner.

Janis returned to her tent and took more heroin. Refusing to talk to a reporter from *Life,* she bellowed, 'I'm not talking to fucking *any*body. Fuck him, man, and fuck the world.' She knew she'd blown it, musically at least, in front of the largest group of people ever assembled in one place. That hadn't prevented the newly christened 'Woodstock nation' from according her the kind of respect usually reserved for heroes and saints. To Wavy Gravy, Woodstock MC and co-ordinator of the freak-out tents, it was Janis who awakened the famous Woodstock spirit with her simple announcement: 'If you have some food left, share it with your brother and sister – the person on your left and the person on your right.'

For breakfast the next day, Janis had her usual junkie special – pie and ice cream. Like most heroin addicts, she consumed sugar compulsively, disregarding dietary considerations. After they'd eaten, she and Peggy drove to Manhattan and stayed in Janis's room at the Chelsea. 'Automatically, I assumed they were holed up at the Chelsea fucking and sucking and doing dope,' says Kim, whom Peggy had left behind on the West Coast. A tall, blond political activist, a friend of both Janis's and Peggy's, came by the Chelsea, shot up heroin, and treated them to a spectacular display of almost Oriental self-control, provoking them to two orgasms each before finally ejaculating into Peggy. His specialty was a relentless rhythm that never varied, even in the throes of passion. Janis's only complaint was that Peggy rather than she had been the recipient of his semen. He must have found Peggy more attractive, Janis bitched.

She recovered quickly, however, and was ready for another three-ways when Motorcycle Richie suddenly appeared at the Chelsea, looking for a good time. Her heroin supply was completely depleted, and she gave Motorcycle Richie five hundred dollars, telling him to go out on the streets and score some junk. When he still hadn't returned three hours later, she grew anxious and suspicious, knowing from bitter experience that people who go on dope runs frequently consume the booty or sell it for profit. Finally, Motorcycle Richie returned, bleeding profusely from twenty knife wounds. He'd been mugged in Bedford-Stuyvesant after he'd asked three guys where to buy dope. Janis undressed him, led him to the bathtub, sponged him off with warm water, and dressed his wounds, carefully inspecting them for authenticity.

Back in San Francisco, Kim was not pleased by Peggy's dalliance with Janis. Says Kim today, 'My relationship with Janis was quite friendly until Peggy and Janis went to Woodstock together. After that, Janis wasn't quite the same with me as she had been.' An emotional bond had been forged between Peggy and Janis, and now, for the first time,

Peggy considered ending her relationship with Kim. Since Peggy and Janis were spending so many nights together, Peggy even thought of going to live with Janis. Still, Peggy could never bring herself to leave Kim, whose physical appeal remained as strong as ever.

Janis appeared at many of the rock concerts of 1969 – Lewisville (Texas), New Orleans Pop, and West Palm Beach – but somehow she missed Altamont, where her good friends the Hell's Angels had been hired as security and one of them killed a man. Her relationship with the Angels had begun to turn sour one night in 1969 when she and Sunshine were helping Sweet William celebrate his birthday. Janis went over to the Keystone Club in North Beach, where Sunshine was a waitress, just in time to see the Hell's Angels roar up on their choppers. They always partied at the Keystone after their club meetings on Wednesday nights, drinking and listening to Nick Gravenites and Michael Bloomfield, who were the house band. Then, says Sunshine, 'Janis and I, Sweet William, and two other Angels went back to Noe Street. It was supposed to be a private party, just us. We got in the house, and there was a stack of *Kozmic Blues* close to the front door.'

Kozmic Blues was just about to be released, and Columbia had sent Janis the usual consignment of complimentary copies. 'Janis and I had just gotten down, shots of dope,' Sunshine says, 'and all of a sudden there's people ringing the front doorbell, there's people looking in the window. All these Hell's Angels started climbing in the window and pouring through the front door.'

Janis looked around and said, 'I didn't invite all these people.'

'You invite me and you invite my brothers,' Sweet William said.

'No, that's not right,' she said. She then became upset and

began to scream. Says Sunshine, 'As the Hell's Angels started filing out, they all grabbed copies of *Kozmic Blues* from the stack.' About thirty of them had helped themselves to Janis's complimentary copies before she went up to a huge six-foot-six Angel. 'You motherfucker!' she said. 'Give me back my record!' Sweet William and another Angel grabbed her and said, 'Hey, you know, by inviting us, you invited them.' But she yelled again at the six-footer. 'Come back here and give me that tape!' He looked her over and then reached out and whopped her across the face. She hit the wall and started sliding down to the floor. He glared at her and said, 'You bitch.'

'I never saw a look on her face like this before,' says Sunshine. 'She just burst into tears.' He was the last of the Angels to leave the apartment, and Janis ended up with about six copies of the LP to give to her friends.

Sunshine believes 'the occurrence with *Kozmic Blues* and getting slapped really destroyed her faith in the Angels. She felt that she'd given them a lot – the appreciation on *Cheap Thrills* and several benefits, including the one for Chocolate George. So why were they treating her so bad? She didn't realize that *that* was who they were.

'After the Noe Street incident, Altamont happened and Janis began to see that she had brought this on herself by her involvement with Freewheelin' Frank.'

The new man in Janis's life in the fall of 1969 was one of the pioneers of heavy metal – Paul Whaley, founder and drummer in the rock band Blue Cheer. Though diminutive, his wiry body was proof that dynamite often comes in small packages. His three-man band was named after a powerful brand of LSD, and they used six Marshall amplifiers, with twenty-four speakers on each, the loudest anyone had ever heard. Gut, the former Hell's Angel who managed them, said,

'They play so hard and so heavy, they make cottage cheese out of the air.' Their revival of Eddie Cochran's 'Summertime Blues' hit the singles chart at number fourteen, and their LP *Vincebus Eruptum* made it to number eleven. Whaley played his drums so hard that he wore thick gloves and filed his drumsticks to get a blunter sound. Critic Lillian Roxon said, 'There are people who see in their music, not the joyous visions of San Francisco acid rock, but the horrors of a bad STP trip, and *that,* they say, is what the sound is all about.'

Whaley had dropped out of the group in April 1969 and now had plenty of leisure time to spend with Janis. She was always in an exceptionally good mood after he made love to her. On September 20, she was positively beaming when Peggy met her at the Landmark shortly before Janis's Hollywood Bowl concert. Janis attributed her high spirits to Whaley, who'd just injected heroin with her and made love to her for hours. To Peggy, Whaley was unappealing on at least two counts – he was skinny and he was married. Janis, however, was a pushover for his punk style, pimples and all.

Shelley Winters, Ann-Margret, and a number of other celebrities attended Janis's Hollywood Bowl concert that night. Janis arrived backstage with Peggy and Sam, who'd given her a lift from the Landmark, where Sam was also registered. Shelley Winters recalls, 'I took my daughter's sweet-sixteen party, and during the concert sixteen thousand people lit up marijuana joints. You could get high from just being there, and when I saw my kid taking deep breaths, I didn't know what to do. You can't tell someone to stop breathing.'

When Janis sang 'Summertime,' Sam allegedly complained to Peggy that the new guitarist was using all his licks. If Janis wasn't going to change the accompaniment, he said, she'd might as well have kept him on. Irate, he walked out in the middle of the show and took Peggy with him. Back at the

Landmark, Sam reportedly used a credit card to break into Janis's room and steal her heroin.

Meanwhile, Janis finished her show at the Bowl and discovered that she was without a ride home. When fans mobbed her in the parking lot, she started stumbling down Highland Avenue toward the Landmark on foot. The spectacle of a star tramping down the Hollywood Hills, pursued by curious onlookers, incensed her less than the fact that Sam and Peggy had had the effrontery to walk out in the middle of her concert.

Peggy performed expert oral sex on Janis that night, which dissipated Janis's anger, if not her ego. Even in the middle of the sex act, Janis couldn't stop gloating over the fact that she'd made sixty thousand dollars for the Bowl performance. Since her set had lasted only half an hour, she figured she was now worth two grand per minute.

A couple of months later, Janis was back in LA for various television commitments, including ABC-TV's 'Music Scene,' produced by her old friend Carl Gottlieb, and the 'Tom Jones Show.' Again she became involved with Sam and Peggy, and they were all doing heroin and getting deeper into trouble with it. While Janis was on the set of the 'Tom Jones Show,' Sam called her from jail and asked her to bail him out. He'd been arrested while riding a borrowed motorcycle on the Strip. Says Sam today, 'I got stopped by the police and they put me in jail for no registration and license. I was just in there for a short time before Janis got me out.'

Kozmic Blues was released to mediocre reviews but shot to number five on the *Billboard* chart on October 18 and remained in the Top 40 for a total of sixteen weeks – deservedly so. It's an underrated album and, if for no other reason than 'Little Girl Blue,' it should be treasured. Sam Andrew acquired an early tape of the LP and took it over to Dave Getz's house, playing it for Peter, James, and Dave.

'They didn't like it,' Sam says. 'I did one sort of guitar smear in a solo on "Work Me, Lord," and James perked up. "That's the best thing on the album," he said, but I think he was just trying to find something there that he could relate to.'

From the first cut, 'Try,' by Jerry Ragovoy, who'd written Janis's hit 'Piece of My Heart,' this is a rousing LP. In 'Try,' Luis Gasca's trumpet is riveting, Sam and Snooky coo the background vocals, and Janis soars over it all, powerful and inventive in her scatlike flights. Opening the next cut, 'Maybe,' are Sam on guitar and Richard Kermode on organ, and Janis again is at her most poignant and appealing. Her supple and melodic voice easily reaches for thrilling high notes. Through part of 'Maybe,' Sam and Janis sing a duet, always a treat. 'Work Me, Lord' is a Nick Gravenites song, and it gives Janis a chance to present her own compelling version of gospel singing.

Janis's great moment on the album comes with 'Little Girl Blue.' It opens with Sam draping guitar chords over Janis's voice like a weeping willow. 'We added a string quartet,' Sam recalls. 'It was just Janis and me on our track, and everything else was added later, strings, drums, and Brad Campbell on bass.' The arrangement is by Gabriel Mekler, though Sam says that 'Michael Bloomfield helped. He was standing around and giving some suggestions.'

When Clive Davis first heard Janis's tape of 'Little Girl Blue,' he was so excited, he played it for the composer Richard Rodgers. 'I want you to hear what this girl from San Francisco is doing with your song,' Davis said. Rodgers hated it, sputtering, 'If I am expected to undergo this kind of humiliation, I don't see how I can ever again cut another record at Columbia.'

In October 1969, Janis had her first real vacation in years. Indicative of the state of her personal life was the fact that her companions were roadies on her payroll – Vince Mitchell and George Ostrow. Vince brought his brother along and they went camping in the woods around Austin, hiking, living in tents, sleeping in sleeping bags, swimming, rowing, and fishing. Janis loved playing hausfrau for the boys, puttering about her makeshift kitchen and cooking all their meals.

Later that month, she did concerts at the University of Texas in Austin and in Houston, and an old classmate, Janice Hayes Cavada, caught the Houston show. 'She was drinking from a bottle,' Janice remembers. 'Her mother was there and her attitude was, We're here, but we don't really like this music.' The following year, her father, Seth, would tell Chet Flippo noncommittally, 'We saw her twice in Houston, at the Coliseum and the Music Hall.' Period.

Returning to San Francisco, Janis again contacted Linda Gravenites in London and promised to stay off smack if Linda would return to the United States and share Janis's new home in Larkspur, a suburban community off Highway 101, just north of the Golden Gate Bridge. She also made numerous other resolutions: She'd learn horseback riding, practice yoga, become a pianist, and lead a wholesome life. One day, Linda called and said, 'I'm ready to come right now.' She flew to New York and Janis met her at One Fifth Avenue, a hotel in Greenwich Village.

'She was seeing cute young boys,' Linda recalls. 'She liked jolly punks and mountain men. She liked a whole lot. She had eclectic taste. She was so funny. If she was interested in someone, you could tell. She started glowing, as if she'd been switched on like a light and one thousand candlepower went on inside.' Asked how Janis managed to take on so many one-night stands without getting robbed or beaten up, Linda says, 'On one tour, there was a pretty young boy in her dressing room, and she took him home to the roadhouse. She said *he* was a mistake!'

While in New York in the autumn of 1969, Linda started designing Janis's clothes for her big Madison Square Garden concert in December. Janis wanted something special not only for the show but for the all-star party that Clive Davis had promised to throw for her at his Central Park West apartment later. Linda shopped around New York and found some rare, costly eighty-dollar chiffon material that had velvet woven into it, and she started to work on the two outfits. Before the Garden, however, Janis played Tampa, Florida, where she had her worst collision with the law since her Berkeley shoplifting bust.

November 16, 1969, the evening of her Tampa show, was unusually cold for Florida. Arctic air had been blowing across the South and the temperature in Tampa had dipped to twenty-eight degrees by the time she arrived at Curtis-Hixon Hall on Sunday night, a few hours before showtime. She and Snooky Flowers were horsing around in the dressing room when a Tampa man came in and invited them to a party after the concert. Sizing him up as a square, Snooky said, 'I'll never go to another party in Florida. I went to one in Miami and it stank.'

'But you don't understand,' the man said. 'You'll have a great time. Besides, the Turtles and Three Dog Night, when they were here a few weeks ago—'

Janis jumped up, do-si-doed with Snooky, and mocked the Tampa man to his face. 'Hot dog!' she said. 'The Turtles! We wouldn't miss it for the world.' He went to the door dispiritedly, and as he left, they could hear the crowd cheering the opening act, B. B. King.

When Janis finally charged onstage and started singing, the excitement was so great that the crowd of 3,500 surged toward the front of the auditorium. Says Linda Gravenites, 'Janis had the idea that a concert wasn't quite a success unless the stage got mobbed.' The city police, loitering backstage, were completely unaware of the initial rush, but the security guards in the auditorium ran back and said they had a 'potential riot' on their hands. The cops appeared in the auditorium seconds later and started shoving people around and ordering them back to their seats. Janis bent over, reached down from the stage, and tapped a cop on the head. 'Listen, mister,' she said, speaking in a concerned but polite tone, 'I've been to more of these things than you have and no one's ever hurt nothing. Leave them alone.' The microphone picked up every word, and the crowd began to cheer her wildly.

Janis resumed her song, leaving the kids blocking the aisles and filling the area in front of the stage. When she finished, she said, 'Now listen, we can't go fuck with each other because that will give them [the police] something to chop on. If we don't hurt nothing, they can't say shit.'

At this point, the manager of the hall, Colonel William Wilson, objected to Janis's language. Though he later said that the crowd 'had not really been unruly,' he ordered the cops to move in with bullhorns and disperse the crowd. Janis was in the middle of the low-key 'Summertime' when Det. L. F. Napoli raised his bullhorn. 'I was trying to build a sensuous mood,' she said, 'when suddenly a cop with a bullhorn comes into my song, yelling at the kids.' Stopping in the middle of the song, she shot Napoli a dirty look. Again a roar went up from the audience, and it was during the next song that Janis finally pushed the cops over the edge. When they once again attempted to clear the aisles, she stopped and said, 'Don't fuck with those people. Hey mister, what are you so uptight about? Did you buy a five-dollar ticket?' Sgt. Ed Williams left the auditorium and went off to secure a warrant for her arrest for using 'vulgar and indecent language.' Someone backstage caught Janis's attention and said, 'Fer chrissakes, tell the kids to sit down!'

'I'm not telling them shit!' she retorted, and the crowd yelled their approval. By now, they were jumping up and down all over the auditorium, trying to get a better look at her and at the unscheduled crisis unfolding before their eyes. Even though reporters covering the event all agreed that 'there was no riot, fight, or physical conflict,' the management now made an uncalled-for decision. The electricity to the stage was cut off and the houselights went up, halting the show in its tracks. 'The main damage,' Colonel Wilson said, 'was that the people responded to her call for disorder.'

Standing onstage in Curtis-Hixon Hall, Janis lost her temper when her amps went dead, and yelled, 'Look here, Mr. Hixon, you coward, get up here. Shit! Look kids, Mr. Hixon is uptight because you're standing on his seats. So everyone, when you leave, walk up to him and apologize.' At that point, the police, their warrants in hand, went backstage to lie in wait for her. Once they had quit the auditorium, everything calmed down and Janis finished her performance without incident.

Linda had been in Janis's dressing room throughout the show 'because there was somebody weird back there and I was guarding her wonderful lynx coat. I gathered there were a lot of people trying to get past the cops and get to the stage, and she was egging them on and I think sort of bad-mouthing the cops, because one of them came wandering backstage and shook his head and said, "She shouldn't have called us pigs!" I thought, Whoops! I found someone and said, "Listen, Janis is going to get busted. Go back to the motel, get it fixed. Any dope in anybody's room, get rid of it! Something's going to happen! It's going to be bad!"'

After Janis took her bows, she went backstage and found it crawling with cops. Spotting Detective Napoli, she went up to him and threatened to kick him in the face. 'Cool it,' he said. She continued to curse him and then abruptly turned and made a beeline for her dressing room. There, at midnight, she was immediately 'chopped' with a warrant and arrested. Sergeant Williams said she was 'somewhat rude but not loud.' She was charged with 'vulgar and indecent language' on two counts: The first was on a warrant sworn out by Sergeant Williams relating to her language during the concert and the second count was added by Detective Napoli for the offstage dressing-down she gave him.

A *Tampa Tribune* reporter was at her dressing room door, but the police refused to let Janis make any statements, a violation of her constitutional rights. Later, they claimed that the reporter hadn't shown proper press credentials. They hustled Janis to the police station and then booked her into City Jail at 12:14 A.M.

'If I have to sit in jail, I would like it to be with the Rolling Stones,' she said. The *Tribune* carried the story atop page one with the banner headline POLICE TOLD JANIS, "COOL IT," THEN THREW HER IN THE COOLER. 'Janis isn't in as deep as Morrison,' said the story, 'who is pending trial in Miami April 27th on six counts: five misdemeanors and one felonious charge of lewd and lascivious behavior in public by exposing his private parts.'

Says Linda, 'It was bad. We went and sat in a cop station almost all night. They had her in a back room, questioning her. We were there in the front, waiting for her to be bailed out. It took a few hours before they released her. I don't know if they searched our motel rooms. If they did, there was nothing there. I had somebody take care of it real early.'

According to the *Tribune*, Janis was released at 1:15 A.M., following payment of a $504 bond, $252 per count. The following day, the paper ran a front-page story questioning the legality of the police action against Janis. Headlined POLICE FACED LEGAL PARADOX, the story pointed out that 'the

Janis Joplin concert Sunday night was as disorderly as the average football game. If fans at a football game crowd the sidelines and ignore the official request to move back, the fans are out of order yet orderly.' The article declared that nothing more serious had happened than 'excited youths dancing and standing on chairs to get a better look at a most entertaining star,' and concluded that 'the authorities were also excited.'

Janis talked to her lawyer, Herbert G. Goldburg, on Wednesday and later appeared before Judge Nick Falsone in municipal court for her hearing on obscenity charges. Her trial was continued, and after the hearing she told reporters that she'd been arrested because 'old people are running scared. They're going to lose their kids and they are trying to get their kids back to them. All the people telling kids what to do, what to wear, where to go . . . that's not going to help. It just makes us [rock 'n' rollers] more attractive.'

She said she would be 'willing to do it again . . . The kids were just like kids everywhere. They wanted to get closer, to be a part of the show. I've played just about everywhere in the country and this is the first time I've ever been arrested. I say anything I want onstage.'

Various city officials managed to take potshots at Janis before she left town. City comptroller Logan Browning, who'd presented a four-thousand-dollar check to the show promoter, stopped payment until damages were determined. While Colonel Wilson admitted, 'The only damage is dirt on the chairs,' he said he'd be 'more cautious [in booking bands] in the future. We don't need this kind of entertainment in Tampa.'

When Mayor Dick Greco confirmed that he would not tolerate her type of performance in Tampa, Janis said she felt it 'strange that they had to drag out the mayor to justify the arrest.' Tampa hadn't been a complete loss, though. She'd 'caught some sun and fish. I caught one catfish and saw a very, very ugly toadfish that someone else caught. The only way I'll ever perform here again is if the promoter hires his own security force.' She'd only come back to Tampa 'if I have to. I'd rather just leave Tampa. Perform other gigs. Go to California.'

On March 4, 1970, Janis would be fined two hundred dollars in absentia on the obscenity charges and the case then became closed. The Floridians had not managed to tame her – the Janis Joplin act remained the wildest in rock. But in personal terms, the arrest represented such a low bottom for Janis that in the following months she consulted doctors about her drinking and drugging and made an effort to kick heroin.

In December 1969, Albert sent her to Dr. Edmund Rothschild, a New York internist specializing in endocrinology, who put her on methadone and Valium and also advised her to do something about her drinking. She told another physician, Dr. Howard Goldin, that she was drinking up to a pint of alcohol a day, in addition to shooting heroin and amphetamines. Medical science proved as helpless as Janis herself in coping with her alcoholism and addiction. She made no attempt to correct the character defects, such as low self-esteem, that drove her to drink and drug.

As the date for her Garden appearance drew near, New York's fashion arbiters saluted her as a style innovator. *Vogue* endorsed her 'wrath and rawness' and asked her where she got her clothes. 'Linda turns them out slowly and turns them out well and only turns them out for those she likes,' Janis replied. The New York boutique Abracadabra ran an ad in *The Village Voice* saying, 'What are you wearing to Janis's concert?' and listed fifty possibilities, including 'velvet gaucho pants' and 'oversized fringe stoles.' *Vogue* gushed, 'Janis Joplin the divine – when she shakes up the places like

Madison Square Garden she's a flashing vision of violets and purples – of panne velvet, silvery chiffon . . . and Janis's audiences are helping to make purple hues big, too.'

Describing the outfit she created for Janis's Garden concert, Linda says, 'From one side of the fabric to the other, the color went from sea-foamy green to a forest green. I used figured velvet woven into chiffon. Part of it was just chiffon see-through, part was with velvet. It was thirty dollars a yard then, which would be eighty dollars now – the most expensive material around.'

Linda called Janis's performance that night 'wonderful. The whole Garden was vibrating like a drum head. It seemed to be bouncing, but maybe that was just the energy from so many people jumping up and down.' Clive Davis, on the other hand, found Janis only 'fairly routine' that night, but the concert improved when she summoned Paul Butterfield and Johnny Winter to jam with her. Winter was from Beaumont, just a stone's throw from Port Arthur, and the chemistry between him and Janis 'was awesome,' wrote Davis. 'Winter played a searing, booming guitar and Janis faced him nose-to-nose, holding the microphone and wailing right back at him, each raising the other to a higher energy level. By the end of the set, Janis was dripping wet, bushy hair flying in all directions.'

The Village Voice went on a rampage, chastising her as 'the virago queen' and dismissing the concert as a 'wing-ding ego trip.' She was 'thoughtless of people's welfare' when she tried to incite them to riot. At the concert, she'd yelled, 'What are you doing just sitting there – this is rock 'n' roll!' A young man had jumped up, grabbed her, and started kissing her. The musicians had had to haul her back into a standing position onstage. 'That's not quite what I had in mind,' she'd said.

The New York Times thought she was 'excellent' and even had good words for the Kozmic Blues Band – a 'powerful and spontaneously happy display of brass blues and rock.' The *New York Post* reviewer pointed out that she hadn't filled the house – the Garden was '6,000 short of capacity.'

At one point in the show, Janis had mentioned Joe Namath, sighing into the mike and saying, 'Joe, where are you?' Namath, who was just a few months younger than Janis, had been an all-American quarterback at the University of Alabama before coming to the New York Jets in 1965 at what was then a record salary – $387,000, plus a Lincoln Continental convertible. 'Joe Willie,' who was six feet two inches tall and weighed 195 pounds, often stood in front of his mirror and said, 'Ah cain't wait until tomorrow, 'cause I get better-lookin' every day.'

Janis had recently met a *Playboy* interviewer who'd written the first magazine article on Namath. 'My God, you know Namath!' she said. 'Listen, you introduce me to Joe Namath and I'll—' And she'd listed exquisite-sounding acts she'd perform on Namath's body, adding, 'I'm serious, just introduce me to him – and you won't be sorry, either.'

One night, she met Namath in the bar he owned, which was called Bachelors III, and later joined him in his pied-à-terre over the bar. She later described the scene to her friend Kenai, who recalls, 'They all got stoned on tequila. Namath passed out on top of Janis, who yelled, "Help me get out of here! He's a big man!" '

Carl Gottlieb also confirms that 'she connected with Namath – at that time he was Broadway Joe – and went to his apartment with him. She fucked him on an expensive white area rug. At the end of the evening, she said, "Hey, man, can I have the rug?"

' "What for?" he asked.

' "As a remembrance of you, man. It was really wonderful."

'Reluctantly, because it was an expensive rug, he said, "Yeah. Sure, you can have the rug."

'So she said, "Thanks, man," took the rug, went downstairs to the limo driver, and said, "Hey, man, you want a rug?" and gave it to him. It was more for the manipulative fun of it than for the trophy. She told me she thought, Let's see how much I can get from this guy. Okay, I got it, but what do I need with this rug? I know she didn't spend the night, because the limo driver was waiting downstairs.'

Janis later told Carl that she'd been 'scalp collecting' at this time and that one of the year's champion track stars was yet another conquest. According to Janis, after she got through with Namath and the runner, 'Namath blew a game, and the sprinter could hardly walk, let alone sprint. I destroyed them all.' Says Carl, 'She was ferocious and very athletic.' Her old friend Henry Carr confirms that she mentioned Joe's name at Madison Square Garden because 'she and Joe got it on.'

She'd expected Namath to attend her Garden performance and was very disappointed when he failed to. Her spirits improved considerably at the dazzling party that Clive Davis threw for her after the concert. 'She'd announced to the crowd at the Garden that this was the last encore because she had a great new dress and she was looking forward to this party,' says Davis. 'Her sense of anticipation for this special party in her honor showed her feminine side, which was just adorable. I'd invited the elite of the music world to meet her, and this was pretty much her first exposure to the industry at that level.'

Again Janis wore a Linda Gravenites creation. 'I cut it from a piece of black paisley,' Linda says. 'It was chiffon and figured velvet, and it went from almost no velvet above to very much velvet toward the bottom.' Clive Davis describes the outfit as 'long black satin pants and a low-cut, see-through black chiffon top.'

Davis had assembled 'a gilt-edged crowd, including Dylan,

Miles Davis, and Tony Bennett. I did not attempt to get down; I wasn't having soul food. I did it in my style of life. It was a catered affair, and it was elegant, with black-tie waiters and waitresses.'

When Janis arrived at 1:00 A.M., Davis noticed that she was 'plainly high.' After her concert, she'd gone back to her hotel room and injected heroin. So much for the methadone treatment, which had proved totally ineffective.

'She literally *glowed* at the attention,' says Davis, 'talking with Dylan . . . and meeting other music luminaries. She said hello to everybody and was very warm to all.' It was a typically high-powered New York soiree, one mixing press, celebrities, managers, and captains of industry in a deceptively calm, low-key setting. It was 'a scene of candlelight and subdued conversations, champagne and caviar,' Davis notes. The guest list included Johnny Winter, Edgar Winter, Paul Butterfield, Rick Derringer, Laura Nyro, Albert Grossman, Lou Adler, Jack Holzman (president of Elektra Records), Neil Bogart (head of Buddah Records), Larry Utall (head of Bell Records), and columnists Earl Wilson and Leonard Lyons.

Linda remembers that 'Bob Dylan was a lot nicer than I thought he'd be. He's a very frail little guy, very small. Janis introduced me to him and told him I made a lot of her clothes. And then I said, "Hey, man, you write some nice songs." He said, "Yes, I do." I felt that if I had made any kind of overstatement, he would have said just as quickly that I was full of shit.'

Laura Nyro, wearing a promlike formal, was so fearful of Janis's anger should she steal any of the spotlight that she remained in a bedroom. When Dylan heard that Laura was at the party, he searched her out and had a tête-à-tête. He'd been playing her songs, he told her, and he really liked them. She was petrified. 'She giggled and could barely talk,' Davis recalls. 'Dylan for once kept the conversation going practically by himself.'

Before leaving New York, Janis was photographed by Scavullo for *Harper's Bazaar*. 'At this point, she didn't have an extra ounce on her little body,' Linda says, showing me one of Scavullo's portraits. 'Look at that body – that's just as tight as can be. She went up and down and she worried about it when she went up.' Linda laughs as she recalls Scavullo's efforts to pose Janis. 'He said, "Look this way" and "Look that way," and Janis just stopped and laughed at him and said, "Aw, man, you're crazy!" He caught her at that moment and it's one of the finest pictures of her.' In another Scavullo photo, she's wearing a trendy outfit designed by Nudie, the popular LA designer for rock and country and western stars. It was a purple bell-bottomed pantsuit with intricate rhinestone embroidery.

When Janis returned to the West Coast, she and Linda moved from Noe to the house Janis had purchased in Larkspur. Though Janis liked to think of Larkspur as the country, it's really just another congested San Francisco suburb. The main drag, Magnolia Avenue, retains a Wild West flavor, with the Silver Peso bar and a ramshackle hotel. Janis loved to shoot pool in the Silver Peso and considered buying it and running it. My visit to the bar is on a quiet Sunday morning, but a mellow crowd of bikers and their ladies are already enjoying their noontime beers. The sign outside is a giant neon martini glass with a golden toothpick in it, and the building is a seedy two-story affair with a stucco bottom and asbestos siding on top.

Branching off Magnolia are various streets leading into the woodsy residential areas, and Janis's house is down Baltimore Avenue. Big redwood and madrone trees give the feeling of a forest, though the houses stand side by side, and deer and raccoon are fairly common sights. Janis's house, the only one in the cul-de-sac at the end of Baltimore, is situated in a stand of redwoods against a green hillside. The house has brown shingles and a sharply angled roof, looking more like a beach house than a cabin in the woods. A basketball hoop is attached to a tall redwood, and a rough-hewn wooden fence separates the property from the street.

'I call it modular because there were three separate sections connected only by a hallway,' says Linda. 'Janis's section had its own bath with a sunken bathtub, and her bedroom opened onto the deck, which had a huge redwood growing through it. My section was a bathroom and bedroom, with a closet in the hallway, which had the washing machine and dryer.' The big living room had lots of stone and glass and a jumbo fireplace.

One day, Dave Richards came riding back into Janis's life on his big Harley. Her former roadie was now a carpenter and Janis hired him to turn the garage into a recording studio. Janis's companion at this time, according to Kenai, was a 'pimply young blond Englishman she'd brought back from her European tour. He stayed a few months, and then she paid his fare home.'

Four hundred people attended her gala housewarming, including Kenai, Kim, Peggy, all of Big Brother except for Sam, who declined his invitation, the Kozmic Blues Band, Arlo Guthrie, Ralph Gleason, Nick Gravenites, Mike Bloomfield, Janis's old friend Jonna Harlan, and, of course, Linda. Kenai recalled that his housewarming gift to Janis was an antique coffeepot and a waffle iron.

According to James Gurley, during the party, Janis confided to him that she was going to fire the Kozmic Blues Band. Again, as she'd been with Big Brother, she was concerned about bad reviews. 'She was so misguided,' says Gurley, 'basing her whole strategy on trying to please highfalutin critics who sit there with their nose in the air sayin', "Oh, this is really not quite good enough." It makes them feel smarter to assume a superior air. She was always sorry [that she'd left Big Brother], and said she had a lot of pressure on her. We talked about *Cheap Thrills,* how we'd had a number-one hit record for eight weeks running, in company with the Beatles, the Rolling Stones, Jimi Hendrix, the Doors, all the heavyweights of that time. We talked about that a lot.' After her smash hit with Big Brother, Janis was acutely aware that *Kozmic Blues,* which stayed at number five, had failed to match her earlier success.

As usual at her parties, her bedroom became a shooting gallery. Secluding themselves, she, Peggy, and Michael Bloomfield injected heroin. Though Janis was drawn to Michael, she didn't try to compete with Peggy, and after the party, Peggy and Bloomfield went to his place in Mill Valley. Peggy became so obsessed with him that she completely got over her fixation on Sam, and Bloomfield became her new fascination.

At the end of 1969, Janis won *Jazz and Pop* magazine's International Critics Poll, which named her Best Female Pop Singer for the year. But with the new decade, 1970, she found little in her life to rejoice over. The isolation of her suburban home terrified her. She climbed in her Porsche and raced around Marin County on a ceaseless search for diversion. She discovered the Trident bar in Sausalito, fell in love with it, and often drank there until closing time. One of the most romantic and appealing bar-restaurants in the world, located on Bridgeway, Sausalito's main street, the Trident, supported by timber pilings, juts out over the water. One of the owners, who'd once managed the Kingston Trio, had given the Trident a look of hip chic – all wood, ferns, large windows, and an open-air deck overlooking San Francisco Bay and the Golden Gate Bridge, with the city, Tiburon, and Angel Island beyond. The waitresses were sexy and staggeringly hip, some sporting tattoos, nose rings, and see-through clothes. The Trident became a second home for Janis, a place to meet her girlfriends, gossip, shoot up, get drunk, and figure out where to go next.

Linda would have nothing to do with the Trident scene. She was enjoying the peace that she thought they'd come to the country in search of and was wondering why Janis refused to stop and smell the flowers. If Janis didn't forgo heroin, and soon, Linda would again have to leave her.

One night, Janis was drinking in a Berkeley bar when she picked up a long-haired dope dealer, gave him her address, and said, 'Race you to the Larkspur exit.' Pushing the Porsche to 80 mph, she beat him to the house, went in, and told a girlfriend, 'Take your clothes off.' When her date arrived, Janis said to the young woman, 'You go warm him up. I'll be there in a minute,' indicating the twelve-point fur rug in her bedroom.

Janis went on methadone again in January 1970. Says Linda, 'When she'd come back from England, she'd asked me what my attitude toward dope was. I said, "As long as I think you're going to quit, I can take it, but if I think you're always going to be on it, I can't stand it." '

Janis suggested that she and Linda do something really amusing, like go to Carnival in Rio, and she'd give up drugs. Ever since she'd seen the movie *Black Orpheus,* Janis had longed to experience Carnival. 'The idea,' Linda says, 'was that Janis could stay so busy having fun that she wouldn't have any time to think about heroin.'

The $2,500 worth of heroin that Janis was still holding, she laid on Peggy during the drive to the airport. She might as well have handed Peggy a loaded gun. Heroin nearly killed Peggy. Kim's habit also worsened. 'Janis's connection came around and he had the best,' Kim says. 'Peggy used to get me or her once a week to fly down to LA and meet one of the dealer's female relatives in the bathroom in the LA airport and she would pass an ounce of heroin under the stall and we would fly back with it. We did most of it and of course the money to pay for it started coming right out of the cash register, so that was the end of that.'

Though Janis was now clean, her life was littered with human wreckage, and in 1970 it would prove to be a land mine.

7

Kristofferson: 1970

Carnival in Rio turned out to be the vacation of Janis's dreams – samba parades, municipal balls, and dancing in the streets. 'It's just like *Black Orpheus,*' Linda recalls. 'The rhythm never stops.'

Janis fell in love with a wholesome, clean-cut, fun-loving world traveler named David (George) Niehaus, who Linda picked up on the beach one day. He'd been hitchhiking around Central and South America, and when he introduced the girls to his friend Ben, Janis whispered to Linda, 'I like the blond one,' indicating George. 'Good,' Linda said. 'I like the other one.'

'Ben was my sweetie, George was hers, and we hung out for the rest of carnival,' Linda recalls. When asked for a precise physical description of George, Sam Andrew, who met him later, immediately replies, 'Gerard Depardieu,' adding, 'big, bluff, and likable.' Best of all, he wasn't a junkie.

In Linda's color snapshots of the vacation, Janis and George look like a carefree, happy, healthy young couple having a tremendously good time. After spending a couple of weeks in Rio and discovering that they were compatible and perhaps even in love, Janis and George decided to take a trip together, just the two of them. They plotted an adventurous excursion that would take them into the jungle and finally up the Brazilian coast to Salvador.

'I'm going into the jungle with a big bear of a beatnik named David Niehaus,' she told *Rolling Stone*. 'I finally remembered I don't have to be on stage twelve months a year. I've decided to go and dig some other jungles for a couple of weeks.'

Richard Bell, who'd soon be the pianist in her next band, the Full Tilt Boogie, says, 'It's a shame that recovery wasn't popular in those days. But she at least started her own recovery in Rio. Albert told her to go there, and she cleaned up her act, got off junk, and examined what she was doing. Of all the things she told me, the one I remember most is: "In Rio, nobody knew me and I just went back to being a hippie bum sleeping and living on the beach." She did her own recovery by herself.'

Linda flew back to the States 'because there were carpenters working on the house and animals to be fed. Janis and George traveled up to Salvador and she decided to stay there for a while. I thought that was super, because that meant longer time without dope, and being happy. They stayed about two weeks, and George was a doll.'

Janis found the local religion fascinating and called it 'voodoo Catholicism.' At night, the beach was alive with animism and magic – people whispering spirit language in the dark and making little offerings that were carried away by the tide. Says Linda, 'The animistic spirit religion blends strange things into Catholicism to create something she was comfortable with.' She loved the bulky macumba rosaries, which were made out of big silver balls, and she bought numerous ones to wear as jewelry.

Since no live entertainment was available in Salvador, they frequented the local whorehouse, where there was a bar and convivial company. A four-piece band played every evening and Janis sang with them for three nights running. Pearl at last was in her true element, belting the blues in a tropical bordello. In Brazil, as she later told *Rolling Stone,* 'I got mv head back.' She also very nearly lost it, smashing up a motorcycle and sustaining a concussion.

'George was in the middle of his round-the-world peregrinations,' Linda says, 'and he kept saying, "Come with me," and she kept saying, "Stay with me." She thought it would be devastating to her career to take off for even three months. It wouldn't, in fact, have wrecked it; she was perfectly capable of taking off three months. She couldn't grasp that George was a real person. He wasn't a silly, dippy groupie. He was healthy and hearty.'

Much as Janis loved George, she loved heroin – and women – even more. Cutting short her three-month vacation after a mere four weeks, she fled to Larkspur, stopping off in LA to score ten thousand dollars' worth of heroin. George followed her to Larkspur, urging her to accompany him to Nepal. But Janis was interested in Peggy again. After spending years as the other woman in Peggy's relationship with Kim, Janis flaunted George in front of Peggy and tried to make her jealous. Twice, Janis and George took Peggy along to the movies, and one night they double-dated with Peggy and Kim. Peggy disliked George intensely, viewing him as a rival for Janis's affections.

When George pressured Janis to make up her mind, Janis went to Linda and said, 'This is getting intense. He's determined to turn me into a schoolteacher's wife. Why can't he see that my way is better?'

'Because he's a real person,' Linda said. 'You can't expect a real person to do that.'

'Why not?' Janis demanded. 'I'm rich. He doesn't have to work.'

'That's wrong even to think of him that way. You just can't

do that. This time, you've got hold of someone real. George is not a toy.'

Looking back, Linda says, 'Unfortunately, she couldn't see that.' One evening, Janis was entertaining George, Linda, and Peggy in the living room. Drawing Peggy aside, Janis invited her to come into the bedroom. Janis had been trying to control her habit, but now she wanted Peggy to shoot up some heroin with her. Peggy claims she attempted to dissuade Janis, but Janis admonished her to stop moralizing about dope. To Janis, the distinction between her and most junkies was that she had learned how to use heroin recreationally, with no dependence, while others let themselves become addicted. However meretricious that argument was, Peggy saw it as an opportunity to get Janis to herself, and the two women shot up together. When the heroin took effect, Peggy became maudlin, dumping all her fears and insecurities on Janis.

As they sat together in the bedroom, what began as sympathetic gestures on Janis's part soon turned to amorous caresses, and they ended up on the floor, undressed. George chose that moment to walk in on them. It is difficult to imagine which was the more loathsome sight for him – Janis's infidelity or her hype kit with its blackened spoon, Pepsi bottle cap, syringe, bloodstained gauze, and bag of heroin.

Janis suggested that he join them and make it a threeways. What George thought of the invitation is not known, but Peggy found it so abhorrent that she got dressed and departed. In the past, she'd been willing to make love with Janis in tandem with various males, but never with one who wanted to take Janis away from her.

Peggy's fears proved groundless. 'George went on to Asia,' Linda says, 'after Janis decided not to go with him.' To the press, and perhaps to herself, Janis expressed her sexual conflicts in terms of socially acceptable polarities, such as career versus marriage. But the real reason was Janis's sexual orientation. She had never led an exclusively heterosexual existence, and to enter into such a relationship with George would have meant going against her nature.

As soon as Linda realized that Janis had slipped back into her addiction full-time, she cleared out of Janis's life once and for all. Asked whether their parting was friendly, Linda replies, 'Well – tense. It got to where every time she went into her room and shut the door, I'd hold my breath until she came out again. I never knew whether she was going to kill herself or not. I was bitching at her one day about it and she said, "If you don't like it, you can just leave!" I said, "Well, I'll be gone tomorrow." I stuck to it because I wanted to shock her and say, "This is what you're doing; this is your choice; this is what it's costing you." '

In April 1970, Linda was replaced in the household by a young woman named Lyndall Erb. Says Sunshine, 'Lyndall was a friend of Linda Eastman's and was supposed to be a clothing designer. A number of people told me she was a groupie. Once Linda [Gravenites] moved out of Larkspur and Lyndall moved in, everything changed. I have to say that I was really strung out, but I never cared for Lyndall. To me, she was not a part of our set and didn't really belong there. Lyndall had this whole collection of groupie friends whom she brought on the set, and they didn't have anything to do with the San Francisco scene.'

Hundgen adds that Lyndall had dated Sam Andrew 'as a way to break into the Haight scene. Lyndall came from Country Joe and the Fish. She was originally hired by Albert to keep an eye on Janis, but they became close. Lyndall would do anything for Janis. She wasn't aggressive on her own, and she had no power in that scene, which was dominated by Janis's drug cronies.'

Life was seldom dull around Larkspur. One day when a new girlfriend had arrived, Janis asked a male guest, 'How can we initiate this chick into our scene? I got it! When she goes to bed, sit on her chest.' Turning to a female guest, she said, 'You give her head while this guy here holds her down.'

Says Hundgen today, 'It was decadent fun.'

Travis Rivers came to see Janis in Larkspur and at one point during their visit she went into the bathroom for about forty minutes. When she came out, she was wretching. 'I don't want to see you like this,' Travis said. They began to argue and he left. 'We didn't speak for six months,' he says.

'I knew she was chipping when she was out at her house in Larkspur,' says Dave Richards, who was finishing some carpentry for her. Friday was payday for his construction crew, and he went into the house to ask Janis for the payroll. She made him wait while she pulled out her hype kit and shot up. 'She did it at the desk,' Dave recalls, 'and sat there and gave me this look like, You want to stop me? I bet you think I shouldn't be doing this, huh?' Aware that she was taunting him, he replied, 'I don't like heroin. It just fucks people up. I've already had eight, nine friends die from it. I can't see any reason for it.' Dave tried but could think of no way to make Janis kick. Says Dave, 'The only way you're going to stop her from using heroin, I thought, is to become her old man and really lay down rules and say, "No, no, Janis." She wants to see me be upset. She wants to see me be concerned. She knows my feelings. She knows I don't like it.' Dave didn't want to be her lover; he was still in love with Helen, as he is to this day.

Janis would never recover from the loss of Linda Gravenites. When she left, it broke Janis's heart, but it also made her give up heroin again. With Linda's departure, Janis could no longer escape the realization that junk had driven most of the decent people out of her life. 'We both talked about kicking on a number of occasions,' Sunshine recalls, 'but it was something that we each had to do on our own. I couldn't help her, she couldn't help me, so we made an agreement that it was something we had to take care of before we could see each other again. I felt and hopefully she felt that we could not continue unless we were both clean.'

Once again, Janis consulted a psychiatrist and went on methadone. 'She went to a spa specializing in kicking,' says Travis. 'Grossman helped her do that, got her into a spa in Mexico. In fact, there were two separate drying outs before her [*Pearl*] recording session.' Unfortunately, she also increased her drinking, and from then on she was loaded most of the time. When she resumed her performance schedule in 1970, her daily routine was to get drunk as soon as she woke up, collapse in the afternoon, come to for a concert, and then drink to oblivion at night. She didn't always revive in time for the concert but went on anyway, performing in an alcoholic blackout.

In the spring of 1970, she was tattooed, setting a kinky style that Cher and thousands of other women would later emulate. Tattoos had traditionally been a male prerogative, but Janis was challenging the double standard on many fronts; for example, her recording of 'One Night Stand,' produced by Todd Rundgren, was an extraordinary breakthrough. The lyrics, the first of their kind in popular music, announced that women could be just as uninhibited as men when it came to screwing around.

Though she was without a band, Big Brother welcomed her anytime they were playing. Nick Gravenites, their new singer, remembers that when they played the Lion's Share in San Anselmo, she joined them onstage but remained in the background, occasionally contributing backup vocals.

The Kozmic Blues Band had never worked out and Janis let them go at the beginning of 1970. When she heard that Big Brother was playing a Family Dog gig one night, she decided to attend. The band spotted her down front and asked her to jam with them. 'I was so jacked,' she said, 'and we hugged and kissed.' Having dropped her songs from their act, no one remembered how to play them, not even their hit single 'Piece of My Heart.' They started improvising onstage, creating new songs as they went along. Bill Graham heard of the reunion and exploited it on April 4, 1970, building a whole Fillmore West concert around them. Janis felt like a prodigal daughter who'd been readmitted into a warm and loving clan. 'It was so much fun,' she said, 'sittin' on the floor, drinkin' tequila, kissin', and talkin' about old times.'

Suffering from a terrible cold that night at the Fillmore, Janis had a drink in one hand and a cup of tea in the other and was popping Dolophine (methadone pills). Mindful of how San Franciscans had crucified her at Winterland following her break with Big Brother, she wondered whether her adopted hometown had forgiven her. Graham certainly had; now that she was an international star, he couldn't do enough for her, painting her dressing room purple – her favorite color – providing fresh flowers and plenty of gin and guacamole dip. One of his ushers, dressed in a tuxedo and top hat, collected her in a taxi.

Making her entrance that night, Janis saluted Big Brother as her true family and staunch friends. They'd rehearsed and were now able to reprise all their old favorites, including 'Easy Rider' and 'Coo-coo.' It was strictly a trip down memory lane, Janis joked. But there was an exciting new song, as well – 'Ego Rock,' which Janis and Nick Gravenites sang as a duet.

'Ego Rock' gave Janis a chance to get even with her native state, whose cruelties to her she'd never forget or forgive. For years, Texas had been celebrated in popular music, from 'San Antonio Rose' to Frank Loesser's 'Big D,' but Janis excoriated Texans in 'Ego Rock' for laughing her off the street just because she'd dared to be different.

On April 12, once again she appeared with Big Brother, this time at Winterland. They were in excellent form, singing 'Bye, Bye Baby' with all its original bounce and charm. Though it was good to guest-shot with Big Brother, she never considered returning to the group. She was ready for another stretch in her career, one that would take her back to her Texas roots: country blues. It was not a sound that she could imagine coming out of an acid-rock band.

Still, she could never quite let go of Big Brother. Later, when Nick had left and they had another girl singer, Kathy McDonald, Janis showed up at the Great Highway, where they were playing, and made trouble. 'She was jealous that there was another woman on with her band,' says Hundgen, who was present as the band's road manager. 'Big Brother had been her family,' Hundgen explains, 'her source of spirituality and sex,' and some of them were an essential part of her drug life. 'She came on the back of the stage,' Hundgen continues, 'grabbed me, and said, "Go over there and get her off the stage. I want to do a number."' Hundgen had to go out onstage, tap Kathy McDonald on the shoulder, and say, ' "Janis wants to come on now. Get off." It was very awkward. Janis did a guest number with the band for old times' sake and as a little ego trip to prove that she could still boss everybody around. As far as she was concerned, we were still her family.'

Finally, she faced the fact that she had to create a new band of her own. Once again, she called on Nick Gravenites and Michael Bloomfield to help her audition musicians. Janis and Neuwirth thought up the name for the new group, Full Tilt Boogie Band. The only holdovers from the Kozmic Blues

A beautiful, and pensive, Janis in beads. This Bob Seidemann photo
was a bestseller. (*Bob Seidemann*)

John Cooke, Mimi Farina and Sam Andrew—a recent photograph. (*Sam Andrew*)

Kim Chappell today, in Carmel Valley, with Arabian mare, Bayreen. Once Joan Baez's lover, Kim captivated both Janis and Peggy Caserta, Janis's lover. Though Janis was obsessed with Kris Kristofferson, both Kim and Peggy slept with him, enraging Janis. (*Kim Chappell*)

Nick Gravenites today. Nick wrote several of Janis's songs, such as "Work Me, Lord," "Buried Alive in the Blues," "Ego Rock," and "As Good as You've Been to This World." (*Bruce S. Gregory*)

Janis on West 23rd Street, New York. She loved the Chelsea Hotel (awning and wrought-iron balconies in background). (*David Gahr*)

Nancy Gurley, 1966, had a profound influence on Janis in Aquarian ideas and hippie fashions. Even though Janis tried to steal her husband, Nancy forgave her. (*Richard Hundgen*)

Linda Gravenites, Jan[...] best friend, roomm[...] and dress designer. (M[...] Green)

One of Linda Gravenit[...] costumes for Janis. (Lin[...] Gravenites)

B DAVIS' PARTY —
SQ. GARDEN NIGHT.

BLOUSE:
BLACK SILK CHIFFON
FIGURED IN VELVET
PAISLEY DESIGN

• ROLLED EDGE AT NECK
• FRENCH SEAMS
• BELLED SLEEVE SHAPE —
  GATHERED INTO WIDE CUF

PANTS: BLACK PANNÉ VELOUR.

linda · 12·69

After her Madison Square Garden triumph in December 1969, Janis wore this Linda Gravenites see-through outfit to Clive Davis's ultra-chic party for her. (*Linda Gravenites*)

At the Newport Folk Festival, 1968, Janis is wearing Linda Gravenites's "push-'em-up" bra dress. (*David Gahr*)

Kris Kristofferson, who wrote the song that made her famous. (*Señor McGuire*)

Albert Grossman, Janis's manager. (*David Gahr*)

Janis was trying to kick heroin in Brazil, and one of the nicest things about George was that he wasn't into drugs. (*Linda Gravenites*)

Seth Morgan, 41, Dies in Crash; His Novel, 'Homeboy,' Won Praise

By ELEANOR BLAU

Seth Morgan, who won acclaim last spring for his first novel, "Homeboy," which drew on his experiences in the drug culture of San Francisco and in prison, was killed early Wednesday morning when the motorcycle he was driving struck a dividing post on a bridge in New Orleans, the police said.

Mr. Morgan, who was 41 years old, and a passenger, Diane Levine, 37, both of New Orleans, were thrown from the motorcycle and were pronounced dead at the scene, the police said, adding that neither of them had been wearing ⁀ets as required by state law.

⁀ Tuesday morning, Mr. Morgan ⁀ ⁀nd charged with driving ⁀e intoxicated, they ⁀wn if he was in- ⁀accident.

⁀ The New ⁀st May, ⁀avagely ⁀t "the

Seth Morgan   Greg Simms, 1990

⁀ld of Mr. Morgan created "an unnerving ⁀ok and utterly persuasive rendition of ⁀ic hell."

Jason Epstein, one of Mr. Morgan's ⁀tors at Random House, said that ⁀eboy" had

In 1970 Janis was going to marry Seth Morgan, dope dealer, pimp, and armed robber. He died in 1990 on his motorcycle. (*Greg Simms*)

Thrift-store chic: Janis in 1966. (*Herb Greene*)

Band were Brad Campbell, bass, and John Till, guitar. Drummer Clark Pierson was commandeered from a San Francisco topless bar, and the others, Richard Bell, piano, and Ken Pearson, organ, were raided from Ronnie Hawkins's Canadian band. These were the musicians who would back Janis on her next album, *Pearl*.

Richard Bell was twenty-two when Janis auditioned him in Larkspur. He remembers arriving at the house and seeing Gabriel, the 'giant erect penis in her front yard.' Janis appeared in a tie-dyed outfit, and the musicians played for about two hours before taking a break. She left the studio. After a while, Lyndall Erb came in and told Richard that he was hired. Somewhat later, Janis invited him and the rest of the band to stay for dinner that night. She served lasagne, salad, and wine, and Richard remembers that 'the lasagne was overcooked.' The other guests included John and Johanna Hall, the songwriting team who provided one of the songs on *Pearl*, 'Half Moon.' In the following days, Bell looked for an apartment and ended up rooming in the Presidio section of San Francisco with Janis's old boyfriend Richard Kermode and John Till and his wife.

From the start, Janis knew that she'd at last found a great band. They were superb professional musicians, and none of them tried to compete with her for control. 'They were willing to play as a backup group,' said her father, Seth, 'rather than as individuals.' Now she needed material for her new album and began to cast about impatiently. Why was it, she wanted to know, that every other rock star of her stature had dozens of people regularly supplying them with new songs and exciting arrangements? Joe Cocker, for instance, had Leon Russell to advise him on every move. Why didn't *she* have someone like that? she wondered. Where were *her* colleagues?

It was a good question. By playing the queen bee, had she

driven people of talent and imagination away from her? Not entirely. Hearing of her plight, Nick Gravenites, Albert Grossman, and San Francisco DJ Tom Donahue came to her aid, spreading the word that she needed songs and ideas. Soon musicians and tunesmiths all the way from San Francisco to New York started coming to Larkspur with material.

Kris Kristofferson arrived one spring day in 1970, bringing with him a song – 'Me and Bobby McGee' – that would ensure not only the success of the new album, *Pearl,* but Janis Joplin's immortality in the annals of rock, pop, country, and folk.

Kristofferson had been playing at the Bitter End in Greenwich Village, and Neuwirth had liked his act so much that he brought all his friends to see him. They met at a boozy bash one night and Neuwirth offered to introduce Kris to Janis, suggesting that they hop on a plane and go to the West Coast immediately. 'Neuwirth brought Kris to town,' says Milan, 'and Kris stayed at our place a couple of times. Mimi [Farina] and I were living at Filbert's Steps in North Beach.' Another source says they stayed with Berkeley friends. When Neuwirth called Janis in Larkspur, she was ready to party, and when he told her that he was with a buddy, she said to bring him along.

Once again, Neuwirth was about to exercise his genius as a galvanizer of momentous rock scenes. First achieving fame as Dylan's roadie, he had found his true calling as a sidekick of superstars. Baez maintained that he was Dylan's model for 'Like a Rolling Stone.' Producer Paul Rothchild used him to keep Jim Morrison in line, and the Doors's record label, Elektra, valued him so highly that they absorbed half his salary, though ostensibly he was doing little more than drinking with Morrison. Now he was about to ignite the synergy of Kristofferson and Joplin, and Paul Rothchild would be their producer.

When Neuwirth and Kristofferson came to party in Larkspur, Kris caught Janis's eye right away. 'She thought he was a honey,' Sunshine says. Thirty-four years old, he wasn't yet wearing a beard and he radiated an early Paul Newman-Greek god look. Stirrings of lust in Janis were immediate and overpowering. Like her, he was a Texan, and he'd hitchhiked around the country, finding love and friendship on the run. He'd spent years in Nashville, struggling to be a songwriter, and now his efforts were beginning to pay off. Roger Miller's recording of 'Me and Bobby McGee' had been a country hit, Johnny Cash recorded Kris's 'Sunday Morning Coming Down,' and Cash was beginning to feature Kris as a guest on his popular TV show.

Recalling his impressions of Janis at this time, Kris said he found her healthy and attractive enough, though she was squawking that she was out of methadone. He compared her to a prizefighter who had to keep in shape to defend his title. She lived in fear that a hotter singer would come along and steal her crown and she'd revert to being the hick-town wallflower who sat at home on Saturday nights.

When they first met, she mixed exotic tropical cocktails, though the meal she was serving was breakfast. She was pleased to see that Kris kept up with her, drink for drink. At lunch, she brought on vodka and orange juice, and again Kris was ready for a refill every time she was. At happy hour, they all piled in cars and headed for the Trident, drinking until last call and then continuing the party at home.

'It didn't strike me that it was that heavy,' says Dave Richards, referring to Janis and Kris's relationship. 'It was more like fun. He was hangin' out at the Trident and pickin' up girls, he and Neuwirth. It was before he was a movie star and he had a lot of charisma. He was a heavy drinker. He was always crocked. Everybody was loaded all the time. It was party time all the time. Her house was like that.'

Janis and Kris developed a classic alcoholic codependency. Though Kristofferson wanted to leave and get on with his life, he allowed himself to become helpless and dependent on Janis. It began when Neuwirth cut out, taking the car and leaving Kris at Janis's house. Each morning, Kris would prepare to leave, but then Janis would cunningly lure him back with the promise of unlimited free booze. Kris loved tequila as much as she did, she'd later tell Jerry Lee Lewis, and Kris was the only man she'd ever met who could drink her under the table. Soon they were lolling about the house all day, two blissed-out lushes in the lap of luxury.

'Kristofferson wanted her to cut "Me and Bobby McGee," ' says James Gurley. 'He was beginning to make waves with his own career. It's not like that would be his only motivation for hanging around her, but the money from a Joplin record would have come in handy.'

At the Trident and the bars in Marin, Janis made the mistake of raving about Kris to her girlfriends. This guy had everything, she said – Rhodes scholar, football star, U.S. Army officer, paratrooper, singer, and a wonderful songwriter. She could go on an intellectual trip with him, discussing William Blake, and then he'd take off his clothes and it got even better: He was built like Hercules. Soon her girlfriends decided to try Kris for themselves. Janis would later confide to Dalton, 'I talk too much. Eric Clapton don't talk about his old lady, man.'

Both Peggy and Kim made love with Kris, driving Janis into jealous rages. Kim describes Kris on the occasion of their meeting at the Trident: 'He was in deerskin with fringe on the arms and around the chest opening and all down the sides of his pants. He looked like he was right out of the old West and right out of the shower. He had a lot of sex appeal – clean-shaven, blue-eyed, and he had this voice that would just melt you. He was purely divine.'

That night, Kim and Kris made love. 'He was so real,' she recalls. 'He wasn't a stud; he was himself and that was all you needed, because he was so brilliant and so sweet and he had a body that you could die for – he had the skin of life, he had the eyes of a god, and he had the voice of honey. And virile! And well-endowed – we're not talking baseball bats, but the guy, to be absolutely accurate . . . he was perfect. He is an excellent lover and he's an excellent man and there's nothing studly about him and there's nothing effeminate about him, either. He was a superior lover, compared to any male or female I've ever been with. Of course, he was just peaking at that time. This was before he had really destroyed himself in any way, shape, or form. Kris did love to drink, but this was before he got into some problems with it.'

Kris's relationship with Janis continued along its bumpy but highly productive course that spring. 'I remember when he introduced "Me and Bobby McGee" to her,' says Dave Richards, who was remodeling the house. 'When I got there that day, she said, "Listen to this song. This is a great song." She was playing the guitar and sang "Me and Bobby McGee" to me.'

Kris was born in Brownsville, Texas, and he'd spent some time in her part of the state, around the Gulf oil rigs, working as a helicopter pilot. In Janis's Jefferson High days, this type of guy, the charming, easygoing jock, had thrown pennies at her in the hall and called her a pig, but Kris sang her beautiful songs. 'They'd drink a lot and get stoned a lot,' Dave Richards says. 'I don't know whether it was a love affair or not, but she certainly found him sexy. At that point, he was wowin' all the girls who liked him. It was a sexual relationship.'

Zelda Fitzgerald once expressed the kind of love Janis felt for Kris. 'I want to love first, and live incidentally,' Zelda told Scott. 'You can't do *anything* without me.' Kris qualified as one of Janis's 'mythic men' – talented, reckless, self-destructive, and unavailable.

As if Janis needed yet another obsession, she began to crave Kris so much that she couldn't stand for him to be out of her sight. 'I got a call at eight or nine one morning from Bobby Neuwirth,' Nick Gravenites recalls. 'He and Janis and Kris Kristofferson had been drinkin' all night, and they wanted to come over. I said, "Sure. Come on over." They got there at about ten. I lived on a hill; they had to walk a little bit and then up some stairs to the house.

'The first person up the stairs was Janis. She had a bottle in her hand and she was cacklin'. They were still partyin' from the night before. Janis comes walkin' in and we sat there talkin' for about five minutes. And then Neuwirth and Kristofferson came up the stairs, and they looked horrible. I mean they were totally fried. They're tired, they're breathing hard, they're collapsing on the couch and on the chair. "What the hell are we doin' here?" Kris said. They were suffering. Partying with Janis could be dangerous.'

Once everyone caught their breath, Janis tried to dominate the conversation, as usual. This was ordinarily easy for her, but not when she was in the company of bright, confident guys like these. Nick and Kris were talking about songwriting when Janis started fidgeting and promoting a quick trip to the nearest bar. Nick hated the idea of hitting a pub in the middle of the day. When the men didn't immediately accede to her wishes, she spoiled the visit. To Nick, who loved her and usually would have gone along and partied, there was something insane about the unholy threesome of Joplin, Kristofferson, and Neuwirth. Triple trouble, they seemed intent on early burnout, and he wanted no part of it.

In May 1970, Janis decided to throw a big party for Michael J. Pollard. 'She instructed me to call Pollard in New York and tell him she was having a party and she expected him to fly from New York,' says Hundgen. 'She said to tell him that if he didn't come, he'd regret it.'

It was to be a tattoo party, she announced, and everyone was going to have to submit to the needle of her friend Lyle Tuttle, the first psychedelic tattoo artist, whose work already decorated Janis's body in three places – the heart on her heart, the bud on her ankle, and the three-color bracelet on her wrist. Tuttle's entire body from neck to wrist to ankles was completely tattooed, including, according to Richard Hundgen, 'his cock and balls.'

There were specific requirements for the women attending the party. They had to agree to let Lyle put a tattooed flower or heart on them. As it worked out at the party, they lay across a chair and exposed themselves while Lyle tattooed them, usually on the thigh or buttocks.

'I ended up falling asleep in the fireplace,' Richard Bell recalls. 'I watched the empty bottles being pushed side by side, building out from one wall and getting huge, and I got pretty drunk.'

There was a keg of beer on the deck that was regularly replenished, and plenty of food sizzling on the outdoor barbecue. Janis chatted animatedly with Mike Bloomfield and Nick Gravenites, periodically checking on Kris, who was contemplating her dog Thurber.

When someone reminded Sunshine that all the women had to get tattooed, she declined. 'I've always thought that tattoos were something that you could be identified by,' she says, 'and I don't know what's going to be happening later in my life, so I don't want a piece of art on me that I might not like in five years.'

Says Richard Bell, 'I saw a couple of girls get tattooed. One was on her rump. The other was on her breast. The one with her rump tattooed had to come back later and have it shaped into a heart. I went down pretty fast after that.'

Michael Pollard wanted a tattoo featuring his wife, Annie, and Bobby Neuwirth started to strip, presumably for Lyle Tuttle, but a sexy blonde got to him first.

Around three o'clock in the morning, Kris said, 'Hey, I'm tired. I'm gonna cut out,' and went to his VW bug and passed out. Janis took a blanket out to the car to tuck him in. While she was struggling with his inert body, trying to arrange the blanket around him, she left the car door open and the roof light was on. 'Shut the fuckin' light off!' Kris said. Well, she thought, if that's all the thanks I get – and she went back in the house and talked to Sunshine. There was a little room off the kitchen, with a couch and a table, and they sat there drinking tequila until 5:00 A.M.

'At five,' says Sunshine, 'we switched to screwdrivers and continued chatting about who's who and who's cute and who isn't. At that point, Janis thought she was having this affair with Kris.' What happened next indicates that by this time the affair may have lost its steam.

They heard a noise in the kitchen and Janis said, 'Oh, that's just Thurber.' She assumed her giant Pyrenees was using the dog door, which opened automatically when touched. But as the scuffling sounds continued, they went out to the kitchen to check. Thurber had made it through the dog door and now stood watching as Kris came crawling in after him, still covered with his blanket. Without speaking to the women, Kris scrambled onto the couch, snuggled under his blanket, and went back to sleep. 'It was real obvious to me,' says Sunshine, 'that if she was supposed to be having this major scene with him, it wasn't happening.'

It had been cursed, of course, from the start – by alcohol. They'd led an unreal existence in Janis's sylvan hideaway, submerged in a sea of booze with a houseful of freeloaders. The idyll turned sour because Janis, like most alcoholics, possessed a Jekyll-and-Hyde personality. No sooner had Kris settled in than she went on the warpath, storming through the house like a beatnik Bette Davis and yelling, 'You're all taking advantage of me!'

According to James Gurley, Janis had asked for it. Says Gurley, 'Guess who'd said, "Oh, please, come over and stay at my house and drink my booze and hang out"? She wanted it both ways.'

Kris inevitably tired of her bitching and rebelled. She knew that it was only a matter of time until he went 'gypsying off down the road to be a star.' When he finally did leave, she must have felt the full force of the 'Bobby McGee' verse that describes how her lover left her high and dry, hoping to find a normal woman and settle down. As it says in the song, she'd sell her soul to the devil for just one more night of passion with Bobby McGee.

In June 1970, Kris made his first major club appearance, singing at the Troubadour in Los Angeles. 'Kris slept on my couch the first time he played LA,' says Carl Gottlieb. 'Seems like everybody who passed through town did – Michael J. Pollard, Judy Collins, Joan Baez, Bobby Neuwirth. My wife and I had quite a salon going at 1628 North Gardner Street. Janis was obsessed with Kristofferson, and no wonder – he was like the Warren Beatty of music, and he cut a swath. Joan Baez would flutter her eyelids at him and get all gooey when he came around. Kris is like the original man's man.'

A few days after the Pollard party, Janis was rehearsing her band in the poolroom at Larkspur. 'There was a bunch of racket out front – motorcycles,' recalls Richard Bell. 'Some guys from the Hell's Angels came up, and they went into a room with Janis and talked for a little bit. After a while, they all came out and exchanged pleasantries and then left. Janis told us that they'd asked if we'd play a party for them, and that was our first gig.'

Held at Pepperland, a dance hall in San Rafael, just north of San Francisco, the Hell's Angels party was attended by 2,300. Richard stood backstage with Janis, waiting to go on. 'She was drinking tequila. She didn't drink Southern Comfort when I played with her [April to October 1970]. We were walking out of the dressing room, and a drunk Hell's Angel came up to her and said, "Give me that bottle of tequila." She told him to fuck off. He nailed her. She fell down, got up, went ahead and played. It put a note of tension in the air. As we began the set, we didn't know, because of what had happened to her as we were walking out, whether the place was going to erupt into a mass fight. It was like being in a powder keg. As we were playing, a pretty rough-looking guy came out onstage. We were sweating a lot and he came over to Clark, the drummer, and Clark didn't know what he was going to do. He had a towel and he wiped Clark's brow with it.'

After the performance, the Hell's Angel who'd punched Janis out came up to her and said she should have told him she was a hotshot rock star. That was his idea of an apology. Her long romance with the Hell's Angels was finally over. Why she let them intimidate her into playing their party in the first place remains a mystery, especially in view of the small fee – $250, of which they paid her only $240. Hundgen offers a clue when he mentions that she got her dope from the Angels.

Two of Janis's old friends, Nick Gravenites and Sam Andrew, were both playing with Big Brother, the opening act at the party, and both saw Janis's performance that night. 'I was dismayed at the change in Janis,' says Sam. 'She was visibly deteriorating and she looked bloated. She was like a parody of what she was at her best. I put it down to her drinking too much and I felt a tinge of fear for her well-being. Her singing was real flabby, no edge at all.'

Nick, Big Brother's lead singer, said two naked freaks came onstage and started dancing during their set. Nick was drinking everything in sight – Benedictine, brandy, tequila, and beer, following the Hell's Angels instructions to the band to get as loaded as they could and still stand. Nick was so carried away that he knelt onstage and lifted his hand like an old-time Holiness preacher. Unlike Sam, he found Janis stupendous that night and says she sang until she dropped. She succeeded in taking several steps after she left the stage before collapsing in a heap.

Later, she asked Michael Pollard to describe her performance at Pepperland, explaining that she'd blacked out and had no memory of it. He assured her that she'd put on a fine show. She began to weep. Pollard had no idea what she was sad about, but any recovering alcoholic could have told him. Any drinker who has reached the blackout stage is indisputably an alcoholic, and life will get progressively worse, never better.

Kris, Neuwirth, and Cooke had all promised to come to San Rafael and take Janis home after the concert. Instead, they were having a party of their own and stood her up. It had started at the Trident that day when they'd run into Kim and Peggy. Cooke warned them that he had to collect Janis after her performance in San Rafael, but soon they were all having such a good time that cocaine lines were laid out on the tabletop for anyone to snort who chose to. From there, it turned into an all-night bash. Says Kim, 'I noticed that Peggy was pickin' up on this guy [Kris] and I thought, Yeah, fine, because she wasn't drinkin', she was getting bored, and he was already totaled, so she took him off to continue the party at Stinson Beach.'

Peggy and Kim had been doing coke all day, and Kim says that Kris tried a little coke. 'I think that was what got Kristofferson going again,' she said. 'It sort of woke him up a little bit. Pretty soon, after his first line on the Trident table, he and Peggy were out of there.'

As she left, Peggy told Kim to pick up some liquor on the way home and handed her a credit card. 'We drank all of her money up,' says Kim. 'Neuwirth and I used to hang out in Boston before we ever knew Peggy. Bobby Neuwirth and I used to make trouble for John Cooke a lot because he was such a nanny, you know. We'd take his motorcycle out and get drunk on bourbon and black out in the middle of the night and do all these crazy things. We tried to see who could worry John the most.'

Finally Kim, Cooke, and Neuwirth left the restaurant. Peggy and Kris had taken the Porsche, but Kim had her Shelby, so they crowded into it, and Kim drove to a liquor store in Sausalito, where they loaded up on tequila and an assortment of other liquors, charging it all on Peggy's card. Then, again with Kim at the wheel, they started driving over Mt. Tamalpais's winding, narrow roads. Somehow they made it to Stinson Beach, where Kim drove through their new fifteen-hundred-dollar wind fence before coming to a halt.

Inside the cabin, Peggy and Kris were up in the loft, naked. Downstairs, Kim and her guests opened the booze and made drinks. Says Kim, 'Those guys were startin' to piss me off. John and Bobby got into their little back-and-forth nit-nit-nit, and John had taken it for granted that he and I were going to sleep together, but he was always sort of on hold.'

Kim was interested in getting in on some of the action in the loft. 'They had just finished fucking or whatever they were doing,' she says, 'and were lying there smoking a cigarette and looking out the window, and Kris looked so good to me, I just said, "Hey, it's my turn."

' "Okay," Peggy said, "I have to go to the bathroom, anyway." She came down nonchalantly and John and Bobby were having fits by this time, but I went up there and we fucked.'

'Kristofferson was conscious?' I ask, because Peggy asserts in her autobiography that Kris had passed out and Kim 'sucked him awake.'

'He was very conscious,' Kim says. 'Very conscious. He was just lying there, neither asleep nor unconscious.'

Neuwirth's head suddenly appeared over the edge of the loft, and he was drinking from a bottle of tequila. 'Okay, Kris,' he said, 'now it's my turn!'

'Wait a minute,' Kim said. 'The buck stops here, Neuwirth.' Says Kim today, 'I kicked him off with one foot. He wasn't expecting it, so the tequila went all over him. He was all pissed off down there.'

Neuwirth and Peggy drove Kris home, going over Mt. Tamalpais. Kim went to bed, leaving Cooke alone in the living room. After a while, Neuwirth and Peggy returned and started the party again, but Kim remained upstairs. Eventually, she got up to go to the bathroom. Half drunk and half asleep, she somehow ended up on the sun deck instead. 'I sat down on what I thought was the toilet, but it was thin air and I fell off the second-story porch, landing in a forked sapling,' says Kim. 'It was easily a ten- or twelve-foot drop. I lay there in the tree, stone naked, and I remember seeing stars and saying to myself, "Oh, what a beautiful night!" Then I passed out.'

A little while later, Cooke discovered her and they took her inside. She had two broken ribs. Despite the agony of that evening, Kim says today, 'I was glad I made the decision to jump up there and fuck with Kris, because he was beautiful, a wonderful man. He was a good friend for a few years until he had his big dilemma with alcohol, and I haven't seen him since.'

'He gave Janis her greatest song,' I say to Kim.

'He sure did, and he loved her so much.'

'*Did* he? You're the only person I've ever heard say that.'

'Oh, God, he just *loved* Janis. He loved her, as I did, for herself, and what was inside and how she could reach in and give it out with her music. He loved her very much and I think it just broke his heart, what happened to her.'

By the time Janis reached Peggy on the phone the following day, she was spitting fire. She demanded to know where Peggy had been, and she fumed that Kris, Cooke, and Neuwith had reneged on their promise to meet her after the Hell's Angels gig. Peggy confessed everything, revealing that both Peggy and Kim had made love to Kris the night before. Janis was crushed. She, too, had been 'screwed' the night before, she said, but hardly in the same way. After she explained about being assaulted by a Hell's Angel, she hung up on Peggy.

To get even with Peggy, Janis telephoned her on June 13 from Louisville, where she was performing, and attempted to arouse Peggy's jealousy. She was holed up at her hotel with a young woman who was expecting Janis to have sex with her. Teasingly, Janis indicated that she'd lost interest and asked for Peggy's advice on how to dispose of unwanted tricks. The surest method, Peggy replied, was to dispatch her on an errand and then lock her out. Janis thanked her for the tip, but whether she followed it is not a matter of record.

The previous night, she'd premiered her new band at Freedom Hall, and though it was a huge venue, an indoor stadium, only four thousand attended. Backstage, she huffed, 'Some dance hall you got here!' A woman reporter asked her whether she customarily drank before a show. Janis replied that she used to start getting drunk hours before a concert and by curtain time she was in a blackout, so she couldn't enjoy her own performance. The blackouts she'd mentioned to Michael Pollard were getting worse, and when people told her about her shows, she could say only, 'Wow, it sounds great. I wish I'd been there.' Her solution to the problem was to wait until minutes before show time and then down all the liquor she could, figuring she could at least be conscious for part of her show before the blackout hit.

In Louisville, she admitted to David Dalton that she had a 'drinking problem.' She was aware that her mind, her keen intelligence, was powerless over alcohol, that indeed her negative thinking lay at the root of her alcoholism. She was also conscious of another alcoholic trait in her character: She lived in a constant state of expectation, never savoring the joy of being fully present in the here and now. She was beginning to get glimpses of the truth that an expectation is the first step to a disappointment – and that it is therefore wise to expect nothing from life. She spoke to Dalton of the importance of 'acceptance.' Intellectually, she knew that happiness is possible only by embracing life on life's terms, rather than trying to control it. Unfortunately, she was still drinking too much to put her newfound knowledge to use in her daily life.

Psychologists William James and Carl Jung and AA founder Bill Wilson have all stated that in order for an alcoholic to recover he must get in touch with the spiritual side of his nature, where incredible power resides. For the alcoholic or addict, this usually requires hitting such a low bottom that he either dies or changes. Afterward, according to Wilson, those who correct the character flaws that led to their drinking or using – selfishness, resentment, anger, isolation, lust – find both sobriety and happiness. AA is a rigorous program of recovery, because the only way to remove personality defects is to change one's behavior: to deflate the self-centered ego by performing daily service for those less fortunate than one's self. It is also a very simple program, because all the recovering alcoholic has to do is go to meetings and not drink. Janis had gotten only as far as realizing that she could not *think* herself into sobriety. That she could *act* her way into sobriety – and happiness – by changing her behavior and devoting herself to the welfare of others was still beyond her comprehension.

When she went onstage in Louisville that night, a woman in the audience yelled, 'Try Just a Little Bit Harder.' Janis fixed her with a stare and said, 'I beg your pardon. I'm doing *my* part, honey.' Janis managed to turn the concert into a crisis by getting everyone up and dancing, despite warnings from security guards. The excitement started during 'Try' as she rapped about cruising the streets for sex, a routine that never failed to please the crowds. On this particular occasion, she went down into the audience and tried to entice a young hunk from his seat. When he reacted to the dare by leaping up and seizing her breasts, absolute mayhem broke out in the stadium.

It was a replay of Tampa, with everyone jumping up and down on their seats, couples dirty dancing, and many in the audience rushing the stage. Though this was Janis's idea of fun, security personnel reacted by brandishing billy clubs and flashlights. Tongue-lashing the guards, she announced that dancing was not only allowed at her concerts; it was mandatory. One guard raised his fist and glared at her with murderous rage. But the good news at Louisville was that everyone loved the Full Tilt Boogie Band and agreed that at last she'd found the proper backup musicians. 'The crowd howled for more,' wrote *Rolling Stone*. The concert became a 'love feast,' said the *Louisville Times*.

At her best, as she was at Louisville, Janis took the blues to the breaking point. In 'Ball and Chain,' she achieved the musical equivalent of a Francis Bacon painting: madness transformed into art. David Dalton said she invoked 'noises full of real terror, the whining of dogs, the croaking of drains, blind helpless screams.' Little Richard awarded perhaps the ultimate accolade when he called her voice, with its almost supernatural ability to harmonize with itself, a manifestation of the Holy Spirit.

The next morning, after a Southern Comfort and Ripple party given by *The Free Press,* she didn't so much wake up as come to. She went to the motel bar as soon as it opened and started talking to a couple of other drinkers. That night, she and Dalton caught a country and western show, and she was depressed to see that Tammy Wynette, George Jones, and Jerry Lee Lewis had no trouble filling twenty thousand seats. As she entered the stadium she suddenly came face-to-face with the guard who'd shaken his fist at her the night before. Now he attempted to take his revenge, rudely ordering her to get out of his way. Janis threatened him with the liquor bottle she was holding, but Dalton and Clark Pierson forced her to back off. She hadn't changed since the days Jim Langdon and Grant Lyons had hustled her out of Louisiana dives.

While Jerry Lee Lewis was singing 'The Beer That Made Milwaukee Famous (Has Made a Loser Out of Me),' Janis was obsessing on his bass player, a blond teenager. She admired his long hair, which was pulled back and glistening like liquid gold. Knowing from past experience that her star prerogatives entitled her to any man she wanted, she caught the kid's eye and started gesturing obscenely. He looked at her as if she was a blithering idiot. Undeterred by his obvious lack of interest, she accosted him after the show and invited him to have a quickie with her backstage. He couldn't get away from her fast enough, and as he fled, she heckled him, casting aspersions on his virility.

Janis went into Jerry Lee Lewis's dressing room and it was an awkward, tense scene. Both hillbillies, they had much in common, but a crucial difference precluded congeniality – Janis was a liberated woman and Jerry Lee remained an unreconstructed redneck. He left all the work of establishing rapport to her, letting her ramble about Kris until he couldn't stand it anymore and cut in with an irate remark about Kris's veneration of Johnny Cash. When he asked Janis about her concert the night before, she boasted that it was a near-riot. Unimpressed, Lewis insinuated that she was out of line when she stirred audiences to violence. He was right – she and Jim Morrison were bad for everyone in the music business, as Janis herself would soon discover. Houston banned her, and her manager was reduced to sending a form letter to the trade, promising that Janis would behave herself if they'd only let her back in their venues.

As they prepared to leave Louisville for the next stop on the tour, Janis had a déjà vu experience. A man in his late thirties came up to her and told her that she was going to die if she didn't change. He was an obvious crank, but she listened to him, intuitively sensing that life often signals us in strange ways. When he tried to warn her about the dangers coming her way in the next two years, she grew defiant. Like Auntie Mame, Janis believed that life was a feast and that most poor bastards were starving to death.

In 1970, Janis was making $300,000 a year, but she still loved sleazy scenes. In New York, she spent most of her time slumming and she caught all of the up-and-coming talent at clubs that were often little more than upholstered toilets. 'When Janis came back from New York the last couple of times, she was talking about Bette Midler,' Sunshine says. 'She thought she was wonderful, that she was the next one up. "That's my next competition," she said.'

The Continental Baths, where Midler sang for fifty dollars a night, was mostly made up of small cubicles where men had sex with one another, and there was a larger room for 'group gropes.' Gay men felt free to wander into the performance area, which was near the pool, wearing only their brief towels, and when they sat down for Midler's act, they didn't bother to conceal their genitals. 'Boys throw their towels at me,' Midler told Johnny Carson. 'When they give me standing ovations, their towels fall to the floor.'

Most New York gays were out of the closet by 1969, thanks to the Stonewall riots. Many of them were moved to tears when Bette sang Bob Dylan's 'I Shall Be Released,' which soon became a gay liberation anthem. But usually the Baths rang with laughter in those days, especially when Bette made cracks such as, 'I was going to Fire Island, but I couldn't find any room in the bushes.'

Later on in the 1970s, Midler would play Janis in the film *The Rose,* and it was uncanny how much the two women had in common. Both were homely girls from working-class backgrounds who had been unpopular in high school. Both had gone back to class reunions after hitting it big; said Bette in 1973, 'I'm now going to a reunion of all the people who couldn't stand me.' Both were influenced by Bessie Smith; both had started as blues singers and flopped. Both would have profound connections to homosexuals – Janis by sexual preference and Bette by her uniquely campy appeal to the gays who launched her career.

From June 29 to July 3, Janis joined the Grateful Dead, Delaney and Bonnie, Eric Andersen, Ian and Sylvia, and Rick Danko on the Festival Express train across Canada. They played concerts in Toronto, Winnipeg, and Calgary. Janis went along strictly for the party, looking forward to nonstop drinking and drugging for five consecutive days.

A *Circus* magazine reporter caught up with her in the lobby of a Toronto hotel, where she was conscientiously cruising the room for potential bedmates. This was a 'groupie's heaven,' she said, the perfect setup for a concupiscent rocker such as herself. Over screwdrivers in the hotel bar, the reporter realized that she was different from most stars. She loved to talk, but she regarded him as an equal and drew him out. Bemoaning the dearth of material for women singers, she accused contemporary composers of ignoring women's feelings, adding that she was writing a song called 'A Woman Knows.'

When she spoke of love now, she sounded resigned and hopeless. Since she was always on the road, she'd given up any chance of a relationship, and music was all she lived for. 'Life's a burn,' she concluded. 'That used to really get me down, but now I've learned to live with the fact.'

Alcohol, which had once numbed her pain, had turned on her. When she dragged herself from bed these days, her skin was dry and flaky, her gums bloody, her tongue parched, her stomach roiling, her bowels griping, and her head splitting. When she slouched from her motel room, the afternoon sun hit her like a nuclear flash. Even worse than her hangover's physical symptoms was the spiritual malaise she felt – that 'pitiful, incomprehensible demoralization' that assails every problem drinker.

She may also have been back on heroin during this trip. Some Joplin observers are under the impression that she stayed clean over the summer, but Richard Hundgen told me, 'Because of heroin, she vomited out the window during the whole train tour.'

At a lonely station in Saskatoon, she saw a lanky cowpoke outside her window and gestured for him to join her on the train. He regarded her with interest, perhaps considering her offer. Whether he knew it or not, he stood at one of the turning points of his life. Would he remain in the Canadian vastness or become a rock star's fetish? Janis yelled through the window, tempting him to come aboard while there was still time. His decision made, he threw her a friendly wave and the train moved on. As they rumbled down the tracks, Jerry Garcia joined her in a chorus of 'I've Just Seen a Face.' The Saskatoon cowboy must have been the only one who escaped her clutches, because she later calculated that she had sex sixty-five times in five days.

The train passed through remote Canadian towns such as Decimal, Lainaune, La Broquerie, Tottenham, Bayswater, Islington, Unaka, Kowkash, Minnipuka, Ophir, Snakes-breath, and Forget. The Grateful Dead's LSD bias had always represented a challenge for Janis, and at last she harangued them into drinking until they were intoxicated. At various points during the journey, she sang a haunting rendition of Merle Haggard's 'The Bottle Let Me Down,' read Thomas Wolfe, and harmonized with Rick Danko on 'Honeysuckle Rose.' For those present, the most haunting memory of the trip was Janis taking her Gibson Hummingbird and singing 'Me and Bobby McGee,' Garcia lending a poignant guitar embellishment. Soon everyone on the train was singing Kristofferson's tune, an early sign of its eventual status as a country blues classic.

In Winnipeg, a brawny frontiersman leapt onstage and demanded a kiss. She granted his wish, and as he walked away, he thanked the crew backstage. Janis kidded him, pointing out that she'd done the kissing, not the guys who worked for her. The Festival Express was such fun that when the last night was upon them, Jerry Garcia suggested a sit-down strike; he and Janis wanted this trip to go on forever. Eric Andersen and Janis joined in a duet of Hank Williams's 'I'm So Lonesome I Could Cry,' and the party was over.

Musically, however, the Festival Express lived on. Much of the Calgary concert is preserved on Janis's posthumous double LP *Joplin in Concert*. When it was released in 1972, Don Heckman of *The New York Times* corrected the rock establishment's judgment that Janis was washed up by 1970.

At Calgary, she revealed a 'musical maturity' far exceeding her previous accomplishments. Clive Davis came in for particularly harsh criticism for prognosticating in his liner notes that Janis might have 'burned less brightly, less intensely' had she survived beyond 1970. Said *The New York Times,* 'The same sort of unknowing remarks were made about Charlie Parker and no doubt about Larry Hart and Franz Schubert. Janis Joplin's talent would have grown and prospered had she lived . . . *Pearl* was the last and finest record she ever made.'

I agree with the *Times* critic that Janis was getting better and better, but on the evidence of the LP *Pearl* rather than her Canadian concerts, which I find somewhat below par. Her 'Ball and Chain,' as performed in Calgary, was no longer arresting. Perhaps due to exhaustion or drunkenness that night, her voice had lost its power and was incapable of pyrotechnics. Instead of the intricate riffs of old, she stopped in midsong and resorted to recitative. And the Full Tilt Boogie Band came no closer to matching Big Brother's definitive rendition of this song than did its predecessor, the Kozmic Blues Band.

Janis landed in Seattle after the Festival Express disbanded in Calgary. She spent July 4, 1970, at the Edgewater Inn, detonating fireworks outside the hotel. Though she did not seem depressed, she foresaw an early death for herself, saying she would only live a few more years, if that. She had emptied her life of everything but music, sex, and alcohol, and that no longer seemed enough to live for. She was struggling along without faith, hope, friends, or any kind of support group. Linda had left her for taking drugs, and now Janis, trying to stay clean, was avoiding Sunshine and Peggy and her other addicted friends for the same reason. That left her with no one.

Bill Wilson, AA's founder, was aware of the vacuum that occurs when an alcoholic or addict gives up his old lifestyle. Daily AA meetings, he suggested, provide a group of new, safe friends to replace the old, dysfunctional relationships, and newcomers in the program are urged to immerse themselves in the fellowship immediately in order to prevent a slip. Rehabs and spas such as Janis went to may be good for drying out but do not provide the opportunity for ongoing personal growth and sober fellowship that can be found in AA or NA (Narcotics Anonymous) meetings. Though Travis Rivers speculates that Janis would not have cared for AA, who knows? She might have felt right at home with fellow recovering alcoholics such as Bobby Neuwirth, James Gurley, Grace Slick, David Crosby, Roy Orbison, Joan Kennedy, Betty Ford, Liz Taylor, Carrie Fisher, and Liza Minnelli.

The concept of Pearl, the all-time good-time girl, was meant to fill the yawning emptiness in Janis's life. She christened her new album *Pearl* and began work on it in July with Paul Rothchild, the Doors's record producer. Tracing the career path that led Rothchild to Janis, Nick Gravenites says, 'Paul was around the Cabal in Berkeley when Paul Butterfield played there in the early days of folk, back in '63. He produced Butterfield's first album, and Butterfield was managed by Grossman. So it was through Rothchild's working relationship with Albert that he ended up producing *Pearl*. He's a real taskmaster, not a one-take guy but someone who'll have you do it over and over until it's right.'

In his folk days, Rothchild also produced albums by Phil Ochs and Tom Paxton and later in his career he would produce two by Bonnie Raitt. Thanks to Neuwirth, who called Rothchild at Elektra Records in 1965 and told him to come down to Albert's house in Gramercy Park right away, Rothchild was present the night that Dylan first played his rough mix of 'Like a Rolling Stone.' Rothchild says he 'made them play the fucking thing five times straight before I could say anything.' When he came out of shock, he realized that folk music was now capable of crossing over into rock and reclaiming rock 'n' roll from the British Invasion.

That Rothchild had been busted and imprisoned in the early sixties would also have made him a man after Janis's own heart. According to *Rolling Stone's* official history of rock 'n' roll, *Rock of Ages,* Rothchild had been 'nosing around Janis Joplin' ever since his days at Elektra Records, when he'd tried 'to convince her to leave Big Brother and sign with Elektra as a single.' According to John Cooke, Rothchild 'was not "hired" in the traditional sense to do this album [*Pearl*].' It all came about one hot day at Larkspur when Janis poured so many piña coladas into Rothchild, Cooke, and Lyndall that she ran out of rum. The party moved on to the No Name Bar. 'John,' Rothchild said the next day, 'Janis Joplin is a *very* smart woman.'

Rothchild had produced the Doors's eponymous first album, which included 'Light My Fire,' 'Break on Through,' 'The End,' and 'Alabama Song.' For *The Doors*, Rothchild used Sunset Sound Recording Studios at 6650 West Sunset Boulevard in LA. As a result, the facility accrued a hit cache and was renowned for its ability to simulate a live-concert feel. Although Janis was a Columbia recording star and committed to using Columbia-owned facilities, she insisted on Sunset Sound for *Pearl.*

In Rothchild, Janis recognized a kindred spirit, an intellectual as well versed in literature as she, and a creative collaborator of great potential. The producer's role, in Rothchild's view, was to identify whatever was special in an artist and bring that to full articulation. 'Whatever his theater is, I try to help him stage that.' Though a strong presence in the studio, Rothchild appreciated the artistic ego and knew when to let the performer take over, an instinct that would serve him well when he worked with Janis.

In July, Janis and the band went to Hawaii on tour. They all started drinking on the plane, and Lyndall got so crocked, she nodded off in midair. Nothing made Janis happier than such antics, and she put on a spirited show in Honolulu. One of her performances there she canceled, forfeiting fifteen thousand dollars in order to return home and pay homage to an old Texas benefactor. Ken Threadgill was celebrating his birthday in Austin and Janis wanted to treat him to a genuine 'Hawaiian lei.'

'We went to the Party Barn,' recalls Jack Jackson, who'd once recorded Janis at Threadgill's. 'It was a big rambling building out in the country, on the way to Lake Travis.' Eight hundred people had bought tickets to hear local bands, but when news circulated that Janis was on the bill, five thousand flocked to the party, where beer and barbecued beef were available for a dollar.

'She could still bust a gut laughing,' says Jackson, 'but she'd changed. At the Ghetto, she had been a restless spirit, a good-humored person of unbridled enthusiasm. Now, she had a cynical, frantic edge. Insulated from people who could have helped her, surrounded by sycophants, she'd lost contact with the real world.'

Janis came onstage inebriated and unable to tune her guitar, but she announced, 'I'm gonna sing ya a great new song. It's by a cat named Kris Kristofferson. He's somebody to watch. Just wait, folks, one of these days, he's gonna be something big. Here it goes – "Me and Bobby McGee." '

'Whatever she was taking that night didn't help,' said Stan Alexander, who'd been a part of the Threadgill crowd in the early sixties, 'but her voice was still strong, still had that quality that could make you break out with a case of shingles after a few bars.'

After her set, Alexander found her sitting on the hood of a pickup truck parked near the stage. When he spoke to her, she made no reply but slid down off the truck, leaned into his body, and mumbled something indistinct. Suzanna, a friend of Janis's from Nacogdoches, saw Janis arguing with one of her companions, and suddenly she pulled down her blouse and flopped a breast in his face, as if to underscore a point.

Later in July, Janis showed a vicious side of her nature when she ran into Chet Helms at a Grateful Dead concert at Pepperland. 'Janis was either extremely drunk or extremely high and cavorting around the stage, just aggravating the hell out of Jerry Garcia,' Chet says. 'She was pestering him, climbing all over him, fondling him on the stage, interfering with his playing, and generally grandstanding. It was fairly evident that he was irritated, but he was trying to proceed and finish playing the set.'

In the dressing room, Janis went up to Chet and kissed him so hard that she bruised his lip. 'It's too bad that we never got it on!' she said. She felt Chet had rejected her when they'd hitched to the West Coast years ago, and she'd been harboring a grudge against him ever since. 'I didn't come to California because you asked me to,' she said. 'I came to California because I was fucked by Travis Rivers.'

Later that month, she reached out just as desperately, though not as brutally, to James Gurley. Big Brother opened for her and Full Tilt Boogie in San Diego on July 11. After the show, on the flight home, 'Janis bought drinks for everyone on the plane,' Jim says. 'She had to have constant attention throughout the flight. She begged me to come to New York with her, but I didn't. I had a relationship going with a woman, and I had my kid, Hongo. She would have been willing for me to abandon them. The only reason I went so often to her house in Larkspur was because I liked to see Lyndall.'

Janis was ecstatic when Milan showed up in Larkspur one day. He always guaranteed her a good time, and they were as hungry for each other as ever. 'She was excited about some singing that she had just done and she was becoming more and more convinced that she *could* sing, if you can believe that,' Milan says. 'She had this feeling that she was just shouting for a long time, but she was getting real control of her singing. At the same time, there was the other emotion in her I sensed and that was resignation, to what, I don't know, unless it was resignation to an unhappiness. I personally felt that I had let Janis down somehow. I don't know why. I don't know that anybody could have given Janis what she wanted.'

Milan told her he was leaving the Bay Area in August to work on a movie called *Medicine Ball Caravan*. Warner Bros. was flying him and his Harley and 160 other hippies to a location site in England. He took her riding on his Harley that day, and he recalls, 'She reached all the way around, like she always did. She gave me this good firm hug, held me that way throughout the ride.'

8

Seth Morgan:
1970

He looked dangerous, but he also looked good enough to eat. His name was Seth Morgan and he came to her house in Larkspur in late July 1970 to make a cocaine delivery. Though he was from a rich eastern family, Seth was a pusher, a thief, and a pimp, and he'd end up in Vacaville state prison in a few years. Sam had run into him at Peggy's, where 'Seth blasted her because she owed him four hundred dollars,' says Sam. 'It was violent and disgusting. Seth almost killed her. She owed me much more than that, but Seth raged at her. If she didn't pay him, which I'm sure she did right away, it would have been really bad.'

James Gurley knew Seth as a heroin user, and Milan says, 'He was pretty spacey.' With her usual candor, Sunshine asserts, 'Seth Morgan was a sleazy motherfucker.' Kenai concurs, informing me that 'Seth was tough-looking. He was a hawker over on Broadway. He had many girlfriends around North Beach. Seth stole things from me and hocked them. Nobody liked Seth.'

His sexuality was ambiguous, at best. A well-known author in West Hollywood encountered Seth Morgan in New York when they were both young men cruising the East Side bars. Asking to remain anonymous, this source, now a distinguished-looking middle-aged man, says, 'We met at a bar called Mike Malkin's in 1967, a couple of years before Seth Morgan became involved with Janis Joplin. Malkin's was a popular place, the sort that would later be called a Yuppie hangout. We met by the coatroom, and he was engaging, nice – and needy. He was wearing a button-down shirt, blue blazer, Levi's, loafers, and I noticed that he had great legs. I told him that I was just leaving, and he said, "I'll go with you."

'We went to another bar, the Madison Pub. After we talked a while, and after a few drinks loosened us up, Seth said, "I'm unsure of my masculinity."

'He was a little preppie of eighteen or nineteen and I was a married man of twenty-six or twenty-seven who hadn't come out yet, and we didn't know what to do. Seth seemed to view himself as a Holden Caulfield type, an Upper East Side wise guy from a social family.

'He led me on, and finally I said, "Do you want to go back to my apartment?" When we got there, I fixed us drinks and we talked a while. He said, "I like to fuck prostitutes, you know, women who've fucked a lot of men." He liked to get drunk so he could be homosexual without guilt. I guess he wasn't drunk enough that night, because when I took him to my bedroom, it didn't work out. There was a narrow single bed in there and he said, "Is this where we're going?" He stood there a minute and then said, "Well, I think I'll leave." I remember at the door, he said, "Good night, Romeo." '

This was the unlikely husband material that Janis got engaged to in the summer of 1970. He appealed to her in many ways. He was a husky, macho, motorcycle type but also, like Kris, a silver-tongued devil who could quote T. S. Eliot. More significantly, he had that edge of anger and discontent that struck sexual sparks from her. When they went to bed together, he startled and enraptured her by slapping her butt at the precise moment of orgasm.

They spent a couple of days together and then she went back to work on her album in LA. After that, she was scheduled to go East for another Cavett show and concerts at Forest Hills and Shea Stadium. She and Seth promised to call each other later in the summer.

At Shea, the *New York Post*'s Alfred G. Aronowitz saw Janis 'take a photographer's camera away and crush his film beneath her heel because he had snapped her picture with a bottle in her hand . . . in the end she tried to get away from the hard-drinking image that went along with being the best woman blues singer of her time. She told the photographer, "I call that fucked up." '

At her last public concert, on August 12, at Harvard Stadium, a young man in the audience of forty thousand screamed, 'I wanna ball you, Janis. We all wanna ball you.' She was game but calculated she'd need a year and a half to accommodate them all.

Janis received a form letter from Port Arthur announcing the tenth annual reunion of the TJ class of 1960, which was to be held in mid-August. She called Dave Richards and asked him to go to Texas with her. 'We're going to go back and raise hell at my high school reunion,' she said. 'I'm flying to Port Arthur with a bunch of crazies – Neuwirth, Cooke [and John Fischer, her sometime chauffeur]. I was shunned by the kids in high school, and I've always had this fantasy of getting even with them one day.'

'I've got some other things going,' Dave said. 'I just can't do it. Sounds like fun.'

'Yeah,' she said. 'Some pretty rough things happened to me back then.'

She sounded as if she might be having second thoughts, but on August 13, drawn by powerful and conflicting motives, she boarded a plane for Houston. Except for former

President Johnson, Texas had never before produced an international celebrity of her magnitude, and she wanted to collect the hero's welcome that she felt her hometown owed her. Most of all, she wanted their acceptance and love, but she didn't know how to get it now any more than she had known as a young girl, and she was about to repeat all her old mistakes.

Arriving in Port Arthur she immediately faced a crisis in press relations – singlehandedly, since Albert, as usual, was doing nothing to help. To prevent Janis from deflecting attention from the class of 1960 to herself, the woman who'd sent out the form letter was now telling reporters, 'This is *not* a reception for Janis Joplin. I'm getting just really tired of hearing about Janis Joplin and all the really nasty things she's said about Port Arthur and the kids I went to high school with. There are five hundred and sixty-six other members of TJ '60 and the reunion is for everybody to have fun, not just for Janis Joplin.'

The organizer invited Janis to her home on Thursday evening to discuss the conflict. At the meeting, Janis was initially defensive, but then they both relaxed and hammered out a compromise solution. To keep the reunion from being mistaken for a Joplin tribute, Janis would be permitted to hold a press conference in the Petroleum Room of the Goodhue Hotel just before the festivities on Saturday. It was an official slap and it stung.

On the night before the reunion, just as in the old days with Langdon, Moriaty, and Lyons, she sought solace by drinking in Louisiana bars. 'I took those Harvard hillbillies across the river to show them what it was like,' Janis said. 'We went over to the Texas Pelican, man.'

Homer Pillsbury, a music promoter who now lives in Beaumont, saw her there and found her behavior somewhat condescending. 'She was in her finery,' he recalls, 'and she looked around and said, "We're freaking out these farmers, aren't we?" But she wasn't – by 1970, Texas had gone completely Ivy League, and everyone was in Bass Weejuns. There wasn't a cowboy in sight. Everyone was trying to look like James Dean. Someone asked her, "Come up and sing, Janis," and she said, "Are you crazy. I get fifty thousand dollars a night." '

After a few drinks, she relaxed and started passing out kisses to any good-looking guy who came up to meet her. 'I *loved* it,' she said. 'They make strong drinks and they have good groups. Everyone had a great time.'

There was more trouble when Janis and the Harvard hillbillies came home that night and tried to crash at her parents' house. The Joplins objected to Janis's companions, some of whom were passed out in a car parked in front of the house. Janis was consigned to a 'cot in the den' and complained vociferously but to no avail.

The situation exploded the next morning when Janis invited the Harvard hillbillies in for breakfast and Bloody Marys. The Joplins cleared out of their own house. 'Of course, they had someplace to go,' Janis said, 'a wedding.' According to Janis's classmate Bill McCuistion, 'She and her motley crew created disruption in her household. It was an awkward situation and her dad laid down the law. They were relieved when she left town.'

On Saturday, journalist Chet Flippo saw Janis arrive at the Goodhue Hotel for her press conference and says she was wearing enough jewelry for a 'Babylonian whore.' The curious – young and old alike – cruised by the hotel in cars, neither waving nor smiling, staring at Janis from icy redneck eyes. Flippo described the downtown area as 'cheap, shoot-'em-up bars and pretentious, 1930ish hotels,' but it sounds positively exciting compared with the ghost town I visit two decades later, in the 1990s. The only things that remain unchanged are the 'noxious oil refineries.' As Janis entered the Goodhue lobby that hot August afternoon in 1970, the muggy air smelled like peroxide hair dye. The press conference was held on the second floor, in the Petroleum Room, where reporters, photographers, and the news crew from KJAC-TV awaited Janis.

When she saw a big white cloth-covered table on a platform at the other end of the room, she said it looked as if someone was about to serve the Last Supper, and she executed a quick detour to the bar. She tried to make it easy for the bartender, ordering anything with vodka – martini, screwdriver, whatever – as long as it was strong. The bartender all but called her a Communist sympathizer – vodka was *not* a Texas drink. Exasperated, she sent one of her flunkies to fetch some vodka, explaining that scotch and bourbon were ruining her voice. Meanwhile, she accepted a gin and orange juice, served in a plastic cup.

The organizer, who was now wearing a green dress and a huge corsage, tried to herd everyone over to the conference table, but Janis hated the harsh lighting and refused to take her seat. She went up to the table, whirled around, and began striking poses for the photographers, wisecracking about Janis Joplin's guest appearance at the Last Supper.

'What have you been up to since 1960?' a reporter asked.

'Tryin' to get laid, stay stoned.'

Eyebrows went up. 'What do you think of Port Arthur now?' someone asked.

'There seems to be a lot of long hair and rock, which also means drug use, you know.'

So far, Janis's strategy – shocking the hometown folks and flaunting her fame and hipness – was working. Then, answering a reporter's question about how she'd differed from her schoolmates at TJ, she suddenly blew it. 'I don't know,' she said, old feelings of shame and humiliation rushing to the surface. 'Why don't you ask *them*?'

'Is it they who made you different?'

'No . . . I . . .'

'In other words, you were different in comparison to them, or were you?'

'I f-felt apart from them.'

'Did you go to many football games?'

'I think . . . *not*. I didn't go to the high school prom and uh—'

'Oh! You *were* asked, weren't you?'

'No, I wasn't. They didn't think . . . they . . . I don't think they wanted to take me.' Frantically attempting to cover her hurt with levity, she joked, 'And I've been suffering ever since – it's enough to make you want to sing the blues.' But clearly she was savaged by this merciless raking of emotional scar tissue.

Before long, she'd recovered sufficiently to drop her next bombshell. Attacking her family on their own turf, she griped that they had failed to provide comfortable bedding for her. She alleged that her mother had said, 'We sold your bed, Janis, when you left home.' Her brother, Mike, and sister, Laura, also came in for criticism. 'My little brother wouldn't give up his room,' she said. 'My little sister wouldn't give up her room.' To the *Port Arthur News,* she confided, 'I've got to check into a motel next time.'

Dolores Jones of the *Beaumont Enterprise* noted that Janis wore 'no makeup and no bra.'

It was 6:30 and time for the cocktail reception to begin in the Petroleum Room. The organizer noticed that some of Janis's young fans, local freaks, had infiltrated the crowd, and she asked Janis to get rid of them. A security guard suddenly appeared, ejecting the long-haired crashers.

The room now began to fill with the class of 1960, most of whom still lived in the Golden Triangle – Beaumont, Port

Arthur, Orange – and worked as football coaches, CPA's, housewives, refinery researchers, gas-station owners, schoolteachers, dietitians, and bus drivers. The women wore hostess gowns, pantsuits, and cocktail dresses and had high, frosted coifs. The men were in polyester blazers ranging in color from bark to mustard. To the 'Dishwater Generation,' as the *Houston Chronicle* reporter called them, Janis looked like Belle Watling, the whorehouse madam in *Gone With the Wind*.

As Janis stood there wondering why she'd come, one of the Harvard hillbillies told her to mix and mingle and maybe people would stop gaping at her. She laughed, thrust her nipples out, waved her long cigarette holder, and plunged into the crowd. Chatting with a crew-cut jock who wouldn't have spat on her ten years before, she reverted to an old attitude of self-abnegation, saying stardom was nothing but tours, buses, and motels. 'Then what you're doing is really a rat race,' he said. Realizing her mistake too late and trying to recant, she said, 'Well, man, it's better than bein' a keypunch operator.'

She was gulping her drink and one of the Harvard hillbillies warned that it was time for another vodka run. Then he got into a squabble with her other escorts over who was to get stuck with the onerous task. Meanwhile, a former classmate was monopolizing Janis, protesting that he was trapped in the Golden Triangle and didn't know how to get out. Janis cited herself as an example of a Port Arthur oddball who'd found wealth by fleeing Texas, urging him to leave for LA at once. *LA?* She must have wanted to make sure he wouldn't show up in San Francisco and bother her.

TJ popularity queen Carol Scalco says Janis 'was dressed like she was going onstage.' Introducing her to Rodney Batchelor, her husband, Carol said, 'We came because they told us in a letter that you'd be here.' Janis looked at Carol, who was as beautiful as ever, and remembered how she'd once envied her. Turning to the Harvard hillbillies, she said, 'This was one of our cheerleaders.'

'Oh, Janis,' Carol said, 'come off that. That was years ago.'

Says Carol today, 'Her flippancy hurt my feelings. Rodney and I both thought she was pretty, and she relaxed, sensing that. She really enjoyed drinking with Rodney.'

There were rumors that the local police had noticed that Janis was 'wasted.' According to John Heath, a Nacogdoches attorney, 'People cut her a lot of slack or she would have been arrested.' When Roy Murphy III told her he was now a lawyer in Houston, she said, 'You think I'm going to get busted and you'll get the case.'

'Janis,' he said, 'I don't even handle criminal law.' Murphy thought that she looked sad in her blue plumed feathers.

At 7:30 everyone went upstairs to the Scenic Room for the dinner dance. Says Jim Guidry, 'She was drunk; there was a slight sway to her.' Michele Sorenson recalls, 'She looked like she was up on something and drinking too. She didn't look real healthy. Her skin coloring didn't look good.' Erin Linn describes Janis's behavior as 'obnoxious, stoned, flamboyant. The fact that she was not even asked to sing one song showed how upset many people were by her.' Ginger Brown recalls that one drunken guy called her 'the pig of the school.' Cooke turned around and said, 'Cool it. She can take care of a squirrel like you.' Janis calmed everyone down by saying, 'Everybody lay whoever you're sitting next to.'

Bill McCuistion says, 'Janis looked like ten miles of bad road – her face, arms, veins. She looked forty years old. I didn't expect her to live very long.'

After dinner, gag gifts were passed out. Jim Tipton, Sr., remembers getting a prize for 'the most gray hair. Janis was given a tire because she traveled the longest distance to get to Port Arthur. Her comment over the microphone was, "What am I going to do with a fucking tire?" It was not said in jest but caustically.' By the end of the reunion, 'she was not particularly ambulatory,' says Charles Williams.

Going down in the elevator, she recognized her old friend Paul Bartlett and said, 'The rednecks booed me but most people were nice to me. I'm surprised everyone treated me so well. We're off to a bar – want to go?' Downstairs, they stood in the lobby, and Janis said, 'I'm making fifty thousand dollars a night, but they've got me moving around so much, I don't know what town I'm in. I'm saving all my money because I don't know how long it will last.' Today a professor of law at Trinity University in San Antonio, Bartlett says, 'She seemed scared about life in general.'

She emerged from the hotel, alone and looking melancholy, dazed, and disappointed. Then she straightened her shoulders, lifted her chin, and swaggered across the street, which looked as wide and empty as a Texas prairie.

After drinking at the Pompano bar, she went with a small party to the Channel Club, where Jerry Lee Lewis was playing. As she had in Louisville, again she made the mistake of going backstage to see Lewis, though it was clear they didn't get along. Laura, Janis's sister, was present, and Jerry Lee sized her up and informed her that she'd be better off if she stopped trying to look like Janis. According to Laura, Janis then slugged Lewis. 'Oh, if you're gonna act like a man,' Lewis said, 'I'll treat ya like one,' and he hauled off and belted Janis.

Dave Richards says that what Janis objected to was 'some racist stuff' that Lewis reportedly said. 'Jerry Lee Lewis is a real asshole,' Janis told Dave.

The fight with Lewis epitomized the horror of her Texas Walpurgisnacht. A terrible truth surfaced from the quagmire of the class reunion: Her life was not livable. She couldn't get along with *anyone* – neither peers nor family, whom she'd also succeeded in outraging.

She returned to Larkspur and within forty-eight hours was discussing marriage with the sickest, most treacherous man she had ever known, Seth Morgan.

In September 1970, Janis checked into the Landmark Motor Hotel in LA to work on her new album, *Pearl*. Seth attended eight recording sessions with her. She doted on him and wanted him around constantly. From her point of view, the only problem in the relationship was that she couldn't prevent him from going back to San Francisco after their weekends together. She bragged to Peggy that he was an animal in bed.

Janis's room at the Landmark, 105, is brownish in color and longer than it is wide. I enter it from a hallway that is formed by large closets on either side. At the far end are sliding glass windows and an air conditioner. There is a view of Franklin Avenue and a derelicts' park across the way. The Landmark is in the middle of downtown Hollywood, a colorful, squalid area of tourist shops, dope peddlers, and a few remnants of the movies' golden years, such as Grauman's Chinese Theater, now renamed Mann's. As I stand in 105 looking out the window, I see a hooker in spike heels and a black miniskirt fighting with her pimp. She jumps on his car and lies spread-eagled on the hood, defying him to take off. He drives a few feet as she clutches at the windshield, trying to hold on. Finally, he stops and they scream at each other in the street.

This would have been a good location for Seth to stage his elaborate sexual fantasies. According to a later girlfriend, Seth would get so high on coke that he was no longer capable of an erection. He'd pay a well-built hustler to fornicate with junkie women while Seth walked around pumping coke into their veins.

What he may have been putting Janis up to can be

surmised from the sexual invitations two of her girlfriends received from her at this time. She wanted to share Seth with Myra Friedman, the woman in Albert's office, and she tried to get Peggy to come to bed with her and Seth. Her language with Peggy was decidedly seductive; she said, for instance, that Seth was just as deft at oral sex as Peggy was, and she frequently crowed about what a 'good fuck' he was. It seems likely that Seth was setting Janis up to provide the elaborate, twisted kind of sexual diversion he required, and there may have been considerable pressure involved.

'Seth and Janis had a lot of similar qualities,' Dave Richards says. 'Both of them were very wounded people, very depressed people. But both were smart. Seth tested people to see if they would like him. He'd put you through seventy-nine paces. He was ruthless when he tested you – intellectually insulting, sexually insulting, anything he could do to crack you, whatever it took. One time, he spent a whole evening humiliating me at a party to see if I would still be his friend. Then as I was leaving, he asked if I'd give him a ride home. I went up the hill and got my truck and started driving it back down the road to pick him up, and there he was, lying across the middle of the road, and I was going about fifty miles an hour. That was a test to see if I'd run over him. When I didn't, he was my friend for life.'

The Landmark, or 'The Land Mine,' as David Crosby called it, was at that time a well-known shooting gallery. From the moment Janis checked in, her relapse into heroin addiction was virtually assured. For the most part, she'd been off heroin since the spring, but in returning to a nest of junkies, she was definitely flirting with disaster. If there is one rule that successful recovering addicts and alcoholics follow, it is: Stay away from slippery people and slippery places. Janis was now back among her old addict friends, such as Peggy, who was in and out of the Landmark that summer, working on a one-hundred-kilo San Diego – San Francisco marijuana run that eventually fell through. Janis's old connection was regularly seen slithering through the Landmark's hallways, pushing heroin to the motel's resident rockers.

'Seth just isn't around enough,' Janis told her pianist, Richard Bell. 'We're supposed to get married, but I don't know. He's in San Francisco most of the time. We talk a lot on the phone. He's got all these emotional problems, and, well, we're just not getting along.'

Peggy's sexual hold on Janis was as strong as ever, and on the weekdays that Seth spent in San Francisco, Janis got lonely. Soon she and Peggy resumed their familiar routine of shooting heroin and making love till dawn. Thus Janis was back on heroin and would spend the rest of her days a junkie. There were the usual complications with Peggy, who now had another girlfriend in addition to Kim.

When Kris learned that Janis was using drugs again, he tried to help. She was at the peak of her career, he pointed out; for once, she had the demon lover of her dreams, Seth, and the perfect producer, Paul. How many people, he asked, could say as much? Why was she so eager to throw it all away? She shrugged, as if it was all worthless.

Like many alcoholics and addicts, Janis was incapable of being satisfied, because she knew on some level that she was destroying herself, that her life was unmanageable, out of control, and hopelessly spiraling downward as long as she drank and used. Reacting to the Seconal overdose that killed Jimi Hendrix on September 18, she said, 'I wonder if I'll get as much publicity?'

As they worked on *Pearl* that early autumn of 1970, Janis and Richard Bell often went to Barney's Beanery after rehearsal and talked about heroin. 'She was ambivalent about it,' Richard recalls. 'She knew that when she took it, she was no longer part of the human experience. "Is there any reason to live if you stop feeling and caring?" she asked. I wish I had beat some sense into her. When I first knew her, she was a heavy drinker, because she was still substituting alcohol for heroin. I know the reasons she went back on it. She'd been keeping it straight, but she returned to a place where she'd been strung out and all her old so-called friends came around and started chippin' on her to try to get her back in their circle.'

Janis asked Seth to help her kick heroin, but he laughed in her face, saying she was just trying to get attention. An alcoholic and addict himself, he was incapable of helping her and, in fact, exacerbated the situation by trying to blame Janis for his all-day boozing.

Strangely, as her personal life dissolved into chaos in September 1970, her artistry blossomed. 'Cutting an album is always a growth experience,' Janis said to Richard. *Pearl* represented her greatest artistic unfolding since joining Big Brother in 1966. With songs like 'Me and Bobby McGee,' she returned to her Texas roots and reclaimed the melodic voice and style she'd perfected in the first phase of her career, as a folksinger. She was excited to be working with terrific musicians in the Full Tilt Boogie Band. One night at Barney's Beanery, she said to Richard Bell, 'This is so great, man! Let's start planning another album right away.'

Says Richard, 'We were talking about a raise for the band. We'd played a lot of concerts, two, three, four times a week, and by now we were a complete unit, and the album was going great. It was exciting to work at Sunset Sound – James Taylor was there doing *Sweet Baby James,* right next to us. For Janis, "McGee" was just the tip of the iceberg, showing a whole untapped source of Texas, country, and blues that she had at her fingertips. In those days, music was strictly categorized into distinct areas – blues, white blues, country and western, whereas now there's much more crossover. When she came to San Francisco, she came as a folksinger and converted over to blues. What we were seeing was how easily she could go back to the old stuff, and with the Full Tilt Boogie, she was going to pursue that area down the road.'

Eight songs were now finished on the LP, and she had done the final vocals on five of them and 'work vocals' on three. A minor crisis developed when they realized there was still enough space on the LP for two additional songs but that she had no more material. For two days, Janis, the band, and Rothchild sat around the studio looking blankly at one another, and then, as she had so frequently in the past, she turned to Nick Gravenites.

Though Nick told her he had only one idea for a song, she implored him to join her in LA. When he arrived, she took him immediately over to Paul Rothchild's house. Nick described the song he was working on, 'Buried Alive in the Blues,' only two verses of which were complete. Janis invited him to the studio to write while she recorded other songs, and 'Buried Alive in the Blues' was finished under those hectic circumstances. When Nick is in the throes of creation, he says, it wouldn't matter if there were a war going on around him. He taught Janis the words and worked with the band on the music. Everyone in the studio loved 'Buried Alive in the Blues.'

He spent some time with Janis before returning to San Francisco and was both heartened and frightened by what he saw. 'Man, I got it made now,' she said. 'I just signed this deal that's gonna guarantee me half a million bucks a year in performance money. Albert did it through his relationships with a bunch of agencies. I've got the papers to prove it. Guaranteed money, man. I'm actually going to be making big money over a long period of time.'

Nick also recognized the great danger she was in and tried to warn her. 'Janis, you're fuckin' up,' he said. 'You're drinkin' too much. You're dopin' too much. This life is bullshit. Your real life is with people, relationships, cookin' breakfast, takin' out the garbage, dumb things, dumb shit.'

'Aw, man,' she said, 'I don't want to live that way. I want to burn. I want to smolder. I don't want to go through all that crap.' Nick finally realized she meant it: 'She wasn't interested in hangin' out and bein' a housefrau and doin' dumb things with some guy, some relationship. She meant it: She wanted to burn. She needed some balance, but she wanted it all one way. That's why people die. She needed people who'd fight with her, not just yes-men. She didn't have anybody who'd say, "Hey, you're fuckin' up, don't do this." '

Shelley Winters remembers seeing Janis at the Montecito, a Hollywood bar that was popular with Method actors. They recognized each other and Janis was curious about *The Great Gatsby* and *Lolita,* two of Shelley's movies that were based on books Janis admired. Janis confided that she was interested in becoming an actress, and Shelley, a member of the Actors Studio, offered to take her to a session as an observer. 'She was thrilled,' says Shelley, 'but she couldn't get up early enough for class. Her life was a twenty-four-hour-a-day party.' Jack Nicholson wanted Janis for *Five Easy Pieces,* but there was such a foul-up in Albert's office that the offer was never forwarded to Janis and was eventually withdrawn.

Jim Morrison and Janis got together at his request shortly before he left for Paris. Calling her his old drinking buddy, he said he wanted to make amends, and they had a warm visit. Morrison was trying to control his alcoholism, drinking only white wine, but the damage had already been done. He had a deathly pallor, his coordination was shot, and he was carrying forty pounds of bloat. Janis, too, was under the illusion that switching from hard liquor to some other drink – in her case, a mixture of alcohol and milk – would help, but for booze hounds like Janis and Jim, any kind of hooch, from Kahlúa to cough syrup, is a killer. When they said good-bye that day, Jim told her that rock 'n' roll was now a part of his past.

Howard Hesseman also saw Janis at this time and spent a night with her at the Landmark. 'She was pretty wrecked that evening,' Howard recalls, and they didn't make love. 'I just spent the night sleeping with her, and we talked most of the night. She showed me several letters that she'd received from people and talked about wanting to design a book that would come out of the sleeve of the album. It was to be a collection of letters from people that had really touched her. "It'll have photos of things that people have sent me," she said. "I want to make something other than just an album to sell people, to have it be a little gift to fans. I really treasure some of the things that they've sent me, and I want to share them with other people." We talked about Paul Rothchild, who was trying to record us –*The Committee* – see if he could get a comedy album out of us.'

Clive Davis talked to her regularly. 'She'd call me and play bits and pieces of the album,' Clive remembers. 'She was thrilled about "Me and Bobby McGee" and played all of it. I knew Kristofferson and we spoke of him. She never sounded incoherent or as if she was on anything.'

Meanwhile, Janis was still trying to get her girlfriends to share Seth Morgan with her, or perhaps take him off her hands altogether. Myra Friedman had been appalled when Janis had attempted to palm him off on her. Now, Janis focused her efforts on Peggy, who went for the bait that Myra had so pointedly declined. At dinner one night in Janis's kitchenette in the Landmark, Janis threw Peggy and Seth together and looked on with satisfaction as her fiancé ogled

Peggy's breasts. Janis served chicken soup, and they all made a date for a three-ways the following weekend.

Some of Janis's actions during this period suggest that she was beginning to see Seth for what he was: a leech. One day while they were shopping, he started indicating the items that he expected her to purchase for him and she told him to go to hell. In retaliation, he returned to San Francisco earlier than planned. Bitterly disappointed, Janis dreaded the prospect of being alone in LA. Seth promised to return in time for their weekend assignation with Peggy, but Janis felt her world was falling apart. Peggy was no longer regularly accessible to her, because Peggy was thoroughly infatuated with her new girlfriend and they were now shacked up at the Chateau Marmont.

On Wednesday, Janis went to her hairdresser for a streak job. Then she looked over her will and, at her lawyer's suggestion, revised it. In 1968, she had left everything to her brother, excluding her parents and sister. She'd also provided for Linda Gravenites. Now, she cut out Linda and bequeathed half her estate to her parents and one-fourth each to her siblings. Lyndall Erb was free to keep anything she wanted in the Larkspur house or give it away to chums. Janis signed the will on October 1 and also reviewed the premarital agreement protecting her monies from her husband-to-be. The premarital papers were to be dispatched to her hotel.

On Friday, when she received the papers, she called her lawyer to inquire about signing procedures. There had to be a witness, he said, but Janis indicated that she and Seth were going to sign the premarital agreement as part of a sexual ritual they were planning. How Morgan could have regarded his exclusion from her estate as anything to celebrate, sexually or otherwise, remains a mystery. Janis contacted City Hall authorities about marriage license requirements.

Following a vague hunch that Janis needed her, Linda

Gravenites showed up in Los Angeles the first week in October. 'I heard she was doing dope and in bad shape in LA,' Linda recalls. 'It was so odd, because I had no plan to go down to LA but found myself getting on a city bus, then getting on an airplane, and arriving at the Burbank airport. There are things that happen that you just don't understand and that was one of them. In LA, on Saturday, I ran into Sunshine and she and I were going to go over to the Landmark and see Janis.'

Sunshine, who'd managed to kick, had made plans with Janis to take in a new Kurosawa film, starring Toshiro Mifune, and Linda was going to go along with them.

On Saturday, Janis and Seth got into another of their fights on the phone; he hadn't arrived in LA as promised and she was angry and upset with him. He calmed her down, promising to show up on Sunday. She also got in touch with her dressmaker and her dope dealer. Lyndall talked to her more than once and learned that Janis had scored heroin, as well as the methadone to cure herself. As Lyndall and Janis spoke on the phone, Danny Fields was visiting Lyndall at the Larkspur house, where he was waiting to take her out to dinner. Just as he entered the living room, Lyndall was suggesting that Janis cancel her plans to take a Mexican vacation after *Pearl* and return to Larkspur instead, since the weather was mild and sunny. Danny added that she could come to Monterey for the weekend and be with old friends like Bobby Neuwirth. The occasion was the Big Sur Hot Springs Folk Festival. Though she had an album to finish in LA, Janis wanted to know more.

Danny took the receiver and explained that the festival had been planned for Esalen but at the last minute had moved to Monterey. All the stars would be living and partying at the Holiday Inn and it would be as much fun as Monterey Pop. They joked about the festival, calling it the Big Ova Festival, the Big Lesbian Conspiracy, and the North California Lesbians in Music Festival. She was tempted but decided to gut it out in LA.

On the day before the scheduled three-way scene with Seth and Peggy at the Landmark, Peggy made a quick trip to San Francisco. At the Trident that night, she was surprised to see Seth dining with Lyndall, and both Seth and Lyndall were drunk. Seth assured Peggy when she stopped by his table that he would be in LA the following day to keep their date with Janis. Both Peggy and Seth were taking the night flight to LA, but when Peggy boarded the plane later on, she didn't see Seth.

Back in LA, Peggy got so involved with her girlfriend, drinking at the Bacchanal-70 bar and shooting up heroin and making love at the Chateau Marmont, that she missed her assignation with Janis. On Saturday, she saw Janis's dealer, who said he'd just delivered fifty dollars' worth of heroin to the Landmark. He added that while he was visiting briefly with Janis, she'd complained about Peggy to him, saying she'd stood her up. In fact, *everyone* had stood her up.

When Janis's connection had come by the Landmark Saturday, he'd left her enough smack to kill a regiment. It hadn't been stepped on, as was customary, and estimates of its purity range from 50 to 80 percent. The dealer wasn't an addict, and when he received a new supply, he usually had a 'taster' check the heroin and cut it. On this particular weekend, the taster was gone but the connection went out and sold the heroin, anyway. According to Sunshine, eight people would die from using that batch of heroin over the weekend.

Janis injected a small amount just before going to work at Sunset Sound. Says Richard Bell, 'We cleaned up everything. It was a good day. We were doing really well. She was satisfied with "Me and Bobby McGee," which we got on the first take, or second. There was a question on the last song, "Buried Alive in the Blues." She said she'd do the vocal the next day.'

Richard thought she looked 'great' that evening, and during a break, they had dinner at a Chinese restaurant. Back at the studio, about two dozen friends came to see her, including Bobby Womack, who'd given her the song 'Trust Me' for the album. Janis played the instrumental track for 'Buried Alive in the Blues' by Nick Gravenites and liked it so much that she romped around merrily, her tassels flying and bells tinkling. Paul Rothchild had produced about one hundred LP's and was convinced that *Pearl* was one of the best. 'That music was full of heart,' he said, 'the way it's supposed to be.' Calling the LP 'a labor of total love,' he saluted the musicians for giving 'a hundred and ten percent' and Janis for giving 'a hundred and fifty percent.'

Someone mentioned that John Lennon's birthday was coming up on October 9, and all the groups who'd worked at Sunset Sound that week had recorded a version of 'Happy Birthday, Dear John.' 'Janis and her band dubbed a casette of the song with Janis happily cackling, "Happy birthday, John! This is for you!" ' says Carl Gottlieb. 'While they were still in the mood and the word *happy* was floating in the air, Janis dove into "Happy Trails to You," and sang it completely.' 'Happy Trails to You,' a classic of the romantic cowboy style, was Roy Rogers and Dale Evans's theme song.

Janis rang Larkspur from the studio, hoping to reach Seth, but Lyndall answered. When she said Seth wasn't there, Janis became testy, taking large gulps from her bottle of Ripple wine.

The session ended around midnight and Janis and a couple of musicians piled into the band's International Harvester station wagon and drove to Barney's Beanery for drinks. Janis ordered tequila, and Richard Bell had a screwdriver. 'She was happy, real excited,' Richards recalls. 'We knew we had something good in the can, that it was going to be a good album, but all of us including her were looking forward to the next one coming up.

'Her next LP was going to be just phenomenal. She was making a big transition. We talked about how she'd been restricted, and she was seeing what the future could be. With her background of Texas and country and folk and California rock, she had a lot more doors open to her for the future.'

They returned to the Landmark, and Richard and Kenny Pearson said good night and headed for their rooms. Seconds later, at about 1:00 A.M., Jack Hagys, the Landmark's manager, saw her 'coming home alone.'

In the solitude of room 105, Janis got out her hype kit and started cooking up a large dose of 'colossal calm.' According to Hundgen, 'Janis at the end gave people a hundred dollar bill and told them, "Take a plane down to my sessions," but nobody showed up; they all spent the money on dope. Peggy and Seth Morgan stood her up. So that's why, you see?' After shooting up, she walked out to the lobby for cigarettes, asking the night clerk, George Sandoz, to change a five-dollar bill. He handed her four dollar bills and four quarters and expected her to go directly to the cigarette machine in the patio, but instead she kept standing there, looking as if she wanted to talk.

To him, she was no one special, just a woman he'd often seen around the hotel, one who never seemed to be happy. That night, she struck him as 'sloppy-looking' in her red ankle-length gypsy costume. Like Blanche DuBois, the tainted southern belle in *A Streetcar Named Desire*, Janis had always depended on the kindness of strangers, and this final stranger didn't disappoint her. Sandoz put aside whatever he was doing and listened. She told him things that people normally share with lovers or spouses – what a long day's work she'd had and how happy she was over her record and how well it was going. They talked for over a quarter of an hour and then she said good night, went to the cigarette machine for her Marlboros, and returned to her room.

Janis pitched her cigarettes on the bed and stripped down to her blouse and panties. Then, quick as a shotgun blast to the brain, death hit her, knocking her to the floor. She fell so hard that she struck her lower lip on a piece of furniture and her mouth filled with blood. She had landed between the bed and a chair, and she lay there all through the night and most of the following day. Her body was not discovered until 7:30 P.M. Sunday, October 4 – eighteen hours after she'd died.

Her old friend Jerry Garcia was playing 'Cold Rain and Snow' during a Grateful Dead set at Winterland when he heard. Janis's timing, he said, had been perfect, checking out just before an inevitable descent into premature senility. 'But going up,' he said, 'it's like a skyrocket, and Janis was a skyrocket chick.'

While Janis lay dead at the Landmark all day Sunday, Seth was in San Francisco trying to reach her by phone. Finally, he was about to board a plane for LA when someone answered the phone at Sunset Sound and told him that Janis had not shown up for work. The session had started at 6:00 P.M., and though Rothchild had experienced a sense of foreboding all day, he'd done nothing about it, assuming she'd stopped to go shopping on her way to work and would show up any minute.

Seth then called Cooke, who was staying in room 223 at the Landmark, and Cooke said he was just leaving for Sunset Sound. Cooke advised Seth to call the studio when he arrived at Burbank airport and someone would come to pick him up. As Cooke left the motel with Vince Mitchell and Phil

Badella, the roadies, he noticed Janis's car in the driveway. Securing the passkey at the desk, he let himself into her room and discovered her body at 7:30 P.M. He called Albert and Janis's lawyer. The lawyer in turn had his brother-in-law, a doctor, come to the hotel. Finally, the police were called and Sergeant Sanchez pronounced Janis dead at 9:10 P.M., an hour and forty minutes after her body had been found. Despite the amount of time that had elapsed, Cooke insisted that only policemen and personnel from the medical examiner's office were permitted to inspect Janis's quarters. When the police arrived, they found no drugs or drug equipment in room 105.

Unfortunately, no inquest was held at the time, and when I contact the Los Angeles Police Department in 1991, I am told, 'We don't have any file on Janis Joplin. It's too old a case.' I visit the LA coroner's office, where the records are scrupulously maintained, and many irregularities immediately come to light. Janis was the subject of two conflicting coroner's reports.

The first call came to the Office of Chief Medical Examiner from Sergeant Sanchez at 9:16 P.M. Sunday. The supervising coroner, A. L. Lorca, went to the Landmark, examined Janis's body, and searched her room. Though he detected needle marks on her arms, he found no drugs, other than 'Dalmane capsules and tablets for pain found on bed.' He could not determine the cause of Janis's death and on his case report (70-10463) he checked all three boxes: Natural, Accident, and Undetermined, adding that 'possibly' she'd overdosed on Dalmane or narcotics.

Janis's body was brought into the morgue and examined. The tattoos on her left breast, wrist, and right heel were duly noted. Her weight was listed at 135 pounds and her height at 66 inches. The inventory of her personal effects included $94.70 in cash, two ankle bracelets, a yellow earring, a red necklace, a key, and a wallet. Her body was then stored in crypt number 9.

Because of the inconclusiveness of the first news reports, wild rumors started to circulate, some saying Janis had been killed by the CIA, others that her room was full of bottles and she'd probably been killed by a lover, still others claiming suicide. According to one theory, the FBI had masterminded an international conspiracy that was responsible for the assassinations of Hendrix, Janis, and Jim Morrison, who all died within a year. Janis's biographer Deborah Landau wrote that attempts were made to squelch speculation about Janis's death by discounting the drug charges and comparing her death to that of Hendrix – 'from an overdose of sleeping pills, followed, in her case, by a fall from the bed.'

In the LA coroner's office, C. R. (Bob) Dambacher wasn't satisfied with Lorca's report. Says Dambacher today, 'There were lots of holes in it. If the needle tracks were fresh, then there should have been a drop of blood and discoloration noted around the puncture wounds. I felt he'd missed some evidence.'

Dr. Thomas T. Noguchi, the chief medical examiner, was also concerned about Janis's needle marks and couldn't understand why no drugs had been found in her room. He entertained the possibility of murder. At 11:00 A.M. on October 5, Dambacher and Noguchi went to the Landmark, broke the public administrator's seal on Janis's door, and conducted the second coroner's investigation, accompanied by Dr. David M. Katsuyama, deputy medical examiner, and William Lystrup. At 11:10, Dambacher discovered the first piece of missing evidence. In plain sight, on Janis's bed, lay a piece of gauze with dried blood on it. More of the bloody gauze turned up in the wastebasket. Janis evidently had dabbed at her puncture wounds with the gauze.

Looking around the kitchen, at 11:20, Dambacher turned

up 'a red balloon or rubber glove' containing heroin and a bloody paper towel. At 11:40, he found Janis's hype kit, containing a smudged teaspoon, more bloody cotton, and a needle and plastic syringe with heroin in it. More heroin was discovered in a paper bag in the top-right dresser drawer in the living room, along with a plastic bag containing marijuana and another plastic bag with four and a half Lilly 172 tablets. The coroner's team left room 105 and resealed it at noon.

Dambacher concluded, 'It was clear that she had OD'd in her room, not at a party or someone's house, that it was self-inflicted, an accident. You have to prove suicide, and there was no suicide note.' That left the question of why Janis's drugs and drug paraphernalia hadn't turned up in the first coroner's report on October 4. Dr. Noguchi asked the LAPD policeman on duty in Janis's room to tell him whether anyone had been in room 105. Yes, indeed, someone had been in there, though Dr. Noguchi couldn't remember whom the cop mentioned. 'He may have removed the drug after her death and then realized it was evidence,' says Dr. Noguchi. 'So he came back and dropped it in the wastepaper basket.' In OD cases, Noguchi explains, well-meaning friends often conceal the stash as an automatic reflex. Then, he says, 'they usually return with it when they have thought things over.'

Dr. Katsuyama performed the autopsy on Janis, making 'the usual Y-shaped incision.' He listed the cause of her death as 'acute heroin-morphine intoxication' due to 'injection of overdose.' His principal anatomical findings were 'pulmonary edema and congestion; visceral congestion; fatty meta-morphosis of liver,' and numerous needle marks on her arms. When he sectioned Janis's left arm, he found 'at least two fresh hemorrhagic areas on the lateral margin.'

There were also 'old needle marks and some are of relatively recent origin.'

She had an old surgical scar 'in the right lower quadrant of the abdomen.' Her mouth was bloody and her blue eyes showed 'moderate dilation of the pupils.' Her recently streaked hair was 'of moderate length and shows a varying shade of, from blond to brunette.' Her uterus contained an intrauterine contraceptive 'of the serpentine type.'

Lab tests solved the riddle of why an average-size injection of heroin had proved fatal in Janis's case. 'The dealer had sold Joplin . . . almost pure heroin, so pure that it had more than ten times the power of the normal heroin she used,' Noguchi found. 'Her system was not prepared for, and could not cope with, the unexpected jolt.'

As Janis's friends learned of her death that Sunday night, their reactions varied widely. Sunshine, who was working as a waitress in a Glendale nightclub called Under the Icehouse, got drunk on tequila. 'I could feel Janis everywhere,' she says. Though she was wearing 'eighty bracelets on one arm and sixty on the other,' she remembers looking at them and wondering, Why didn't I wear any *beads* today? Two of Janis's girlfriends were at the bar, peaking on mescaline, and they all took off in Sunshine's car. After visiting Linda Gravenites, they were stopped by the LA county sheriff, who discovered a box of Seconals on Sunshine. She spent a few hours in jail, where all 140 bracelets were sawed off her arms .

Sunshine then went to Sunset Sound, where Janis's friends were convening. The Full Tilt Boogie Band was sitting around in shock. Says Richard Bell, 'Paul Rothchild came and told us. It was pretty weird, just out of the blue, like somebody bringing a knife and shoving it right through you.' Linda Gravenites recalls, 'They were playing the first tapes of *Pearl* and it was too much to take. Sunshine was falling apart. Lyndall was on the phone falling apart. Albert was there.

There were a lot of people to talk to.'

Rothchild played the birthday cassette Janis had made for John Lennon, and at the end of the cassette, Janis had sung 'Happy Trails to You,' signing off with the touching wish that everyone achieve their dreams. Says Carl Gottlieb, 'We were listening to it and she had not been dead twenty-four hours.' If the tape ever reached Lennon, it would probably have appalled him. A heroin addict himself, Lennon was spooked when he heard of Janis's death, seeing it as a sign that he, too, was doomed to an early grave. His premonition proved correct. He had just turned forty when he was shot and killed in 1980.

Lyndall Erb was in LA and realized that she needed to alert someone in San Francisco to look after the Larkspur house. She reached Dave Richards, who'd been constructing a carport for Janis that had a sun deck on top and resembled a flying saucer. 'We'd just begun to build that,' says Dave. 'We were staking it out to pour the concrete for it the same evening she died.' After talking with Lyndall, he immediately called each member of Big Brother, and they all rushed to his house in Fairfax, where Seidemann also joined them. 'She barely scratched the surface,' Sam says. ' "Little Girl Blue" shows where she could have gone. It's so stupid.'

Dave Richards then went to Larkspur to house-sit until Lyndall returned. 'I took care of business first,' he says, 'and then I cried.' At Larkspur, onlookers were already gathering in the cul-de-sac in front of Janis's house. 'Then came the press,' says Dave, 'a horrendous experience. Some blond anchor-type woman with a microphone was rude, and I told her to go fuck herself. She kept saying, "Who are you?" and I kept saying, "Fuck you. Go away."

'Then different people who were friends of Janis's showed up at various times during the day. Jeffrey, a drummer, brought a case of beer and sat there and got crocked. I stayed there all that day and until somebody, maybe Lyndall, showed up to take charge of the house.'

Nick Gravenites was in a recording studio control room in San Francisco when he heard. 'I had a real hard time facing it,' says Nick. 'I liked Janis a lot. She was real generous, intelligent, funny, and kind. I was glad that she was a success. For her to succeed was for me to succeed. Not only just making a few bucks off her records. If I wanted to go hang out at Janis's house, sit around on the cushions in the lap of luxury, I could do it. Welcome anytime. I liked her because she was real, even to the point of dying like she did in LA. She lived and died the blues life.'

Rothchild asked Nick to return to the studio and supply the vocal track for 'Buried Alive in the Blues.' Nick was willing, but somehow the plan never materialized, and *Pearl* was issued as an unfinished album, 'Buried Alive in the Blues' remaining an instrumental track.

After hearing of Janis's death on October 4, Peggy had gone to the Landmark, where she'd encountered John Cooke, Paul Rothchild, and Kris Kristofferson. From the way Cooke looked at her and a harsh remark he allegedly made, Peggy knew he blamed her. Less judgmental, Rothchild embraced her and they held each other for a long time. Arriving somewhat later, Kristofferson said he'd been in Big Sur at the Hot Springs Folk Festival and had just flown down from Monterey. Grabbing Peggy in a hug, he wondered aloud whether they'd failed Janis. He was crying.

Intent on avenging Janis's death, Seth Morgan cheated her connection out of one thousand dollars, giving him a bad coke count at Barney's Beanery. The connection then cleared out of town, fearing that the police were going to find his name in Janis's address book and arrest him. Seth was misty-eyed, but years later he sounded about as emotional as a rattlesnake when he callously referred to Janis's death as 'her untimely checkout.' According to Peggy, he asked her to sleep with him only hours after Janis's body was found and then complained when she turned him down for her girlfriend. He and some other male friends of Janis's tagged along with Peggy and her girlfriend when they went off to the Bacchanal-70. The evening became even more ludicrous as the guys got drunk and tried to seduce the lesbian clientele.

In Port Arthur, Janis's family was barraged with hate calls. Her father said both the townspeople and the local media disliked her because of the derogatory remarks she'd made about Port Arthur. During her life, the calls had poured in every time she'd knocked the town on national TV. Now that she was dead, people were calling and either remaining silent or, worse, laughing.

On hearing of Janis's overdose, Jim Morrison rolled his eyes and said, 'You're drinking with number three.' When he died the following July, as with Janis's death, at first a cover-up was attempted, and the press was told that Jim had died of a heart attack. But when his wife, Pam Courson, died a few years later of a heroin overdose, Morrison biographers concluded that Jim had gotten into Pam's stash and taken too much.

Albert Grossman's feelings about the loss of his most valuable client are not known, but no doubt he was consoled by the fact that her earnings for 1970 would exceed $1 million. Neuwirth called Patti Smith and said simply, 'Well, the lady's dead.' The following year, he would use the identical words when he told Patti that Edie Sedgwick, an Andy Warhol superstar, had died of a barbiturate overdose. At *Rolling Stone,* when Jann Wenner's secretary told him Janis was dead, he said, 'Cancel her subscription.'

'I heard about it on television in the morning,' says Clive Davis. 'That just shocked me.' When he went to his office, he shut the door, put on his tape of *Pearl,* and wept.

The bright young men Janis had run around with in high school all called Jim Langdon. 'I've been coming to terms with the loss ever since,' says Jim. 'She's still very much a part of my life.'

Grant Lyons says, 'Beginning with Hendrix's death earlier in the month, I'd begun to realize that behind the flashy LSD facade that the media were focusing on, it was heroin that had hooked the rock 'n' roll culture. Her death had the inevitability of fate.'

Like Grant, Janis's obituary writers also saw her as a victim of outside circumstances. *The New Yorker*'s Ellen Willis wrote, 'Her doping was not a personal but a cultural idiosyncrasy.' *The New York Times* editorialized, 'God, what a year [1970] this is turning out to be. The king and the queen of the gloriously self-expressive music that came surging out of the late sixties are dead, the victims, directly or indirectly, of the very real physical excesses that were part of the world that surrounded them.'

Fortunately, Janis's death had the effect of reversing the heroin trend as the late sixties drug of choice. According to Dr. Noguchi, whose office kept track of drug trends, a precipitous drop in heroin use occurred immediately following news of her death.

Travis Rivers was watching the 'Today' show and immediately called Larkspur to confirm the terrible report. 'She was still clutching the change from her cigarette money when she died – a good businesswoman to the end,' he says. 'I miss her a lot. It was always my intention to be friends with her forever.'

Milan read of Janis's death in the *International Herald Tribune* in Paris, where he had gone after finishing his movie. Says Milan, 'As I was driving around Paris on my Harley, I had a strange experience. She came and said goodbye. It's like she was on the back of the Harley again, holding on to me like she used to, reaching all the way around. She gave me this good firm hug. Then she was gone – and so was I. It was winter in Paris and I wasn't with anyone. I just got on the scooter and rode until the sun was shining down in Morocco and didn't stop until I buried the axle in the sand.'

Shortly after Janis died, David (George) Niehaus returned from Nepal and came to see Linda Gravenites, bringing her some silk to make him a pair of trousers. 'He had an if-only feeling about her,' Linda says. 'We all had that.'

Janis's will specified cremation, and funeral services were held at Westwood Village Mortuary on October 7, 1970. Six days later, her ashes were scattered from a plane over the California coast, off Marin County. In Port Arthur, under the headline SINGER'S DEATH LAID TO DRUGS, the *News'* obit writer noted, 'She never sang in her hometown and visited only infrequently.'

9

Drinks Are on Pearl: 1970

Janis's will provided for a wake, specifying a budget of $2,500. The party was held at the Lion's Share nightclub in San Anselmo, and the invitation stated, 'Drinks are on Pearl.' Among the guests were Chet Helms, Peggy Caserta, Seth Morgan, James Gurley, Kim Chappell, Linda Gravenites, Sunshine, Pattycakes Josephson, Sam Andrew, Kenai, Nick Gravenites, David Getz, Dave Richards, Albert Grossman, Bobby Neuwirth, Howard Hesseman, John Cooke, and Lyndall Erb.

James Gurley remembers having a very good time.'Everybody just got as drunk and as fucked up as they could,' he says. 'I think it was fitting to send her off that way. I made a toast: "Here's to what's-her-name?" There was no talking about her at all.'

Chet danced with Cheryl Littledeer, who had given Gurley a second son, Django, named after Django Reinhardt, a European jazz guitarist of the thirties and forties. 'I had a reasonably good time,' says Chet, 'given the circumstances.'

Seth Morgan cruised the room and when someone pointed out Linda Gravenites, he approached her and said, 'I'm Seth. Hi.' She frowned at him and thought, Euch! Like, so what, you smarmy little ass. Says Linda today, 'There was no need for them to get married. It would have lasted two weeks. She went through people at an alarming rate.' When someone played the song Joe McDonald had written for Janis, Linda started to get emotional and ran for the ladies' room in back. 'I bumped into Dave Richards in the hallway,' she says, 'and broke down and cried.'

When she returned to the party, Big Brother was playing and she started feeling good again, going up to Grossman and asking him to dance. He was already doing a tiny jig in place and said, 'I am dancing.' According to Linda, Kris was not at the party. 'He was in LA,' she says. 'I met him when I was down there and I didn't care much for him.'

Kenai attended the wake with Howard Hesseman, and when he spotted Seth, he wanted to go up to him and demand payment for all the things he'd stolen from him.

'Peggy had gotten me on dope and I was strung out,' recalls Kim Chappell. 'Sam, Peggy, and I were dying for some heroin. We were in terrible shape and I remember one of us saying, "What would Janis say if she were here? Get down! Get some heroin." So we did.'

What Sunshine remembers most about Janis's wake was 'Kenai's killer pot brownies.' After the party, she and Seth went to Janis's house in Larkspur, where Laura, Janis's sister, was 'being very straight and wringing her hands.' Nick Gravenites joined them and they all spent the night together at Janis's.

During the following week, Sunshine helped earmark Janis's possessions for distribution among her friends, going around the house and saying, 'Sam should have this and so-and-so should have that.' It turned out to be anything but an orderly process. When Kenai went to Larkspur to collect some of Linda Gravenites's things, Lyndall Erb made him wait three hours. 'But I managed to get Linda's teapot,' he says. 'The house was a mess. Eric Andersen and Debbie Greene were staying there with Lyndall, and she was selling stuff. Jerry Garcia got a Chinese room divider.'

A few months after Janis's death, *Pearl* was released. The LP debuted on the *Billboard* chart February 6, 1971, and went to number one. 'Me and Bobby McGee,' the album's hit single, charted on February 20 and also sailed to number one. Had Janis lived to collect *Pearl* royalties, she'd have been a millionaire by 1971. Praised by critics on its release, the album continued to grow in stature over the years, and after two decades, *New York* magazine, in 1990, placed it as number one on their list of the ten best albums ever recorded by women. In addition to 'Me and Bobby McGee,' which became one of the anthems of Janis's generation, *Pearl* includes the wonderful 'Mercedes Benz,' 'A Woman Left Lonely,' and 'Get It While You Can.' The most impressive thing about the album is the country-style voice she unveiled in 'Me and Bobby McGee,' harking back to her roots in folk music.

'Her legacy will survive the changing trends of pop music,' wrote *Billboard*. Her old bête noire, *Rolling Stone*, canonized her as the 'premier white blues singer of the '60s,' and *The Who's Who in Rock* called her 'one of the brightest stars rock has ever produced.' Eighteen years after her death, *Time* put her on its cover, writing, 'Janis Joplin expressed one side of 1968 fairly well: ecstatic and self-destructive simultaneously, wailing to the edges of the universe.'

Epilogue

From classmate Gayle Blakeman, today a housewife in Lafayette, Louisiana, to movie star Kris Kristofferson, Janis profoundly influenced almost every life she touched. Gayle tells me that she gave up drugs the minute she heard of Janis's death. Different but equally dramatic was Janis's effect on Kris: She gave him his first number-one hit when 'Me and Bobby McGee' was released in January 1971.

'When I first listened to it,' says Kris, 'I could just hear her laughing to herself and saying, "Wait till that motherfucker Kris hears this!" ' At the end of the year, the Nashville Songwriter's Association voted him Songwriter of the Year. Later, he became a top movie star, appearing opposite Barbra Streisand in *A Star Is Born*, but by the mid-1970s, his alcoholism and drug addiction trashed his career. Perhaps following Janis's example, he tried to charm the media into accepting him as a hard-drinking rogue, but it backfired in his face. *Esquire* was not amused when he said he started his drinking each day at dawn. 'Let's have some dope,' he suggested to their interviewer Laura Cunningham, who later wrote, 'I remain high just by breathing Kris's exhaust.'

He further damaged his reputation, and his marriage to Rita Coolidge, by posing for a nude *Playboy* spread with Sarah Miles. Kris was shown plunging into Sarah, exposing his naked buttocks, and in another shot he was pressing his face into her genitals. 'That was just about the worst thing I ever have done,' he admitted. 'My face where it was for ten million people.' He stopped drinking in 1976 and became active in progressive causes, and though he continues to sing and act, his career has never quite recovered its initial impetus.

James Gurley got clean and sober in 1984, when his eighteen-year-old son, Hongo, was almost killed in a motor-cycle accident. Asked to reveal how he recovered from alcoholism and heroin addiction, Gurley says, 'I turned my life and my will over to God.' He still plays with Big Brother, who get together on special occasions, such as their October 1991 appearance at the Rock 'n' Roll Hall of Fame in Cleveland, where Jann Wenner announced the acquisition of a major Joplin collection. Jim records with the drummer Muruga (their tape is available from Musart Co., POB 160461, Cupertino, CA, 95016) and is currently working on a solo album, with computer-controlled keyboard, entitled *Fingers of Brutality.* Popular in Japan, Jim was the hit of the summer 1991 Hiroshima music festival and may return there with Big Brother and singer Michele Bastian.

As suave and prepossessing as ever, Sam Andrew has been off heroin since 1975. 'I started reading Aleister Crowley,' he says. 'A lot of the upper class in England between the wars were addicted to cocaine and heroin, and Crowley showed me a way out from an urbane, intelligent English-man's point of view.' Today, he leads a life of impeccable decorum in the Pacific Northwest, where he lives with his attractive, soft-spoken wife, Suzanne, whom he married in 1983, and their five-year-old daughter, Mari. Describing himself as an agnostic with an open mind, Sam attends University Presbyterian Church, where his wife was baptized. 'Part of the reason for our moving to Seattle was our return to the bosom of the church,' he says. Employed as a financial adviser with Dwight H. Olson Company, he also performs with the Sam Andrew Band at the Scarlet Tree and the Central Club.

In 1991, Sam served as a consultant on the musical *Janis*, which was shut down by court action from the Joplin family. Even though Janis had been dead over twenty years, the Joplins, who were planning their own musical, movie, and radio show, in addition to Laura's book, claimed exclusive rights to Janis's 'voice, delivery, mannerisms, appearance and dress, and the actions accompanying her performances.'

Susan Ross, the playwright, countersued for $3 million, stating, 'Janis Joplin is a part of our national heritage. Her influence on us today, on the music business and on the way women in music perform is tremendous. She is not a part of someone's personal property.' The court agreed: The Joplins lost when U.S. District Judge John C. Coughenour ruled that 'the right of publicity cannot rationally reach so far' and warned that such suits 'would bar even a comedian's imitation of a famous figure or a photograph of a celebrity on the cover of a biography.'

Ralph J. Gleason, the provincial reviewer who attacked Janis for leaving Big Brother, died of a massive heart attack in 1975.

Owsley, the acid king, was busted in Orinda, California, by thirteen federal and state narcotics agents, who confiscated his stash of 868,000 doses of LSD. Sentenced to three years in prison, he suffered a broken nose during a bout with a fellow convict. When last heard of, he was out of jail and working as a beekeeper, though Richard Hundgen believes he's designing gold jewelry in Lake Tahoe.

In February 1992, Milan Melvin moved to a ranch in Oregon, where he is 'up at the crack of dawn, splitting logs and running a tractor.'

Bobby Neuwirth has a decade of sobriety under his belt, lives in Venice, California, and has resumed painting. 'He went back to it like I did,' says Dave Getz, who is also an artist (and also clean and sober).

Stanley Mouse sells his posters, paintings, and T-shirts out of a little gallery in Sonoma, California.

I found Mark Braunstein in Cotati, near Santa Rosa, where he'd been running a cabaret. He was selling off the business as I interviewed him, but he was still the cheery, upbeat, glossy-haired swain who'd dazzled Janis.

Travis Rivers worked for Tracy Nelson from 1967 to 1979. Today, Travis is a computer expert in New York and lives in Greenwich Village with documentary filmmaker Mary Brown, who produced the five-part *Portraits of America* for Ted Turner.

Chet Helms lives in San Francisco with Judy Davis, a pretty woman who looks as if she just stepped off a 1960s commune. Chet runs the Atelier Dore, an art gallery on Bush Street. Janis's other impresario, Bill Graham, sounded as excited as a kid when I talked with him in 1991. He was to appear in a movie – *Bugsy* – and he acted as if it was the most important thing that had ever happened to him or anyone else. A few months later, he died in a helicopter crash, returning from a rock concert.

As Peggy Caserta stated in her autobiography, heroin ruined her life. Eventually, she became a pusher herself, and only when heroin stopped getting her high, regardless of how much she injected, did she resort to methadone in an effort to kick. She ended her book on a rueful note, saying that all she had left was Janis's memory.

Kim Chappell says that she was almost murdered as a result of Peggy's book, which was published in 1973. One night, Kim was in the Bacchanal-70 with Peggy's lover and went out into the alley for a while. A carful of dope dealers came by and asked for Peggy's girlfriend. One of them said, 'Sounds like a party going on in there.' Kim started to go back in but said, 'Yeah, why don't you come on in?' They leapt out and stabbed her three times in the chest, puncturing both lungs.

Kim staggered into the bar and then was taken to the Hollywood hospital, where she wasn't expected to live. 'But I pulled through,' says Kim. 'I was stabbed because, when Peggy's book came out, her dealer, the same one who'd given Janis her last fix, didn't like it that he was referred to and was out to get Peggy. He couldn't find her, so he went for her lover. When they realized who I was, they felt that my death would also hit Peggy, and so they stabbed me.

'I finally managed to get clean; though I still enjoy marijuana and a glass of wine with a meal, I'm careful not to abuse. Janis was a real pig when it came to alcohol and drugs.'

As for Peggy, Milan Melvin reports that 'she's still exactly the same Peggy as she was back then. Exactly. Peggy's new girlfriend is a Janis look-alike and affects singing in a Janis style. When Peggy lived here in Santa Barbara, she invited me over to her place and had an all-girl band playing. Peggy was trying to get her recorded and get her singing in clubs.'

Albert Grossman's downfall came in the 1970s. His gross income during his peak years at the end of the sixties was $1.8 million, but his music empire began to crumble with the departure of Bob Dylan in 1969 – who, according to one theory, decided that he had been 'ripped off' by Albert – and Peter, Paul and Mary, who left him in 1970. Janis's death was the coup de grace. 'He was someone big who finished up badly,' says one former colleague.

By 1974, Grossman was so short of cash that he tried to collect on his $200,000 accidental death policy on Janis. The San Francisco Associated Indemnity Corporation refused to pay, rejecting the LA coroner's finding that Janis's death was an accident. The insurance company said she had committed suicide and that if they had been told of her drug use and drinking, they'd never have issued the policy. A six-person jury tried the case in New York State Supreme Court in 1974, and Albert swore under oath that he did not know that Janis was a heroin addict, claiming that he had taken out the policy 'with air crashes in mind.' After a three-week trial, the defense failed to show that Janis's death had been intentional, and Albert collected $112,000. Friends say Albert 'needed the cash.' He died of heart failure in the 1980s.

Seth Morgan tried his hand at various enterprises, including running a movie house and pimping. Dave Richards helped him build the theater, where he showed foreign art films, hoping to attract students from nearby Marin College. When that failed, he turned it into a porn house, but that flopped, too. Unable to pay Dave for his labor, he let Dave live in his home rent-free, but eventually they were all evicted for nonpayment of rent. Driving while drunk, Seth cracked up his motorcycle, and the girl who was riding behind him was so severely injured that part of her face remained immobile. He worked as a hawker for a strip joint and pimped for a girl he led into prostitution.

A few years after Janis's death, Seth pulled an armed robbery and pinned his victim's hand to the floor with a dagger. When he was locked up in Vacaville from 1977 to 1980, he learned to write in the prison's creative-writing program and ultimately published his novel, *Homeboy,* which portrayed life in the sexual and criminal underworld m pretentious poetic prose. A prostitute character named Ring 'n' Things was thought by reviewers to resemble Janis. Critics praised the novel, but shortly after its publication, Seth, then forty-one and living in New Orleans, went on his final binge.

He was upset because his father, Frederick Morgan, heir to a soap fortune and editor of the *Hudson Review*, regretted having appeared on a TV show, NBC's 'Sunday Today,' on behalf of *Homeboy*.

On October 17, 1990, Seth, drunk and stoned, forced his reluctant girlfriend, Diane (Suzy) Levine, thirty-seven, into going riding with him on his 1972 Harley-Davidson. Moments before the crash, someone saw them speeding toward a bridge and said Suzy was holding on to him with one hand and pounding him on the back with the other. Seconds later, the front wheel hit the median and Seth flew facefirst into a bridge piling at 40 mph. The impact was so great that his body dislodged the piling, which was made up of eight telephone poles bound together.

Little was left of the face that had charmed so many women, including Janis, who'd once dreamed that she was going to die with Seth on his motorcycle. Neither Seth nor Suzy had been wearing helmets, and both were killed instantly. Seth had been drinking, and only the day before the fatal crash, he'd been arrested for drunken driving. In the morgue, his tattooed arms still bore needle tracks from days of drugging, and on his shoulder there was a spider tattoo.

Following her success at the Continental Baths, Bette Midler turned into a recording star, specializing in retrorock hits such as 'Da Do Run Run' and 'Leader of the Pack.' It was producer Peter Guber who came up with the idea of Bette playing Janis; and the film biography based on Janis's life, *The Rose*, came out in 1979. The original story, at first entitled *Pearl*, was written by William Kerby, and by the time Bo Goldman and Michael Cimino fashioned it into a screenplay for Bette, she and her manager, Aaron Russo, insisted that it was not about Janis. Their statement read: '*The Rose* is a composite: Janis, Jimi Hendrix, Jim Morrison,

Marilyn Monroe and James Dean, characters who got too caught up in the momentum of their lives to know when to stop.' Paul Rothchild was hired as musical director. When the film was released, Midler was hailed as a new movie star and received an Oscar nomination as Best Actress.

Sunshine would have preferred Sissy Spacek to play Janis in *The Rose*, but she went to see the movie, anyway. 'I was still drinking heavily,' she says. 'I took a bottle of brandy in with me and threw it at the screen. I thought Bette was wonderful, but the stuff with the chauffeur was terrible, and the talk about her taking on the football team – that's not how Janis felt about it. She was ashamed of having made it with everybody, including the football team. That's the kind of hurt you'll do anything – be a loudmouth, be a rebel – to get beyond.'

A Janis Joplin imitator named Pearl Heart appeared in a nightclub scene in *The Rose*, and Sam later became part of Pearl Heart's act, playing guitar in his backup group. Sam loved Bette Midler, as well as the title song, 'The Rose,' but says of the film, 'I don't think it got too close to Janis.' Asked how his own experience as a rock 'n' roller compared with the depiction of rock life in *The Rose* – private planes, limousines, and great wealth – he says, 'Not at all. *The Rose* was a late '70s take on the whole thing. Rock had really moved along. In the '60s, no one got rich, that's for sure. It wasn't the same numbers as even five years later. Things got big in the '70s. Monterey Pop is insignificant in comparison with anything happening in Tacoma Dome tonight [1991], in terms of box office.'

Sunshine managed to kick heroin after a final, harrowing bottom. 'I was getting three ounces of uncut dope delivered to me on a daily basis from La Familia, the Mexican mafia, and turning ounces over to people. I had an apartment that I went and sat in for an hour every afternoon, and people came and picked up their dope. I never really saw the money, because I just kept my cut, and I was doing about a half an ounce a day. Then one time I was sitting in the bathtub, trying to find a place to shoot up, but there were no veins left. I sat there adding hot water for forty-five minutes, and while I was trying to fix, the water turned pink. "This is it," I said, and threw the syringe away, got dressed, went to the airport, called my connection, and told him, "There's two ounces that you delivered yesterday. It's in the drawer. That's five thousand dollars. I'm gone." '

'Did you have any help kicking?' I ask.

'The Great Spirit,' she says. 'My Indian grandmother was hooked to a medicine woman. I tried to keep that no matter what else was going on, to keep a little portion of my soul clean and clear. That's really what saved me. I went to my aunt and she took me in. I didn't sleep for twenty-three days, had convulsions. I had such a hard time because I hadn't been using cut dope.'

At Christmas 1991, Linda Gravenites sends me a photograph of the church window she was starting to design when I'd visited her in Cazadero earlier in the year. The golden cross radiating light through the redwoods turned out to be a work of art, and it pleased St. Colman's Church so much that they gave her a big bonus. I call Linda to wish her Merry Christmas and thank her for the photo. We get into a conversation about the Joplin family's efforts to stop the Seattle musical on Janis, and I ask, 'What would Janis think about what I'm doing?'

'Oh, she'd love it!' Linda says. 'She wanted everybody to talk about her all the time, to listen to her *and love her.*'

Just as Orson Welles pinpointed the sled 'Rosebud' as the key to Citizen Kane's psyche, every biographer looks for a symbol that will explain his subject. In Janis's case, for me at least, it's those jodhpurs she wore to Sunday school as a kid. In Port Arthur, they've been talking about how she wore pants ever since. Self-expression was important in the Joplin household, but no one could have foreseen the ridicule that would result for Janis – nor the disgrace when her mother suggested that Janis take mechanical drawing in high school, ending up as the only girl in an all-male class. As Janis went through adolescence, taking nonconformity and rebellion to heights never before imagined by the burghers of Port Arthur, the rules were suddenly reversed and she was ordered to be more like everybody else. No wonder she cracked up.

Though she survived into adulthood, the emotional deformities sustained in youth prevented her from having a normal life. At least she had her talent and her drive for stardom. The yearning of her great soul was to stand in the spotlight and entertain people, reach out and make them laugh and cry, make them more human by touching their hearts. But even this became agony for her. The kids at TJ High did such a thorough job of stomping on her joie de vivre, her energy, and her self-esteem that the only way she could go onstage was by first getting drunk and drugged.

Once she was in the grips of alcohol and drugs, she was finished. As they say in recovery groups, only three fates await the alcoholic or addict – jails, institutions, and death. Not one alcoholic or addict has ever been known to get better as long as he or she continued to drink or use – and continue she did, right up to those last shots at Barney's Beanery and the Landmark. She was doing the best she could to medicate intolerable pain and lead some kind of life. That she achieved as much as she did, considering the burden of suffering she carried, makes her a shining example of the triumph of the human spirit.

APPENDICES

Coroner's Report

File #70-10463

OFFICE OF CHIEF MEDICAL EXAMINER-CORONER

Date <u>October 5, 1970</u> Time <u>0935 Hours</u>

I performed an autopsy on the body of JANIS JOPLIN
at OFFICE OF CHIEF MEDICAL EXAMINER-CORONER, HALL OF
JUSTICE, LOS ANGELES, CALIFORNIA
and from the anatomic findings and pertinent history I ascribe the
death to:

ACUTE HEROIN-MORPHINE INTOXICATION

DUE TO: INJECTION OF OVERDOSE

Final Oct. 28, 1970

<u>ANATOMICAL SUMMARY</u>

    I.   Pulmonary edema and congestion
    II.   Visceral congestion.
    III. Needle marks, arms, bilateral.
    IV. Fatty metamorphosis of liver.

EXTERNAL EXAMINATION:

The unembalmed body is that of a Caucasian female, appearing the stated age of 27. A tattoo of a bracelet is present around the left wrist. A small tattoo of a flower is present just behind the lateral malleolus on the right heel. There is also a small heart tattooed over, and medial to, the left breast. Numerous needle marks are present in the arms bilaterally, both in the antecubital fossa and on the left lateral anterior margin of the left arm. On sectioning, there appears to be at least two fresh hemorrhagic areas on the lateral margin of the left arm. The antecubital fossa shows, what appears to be, old needle marks and some are of relatively recent origin. An old surgical scar is present in the right lower quadrant of the abdomen. There is a slight amount of bloody material present in the mouth and on further examination, some disruption of the mucosa is noted. No evidence of major trauma or of violence is present. The hair is of moderate length and shows a varying shade of, from blond to brunette. The eyes are blue and show moderate dilation of the pupils. The external genitalia is female. There is some irregular dependent livor with the pressure changes chiefly on the left side, suggesting body rest on the left side.

Discography

ALBUMS (33$^1/_3$ rpm) AND CASSETTES

Big Brother and the Holding Company. September 1967. Mainstream S/6099. Side I: 'Bye, Bye Baby' by Powell St. John (Brent Music Corp./BMI). 'Easy Rider' by James Gurley (Brent Music Corp./BMI). 'Intruder' by Janis Joplin (Brent Music Corp./BMI). 'Light Is Faster Than Sound' by Peter Albin (Brent Music Corp./ BMI). 'Call on Me' by Sam Andrew (Brent Music Corp./BMI). Side II: 'Women Is Losers' (author unlisted) (Cheap Thrills/ASCAP). 'Blindman' by Peter Albin, Sam Andrew, David Getz, James Gurley, and Janis Joplin (Brent Music Corp./BMI). 'Down on Me' arranged by Janis Joplin (Brent Music Corp./BMI). 'Caterpillar' by Peter Albin (Brent Music Corp./BMI). 'All Is Loneliness' by Moondog (Prestige Music, Inc./BMI).

Cheap Thrills: Big Brother and the Holding Company. September 1968. Columbia KCS 9700. Also Columbia Stereo Cassette PCT 00488. Also *Pearl/Cheap Thrills*, Columbia Stereo Cassette GT 38219. Side I: 'Combination of the Two' by Sam Andrew (ASCAP) – lead guitar: James Gurley; vocal: Sam Andrew. 'I Need a Man to Love' by Sam Andrew and Janis Joplin (ASCAP) – vocal: Janis Joplin; lead guitar: Sam Andrew. 'Summertime' by DuBose Hayward and George Gershwin (ASCAP) – vocal: Janis Joplin; arranged by Sam Andrew. 'Piece of My Heart' by Bert Berns and Jerry Ragovoy (Web IV Music Inc., and Ragmar Music Corp./

Pearl

BMI) – vocal: Janis Joplin; lead guitar: Sam Andrew. Side II:
Blues' by Janis Joplin (ASCAP) – vocal: Janis Joplin; piano: ِ
Simon; guitar: Peter Albin. 'Oh, Sweet Mary' by Janis Jo[
(ASCAP) – vocal: Sam Andrew; lead guitar: Peter Albin. 'Ball aι
Chain' by Willie Mae (Big Mama) Thornton (Swampwater Musι
& Bradbury Taylor, d/b/a Bay-Tone Music Publishing
Company/BMI) – vocal: Janis Joplin; lead guitar: James Gurley.
Engineering: Fred Catero, Jerry Hochman, Roy Segal, Janis Joplin,
and James Gurley.

I Got Dem Ol' Kozmic Blues Again Mama!: Janis Joplin.
November 1969. Columbia PC 9913. Also Columbia Stereo
Cassette PCT 00748. Side I: 'Try (Just a Little Bit Harder)' by Jerry
Ragovoy and Chip Taylor (Ragmar Music Corp./BMI). 'Maybe'
by Richard Barrett (Nom Music, Inc./BMI). 'One Good Man' by
Janis Joplin (ASCAP). 'As Good as You've Been to This World' by
Nick Gravenites (ASCAP). Side II: 'To Love Somebody' by Barry
Gibb and Robin Gibb (BMI). 'Kozmic Blues' by Janis Joplin and
Gabriel Mekler (ASCAP). 'Little Girl Blue' by Lorenz Hart and
Richard Rodgers (T. B. Harms Company/ASCAP) arranged by
Gabriel Mekler. 'Work Me, Lord' by Nick Gravenites (ASCAP).
Produced by Gabriel Mekler/Lizard Productions. Engineering: Sy
Mitchell, Jerry Hochman, Alex Kazanegras. Personnel – Guitar:
Sam Andrew; organ: Richard Kermode, Gabriel Mekler; bass: Brad
Campbell; drums: Maury Baker, Lonnie Castille; baritone sax:
Cornelius Snooky Flowers; tenor sax: Terry Clements; trumpet:
Luis Gasca; background voices: Sam and Snooky.

Pearl: Janis Joplin/Full Tilt Boogie. January 1971. Columbia KC
30322. Also Columbia Stereo Cassette *Pearl/Cheap Thrills* GT
38219. Side I: 'Move Over' by Janis Joplin (ASCAP). 'Cry Baby' by
Bert Russell and Norman Meade (Robert Mellin, Inc., and
Rittenhouse Music, Inc./BMI). 'A Woman Left Lonely' by Spooner
Oldham and Dan Penn (Equinox Music, Central Star Music, and
Dann Penn Music/BMI). 'Half Moon' by John Hall and Johanna
Hall (ASCAP). 'Buried Alive in the Blues' by Nick Gravenites
(ASCAP). Side II: 'My Baby' by Jerry Ragovoy and M. Shuman
(BMI). 'Me and Bobby McGee' by Kris Kristofferson and Fred
Foster (Combine Music Corporation/BMI). 'Mercedes Benz' by

Joplin and Michael McClure (ASCAP). 'Trust Me' by Bobby mack (Metric Music Company, Inc., and Tracebob Music/ MI). 'Get It While You Can' by Jerry Ragovoy and M. Shurman 3MI). Produced by Paul A. Rothchild. Engineer: Phil Macy. Full Tilt Boogie: Janis Joplin – vocals. Brad Campbell – bass. Clark Pierson – drums. Ken Pearson – organ. John Till – guitar. Richard Bell – piano. Sandra Crouch – tambourine. Bobbie Hall – conga/bongos. Bobby Womack – acoustic guitar (on 'Trust Me'). Pearl – acoustic guitar (on 'Me and Bobby McGee'). Chorus voices: Pearl, Full Tilt Boogie, Vince Mitchell, Phil Badella, and John Cooke.

Joplin in Concert. July 1972. Columbia C2X31160. Also Columbia Stereo Cassette CGT 31160. Side I: Big Brother and the Holding Company. 'Down on Me' arranged by J. Joplin (BMI). Recorded by Fred Catero at the Grande Ballroom, Detroit, Michigan, March 2, 1968. 'Bye, Bye Baby' (ASCAP). Recorded by David Diller at Winterland, San Francisco, April 12, 1968. 'All Is Loneliness' (ASCAP). Tape recorded and supplied by the Bill Graham Organization. Recorded at the Fillmore West, April 4, 1970. 'Piece of My Heart' (BMI). Recorded by Fred Catero at the Grande Ballroom, Detroit, Michigan, March 2, 1968. Side II: Big Brother and the Holding Company. 'Road Block' by Janis Joplin and Peter Albin (ASCAP). Recorded by Dan Healey and Owsley at the Carousel Ballroom, San Francisco, June 23, 1968. 'Flower in the Sun' by Sam Andrew (ASCAP). Same as above. 'Summertime' (ASCAP). Same as above. 'Ego Rock' by Nick Gravenites and Janis Joplin (ASCAP). Sung with Nick Gravenites. Tape recorded and supplied by the Bill Graham Organization. Recorded at the Fillmore West, April 4, 1970.

Side III: Full Tilt Boogie Band. Recorded during the Canadian Festival Express, June–July 1970. Tape supplied by Maclean-Hunter, Ltd. 'Half Moon' (BMI). Toronto, June 28, 1970. 'Kozmic Blues' (ASCAP). Toronto, June 28, 1970. 'Move Over' (ASCAP). Calgary, July 4, 1970. Side IV: Full Tilt Boogie Band. 'Try (Just a Little Bit Harder)' (BMI). Calgary, July 4, 1970. 'Get It While You Can' (BMI). Calgary, July 4, 1970. 'Ball and Chain' (BMI). Calgary, July 4, 1970.

Collected and assembled by Elliot Mazer. Re-recording and

editing engineers: Don Puluse, Larry Keyes, and Tim Geelan. notes by Clive Davis.

Janis Joplin's Greatest Hits. July 1973. Columbia PC 32168. Al Columbia Stereo Cassette PCT # 32168. Side I: 'Piece of My Heart (BMI). Big Brother and the Holding Company. 'Summertime' (ASCAP). Big Brother and the Holding Company. 'Try (Just a Little Bit Harder)' (BMI). Kozmic Blues Band. 'Cry Baby' by J. Ragovoy and B. Berns (BMI). Full Tilt Boogie Band. 'Me and Bobby McGee' (BMI). Full Tilt Boogie Band. Side II: 'Down on Me' arranged by J. Joplin. Big Brother and the Holding Company. Recorded live by Fred Catero. 'Get It While You Can' (BMI). Full Tilt Boogie Band. 'Bye, Bye Baby' (ASCAP). Big Brother and the Holding Company. 'Move Over' (ASCAP). Full Tilt Boogie Band. 'Ball and Chain' (BMI). Full Tilt Boogie Band.

Farewell Song. January 1982. Columbia PC37569. Also Columbia Stereo Cassette PCT 37569. Side I: 'Tell Mama.' Recorded Toronto, June 28, 1970, during the Canadian Festival Express. Tape supplied by Maclean-Hunter, Ltd. Full Tilt Boogie Band. 'Magic of Love.' Recorded at the Grande Ballroom, Detroit, Michigan, March 1, 1968. Big Brother and the Holding Company. Originally produced by John Simon. 'Misery'n.' Recorded at Columbia Studio E, New York, April 1, 1968. Big Brother and the Holding Company. 'One Night Stand.' Recorded at Columbia Studio D, Los Angeles, March 28, 1970. Paul Butterfield Blues Band. Originally produced by Todd Rundgren. 'Harry.' Recorded at Columbia Studio E, New York, June 1968. Big Brother and the Holding Company. Originally produced by John Simon. Side II: 'Raise Your Hand.' Recorded Frankfurt, West Germany, April 12, 1969. Tape supplied by Bavaria Atelier GmbH. Kozmic Blues Band. 'Farewell Song.' Recorded at Winterland, San Francisco, April 13, 1968. Big Brother and the Holding Company. Originally produced by John Simon. Medley: 'Amazing Grace/Hi Heel Sneakers.' Recorded at the Matrix, San Francisco, January 31, 1967. Tape recorded and supplied by Peter Abrams. Big Brother and the Holding Company. 'Catch Me, Daddy.' Recorded at Columbia Studio E, New York. Originally produced by John Simon.

olumbia PG 33345. Part One: from the sound track of the picture *Janis* (with substituted performances of 'Piece of Heart' and 'Cry Baby') produced by Crawley Films – executive ucer F. R. Crawley. Directed and edited by Howard Alk and ton Findlay. A Universal release. Side I: 'Mercedes Benz' SCAP). Full Tilt Boogie Band. Taken from the Columbia LP *Pearl*. 'Ball and Chain' (BMI). Kozmic Blues Band. From the Frankfurt, Germany, concert, 1969. Courtesy of Bavaria Atelier GmbH. Rap on 'Try.' From the Toronto, Canada, concert, 1970. 'Try (Just a Little Bit Harder)' (BMI). From the Toronto, Canada, concert, 1970. Full Tilt Boogie Band. 'Summertime' (ASCAP). Kozmic Blues Band. From the Frankfurt, Germany, concert, 1969. Courtesy of Bavaria Atelier GmbH. Albert Hall interview (1969). Courtesy of Bavaria Atelier GmbH. 'Cry Baby' (BMI). Full Tilt Boogie Band. Taken from the Columbia LP *Pearl*. Side II: 'Move Over' (ASCAP). Full Tilt Boogie Band. From the sound track of the 'Dick Cavett Show' TV appearance (1970). Dick Cavett TV Interview (1970). 'Piece of My Heart' (BMI). Big Brother and the Holding Company. Taken from the Columbia LP *Cheap Thrills*. Port Arthur High School Reunion. Courtesy KJA TV, Port Arthur, Texas (Listed as 1969 on LP but the date shou. 1970.) 'Maybe' by R. Barrett (BMI). Kozmic Blues Band. m the Frankfurt, Germany, concert, 1969. Courtesy of Bavar. telier GmbH. 'Me and Bobby McGee' (BMI). Full Tilt Boogie Ba

Part One produced by Paul A. Rothchild, except for 'I of My Heart.' Remix engineering: Fritz Richmond, Elektra d Recorders, Los Angeles Mastered at Sterling Sound, New York

Part Two: Janis Joplin: Early Performances. Side I: 'Trouble Mind' by R. M. Jones (ASCAP). Recorded 1963, 1964, Austi. Texas. 'What Good Can Drinkin' Do' by Janis Joplin (ASCAP). Same as above. 'Silver Threads and Golden Needles' by J. Rhodes and D. Reynolds (BMI). Same as above. 'Mississippi River' (public domain). Same as above. 'Stealin'' by L. Stock and A. Lewis (ASCAP). Same as above. 'No Reason for Livin'' by Janis Joplin (ASCAP). Same as above. 'Black Mountain Blues' by H. Cole (ASCAP). Recorded in San Francisco, 1965, with Dick Oxtot Jazz Band. 'Walk Right In' by G. Cannon and H. Wood (BMI). Recorded in Austin, Texas, 1963, 1964. Side II: 'River Jordan' (public domain). Recorded in San Francisco, 1965, with Dick Oxtot

Jazz Band. 'Mary Jane' by Janis Joplin. Same as above.
City Blues' by C. Parker (BMI). Recorded in Austin, Texas
1964. 'Daddy, Daddy, Daddy' by Janis Joplin (ASCAP). Same
above. 'C. C. Rider' by M. Rainey (pending). Same as above.
Francisco Bay Blues' by J. Fuller (BMI). Same as above. 'Winner
Boy' by J. R. Morton (ASCAP). Same as above. 'Careless Love' by
H. Ledbetter (BMI). Same as above. 'I'll Drown in My Own Tears'
by H. Glover (BMI). Same as above.

Part Two produced by Paul A. Rothchild. Remix engineering:
Fritz Richmond. Elektra Sound Recorders, Los Angeles. Special
thanks to Bob Simmons, Jack Jackson, Henry Carr, and Dick Oxtot
for providing the early performances and to Budge Crawley for
sound track materials. Liner notes by Jim Rooney. Includes a
16-page photographic insert.

Janis Joplin: Anthology (made in England). CBS 22101. Side I:
'Piece of My Heart' (Planetary Nom [London], Ltd.). Big Brother
and the Holding Company. 'Summertime' (Chappell Music, Ltd.).
Same as above. 'Maybe' (Planetary Nom [London], Ltd.). Kozmic
Blues Band. 'Try (Just a Little Bit Harder)' (Ragmar Music
Corp.[MCPS]). Same as above. 'To Love Somebody' (Abagail
Music, Ltd.). Same as above. Side II: 'Kozmic Blues' (Carlin Music
Corp./Leeds Music, Ltd.). Same as above. 'Turtle Blues' (copyright
control). Big Brother and the Holding Company. 'Oh, Sweet Mary'
(copyright control). Same as above. 'Little Girl Blue' (Chappell
Music, Ltd.). Kozmic Blues Band. 'Trust Me' (United Artists Music,
Ltd.). Full Tilt Boogie. Side III: 'Move Over' (Carlin Music Corp.).
Same as above. 'Half Moon' (Intersong Music, Ltd.). Same as
above. 'Cry Baby' (Robert Mellin, Ltd.). Same as above. 'Me and
Bobby McGee' (Keith Prowse Music Pub. Co., Ltd.). Same as
above. 'Mercedes Benz' (Carlin Music Corp.). Same as above. Side
IV – Live. 'Down on Me' (Bocu Music, Ltd.). Big Brother and the
Holding Company. 'Bye, Bye Baby' (Mainspring Watchwork Music
Co. [MCPS]). 'Get It While You Can' (Carlin Music Corp.). Full
Tilt Boogie. 'Ball and Chain' (Chappell Music, Ltd.). Same as
above. Liner notes by John Rogan.

Big Brother and the Holding Company Live. Rhino RNLP 121.
Also issued on Made to Last Records, produced by David Getz, as

r Thrills, April 1984, MTL00l. Side I: 'Come on Baby Let
ood Times Roll' by Leonard Lee (Atlantic Music Corp./Unart
c Corp./BMI). 'I Know You Rider' – traditional arranged by
Brother and the Holding Company (Cheap Thrills
usic/ASCAP). 'Moanin' at Midnight' by Chester Burnett (Arc
Music Corp./BMI). 'Hey Baby' by Big Brother and the Holding
Company (Cheap Thrills Music/ASCAP). 'Down on Me' traditional
arranged by Big Brother and the Holding Company (Cheap Thrills
Music/ASCAP). 'Gutra's Garden' by Big Brother and the Holding
Company (Cheap Thrills Music/ASCAP). 'Harry' by David Getz
(Cheap Thrills Music/ASCAP). Side II: 'Whisperman' by Big
Brother and the Holding Company (Cheap Thrills Music/ASCAP).
'Women Is Losers' by Janis Joplin (Cheap Thrills Music/ASCAP).
'Blow My Mind' by Jimmy McCracklin (Metric Music Corp./BMI).
'Oh My Soul' by Richard Penniman (Venice Music/BMI). 'Coo-
Coo' traditional arranged by Big Brother and the Holding
Company (Cheap Thrills Music/ASCAP). 'Ball and Chain' by Willie
Mae Thornton (Baytone Music Corp./BMI). Recorded live at
California Hall, San Francisco, July 28, 1966. Recorded by Peter
Abram. Remixed and edited at Harbor Sound, Sausalito,
California. Engineered by Dana Chappele and Jon Gass. Mastered
by Joe Gastwirt at JVC Cutting Center, Los Angeles. Includes 4-
page photographic and text insert, *Big Brother and the Holding
Company Scrapbook*. Text by David Getz, 1984.

VIDEOCASSETTES

Monterey Pop. 1969. Sony Video. Features Janis, along with many
other acts, at the 1967 concert.
Janis. 1975. MCA Home Video. 97 minutes of Joplin interviews
and concert footage.
The Rose. 1979. CBS/Fox. Closely patterned on Janis's life, this
film stars Bette Midler.
American Pop. 1981. CBS/Fox. In this animated film, Janis sings
'Summertime' with Big Brother. Audio only.
Cool Cats. 1984. MGM/UA. Janis sings 'Ball and Chain.'
Closet Classics. Janis performs 'Tell Mama' on this MTV clip.

Bibliography

Alcoholics Anonymous. *Alcoholics Anonymous* (The Big Book). New York: Alcoholics Anonymous World Services, Inc., 1939.

———. *Alcoholics Anonymous Comes of Age.* New York: Alcoholics Anonymous World Services, Inc., 1957.

———.*Twelve Steps and Twelve Traditions.* New York: Alcoholics Anonymous World Services, Inc., 1952.

Anson, Robert Sam. *Gone Crazy and Back Again.* New York: Doubleday, 1981.

Anthony, Gene. *The Summer of Love.* Foreword by Michael McClure. Berkeley, California: Celestial Arts, 1980.

Baez, Joan. *And a Voice to Sing With.* New York: New American Library, 1987.

Bane, Michael. *Who's Who in Rock.* New York: Facts on File, Inc., 1981.

Berry, Chuck. *The Autobiography.* New York: Fireside, 1987.

Booth, Stanley. *The True Adventures of the Rolling Stones.* New York: Vintage, 1984.

Brandelius, Jerilyn Lee. *Grateful Dead Family Album.* New York: Warner Books, 1989.

Broven, John. *Rhythm & Blues in New Orleans.* Gretna, Louisiana: Pelican, 1974.

Carey, Gary. *Lenny, Janis and Jimi.* New York: Pocket Books, 1975.

Caro, Robert. *The Path to Power.* New York: Vintage, 1982.

Casale, Anthony M., and Phillip Lerman. *Where Have All the Flowers Gone?* Kansas City, Missouri: Andrews and McMeel, 1989.

Peggy, as told to Dan Knapp. *Going Down with Janis.* York: Dell, 1973.

.t, Dick, and Christopher Porterfield. *Cavett.* New York: rcourt Brace Jovanovich, 1974.

/ Lights Books. *Names of 12 San Francisco Streets Changed to Honor Authors & Artists.* San Francisco: City Lights Books, 1989.

Clark, James A., and Michel T. Halbouty. *Spindletop.* Houston: Gulf Publishing Company, 1952.

Clark, Tom. *Jack Kerouac.* New York: Paragon House, 1984.

Crosby, David, and Carl Gottlieb. *Long Time Gone.* New York: Doubleday, 1988.

Crowley, Aleister. *Diary of a Drug Fiend.* York Beach, Maine: Samuel Weiser, Inc., 1922.

Crumb, Robert. *R. Crumb's Head Comix.* New York: Fireside/Simon & Schuster, 1968.

Dalton, David. *Janis.* New York: Stonehill/Simon & Schuster, 1971. Subsequently published in a different format as *Piece of My Heart* by St. Martin's Press, New York.

Dannen, Fredric. *Hit Men.* New York: Times Books, 1990.

Denselow, Robin. *When the Music's Over.* London: Faber and Faber, 1989.

Densmore, John. *Riders on the Storm.* New York: Delacorte Press, 1990.

Des Barres, Pamela. *I'm with the Band.* New York: Jove, 1988.

Eisen, Jonathan, ed. *The Age of Rock 2.* New York: Random House, 1970

Fitzgerald, F. Scott. *Letters of F. Scott Fitzgerald.* Edited by Andrew Turnbull. New York: Charles Scribner's Sons, 1963.

Frazier, George. 'Brief Candle,' *No One Waved Good-Bye.* Edited by Robert Somma. New York: Outerbridge & Dienstfrey, 1971.

Friedman, Myra. *Buried Alive.* New York: William Morrow, 1973.

Gans, David, and Peter Simon. *Playing in the Band.* New York: St. Martin's Press, 1985.

Gaskin, Stephen. *Haight Ashbury Flashbacks.* Berkeley: Ronin Publishing, Inc., 1990.

Goldman, Albert. *The Lives of John Lennon.* New York: William Morrow, 1988.

Greene, Herb. *Book of the Dead.* Foreword by Robert Hunter.

New York: Delacorte Press, 1990.

Grushkin, Paul, Cynthia Bassett, and Jonas Grushkin. *G____ Dead*. New York: Quill, 1983.

Harris, Sheldon. *Blues Who's Who*. New York: Da Capo, 197__

Helander, Brock. *The Rock Who's Who*. New York: Schirn__ 1982.

Hite, Shere. *The Hite Report*. New York: Macmillan, 1976.

Holiday, Billie, with William Dufty. *Lady Sings the Blues*. London: Penguin, 1956.

Hopkins, Jerry, and Danny Sugerman. *No One Here Gets Out Alive*. New York: Warner Books, 1980.

Kandel, Lenore. *The Love Book*. San Francisco: Stolen Paper Editions, 1966.

Kerouac, Jack. *The Dharma Bums*. New York: Signet, 1958.

———. *On the Road*. New York: Penguin, 1957.

———. *The Subterraneans*. New York: Grove Weidenfeld, 1958.

Kratochvil, Laurie, ed. *Rolling Stone: The Photograph*. New York: Simon & Schuster, 1989.

Landau, Deborah. *Janis Joplin: Her Life and Times*. New York: Paperback Library, 1971.

Lazell, Barry, with Dafydd Rees and Luke Crampton. *Rock Movers & Shakers*. New York: Billboard Publications, Inc., 1989.

Lobenthal, Joel. *Radical Rags*. New York: Abbeville Press, 1990.

Lydon, Michael. *Rock Folk*. New York: Delta, 1971.

Makower, Joel. *Woodstock*. New York: Doubleday, 1989.

Malone, Bill C. *Country Music U.S.A.* Austin: University of Texas Press, 1985.

Matson, Robert W. *Sonoma Coast*. Santa Rosa, California: Sea Wolf Publishing, 1991.

Mellers, Wilfrid. *Angels of the Night*. Oxford, England: Basil Blackwell, 1986.

Mezzrow, Milton (Mezz), and Bernard Wolfe. *Really the Blues*. New York: Citadel Press, 1946.

Miller, Jim, ed. *The Rolling Stone Illustrated History of Rock & Roll*. New York: Random House, 1980.

Millett, Kate. *Flying*. New York: Alfred A. Knopf, 1974.

Mitchell, Mitch, and John Platt. *Jimi Hendrix: Inside the Experience*. New York: Harmony, 1990.

Money, John. *Gay, Straight and In-Between*. New York: Oxford

Bibliography

...versity Press, 1988.

...an, Tom, and Tom Sewell. *Fantasy by the Sea*. Culver City, California: Peace Press, 1980.

...organ, Seth. *Homeboy*. New York: Random House, 1990.

...urray, Charles Shaar. *Crosstown Traffic*. New York: St. Martin's Press, 1989.

Noguchi, Thomas T., and Joseph DiMona. *Coroner*. New York: Pocket Books, 1983.

Ouspensky, P. D. *In Search of the Miraculous*. New York: Harcourt, Brace & World, 1949.

Pareles, Jon, and Patricia Romanowski. *The Rolling Stone Encyclopedia of Rock & Roll*. New York: Rolling Stone Press/Summit Books, 1983.

Pavletich, Aida. *Rock-A-Bye, Baby*. New York: Doubleday, 1980.

Perry, Charles. *The Haight-Ashbury*. New York: Random House/Rolling Stone Press, 1984.

Phillips, John, with Jim Jerome. *Papa John*. New York: Dell, 1986.

Pollock, Bruce. *When the Music Mattered*. New York: Henry Holt, 1983.

Reich, Charles A. *The Greening of Amenca*. New York: Random House, 1970.

Reid, Jan. *The Improbable Rise of Redneck Rock*. New York: De Capo, 1974.

Riese, Randall. *Nashville Babylon*. New York: Congdon & Weed, Inc., 1988.

Riordan, James, and Jerry Prochnicky. *Break on Through*. New York: William Morrow, 1991.

Rolling Stone editors. *The Rolling Stone Interviews: The 1980s*. Edited by Sid Holt. New York: St. Martin's Press/Rolling Stone Press, 1989.

Roxon, Lillian. *Lillian Roxon's Rock Encyclopedia*. New York: Grosset & Dunlap, 1971.

Sander, Ellen. *Trips*. New York: Charles Scribner's Sons, 1973.

Smith, Steve, and the Diagram Group. *Rock Day by Day*. Enfield, England: Guinness Books, 1987.

Spada, James. *Divine Bette Midler*. New York: Macmillan, 1984.

Spitz, Bob. *Barefoot in Babylon*. New York: W. W. Norton, 1979.

———. *Dylan*. New York: McGraw-Hill, 1989.

———. *The Making of Superstars*. New York: Doubleday, 1978.

Spungen, Deborah. *And I Don't Want to Live This Life.*
York: Fawcett Crest, 1983 .

Stambler, Irwin. *The Encyclopedia of Pop, Rock & Soul.* N
York: St. Martin's Press, 1989.

——— and Grelun Landon. *The Encyclopedia of Folk, Country &*
Western Music. New York: St. Martin's Press, 1984.

Stein, Jean, edited with George Plimpton. *Edie.* New York: Alfred
A. Knopf, 1982.

Thorgerson, Storm. *Classic Album Covers of the 60s.* New York:
Gallery Books, 1989.

Turner, Florence. *At the Chelsea.* New York: Harcourt Brace
Jovanovich, 1987.

Uslan, Michael, and Bruce Solomon. *Dick Clark's First 25 Years of*
Rock & Roll. New York: Dell, 1981.

Ward, Ed, Geoffrey Stokes, and Ken Tucker. *Rock of Ages: The*
Rolling Stone History of Rock & Roll. Introduction by Jann S.
Wenner. New York: Rolling Stone Press/Summit Books, 1986.

Whitburn, Joel. *The Billboard Book of Top 40 Albums.* New York:
Billboard Publications, Inc., 1987.

———. *The Billboard Book of Top 40 Hits.* New York: Billboard
Publications, Inc., 1987.

Whitcomb, Ian. *Rock Odyssey.* New York: Dolphin, 1983.

White, Timothy. *Rock Lives.* New York: Henry Holt, 1990.

Wolfe, Tom. *The Electric Kool-Aid Acid Test.* New York: Bantam,
1968.

Index

Index

Index

369

Warner now offers an exciting range of quality tit:
both established and new authors. All of the book:
this series are available from:
Little, Brown and Company (UK) Limited,
P.O. Box 11,
Falmouth,
Cornwall TR10 9EN.

Alternatively you may fax your order to the above
address. Fax No. 0326 376423.

Payments can be made as follows: Cheque, postal
order (payable to Little, Brown and Company) or by
credit cards, Visa/Access. Do not send cash or
currency. UK customers: and B.F.P.O.: please send a
cheque or postal order (no currency) and allow £1.00
for postage and packing for the first book, plus 50p for
the second book, plus 30p for each additional book up
to a maximum charge of £3.00 (7 books plus).

Overseas customers including Ireland, please allow
£2.00 for postage and packing for the first book, plus
£1.00 for the second book, plus 50p for each
additional book.

NAME (Block Letters) ....

ADDRESS...

....

☐ I enclose my remittance for _____

☐ I wish to pay by Access/Visa Card

Number ☐☐☐☐☐☐☐☐☐☐☐☐☐☐☐☐☐☐

Card Expiry Date ☐☐☐☐